Beeston Castle, Cheshire
a report on the excavations 1968–85

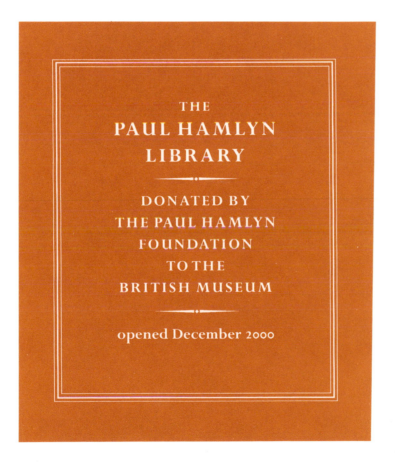

Archaeological Report no 23

Beeston Castle, Cheshire
a report on the excavations 1968–85
by Laurence Keen and Peter Hough

compiled and edited by Peter Ellis

with contributions by
Marion Archibald, Angela Bliss, Sarnia Butcher, Peter Carrington,
Robert Charleston, Tony Clark, Paul Courtney, Elisabeth Crowfoot, Peter Davey,
Ian Eaves, Jane Edwards, Blanche Ellis, Jennifer Foster, Maureen Girling,
Alison Goodall, Janet Henderson, Don Henson, Duncan Hook, Hilary Howard,
Linda Hurcombe, Marjorie Hutchinson, Glynis Jones, Laurence Keen,
Gerry McDonnell, Richard Macphail, Richard Moss, Jacqui Mulville,
Stuart Needham, Penny Noake, Cathy Royle, Rebecca Smart, Ian Stead,
and Ann Woodward

Historic Buildings & Monuments Commission for England
1993

Copyright © English Heritage 1993

First published 1993 by English Heritage, Keysign House, 429 Oxford Street, London W1R 2HD

Typeset from Ventura page layouts
Set in 10/11 and 8/9 point Palatino
Printed on 100gsm matt-coated cartridge by Hobbs the Printers Limited, Second Avenue, Millbrook, Southampton, SO9 2UZ.

A catalogue record for this book is available from the British Library
ISBN 1 85074 429 7

Edited by Kate Jeffrey and Kate Macdonald
Designed by Chris Evans

Contents

Microfiche contents list

List of illustrations

List of tables

Acknowledgements

The successful completion of the excavation campaigns and the post-excavation programmes were only achieved as the result of the combined effort and assistance of a large number of people.

The 1968–73 excavations

For the archaeological work carried out between September 1968 and August 1973, Laurence Keen is indebted to O J Weaver, Inspector of Ancient Monuments of the then Ministry of Public Building and Works, for the invitation to direct the excavations, and for his great interest in the project. Thanks are due to the direct labour team at the castle, under J Bell, for providing manpower during the earlier seasons in 1968–70, and also to the staff of the area office, particularly G Davies and A Griffiths. Considerable support was given throughout the project by E G Wilson at the London headquarters, who bore the weight of administrative arrangements and sorted out many problems. Debts of gratitude are owed to D Price-Williams, R Barlow, I Stuart, and R A Hall, who provided archaeological support during the early seasons. In the spring and summer of 1972 and the summer of 1973 full teams of volunteers were engaged and their personal interest and hard work should not go unrecorded: H Arnold, P Boland, Jane Bowden, M Clark, D Clarke, M Clerk, T Coleshaw, Sheila Colfer, I Collingwood, S Cracknell, A Darlington, A de Lewandowicz, Elizabeth de Lewandowicz, M de Lewandowicz, Karen Done, D Earnshaw, Shirley Forwood, Sara Gibbons, Heather Gibson, M Hallett, N Hawley, P Holdsworth, J Inman, Hilary Jennings, R Lawrence, B Moore, Helen Nicholson, M O'Connell, Barbara Pedge, S Pigott, A Pinder, Gina Porter, Susan Porter, T Pritchard-Barnett, Cheryl Pritchett, Margaret Rodgers, A Thomas, M Thomas, Ann Waldsax, Joyce Wallis, Helen Ward, M Ward, and Penny Wyatt. Thanks are due to D Hayns of the Beeston Field Centre, who, through the Cheshire Education Committee, provided accommodation in the spring of 1972.

In 1972 R A Hall and in 1973 D W R Thackray were assistant supervisors; other members of the staff were Heather Gibson and Helen Nicholson, who looked after the finds, and N Hawley, D Jones, and C J Arnold, to all of whom a special debt of gratitude is owed.

At the completion of Laurence Keen's work in 1973 a programme of post-excavation work was initiated. Thanks are owed to the staff of the Ancient Monuments Laboratory, at the then Department of the Environment (subsequently English Heritage), for conservation and analysis of the finds, and for commissioning the human and animal bone and mollusca reports, which have been incorporated into this volume. Work on the pottery was started by S Rollo-Smith. This was carried on by C Tracy, who also provided a text describing the excavations from numerous drafts and notes, and produced sections and plans ready for publication. C J Arnold provided a report on the clay pipes.

With the start of further archaeological work by P Hough the production of a full report on the 1968–73 excavations was abandoned, pending a decision on if, and how, the two reports could, or should, be amalgamated. The production of this volume, describing all of the archaeological work, could not have been achieved without the commissioning of Peter Ellis to combine the results of the two separate archaeological campaigns. Laurence Keen is particularly grateful to him for his forbearance and enthusiasm in resurrecting a report, the bones of which had been gathering dust for far too long. He would like to thank also Dr C A R Radford for discussing with him references to Richard II's treasure; H Jaques and R N R Peers for their generous efforts in improving his text; Dr P Dixon for helpful comments on the history of the castle – not least for noticing one serious mistake, which could be corrected before the text went to press; and Dr C P Lewis for his comments on the historical account.

The 1975–85 excavations

O J Weaver again oversaw the excavation programme. Thanks are due to him and to Glyn Coppack of English Heritage, who took over supervision at a later stage. The excavations were directed by Peter Hough with the assistance of Catherine Hough and Noel Edwards. Amongst a large excavation team, including many volunteers, the following took on additional responsibilities: Duncan Brown, Robin Brown, Anthony Burt, Paul Courtney, Graham Darlington, Jane Edwards, Joe Edwards, Mark Fletcher, Dot Francis, Robina MacNeil-Sale, Penny Noake, Carol Siddon, Kerry Wiggins, and John Wood. Much work on the documentary background was carried out by Catherine Hough. Thanks are due to a Department of the Environment survey team who established an accurate grid. The finds from the excavations were conserved at Fortress House by the Conservation Section of the Ancient Monuments Laboratory.

The post-excavation project was undertaken over a period of ten months in 1988–89. Thanks are due to Colin Hayfield for an initial assessment of the project and to Andrew Brooker Carey. Peter Ellis would like to thank colleagues at Birmingham University Field Archaeology Unit, in particular Simon Buteux, Caroline Gait, Liz Hooper, Ann Humphries (who prepared the microfiche and typed much of it), Peter Leach, Jackie Pearson, Andrew Rutherford, and Ann Woodward. At Birmingham, the site and some of the finds drawings were prepared by Trevor Pearson, who also gave invaluable advice and assistance on many aspects of the project, and by Sonia Hodges and Tim Watkin. Photographs are credited in the text, but acknowledgements for the drawings are made here. For Figures 1–5, 7, 9–11, 14, 15, 19–26, 38–40, 51, 52, 62, 71–3, 76–80, 84, 86, 89, 92, 117–121, and 123–129, T Pearson; for Figures 30–33, K

Hughes; for Figures 34, 35, 37, 43, 110 and 111, C Evans; for Figures 36, 44, 93–109, and 112–115, the Drawing Office at Academic & Specialist Publications, English Heritage; for Figures 41 and 42, S Hodges; for Figures 45–50, T Watkin; for Figures 63, and 130–145, the Beeston Castle excavation team; and for Figure 116, J Stringer. Figures M54–M61 were prepared by G Jones. Chris Evans of the Drawing Office is additionally thanked for ordering the drawings. Also at English Heritage thanks are due to Marjorie Hutchinson and Barry Knight for facilitating the finds reports; to Glyn Coppack, the supervising Inspector; and to Stephen Johnson and Margaret Wood at Academic and Specialist Publications. The onerous task of copy-editing was undertaken there by Kate Jeffrey, and the report was put through production by Dr Kate Macdonald. The many specialists contributing to this volume were most tolerant of the difficulties arising from the changes in the post-excavation programme. Some very kindly re-worked their reports as a result of alterations to the phasing. At Beeston Castle, Doreen Evans is thanked for her help with the finds stored there. For discussion and interpretation of the site thanks are owed to Paul Courtney, Peter Davey, Glynis Jones, Laurence Keen, Richard Macphail, Stuart Needham, and Ann Woodward. They have suggested many improvements but the final responsibility for the report is the author's. Laurence Keen also assisted with many aspects of the report in addition to the part dealing with his excavations. Ian and Alison Goodall kindly commented on aspects of the medieval and post-medieval finds. The cover photo of *View of the Upper Ward of the Castle, River Gowy in the distance* by George Barret (Snr), is reproduced by kind permission of the Grosvenor Museum, Chester.

Specialist reports

The authors who have contributed specialist reports to this volume would like to make the following acknowledgements.

Angela Bliss is grateful to Michael Heyworth and Gill Spencer for the X-ray fluorescence analysis of the rings.

Peter Carrington is grateful to Mrs Margaret Ward and Mrs K F Hartley for their comments on the samian and mortaria sherds respectively.

Robert Charleston would like to thank Jennifer Stringer for the care taken with the glass-drawings.

Paul Courtney is most grateful to Mrs J Rutter (Grosvenor Museum, Chester), Mr I Scott (Test Valley Archaeological Unit), Mrs R Weinstein and Mr C Manton (Museum of London), Ian and Alison Goodall, and Mr R Ellis, for their advice on specific points.

Peter Davey is grateful to David Higgins, Adrian Oswald and Janet Rutter, who made valuable suggestions and gave freely of their knowledge.

Jennifer Foster is grateful to Noreen Kay for calculating the probable capacity of vessel no 1.

Janet Henderson would like to thank Dr Juliet Rogers.

Marjorie Hutchinson is indebted to Dr Roger Harding, then Curator of Gemstones, the Geological Museum, London, now Director of Gemmology, GAGTL (Gemmological Association and Gem-testing Laboratory of Great Britain) for the use of his heavy liquid, to Michael Heyworth for ED-XRF analyses, and to Andrew David, Ancient Monuments Laboratory, for checking flake identifications.

Glynis Jones and Richard Moss would like to thank Claire Hoare who supervised the collection and on-site processing of samples and all those who took part in this work. Particular thanks are extended to Ian Smith who spent a considerable amount of time sorting flots and residues from samples collected in 1985. Thanks are also owed to Paul Halstead who read and commented on an earlier draft of this report. The report was completed in December 1988.

Richard Macphail wishes to thank Jill Walker of the Isotopes Measurements Laboratory, Harwell for the radiocarbon dates, the Institut National Agronomique, Paris-Grignon for thin-section manufacturing facilities, Dr Marie Agnès Courty-Fedoroff and Peter Ellis for useful discussion, and Ken Whittaker for the soil pollen analysis.

Stuart Needham is grateful to Paul Craddock for discussing aspects of axe-casting technology. The drawings are the work of Karen Hughes.

Penny Noake and Jane Edwards would like to thank all those who worked on the processing and reconstructing of the pottery; D Brown is thanked for thin-sectioning and identifying fabric inclusions; P Hough, P Davey, B Noake, J Greaves, D Higgins, and J Rutter are thanked for their helpful comments and discussion.

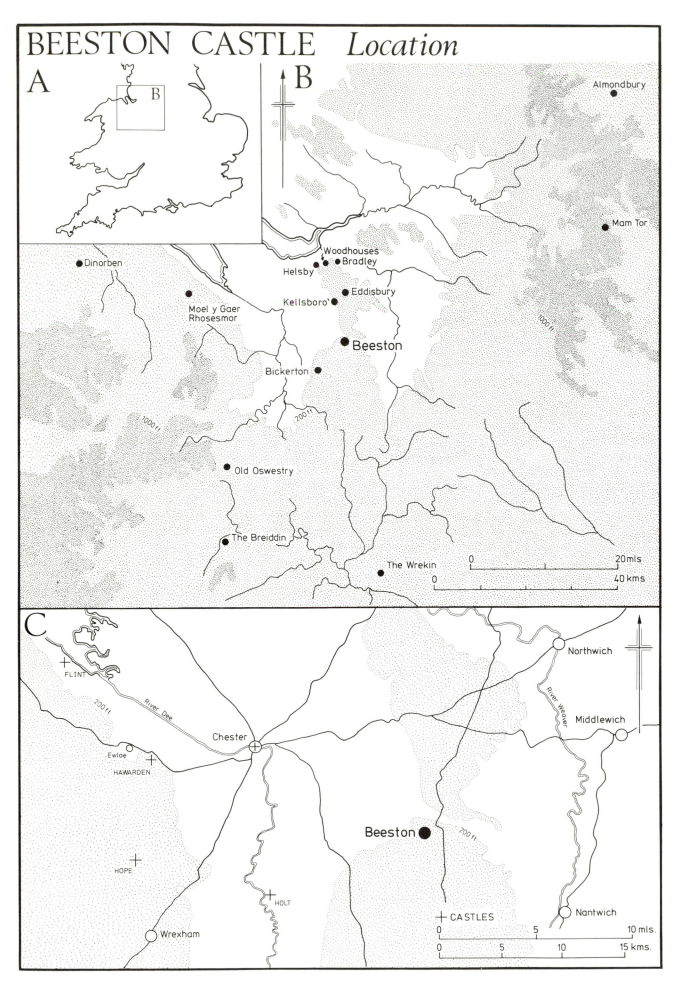

Fig 1 *Beeston Castle, Cheshire: site location; B with prehistoric and C with medieval sites discussed in the text; scales as shown*

1   Introduction

by Peter Ellis

Topography and geology (Figs 1, 2, & 63)

The rock outcrop on which Beeston Castle is sited is an impressive natural feature dominating the surrounding plain. It lies (National Grid reference SJ 538 592) at the north end of the Peckforton hills, the southernmost of a group of hills which divide the Cheshire plain in a line running south from the Mersey estuary. Its rocky sides present a vertical face to the north and west, and the other sides are steeply sloping with occasional rock outcrops. From below, the ruins of the great medieval castle can be seen in places through a surrounding fringe of trees.

It is virtually inaccessible except from the east. From the nineteenth-century gatehouse a track winds up the steep hill slope, through the ruins of the medieval gatehouse to the Outer Ward, and on to the sloping plateau behind the outer defences. A number of trackways lead past heavily quarried areas to the highest part of the crag where the core of the castle defences, the Inner Ward, is sited. The inner curtain wall with its interval towers and gateway are defended by a large, deep, dry moat, cleared to bedrock in the 1970s. These inner defences are now approached by a modern concrete bridge, its single span across the moat providing the only access. From here, at 160m above sea level, the cliffs fall away sheer on two sides down to the level of the surrounding land 100m below. There are views across the Mersey estuary to the north, east to the Peak District, west to Wales, and south as far as The Wrekin 50km away. Also to the south, Peckforton Castle, built in Gothic style between 1844 and 1850, mirrors the castle on the opposite side of the valley between the crag and the Peckforton hills.

The ridge of higher ground of which Beeston crag and the Peckforton hills form a part was a favoured settlement area in prehistory judging by the distributions of pottery (Fig 51), metalwork (Longley 1987, fig 17), and Iron Age sites (Fig 1). The excavations reported on here have shown that Beeston was a major defended site in the first millennium BC. In Roman and medieval times the Cheshire Plain was seen as of strategic importance. In both periods the county town of Chester, 16km north-west of Beeston, represented the key to dividing and controlling potential enemies in the upland areas of Wales and the north of England. At Beeston some indications of a Roman settlement were found at the foot of the crag, while in the medieval period and at the time of the Civil War, the crag was dominated by the castle, a thirteenth-century fortification, which played a significant local role.

Like the Peckforton range, the crag is of sandstone, capped with sandy drift deposits of Ice Age origin (Fig 2). The surrounding area was heavily glaciated leaving a blanket of Boulder clay. These deposits are thought to be the product of separate ice sheets, one from south-west Scotland, and the second from north Wales. There are copper deposits at the foot of the crag and along the Peckforton range, and a seam at Bickerton was mined in the nineteenth century (Tylecote 1987, 29). Numerous non-local erratic stones are found and these derive in the main from Scotland and the Lake District (Poole and Whiteman 1966, 60).

The geology of the area and the interrelationship of the landscape and the inhabitants of the crag in prehistory are discussed in detail in a number of specialist reports. The range of stone locally available is analysed in the report on the non-flint lithic finds (p 59); soil formation in prehistory and the likely resulting landscape is dealt with in the report on the soils and pollens (p 83); the local clay sources are described in the reports on the prehistoric pottery (p 63), and on the metalworking evidence (M1:C8); while finally the possibility that copper was mined in prehistory is raised in the report on the Bronze Age metalwork (p 48)

The excavations

Topographical descriptions of Beeston crag are dominated by the structure of the medieval castle, the Inner and Outer Wards defined by wall circuits, and, in the case of the Inner Ward, by the Inner Ditch (the dry moat) on its south and east sides. The Outer Gateway is located on the east side of the outer curtain.

In 1959 the monument was placed in the guardianship of the then Ministry of Public Buildings and Works. The subsequent campaign of consolidation and preparation for public display gave rise to successive campaigns of archaeological excavation. Those reported on here took place in the Inner Ward, the Outer Ward, at the Outer Gateway, and at the 'Lower Green' by the nineteenth-century entrance.

The 1968–73 excavations (Figs 3 & 71)

These excavations, directed by Laurence Keen, were intended principally to clear modern material and display more of the medieval structure. In the Inner Ward it was hoped that excavation might reveal medieval walls surviving to a greater height, thus increasing safety for the visitor, who was at that time prohibited access. Although levels were intended to be reduced to the top of the medieval ground surface, in the event there was so little *in situ* medieval occupation that the excavations were carried through to bedrock in most areas. The excavation trenches were lettered from A to Z. In this report the original 18 trenches have been amalgamated into six areas lettered A, H, N, X, K, and W (Fig 71), maintaining the original principal areas. The dates of successive excavations of the different areas are shown on the same figure. Labour for most of the work in the Inner Ward was provided by the castle's direct labour team, and by H M Borstal and a local prison, with

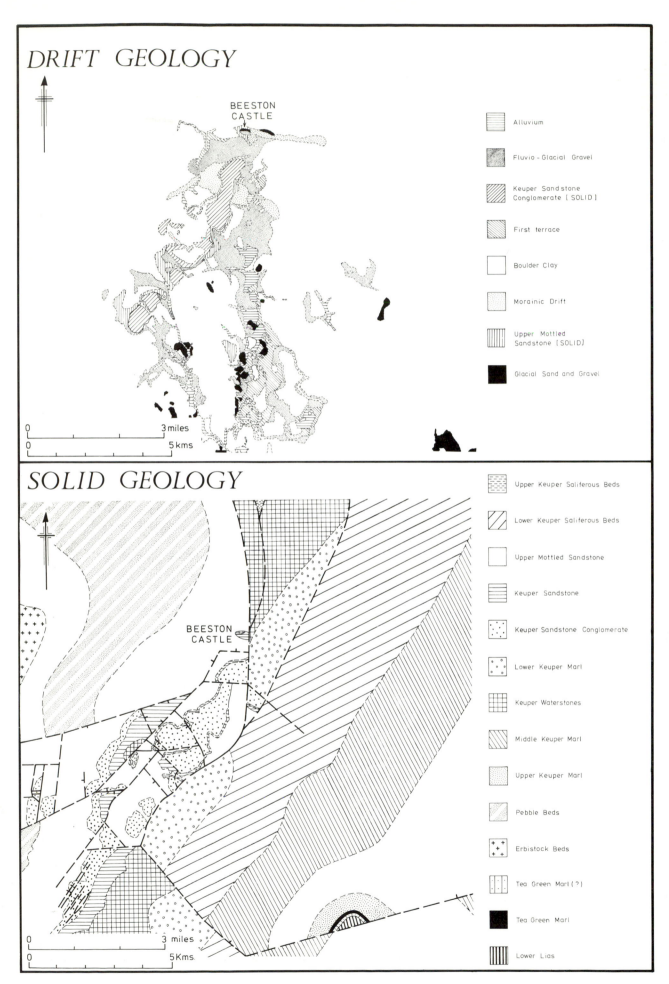

Fig 2 Local drift and solid geology; scales as shown

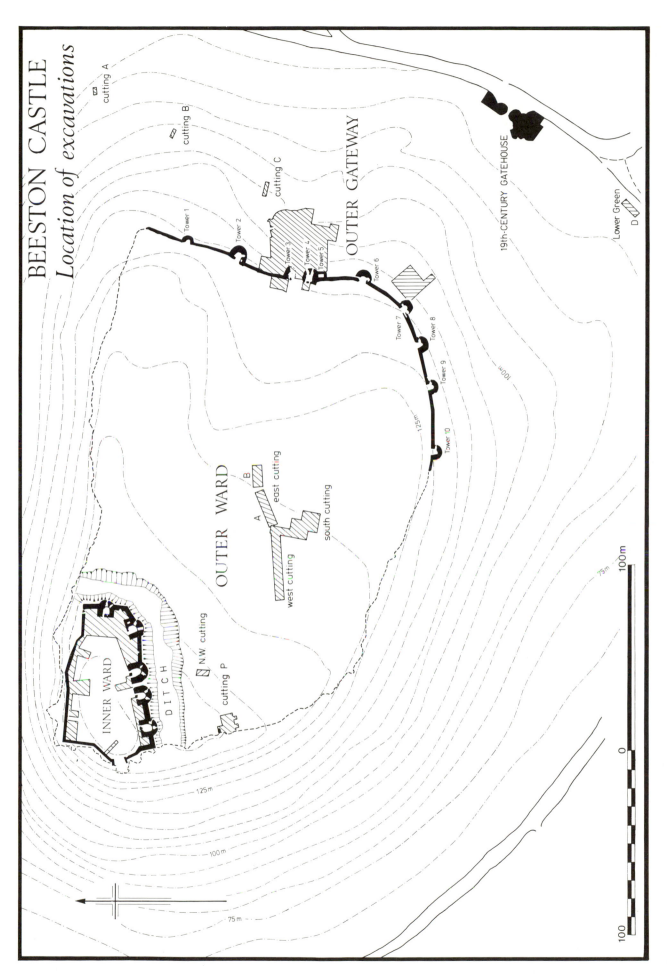

BEESTON CASTLE
Location of excavations

cutting A

cutting B

cutting C

OUTER GATEWAY

19th-CENTURY GATEHOUSE

Lower Green

D

Tower 1

Tower 2

Tower 3

Tower 4

Tower 5

Tower 6

Tower 7

Tower 8

Tower 9

Tower 10

100 m

125 m

OUTER WARD

B

A

east cutting

south cutting

west cutting

INNER WARD

DITCH

NW cutting

cutting P

125 m

100 m

75 m

75 m

100 m

0

100 m

Fig 3 Location of excavations; scale 1:2000

archaeological supervision. Only in 1972 and 1973 were full archaeological teams engaged. Large quantities of spoil from the excavations of the well in 1842 and 1935 were removed from areas A and H by labourers after being initially identified by archaeological trial trenching. Some small-scale work was carried out in the Inner Ditch in 1972. In the Outer Ward, Area P was excavated in 1972, and Towers 5 and 7 at the Outer Gateway were partly excavated in 1973.

The excavation contexts were numbered from 1 for each of the areas with the area or tower initials prefixed. Because of the large quantity of finds the original numbering sequence for the finds has been maintained as far as possible although the provenances of some of the finds have been given with less accuracy, to conform with the reduced number of area descriptions. A concordance of the alterations is available in the archive.

The 1975–85 excavations (Figs 3 & 4)

Mechanical clearance of the Inner Ditch was preceded by further archaeological work in 1975–6 under the direction of Peter Hough. The results of these excavations have been published (Hough 1978). Subsequently excavation was undertaken by Peter Hough at the Outer Ward, the Outer Gateway, and on the hillslopes to its east, together with further work in the Inner Ward.

The Outer Gateway excavations took place prior to the construction of new access routes to the castle, and were carried through in almost all areas to the natural surface. The earlier excavations at Towers 5 and 7 were reopened and enlarged. The dates of successive excavations are shown on Figure 4. Excavation in the Outer Ward commenced in 1980 following the discovery, as a surface find, of a Bronze Age palstave, and continued in 1981 to clear the area designated as the South Cutting in this report. In 1985 West Cutting C and East Cuttings A and B were excavated in advance of a new pathway through to the Inner Ward. A small area was opened on the south side of the entranceway across the Inner Ditch (North West Cutting, Fig 3). Further work was carried out in the Inner Ward and Ditch. The West Gatehouse Tower was excavated in 1980, and a burial found by workmen against the north wall of the Inner Ward was recorded. Recording of contractors' work in the Inner Ditch took place in 1977, 1979, and 1982. Three small trenches were opened to the north of the Outer Gateway excavations along the line of a trackway (Cuttings A, B, and C, Fig 3). Finally, south of the modern entrance an area was opened up at the foot of the hill slope (Lower Green, Fig 3).

A brief account of the results up to 1981 has been published (Hough 1982).

Post-excavation and presentation

Direction of the post-excavation project to bring all the separate excavations to publication was handed over to the present writer in 1988, when Peter Hough left the project to take up a post in teaching. By that time all the specialist reports for the Hough excavations had been commissioned and some had been completed. Although a start had been made on the post-excavation work, the data was approached afresh. The Keen excavations had been summarised in a text by the excavator describing the excavated features; the architectural evidence, pottery, animal bone, and clay pipes had been reported on, and the remaining finds identified and described.

The following report presents all the evidence from the separate excavations within a single unified period scheme. It is divided in two parts: Part I details the evidence prior to the construction of the medieval castle, while Part II describes the medieval and post-medieval evidence. In Part I the site evidence and the accompanying illustrations are followed by presentation of the finds, with a final summary and discussion section ordering the data and placing it in context. Part II begins with an outline of the historical and documentary evidence, followed by an architectural description of the Inner Ward, and the Outer Gateway and curtain wall. A report on the landscape setting of the castle is presented in microfiche (M2:E5–9). The excavation evidence is then followed by descriptions of the finds, and a final discussion section integrating the various types of evidence.

The site texts refer specifically only to layers and features which are shown on the illustrations. The main sequences are presented here; inevitably a large amount of detail has been omitted. A few minor changes have been made to the field numbering of contexts and finds to simplify the presentation. New feature numbers have been provided in some instances. A full description of the changes carried out is available in the archive. A list of all the site contexts and features, grouped by period, is available in the archive (F19).

Because of the large quantities and the wide range of the medieval and post-medieval finds, many of the specialist reports have had to be shortened in the text presented here. Further details of the medieval and post-medieval objects, the spurs, the vessel glass, the clay tobacco pipes, and the medieval and post-medieval pottery may be found in the microfiche. The reports on the human and animal bones, including Tables M58 and M59, the industrial residues, including Table M60, the post-medieval glass beads, the medieval and post-medieval window glass, the post-medieval buildings material, and the environmental data from the Inner Ward are all available in the microfiche (see microfiche contents, p 6).

In the microfiche the presentation of finds uses the Ancient Monuments Laboratory six- or seven-figure accession number or a site finds number, followed by the site (IW Inner Ward; OG Outer Gateway; OW Outer Ward; LG Lower Green), the layer, and the period. Concordances exist in the archive to relate site find numbers with Ancient Monuments Laboratory numbers and vice versa. Some of these details have been omitted from some of the finds reports in the printed text.

Periodisation

The relatively simple stratification, and the presence of artefacts which broadly indicated the date of deposits, allowed a single period system to be used for all the

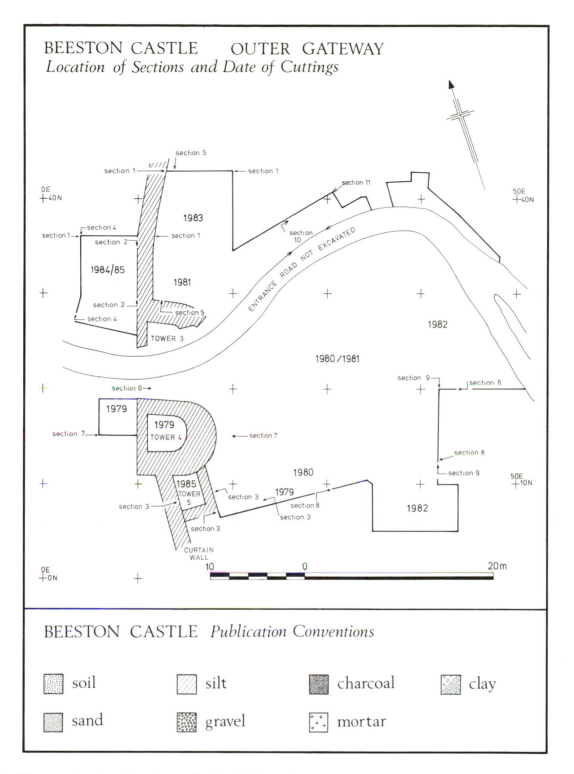

Fig 4 Outer Gateway: location of sections and grid, with date of excavation cuttings and section conventions; scale 1:400

sites. The drawbacks of such a system – namely that stratigraphic links cannot be proven – would still have occurred if a site-specific phasing had been used. Within the separate sites there were often few stratigraphic links between different areas. This was particularly so in the Inner and Outer Ward, but even at the Outer Gateway, where there was a good depth of deposits, for the prehistoric period at least, the castle gateway itself, the entry tracks, the sharp slopes, and erosion, all denied the possibility of establishing a stratified framework for the whole area. Thus deposits have

had to be grouped together on the basis of their artefactual contents rather than their stratigraphic relationship. Under these circumstances the choice of a single periodisation for all the sites has the justification of accessibility and simplicity. The main divergence between the phasing presented here and earlier periodisations (Hough 1982) occurs with the Outer Gateway data; a concordance of the two systems is available in the archive.

For the prehistoric period, the main phasing and dating evidence derived from the rampart sequence at the Outer Gateway. The ramparts had been cut into unconnected areas by the medieval castle defences, and this caused difficulties in excavation and interpretation. It should also be noted that absent or ambiguous correlations between drawn contexts and the written record at the Outer Gateway gave rise to further difficulties. The periodisation here is thus based on a 'best fit' of the evidence given by the stratification and the artefacts from the different surviving areas. The pre-Late Bronze Age evidence was slight; a handful of features at the Outer Gateway suggested a Neolithic and Middle to Late Bronze Age presence (Periods 1A and 2A), while other Bronze Age evidence (Period 1B) was suggested only by finds. There was no prehistoric evidence from the Inner Ward. The weight of the archaeological evidence starts with Period 2B.

The medieval and post-medieval periodisation was achieved by linking deposits which were clearly datable by their finds. Pottery and clay pipes in particular served to separate Periods 5, 7, and 9, while Periods 6 and 8 were defined more clearly by the stratigraphic evidence and were confined to the Outer Gateway. The medieval evidence derived from the Inner Ward and Outer Gateway, and the post-medieval evidence from all the main areas excavated. The archaeological evidence was divided into twelve periods, as follows.

Part I
    Period 1A: Neolithic
    Period 1B: Early/Middle Bronze Age
    Period 2A: Late Bronze Age to c 900 BC
    Period 2B: Late Bronze Age, c 900 BC to c 650 BC
    Period 3A: Early Iron Age, c 650 BC to c 450 BC
    Period 3B: Middle/Late Iron Age, c 450 BC to first century BC
    Period 4: Romano-British to thirteenth century AD

Part II
    Period 5: Thirteenth to fourteenth centuries AD
    Period 6: Later medieval
    Period 7: Civil War
    Period 8: Late seventeenth century
    Period 9: Eighteenth to twentieth centuries

The sequence of events, separately tabulated for each area excavated, is shown in brief for the prehistoric period (Table 1) and for the medieval and post-medieval periods (Table 34).

The full site record is available in the archive which is held, together with the finds, by the English Heritage Museums Division. The main categories of archive evidence will also be available on microfilm at the National Archaeological Record of the RCHME and at the Grosvenor Museum, Chester. An archive index is presented in the microfiche (M3:G9–13).

Table 1   The prehistoric and Roman sequence: location and period of the main events

	Outer Gateway	Tower 7	Outer Ward	Lower Green
Period 1A	Structure on hillslope; pit		flints	
Period 1B			pottery; flints; ?barrow	
Period 2A	?posthole palisade		?posthole palisade	
Period 2B	rampart; metalworking	?rampart	?crop-processing; metalworking; buildings	
Period 3A	rampart; platform; ditch; entrance track	ditch; ?rampart	buildings	
Period 3B	rampart; ditch; ?structures on hillslope; entrance track	ditch; ?rampart	buildings	pottery salt containers (VCP)
Period 4	entrance track		RB finds	RB occupation

PART I PREHISTORIC AND ROMAN

2 The excavations

by Peter Ellis

Period 1A: Neolithic (Figs 5 & 6)

The Outer Gateway excavation was sited where a natural valley, with a shallower gradient than the steep hillslopes to north and south, was floored with sand deposits, except at the scarp edge where natural rock was encountered. Half way up the valley, to the east of the excavation area, the gradient was less sharp. Here a group of features was found sealed beneath a Period 2A hillwash layer. The hillside had been modified by a series of slight circular terraces and hollows, F543. Below them a stone spread defined by a slight bank, F694, may have been associated. Two postholes, F548 and F552, were located to the south on the edge of a further slight bank, F693. The area of terracing was clearly defined by a spread of charcoal-rich soil, 542, up to 0.1m thick, containing occupation debris. Further layers of charcoal and sand were recorded sealing 542. A steep-sectioned stone-packed posthole, F545, and a pit, F509, were also located.

It is clear that some attempt was made to modify the hillslope and to create a level, and the occupation debris and spread burnt deposits indicate the use of this levelled area on more than a temporary scale. The embanked area downslope from the hollows might represent the remains of an enclosure.

A small number of sherds of Early to Middle Neolithic pottery was found within the layers overlying the burnt spread, 542 (Fig 45.2). Attribution of a Neolithic date to the hollows was strengthened by a radiocarbon date of 4340–4003 cal BC from layer 542. A further date of 4036–3816 cal BC from charcoal in the later Iron Age hillfort ditch, F490 (Fig 11), must be associated. The charcoal was found in a primary fill on the east side of the ditch and must have derived from layer 542 when the ditch was initially open.

Two clay-filled gullies to the south, F480 and F517, may be associated features, although their sharply defined edges and uniform fills suggest a natural origin. They were cut by a group of features described below under Period 3B (Fig 14), but which may also represent Neolithic occupation.

Further possible Neolithic features were found on the plateau edge (Figs 5 and 18, Sections 1 and 4). Here the corner of a deep pit, F950, and a smaller pit or

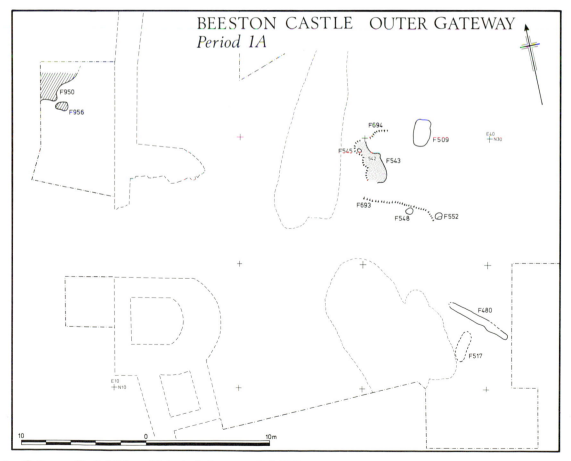

Fig 5 Outer Gateway: Period 1A prehistoric features; scale 1:300

Fig 6 Outer Gateway: Period 1A occupation area F543, view west (Photo P Hough)

posthole, F956, were located beneath the platform behind the Period 3A rampart, F680. F950 had been cut into bedrock with a stepped edge and was infilled with sand and stony silt. A single sherd of Early to Middle Neolithic pottery was found at the base of the pit.

The size of F950 indicates a substantial pit, perhaps marking an entranceway. It is possible that other features found beneath the rampart and discussed under Period 2A are associated. The location of this activity on the scarp edge must raise the question of whether these features represent some defensive arrangements, as was to be the case in later periods.

A few sherds of possible Late Neolithic pottery were found in the Outer Ward (Fig 3), in overall post-medieval layers in South Cutting and East Cutting A, and in a post-medieval posthole in West Cutting. An assemblage of undated flint (mostly debitage) was found, again in overall post-medieval layers and the fills of later postholes. Two dense concentrations in South Cutting may denote working areas (M1:C14).

Although only a small number of sherds is involved it may be significant that the Early/Middle Neolithic Fabrics 10, 11, and 12 (Table 22) were not found on the plateau, Neolithic pottery there being limited to the possibly Late Neolithic Fabric 13.

Period 1B: Early/Middle Bronze Age

Pottery of Late Neolithic, Early Bronze Age, and Middle Bronze Age date was found in later features. At the Outer Gateway, layers forming the Period 3A platform

to the rear of the rampart provided a number of sherds of Late Neolithic (Beaker) and Early Bronze Age pottery from Fabrics 14 to 18 (Table 22). It is clear that this material together with later Bronze Age finds was residual. A small number of sherds was found in the Period 3A rampart itself. At the Outer Ward a similar group was found in overall post-medieval layers, and, occasionally, in the fills of Late Bronze Age and Iron Age postholes. This material was particularly concentrated in South Cutting and East Cutting A overall layers, although more widespread in the posthole fills. Amongst the postholes, five contained Late Neolithic (Beaker)/Early Bronze Age pottery alone: two Period 2 postholes, F201 and F238, in West Cutting (Fig 22), and three Period 3 postholes, F84 in South Cutting, F242 in West Cutting, and F253 in East Cutting A (Fig 23).

The presence of probable funerary material amongst this pottery assemblage at the Outer Ward, together with flints that might occur both as grave goods and as finds from pre-barrow activity, has led to the suggestion (by Ann Woodward) that the Early Bronze Age finds might indicate the former presence of round barrows on Beeston crag. Of the six diagnostic sherds, four occurred in East Cutting A, and two in South Cutting. The diagnostic flint on the other hand was concentrated in South Cutting. It is possible that these foci indicate the former location of a barrow centred between South Cutting and East Cutting A.

If it is correct to envisage Bronze Age burial on Beeston crag (and the evidence from nearby upland areas suggests that it is likely), then any earthworks were entirely removed in the excavated areas in the later Bronze Age. A detailed field survey (M2:E5–9) did not suggest the existence of barrows elsewhere on the plateau, which has in any case suffered from extensive quarrying and levelling.

Period 2A: Late Bronze Age (Figs 7 & 8)

On the scarp edge to the east of Tower 5, a group of features was cut into a thin deposit of natural sand. To the north, a dark stain in the sand, F334, was continued southward as a vertical-sided trench, F307, 0.2m deep (Fig 8). Southward again, two edge-set stones continued the line together with a further linear stain, F682, while in section was a possible cut, F683 (Fig 18, Section 3). A stone-packed posthole, F215, cut F307. Northward, two further postholes, F213 and F241, were recorded cutting the natural surface.

East of the curtain wall and north of the gateway, further postholes may be attributed to a pre-rampart phase. These were sealed by collapsed rampart material from later periods rather than by the *in situ* Period 2B bank, and may be of Period 3 date. A large depression, F699, and a pit, F690, were also recorded. East of the later rampart line a hollow, F696b, predated posthole F697. A layer of bleached sand was recorded overlying bedrock within which charcoal was present.

The southern group of features represents a reasonably convincing linear group, perhaps representing a

Fig 8 Outer Gateway: Period 2A possible palisade trench and postholes, view south (Photo P Hough)

palisade placement. Three of the five postholes to the north on the scarp edge could also be seen as representing further posts. The line is as close to the scarp edge as is the case with the southern group, and it may well be that erosion has removed other indications of the line to the north.

Late Bronze Age pottery was found in the depression F698, although the feature was not sealed by the later ramparts and the sherds may be intrusive.

There was no evidence of similar features at Tower 7 (Figs 3 and 21). However, excavations in the Outer Ward at area P, to the south-west of the summit plateau, revealed three postholes, F20, F22, and F26, sealed beneath topsoil and subsoil sand (Figs 3 and 86). The postholes were all *c* 0.6m in diameter and 0.3m deep, with fills of silt and charcoal. Disturbed stone packing was recorded in F22. These postpits may possibly be seen in a prehistoric context, and represent further evidence of an early palisade, although, in contrast to the evidence from the east side of the plateau, the line was sited some 6m back from the scarp edge. They may alternatively be Civil War features (p 126).

There is thus a suggestion in three places of a possible palisade structure prior to the Late Bronze Age Period 2B rampart on the scarp edge of the plateau. There is no dating evidence beyond a possible *terminus ante quem* provided by the radiocarbon sample from the overlying Period 2B bank (p 85). If taken together the features may

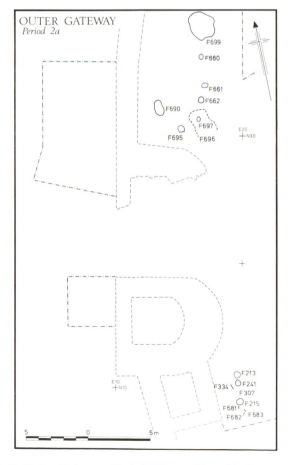

Fig 7 Outer Gateway: Period 2A possible palisade features; scale 1:300

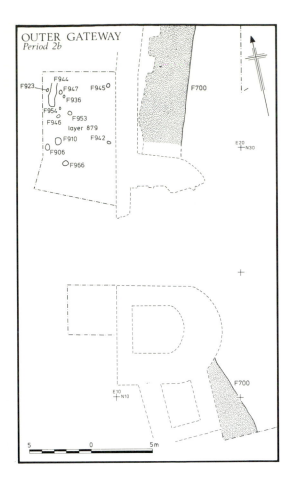

Fig 9 Outer Gateway: Period 2B; scale 1:300

be interpreted as representing defences of any date from the Neolithic to the Late Bronze Age, or alternatively as marking out lines for the Period 2B rampart.

A small amount of pottery of Middle to Late Bronze Age date (Fabrics 19–21), was found solely in the Outer Ward East Cutting A. Overall post-medieval layers here contained a few sherds as did posthole F268, unaccompanied in this case by other pottery fabrics.

Period 2B: Late Bronze Age (Figs 9 & 10)

On the plateau edge were indications of the provision of a bank, F700, formed of a dump of sand laced with timbers (Fig 9). In the area north of the entrance and east of the curtain wall, this comprised an initial layer of small stones and a number of large boulders, beneath two main deposits of sand. Layers 669 and 652 at the base of the bank were composed of sand and stone, sealed by a second deposit, layer 641, of orange sand with occasional humic lenses (Fig 18, Sections 1 and 5). The charcoal outlines of timbers lying east–west were noted within more generalised charcoal spreads on the surface of layer 641 (Fig 10). Stones may have formed part of a deliberate placement. To the north, a large piece of charcoal indicated a possible timber 1.4m long and 0.35m wide. Elsewhere smaller fragments were noted. In section, three features F962, F677, and F645 were noted, the latter two cut from the base layer, and F962 from the surface of 641 (Fig 18, Sections 2 and 5).

They may indicate the presence of otherwise unrecognised structural elements. Eastward the bank layers terminated at the sharp break of slope at the scarp edge. There was no evidence of a revetting face, but this may have been removed by the later Period 3B rampart. The layers conformed to the ground slope beneath and it is possible that the boulders below, and the compact layer 641, were intended to stabilise the bank. The timbers on the surface of 641 may represent a timber lacing or the collapsed remnants of a timber structure.

To the west of the curtain wall evidence was found of occupation to the rear of the rampart (Fig 9). The Period 1B features here were cut by a gully, F944, and a number of postholes and stakeholes. These were associated with charcoal-rich layers of soil and sand, 879 and 938, of which only the latter was recorded in section (Fig 18, Section 1). The contrast between the extent of use of the ground surface to the east and west of the curtain wall is marked, and there seems little doubt that the occupation evidence to the west, and its absence to the east, indicate the existence of an associated bank along the scarp edge.

Within and to the east of Tower 5 a layer of grey sand with some stone, 324, was recorded overlying the Period 2A features (Fig 18, Section 3). On its level surface and sloping face to the east, deposits of charcoal and burnt stone, 160, were noted in which, again, were the clear outlines of timbers running east–west. Within the tower the level of bedrock was not established. Layer 937 may represent an initial dump of red sand, or be equated with layer 324. Alternatively it may represent a continuation of layer 115, perhaps filling a discontinuity in the bedrock. If this is so then layer 935 may represent the westward continuation of layer 324.

The resulting bank of sand was over 0.4m high and was at least 4m wide. The angle of rest of the layers was more marked than to the north, although the level established on the surface of 324 is comparable with that formed by 641 to the north.

Excavations below the floor of Tower 7 encountered deep deposits overlying bedrock which may be elements of the prehistoric ramparts (Fig 21). Layer 22 overlying bedrock comprised a deposit of sand and large stones, and three areas of charcoal were noted on its levelled upper surface at its interface with layer 17.

The three separate exposures suggest a rampart on the scarp edge. This would have been very much compressed and degraded by later ramparts, but the evidence suggests two alternatives, either that the bank was timber laced, or that it formed a level on which a timber superstructure was constructed.

Pottery of Late Bronze Age date was found in a number of rampart layers: to the south, in layer 160, and to the north, in layers 641, 654, 658, and 667 (Table 2). West of the curtain wall to the rear of the rampart pottery was also found in posthole F910 and in layers 879 and 907 (Figs 48.40 and 49.64). In addition metalwork of the Ewart Park phase was found, comprising two socketed axes in layers 641 and 676 (Fig 30.1 and 2). A shale ring was found in layer 641 and another to the rear of the rampart in layer 879 (Fig 43.1 and 2). A radiocarbon determination made from the timbers located in layer 160 to the south gave a date of 1160–920 cal BC (HAR-4405).

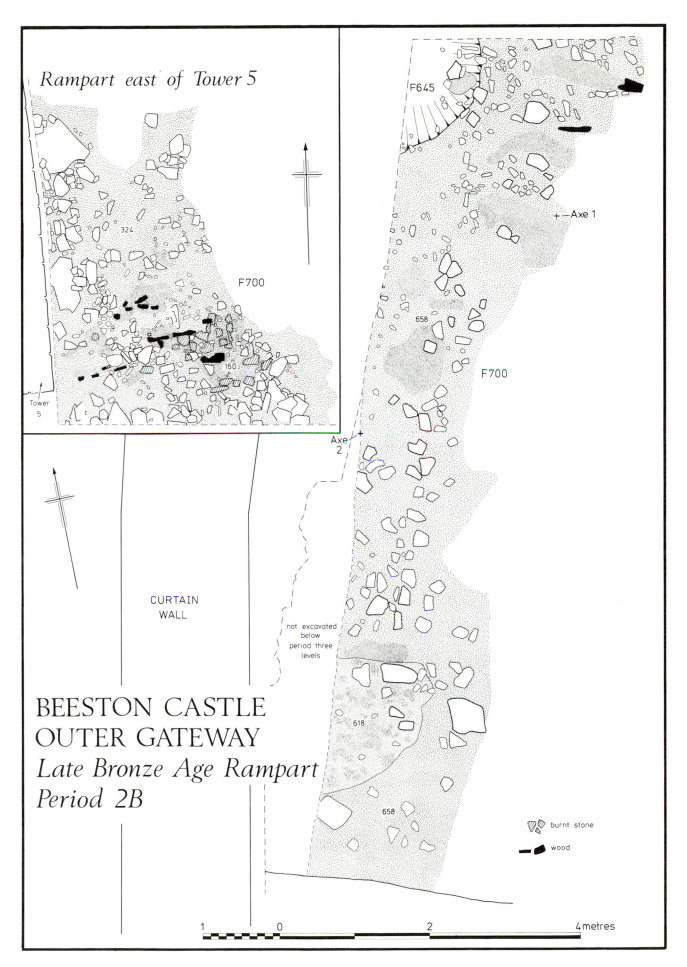

Rampart east of Tower 5

324

F700

Tower 5

F645

+—Axe 1

658

F700

Axe 2 +

not excavated below period three levels

CURTAIN WALL

BEESTON CASTLE
OUTER GATEWAY
*Late Bronze Age Rampart
Period 2B*

618

658

burnt stone

wood

1   0   2   4 metres

Fig 10 Outer Gateway: Period 2B rampart F700; scale 1:50

Table 2 Selected finds associated with rampart phases

Category	Period			
	2A	2B	3A	3B
LBA and IA pottery fabrics	2, 7, 8	2, 4 7–9, 24	1, 2, 4–9, 22, 24, 25	1, 2, 4–9, 23–25
Copper alloy metalwork		two axes (Fig 30.1–2)	shank fragment (No 3)	drinking vessel (Fig 34.1)
Iron metalwork			dagger (Fig 36.1) pin (Fig 36.5) riveted strip (Fig 36.7)	?adze (Fig 36.3) strip (Fig 36.6)
Shale		two rings (Fig 43.1–2)	ring (Fig 43.3)	
Clay objects			three spindlewhorls (Fig 52.1–2) three loomweights (Fig 52.3–5)	
Other			stone artefacts (Table 20) crucibles (Fig 38.8–9)	
Radiocarbon dates		HAR 4405 (1160–920 cal BC)		HAR 5609 HAR 6464 HAR 6465 HAR 6468 HAR 6469 HAR 6503 (range 765–257 cal BC: Table 33)
Archaeomagnetic date				360–240 cal BC

From layers forming a later, Period 3A, platform to the rear of the 2B, 3A, and 3B defences came an assemblage of pottery and other finds which indicates a major focus of activity at what is suggested below to be the entranceway (Table 2). The layers would have comprised material lying west of the excavated area within the gateway. Metalworking debris, stone artefacts, and evidence of high-temperature hearths were associated with Late Bronze Age pottery, and give a strong indication of occupation and metalworking just outside the excavation area, associated with the Period 2B occupation evidence sealed beneath the later platform.

Down the slope below the rampart, a hillwash layer (535) sealed the Period 1 features. Layers 432 and 527, respectively beneath and to the south of the 3B entrance tracks, appeared to represent equivalent horizons (Fig 19, Sections 6 and 8; Fig 20).

Layers 535 and 527 contained Late Bronze Age pottery, and a polished flake from a Neolithic axe was also found in layer 535 overlying the suggested Period 1 focus of activity.

At the Outer Ward excavations a number of features were located, some of which could be shown to predate the prehistoric posthole evidence discussed in Period 3 below (Fig 22; Tables M3–M5, M1:A7–8). The features comprised the surviving remnants of pits cut into the underlying bedrock. In the West Cutting, F185 predated a Period 3 posthole, while F148, F201, F196, F198, F205, F218, and F225, although not stratigraphically related, shared similar sand fills (Fig 24). Similar pits (F85, F102, F50, and F37) were recorded in South Cutting (Fig 25); of these F50 and F85 predated later postholes. F262 in East Cutting A (Fig 26) was also cut by later features. In East Cutting B, F260 and F273 are similar features. Large shallow cuts into bedrock were also recorded. These comprised F60, F115, and F226 in South Cutting, and F286, F289, and F272 in East Cutting B (Fig 22). To this period may also be attributed a number of the postholes which, for convenience, are described together in Period 3.

Groups of two or three related pits may mark a type of some significance. In West Cutting, three examples were noted (Fig 22). F179, F175, and F181 were located to the west of two further groups: F182, F190, and F189; and F183, F184, and F192. Further east, intercutting pits F233 and F232 may be associated with F238. In all these cases later postholes cut the suggested Period 2B features. In East Cutting B a rather different group of pits seemed to be linked (Fig 22). F270 and F271 may be related to F273, while F275 and F276 were also closely placed.

The effect of soil erosion makes interpretation of these features difficult. There were no associated occupation levels. The grouped pits may have an association with crop processing or storage functions, or possibly be associated with metalworking. The wide, shallow pits may well be quarry features to extract stone.

Some indication of former associated levels is offered by the plant remains (p 80). These may have collected in a widespread layer or layers which have been subsequently eroded, and survived only in features. Analysis of the evidence in the West and East Cuttings clearly shows that such a layer must have been *in situ* at the time the features described above were cut, since many of them contain plant remains argued to derive from earlier deposits. The implications of this evidence are discussed more fully in Chapter 4.

Two complete Late Bronze Age vessels were found, one in a Period 9 layer just above the bedrock (Fig 49.54), and the other, recorded as Late Bronze Age on site but lost before analysis, was placed in a slight hollow, F269, in East Cutting B (Fig 22). Building 9, a posthole structure described with other similar structures in Period 3 (Fig 23), may have been associated with the buried pot which was perhaps used for storage. The presence of metalworking debris in three of the postholes of Building 5, uniquely amongst the other Period 3 circular

structures, may suggest that this too is a Period 2B building.

Pottery from the pits and postholes described under Period 3, and from the overall layers allocated to Period 9, represented the main fabrics identified as Late Bronze Age (Figs 46.21–35; 48.43–4, 47–8, 50–1; 49.55, 57). Metalwork of this phase was also found comprising an axe apparently buried deliberately in F50 (Fig 31.5). Throughout the cuttings evidence of metalworking was found dispersed in later layers, in the form of crucibles and moulds (Fig 38.1–7), probable Late Bronze Age pieces (Figs 31.6; 32; 33.7–12), and pieces of metalworking waste. Some of these are likely to be in secondary positions, having been disturbed by later activities.

The numerous finds of Late Bronze Age pottery, metalwork, and refractory debris suggest substantial activity in Period 2B, although features are hard to find. A Bronze Age date is likely for one of the postholes, F25 in South Cutting, from which charcoal provided a radiocarbon date of 843–777 cal BC (HAR-4401). This and the other postholes are described under Period 3, as are the range of finds from later layers, of which a proportion are likely to be from the Late Bronze Age. The difficulties in interpreting the evidence are discussed at the end of Part I.

Period 3A: Early Iron Age (Figs 11–13)

North of the entrance and east of the curtain wall, the upper surface and timberwork of the Period 2B rampart

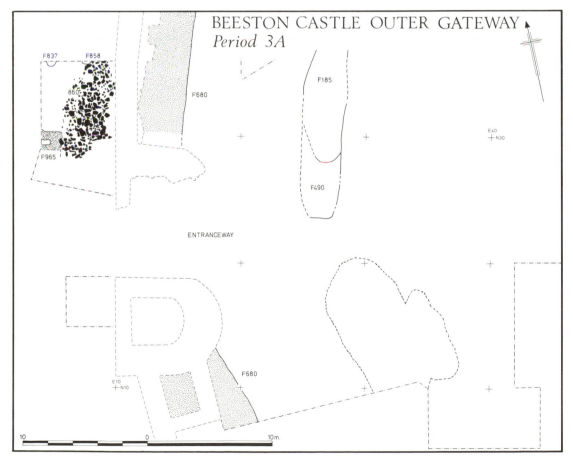

Fig 11 Outer Gateway: Period 3A; scale 1:300

was sealed by a layer of brown sand and charcoal, 618, and a layer of mottled brown and white sand with charcoal inclusions, 637 (Figs 11 and 18, Sections 1 and 5). This latter layer contained a large amount of burnt stone. West of the curtain wall a layer of clean sand, 908, covered the Period 2B levels, and above, successive dumps of sand were recorded, comprising layers 889, 887, 877, and 872. At the surface of 877 a shallow depression, F962, was apparent in Section 2 (Fig 18, Sections 1, 2, and 4).

These sand layers sloped from west to east conforming with the surface below. There was no sign of a diminution of the depth of the deposits to the west, where a massive boulder was located with the sand dumps apparently accumulated around it. A posthole, F837, was cut from the top of layer 872 (Fig 18, Section 1). In the south-east part of the excavated area a group of similarly sized stones, no bigger than 80mm across, had been collected and deposited in a shallow pit, F965, together with a large boulder (Fig 11 and Fig 18, Section 4). These layers and features were sealed by a layer of dark sand and charcoal on which lay a deposit of flat stone slabs, 860, thinning out to the west and terminating within the cutting (Figs 11 and 13). A deposit of clay and sandy soil, 853 and 858, about 1.5m across overlay 860 against the north section. These layers had been burnt and may be associated with a spread of charcoal-rich dark sand, 852, which thickened noticeably to the west (Fig 18, Section 4).

A succession of embanking layers are indicated by the sand deposits 908 to 872, with the cutting of the postpit, F837, and the deposition of stones in F965 marking a termination of the dumps. Subsequent events led to the deposition of charcoal-rich layers, which in turn were sealed beneath a deposit suggesting a levelled stone surface. On this layer were the remnants of a hearth, F858, and associated rake-out material 852; analysis suggested ironsmithing (M3:G6). The deposition of the stone layer 860, and subsequent activity represented by F858, represent successive uses of the platform. The collection of stones in F965 may well be a cache of slingstones deliberately placed for defence near the entrance.

Comparison of the levels east and west of the curtain wall indicate that these deposits may have been associated, and had formed a bank, F680, at least 0.6m high with a total width of 12m. This latter measurement suggests that there is either an inturning of the bank to run westward, or that a fighting platform was deliberately provided to the rear of the rampart. The entranceway must lie just to the south of the excavated areas and the evidence suggests an additional defence at a gateway with a platform and a ready supply of slingstones. It may be that initially a platform was provided beside an inturned entrance, and it is possible that layer 860 represents the floor of a subsequent guard chamber with a hearth, but no structural evidence was found.

Beneath and to the east of Tower 5 a layer of pale sand and stone, 164, was recorded overlying the Period 2B bank (Fig 18, Section 3). This in turn underlay a similar layer, 159. Although medieval pottery was recorded in 159, it is likely to be a further part of the bank, with material intrusive from Period 6 activity above. Com-

parable layers within Tower 5 were 934, 933, and 932. A possible posthole, F931, was noted at the upper surface of these sand horizons.

This bank of sand overlying the Period 2B layers thus survived to a height of over 1m above the ground surface at the scarp edge, and was over 6m wide. The angle of rest of the layers within Tower 5 contrasts with the level horizons over the Period 2B bank to the east. It is possible that the stone present in the eastern part of 159 and 164 indicates a collapsed revetment rather than the decay of the later Period 3B rampart.

Layer 22, overlying bedrock beneath Tower 7, may have been part of the Period 2B bank, but the overlying layer of sand and stone, 17, may well be equated with the other Period 3A deposits to the north (Fig 21).

Pottery of Late Bronze Age date was found together with earlier fabrics in a number of rampart layers from the northern area. West of the curtain wall, eight of the platform layers contained pottery (Figs 45.18 and 20; 48.38 and 42; 49.56 and 63) as did 12 layers east of the medieval curtain (Figs 45.5–7, 9–10, and 17; 48.39 and 53). However, an Iron Age fabric, Cheshire stony-tempered VCP – the acronym for Very Coarse Pottery (p 71) – was found in layer 639 forming the rampart, and layer 889 at the base of the platform. This fabric was used for salt containers in the Iron Age. Hereafter the pottery composed of this fabric is identified as VCP. Two copper alloy fragments were found in layers 637 and 674 east of the curtain wall (nos 3–4, p 49), and refractory debris, comprising crucible and furnace lining fragments, in layers 618 (Fig 38.8–9) and 644, together with an undiagnostic piece in 637. West of the curtain wall a further undiagnostic piece was found in layer 886, and five fragments of metalworking moulds in layers 860 and 854, forming the upper part of the rearward platform (p 56). A broken shale ring was found here in layer 872 (Fig 43.3). In the upper surface, pieces of ironwork were found: a pin and fragment in layer 860, and a dagger, possibly of La Tène 1 date, in layer 854 (Figs 36.1, 5, and 7). Items of worked stone were found in both rampart and platform, represented by a quern fragment from layer 860, two whetstones (Fig 42.4–5), two possible spindlewhorls (Fig 42.7–8), as well as roughly worked lids and utility stones (Table 20). Fired clay pieces comprised three spindlewhorls from the rampart (Fig 52.1–2), and three loomweights (Fig 52.3–5) from the platform. The layers making up the platform and rampart contained much occupation material (p 84), and, as noted above, a hearth bottom from F858 indicated ironsmithing.

Below the rampart a ditch, F185, was obliquely sectioned on either side of the modern access route (Fig 20, Sections 10 and 11). Both sections revealed a deep V-sectioned ditch, whose base levels demonstrated a sharp drop to the south. The ditch was continued southward with a shallower flattened profile to a terminal, F490, cutting Period 1A and 2B layers.

Further evidence of the ditch was found in excavations downslope from Tower 7 in 1982 (Fig 21). Here a deeply cut ditch similar in profile to F185 occupied the same position and contour on the hill slope. The ditch, F1000, contained a base fill of dark, humic, charcoal-rich silt, which was both sampled for pollen and dated by radiocarbon. The results are discussed by Richard Mac-

Fig 12 Outer Gateway: Period 3 ramparts, view south (Photo P Hough)

phail (p 84), and the date of 791–410 cal BC may indicate that the ditch was cut in Period 2B.

The ditch terminal at the Outer Gateway must indicate the position of an entranceway located at the same site as that into the medieval castle. A southern ditch terminal would have been removed by medieval ditch cutting.

Period 3B: Middle/Late Iron Age

The rampart and entrance (Figs 12, 14–16)

At the Outer Gateway, excavation to the north of the medieval gateway produced evidence for a massive rampart, F679, constructed on the line of the Period 2B and 3A defences. Excavations to the south at Tower 5 and Tower 7 showed possible evidence of its southward continuation.

To the north a line of massive boulders, F616, was recorded above the scarp edge east of the curtain wall (Figs 14 and 15). These did not reach the north section, but here a sharp cut down the face of the Period 2B and 3A layers 641 and 637 may indicate the former trench position (Fig 18, Section 1).

Above the Period 3A bank of sand, stone blocks, many with evidence of burning, had been deposited in different sections, layers 635, 685, 638, and 625 (Figs 15 and 18, Sections 1 and 5). Within two of these groups, the remains of charred timbers, F621 and F624, were recorded at successive levels from the base of the se-

quence upward. F621 was of oak and F624 of ash. Plans of their positions at successive levels show that they represent the remains of two uprights embedded in compacted stonework (Fig 15), with diameters of about 1.2m and depths of 0.4m. In addition pieces of vitrified stone, 634, were recorded. Above, less burnt stone was noted while the upper rampart layers were composed of stone in a brown sand matrix (Fig 16).

West of the curtain wall the Period 3A layer 860 was cut by a deep trench, F874 (Fig 13), in which massive boulders, F882, were located (Fig 15, Fig 18, Sections 1 and 2). Other boulders just to the east, forming the base courses of the curtain wall, may be associated. The trench line ran parallel to the line of boulders east of the curtain wall. Cutting the infilled construction trench and 2m to the west, two large postpits were recorded, F844 and F855 (Figs 13 and 14). These pits were steeply edged and flat-based, respectively 0.7m and 0.8m deep with similar fills of grey sand and small stones. The postpits were cut from the surface of a deposit of mixed sands and charcoal, 836. Subsequent to their disuse a further deposit of sand and charcoal, 831, sealed the pits and was in turn cut by an apparent line of stone-packed postholes, F838, F841, and F847 (Figs 14 and 17). In all three, postpipes of grey silt and charcoal and surrounding packing stones were recorded. A fourth, stone-defined postpit, F834, lay to the east at the same horizon.

Below and to the east of Tower 5 were layers of rubble overlying the Period 3A bank (Fig 18, Section 3). Layer 914, of grey loam and stone, may represent the

Fig 13 Outer Gateway: Period 3A platform behind rampart, layer 860, view south (Photo P Hough)

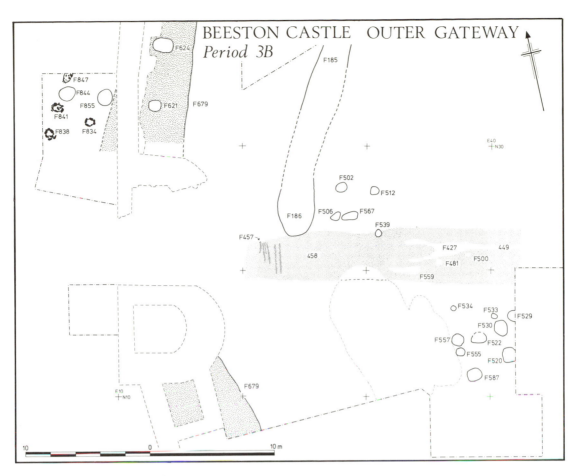

Fig 14 Outer Gateway: Period 3B; scale 1:300

remnants of a disturbed upper level, with soil inclusions from pre-Period 5 ground levels. Similarly layers 36 and 46 to the east, although containing post-medieval material, may also be disturbed elements of the Period 3 rampart. A posthole, F213, lay just forward of the disturbed rampart edge.

Excavation beneath Tower 7 showed probable Period 4 layers overlying the Period 3A rampart, but the east face of layer 21 may mark a cut into the earlier rampart, and perhaps the site of the eastward boulder-filled trench (Fig 21).

There is no ground evidence to suggest the location of the Period 3B rampart to the south, although a position on the scarp edge seems inescapable. The removal of Period 3B evidence is likely to have occurred during subsequent use of the hill, and natural erosion of its scarp edge.

The rampart boulders, all larger than 1m in length and some up to 2m, were paralleled by very large boulders found tumbled down the hillslope. Other boulders located beneath the south gate tower, Tower 4, may well have derived from the rampart. The intention would seem to have been to form a stable base for the subsequent stone bank. These boulders lay on the natural surface and thus additionally maintained the eastern part of the Period 2B and 3A banks *in situ*. There were no indications that posts penetrated through to the Period 2 bank below, and it would seem likely that stability was provided by the underlying boulders and perhaps by a stone face.

Although much tumbled to the east it was clear that the main body of the bank was formed of different construction zones each around 3m long. There was little indication of a timber frame although some fragments of carbonised wood, not associated with F621 and F624, were found. The layout of the latter suggests a row of massive posts along the line of the rampart. In addition, F855 and F844, to the west of the curtain wall, are aligned with F621. This might suggest that the main part of the defences was a timber structure based on and to the rear of a stone raft. The position of the postpits cutting through the rear boulder-filled trench indicate that, if there is a relationship with F621 and F624, either the entire timber frame was secondary to the initial stone structure, or the rearward posts were secondary to a main structure on the top of the bank.

Very intensive burning within the body of the rampart was recorded. Vitrified and scorched stones, and the quantity of charcoal, suggested burnt timberwork and consequent intense heating of stones. Archaeomagnetic dating from the area of vitrification is later than the radiocarbon dates for the timbers F621 and F624 (p 86). However, burnt stones occurred in some of the construction sections of the rampart and not in others, suggesting that in this case the burning predated its construction. The timbers, F621 and F624, were infested with larvae (p 79) – their carbonisation must have occurred later. Two episodes of burning are indicated, one predating the rampart, and one having occurred when it was *in situ*.

It is possible to suggest a timber structure on top and to the rear of the stone bank, or alternatively an entrance

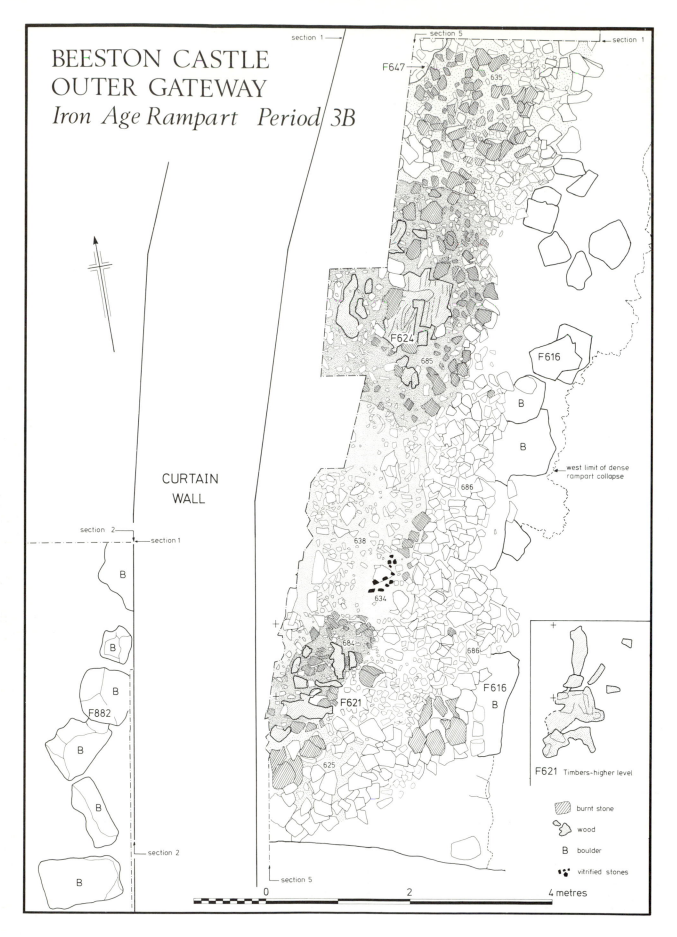

BEESTON CASTLE OUTER GATEWAY
Iron Age Rampart Period 3B

CURTAIN WALL

section 1

section 5

section 1

F647

635

F624

685

F616

B

west limit of dense rampart collapse

686

638

634

684

686

F621

F616

B

625

section 2

section 1

B

B

B

F882

B

B

section 2

B

section 5

F621 Timbers–higher level

burnt stone

wood

B boulder

vitrified stones

0   2   4 metres

Fig 15 Outer Gateway: Period 3B rampart F679; scale 1:50

tower. Following disuse of this structure, it is clear that the postpits to the rear of the rampart were deliberately emptied of their contents, while charred timbers remained *in situ* in the postpits on the rampart line.

A later phase is indicated by the stratigraphic position of the four postholes, three in line, to the west. These postholes are likely to have supported structures behind and parallel to the rampart; the latter was presumably entirely of stone, although other elements may well have been lost.

Beneath Tower 5 and to the east there are some indications of an upper level of stone which may be associated with the Period 3B rampart; here, however, there was no evidence of a boulder-filled trench. The presence of medieval pottery indicates disturbance in this area. The Period 2B and 3A ramparts here lie on a spur bowing out eastward of the scarp edge and it may be that the Period 3B rampart lay further west. However, the radiocarbon date (HAR-4402) from posthole F213 suggests that this may be a rampart feature and mark a setting for a timber revetment support.

As with the earlier rampart a quantity of pottery and artefacts was found in association with the rampart material. The majority of the pottery was of the Late Bronze Age. The sherds of a Late Bronze Age vessel (Fig 47.36) were recorded in the layer representing the fill of the outer boulder-filled trench, at a level below the upper limits of the Period 3A bank. It is possible that the vessel was introduced into the trench in backfill or collapse of Period 2B or 3A layers. Other illustrated vessels are Figures 45.19; 48.37, 40–1, and 49. However, VCP sherds were found in the rampart, with one sherd in the backfill of the eastern boulder-filled trench. A vessel of Iron Age date, probably of leather with copper alloy mounts, was located in the pit F833, and must have been deliberately deposited there (Figs 34.1 and 35). An iron tool was found in the inner boulder-filled trench (Fig 36.3). Other metalworking debris may have been residual. Further VCP sherds were found in F833 and in layers west of the curtain wall at the level of the group of four stone-packed postholes. This together with VCP sherds in overlying Period 4 layers suggests that some Period 3B activity associated with the salt containers was located here.

Radiocarbon and archaeomagnetic determinations are available for timbers from F621 and F624 and for

Fig 16 Outer Gateway: Period 3B rampart under excavation, view south (Photo P Hough)

Fig 17 Outer Gateway: Period 3B postholes to rear of rampart, view west (Photo P Hough)

burnt stone within the rampart body. Five radiocarbon dates from F621 and F624 lie within a range of 2430 and 2290 ± 70 BP (HAR-6464, 6465, 6468, 6469, and 6503). A date of 2400 ± 70 BP came from an associated fragment of charcoal (HAR-5609), while further similar dates came from a posthole and a displaced piece from a later context east of Tower 4 (HAR-4402 and 6459). Calibration of these dates (p 85) offers a range from 800–257 cal BC, but can be interpreted as centring around 400 cal BC. An archaeomagnetic date of 360–240 cal BC was indicated by measurements on pieces of burnt sandstone in the upper part of the rampart.

The ditch and entranceway below the rampart (Fig 14)

The Period 3A ditch, F185, was recorded to the north of the Outer Gateway site in two places. The deep V-sectioned ditch dropped sharply down to a terminal to the south. Differing fills were apparent in the two cuttings (Fig 20, Sections 10 and 11), and there was evidence of a possible recutting in the northern section, but in both transects the ditch fills were sealed beneath a layer of compact blue clay and stone, 177. The Period 3A ditch terminal, F490, had been infilled with layers of mixed sand, silt, and rubble, and the ditch had been recut to a terminal, F186, higher up the slope. There was some evidence of the recutting in Section 11 (Fig 20), where there appears to be a secondary cut into bedrock west of the ditch. F186 may have been associated with two postholes, F502 and F506, cutting the eastern lip of F490

(Fig 14). With the exception of the fills of F490 which can be placed in Period 3B, the ditch fills may be of Period 3B or 4. The sealing clay layer, 177, may represent a Period 4 deposit, perhaps at the base of a stream.

A southern extension of the ditch was located below Tower 7 (Fig 21), with, as noted above, a radiocarbon determination of 791–410 cal BC from the lowest silts (HAR-8102). The base fill of ditch F1000 was overlain by sand and silt layers beneath a thick deposit of sand and stones. A horizon of dark grey silt, 1008, represented its uppermost fill. No recuttings could be seen.

A sherd of Iron Age pottery was located in the lowest fill of the shallower terminal end of ditch F490. This sherd was one of only two found during the excavation campaigns attributable to the later Iron Age Fabric 26 (Table 22). The absence of any other pottery is presumably an indication that the ditch can be assigned to the virtually aceramic Iron Age. The dating evidence is confused by the result of the radiocarbon determination sought from charcoal in the same layer as the sherd of pottery. The date of 4036–3816 cal BC (HAR-6462) has been discussed with regard to the Period 1 features cut by the ditch, and this date is evidently associated with the Neolithic features to the east. A sherd of Neolithic pottery in the fill of posthole F502 is likely to derive from the Period 1A layers below.

The stratigraphic evidence for a recutting of the V-sectioned ditch in its northern section, and the evidence for the reworking of the ditch line following its silting, indicate a lengthy period of time during which the ditch formed a significant aspect of the defences.

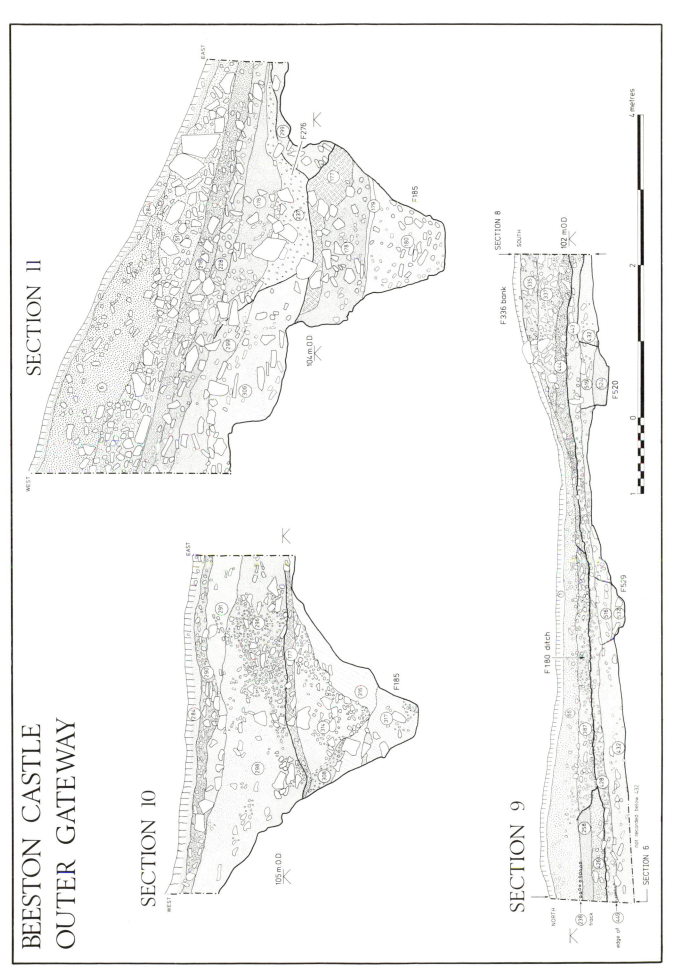

Fig 20 *Outer Gateway: sections 9–11; scale 1:50*

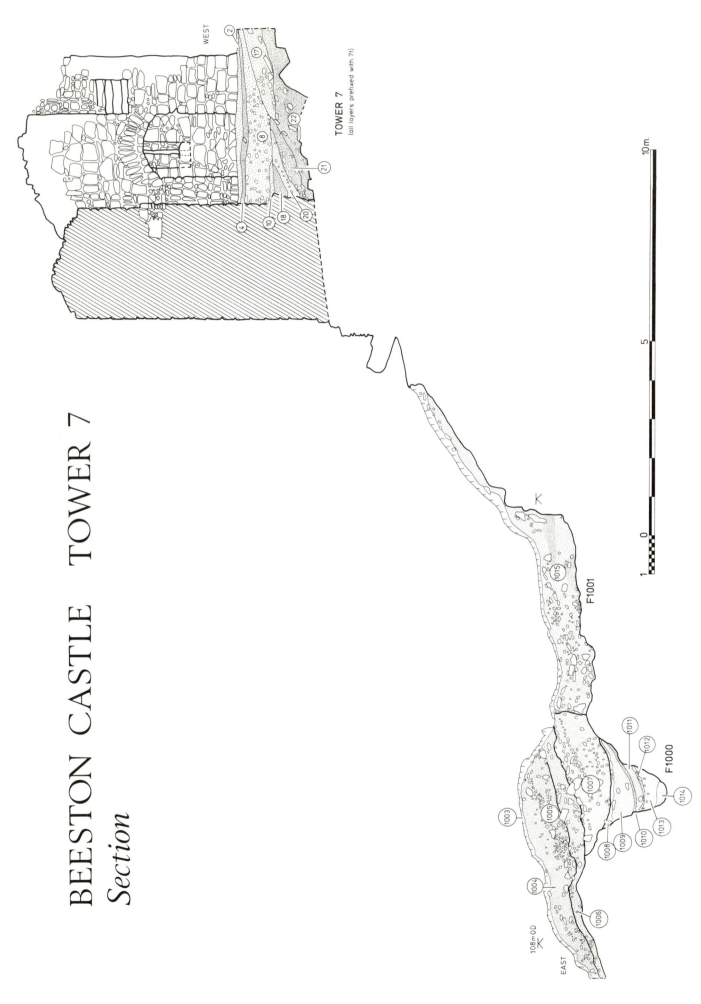

Fig 21 Outer curtain wall, Tower 7: section; scale 1:100

The ditch clearly indicated an entranceway – a southern continuation would have been removed by medieval ditch cutting. On the natural bedrock surface, a succession of trackway features and interleaving hillwash layers was recorded overlying the Period 2B layers. The indications of trackways were all confined to a line running up the natural valley leading to the plateau respecting the ditch terminal, F186.

To the west, parallel dark stains, F457, 2m long and 0.05–0.2m wide, separated by grey silt, were located 6m east of the scarp edge (Fig 19, Section 6). They lay at the westward limit of a layer of pebbles and brown silt with some charcoal inclusions, 458, and were overlain by a layer of flat and pitching stones, 456, at the level of 458. Layer 458 was traced eastward for 12m and formed a zone of trackway c 3m wide, overlain by a band of silt, 442. A shallow cutting, F559, may have been an eroded hollow associated with the trackway. A further element of trackway, 449, similar to 458 and in the same stratigraphic position, was located further east again, sealed beneath the silt layer 442. Other features appeared to have a spatial and stratigraphic relationship with the trackway spreads. A shallow cut, F567, lay just to the north of 458, as too did a stone-packed posthole, F539. Both shared the same Period 4 sealing horizon, as did F506, the posthole cutting the infilled F490. Further north a second postpit, F512, cut the Period 2B layer, 535, with F502 to the west.

The soil-marked features, F457, may well represent the remains of a timber base at a point where traffic was funnelled towards a narrow entrance point. Further downslope the remains of metalling were apparent, together with gullies and hollows possibly resulting from rutting and erosion. Layer 442 may represent a trampled horizon or a later Period 4 hillwash deposit. The function of the postholes north of the track is unclear.

VCP sherds were found on the trackway surface. All the trackway features seemed to belong to a period when the southern ditch terminal was in place, the tracks skirting its southern limit. This may suggest that the surviving trackway elements can all be assigned to Period 3B.

South of the trackway a number of other features were recorded lying beneath a Period 4 layer of hillwash soil, some cutting the Period 1A gully F517. These comprised a group of stone-packed postholes of which F520, F535, F557, and F587 may indicate a four-post structure. The postpits were laid out across the shallower line of the contours at the foot of the main scarp, and west of the sharper slope down to the valley floor. There seems little doubt from the density of postpits that some structure was located here, repeating the use made of the shallower hillslope in Period 1A. A gully, F480, and pit, F534, may not be associated but represent later erosion features. There was no dating evidence from the postpits, which may be of any prehistoric period.

The Outer Ward occupation (Figs 22–27)

Excavations in the Outer Ward revealed 146 postholes with stones present in the postpit backfill. Deliberate stone packing round a postpipe was identified in 61 of these postholes, and stones in the fill of the remainder seem likely to represent disturbed stone packing. As will be discussed below, the great majority of these postholes cannot be closely dated within the Late Bronze Age and Iron Age, and all are described here.

The postholes were cut into bedrock but only rarely were their outlines visible in overlying soil layers, except in the form of groups of end-set stones. Although excavation was by means of a succession of spits, each level being carefully planned, there was no evidence of occupation horizons. Recent pottery and clay pipe fragments were found at all levels down to bedrock or natural sand in all the cuttings. The soils were examined by Richard Macphail (p 83); it is clear that the loss of occupation evidence above the natural surface was due to the loose and uncompacted nature of the soils, and some movement of artefacts within the unstable matrix is suggested. The upper soil levels suffered disturbance in Periods 7 and 9 (see Part II of this volume), and, in addition, use of the pathway preceding excavation along the line of the West and East Cuttings must have resulted in some compaction and movement of the subsoils.

Where stone-packed postholes and other prehistoric features (discussed under Period 2B, p 24) were contiguous, the postholes were later. Prehistoric and post-medieval postholes were distinguishable by the visibility of most of the latter just beneath the topsoil. Later terracing, F297 (Fig 92), may have removed posthole evidence from the northern end of South Cutting and the eastern end of West Cutting, but there was no evidence that terracing had affected more than the eastern end of West Cutting, and it is probable that the absence of features over the eastern third of West Cutting, and in the south-eastern part of South Cutting, reflects a real distribution. A post-medieval quarry, F301, at the eastern end of East Cutting B affected only a small area.

The postholes were all relatively similar (Tables M6–M11, M1:A9–B3; Figs M28–M29, M1:B4–5). A large postpit (sizes ranging from 0.3–1.36m diameter, with an average of 0.75m) was filled with stone packing enclosing a postpipe ranging from 0.1–0.5m diameter. Most of the postpipes were around 0.35m in diameter, and were visible in a number of cases. In all recorded cases except two, where rectangular posts were used (F10 and F11), round posts were recognised, and similar posts may be assumed from the remainder of these pits. Some intercutting of postpits was observable, but this seemed in most cases to represent a replacement of an earlier post.

It is clear that the area had been intensively used, particularly in South Cutting and the western part of West Cutting, and different phases of use and rearrangements of layouts are to be expected. The absence of occupation floors or working zones confines the available information simply to the postholes. Two types of layout may be expected from prehistoric parallels: rectilinear and linear four-post and two-post structures, or circular roundhouses. There is little to suggest rectilinear or linear layouts, with the exception of two pairs of postholes in East Cutting A which appear to have been replaced slightly to the south: F256 and F265, replaced by F258 and F261.

The remainder of the evidence suggests the former existence of circular roundhouse structures. Given the criteria suggested by Guilbert (1981, 1982), none of the suggested Beeston structures is wholly convincing. Both Bronze Age and Iron Age double-ringed structures are seen as displaying a careful plan, with postholes mirroring each other either side of a supposed axial line through the entranceway to a posthole at the rear of the building. An odd number of postholes is suggested, with the widest spacing at the entrance (Guilbert 1982). At Beeston, possible structures have been sought where the posts are relatively evenly spaced along their suggested arc, although the slight depths of some of the postholes (Figs M28 and M29, M1:B4–5) show how easily the evidence could be lost. Only one of the suggested plans is complete, and elements of all the plans may have been lost.

Nevertheless, a number of former structures can be suggested, and they are discussed in detail in the microfiche (M1:A4–6). In West Cutting, Building 1 seems a possible attribution, while Buildings 2 and 3 are more speculative. In South Cutting, three further possible buildings, 4, 5, and 6, are marked by circular rings of postholes. The absence of postholes from the northern sector of Building 4 may be the result of later terracing. In East Cutting A, two intersecting arcs of postholes appear to be represented (Buildings 7 and 8). A possible final structure, Building 9, was located in East Cutting B.

Some pottery evidence was associated with the postholes suggested to represent buildings (Tables M6–8, M1:A9–13). Postholes F177 and F161 (Building 1), F241, F234, F242, F235, and F239 (Building 3), F86 (Building 4), F101 (Building 4 or 5), F77 (Building 5) F108 (Building 5 or 6), F245, F249, and F251 (Building 7), F244, F260, and F263 (Building 8), and F287 and F279 (Building 9), all contained a range of Late Bronze Age pottery fabrics. F28 in Building 6 and F220 in Building 3 contained sherds of Iron Age VCP fabric. To complete the pottery evidence the Period 2A data of Early Bronze Age pottery found in F242 (Building 3) and F253 (Building 7), and Middle Bronze Age pottery in F268, unaccompanied by later material, needs to be remembered. How

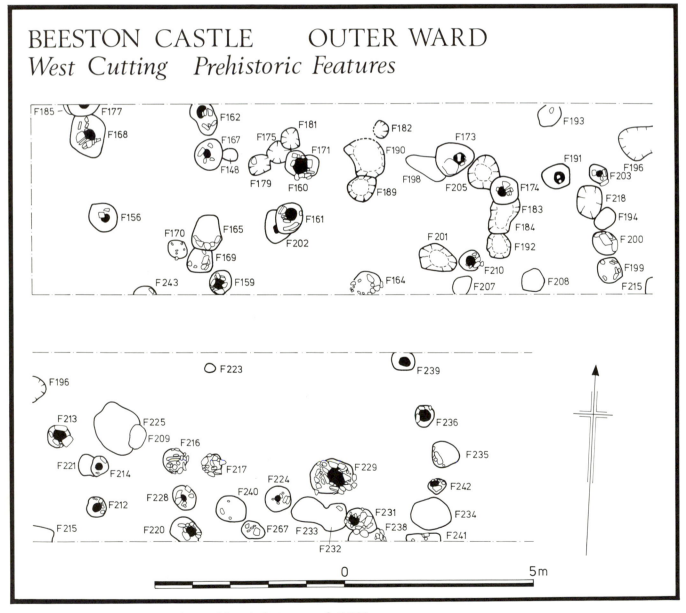

Fig 24 Outer Ward: West Cutting prehistoric features; scale 1:100

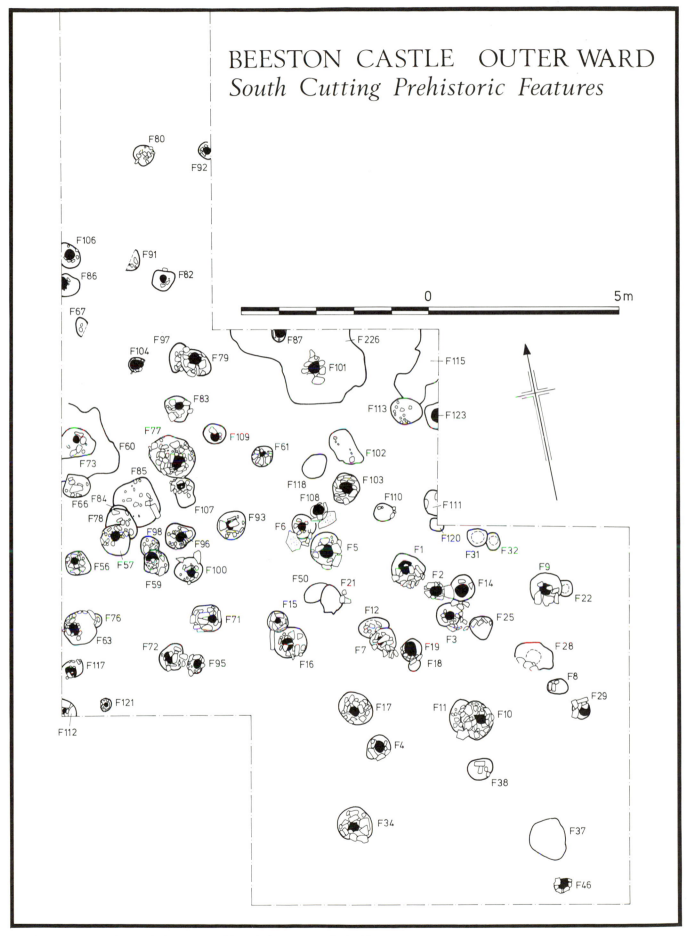

Fig 25 Outer Ward: South Cutting prehistoric features; scale 1:100

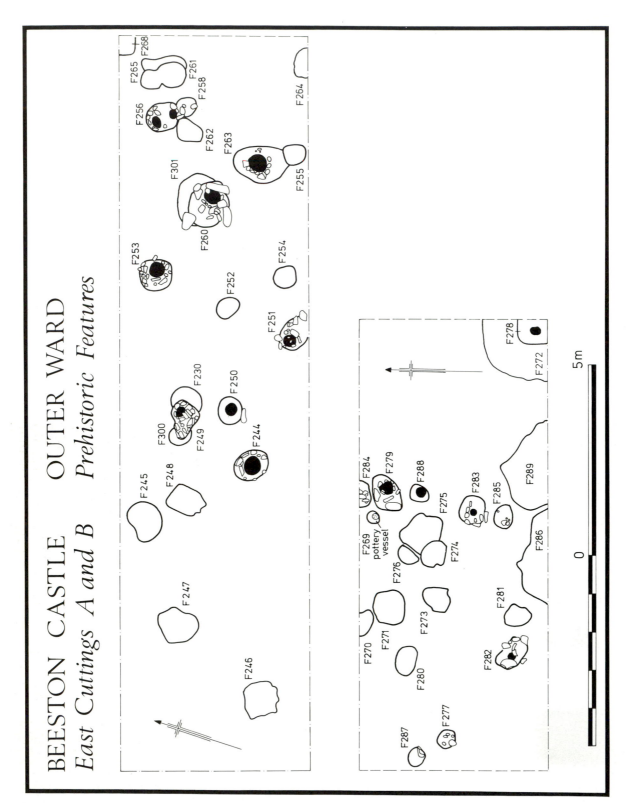

Fig 26 Outer Ward: East Cuttings A and B prehistoric features; scale 1:100

far this evidence can be used to indicate dates for the suggested buildings is not clear. The deposition of pottery in posthole fills may reflect material either from long pre-existing occupation areas, or associated with the structures, or fallen into pits left open after the structural timbers were removed.

A radiocarbon determination was obtained from charred post residues and charcoal in posthole F29, forming part of the suggested porch of Building 6, giving a date of 402–234 cal BC (HAR-4406). Four postholes associated with Building 5 contained metalworking scraps (F77, F93, F101, and F108, the latter shared with Building 6). Although this may signify no more than that the structure is placed at the apparent focus of metalworking, expressed in the distribution of finds (Fig 22), Building 5 is smaller than Buildings 4 and 6 on either side. The structure cannot have been contemporary with its neighbours, and it is possible that it represents a Period 2 structure. On different grounds it may be possible to suggest a late Bronze Age date for Building 9. The location of the Late Bronze Age pottery vessel buried in F269 (discussed under Period 2B, p 25) may be associated with the building, representing a storage container sited just within the confines of the building. There is evidence of ceramic containers within Late Bronze Age structures, sometimes stabilised by being set within pits. A good parallel for this practice is from Hut 1 at Weston Wood, Surrey (Harding 1964). The position and spacing of the postholes, apparently in pairs, may suggest some difference between Building 9 and the others. Other finds made from these posthole fills included a whetstone

found in F79 from Building 4 or 5, and a quern fragment in F97 from Building 4.

The problem of dating the structures can also be approached by way of their size. The evidence from southern England (Guilbert 1981, 1982; A Woodward, pers comm) suggests that the diameter of double-ringed structures increased from the Middle Bronze Age to the Middle Iron Age. On the basis of size the smallest suggested Beeston structures (Buildings 1, 2, 4, and 5) may be assigned to the Late Bronze Age, Buildings 3, 6, and 9 to the Late Bronze Age/Early Iron Age, while Buildings 7 and 8 have Iron Age counterparts. The dating of the Outer Ward occupation evidence is examined further in Chapter 4.

The remaining postholes unattributed to a structure are principally grouped in South Cutting, within and to the west of Building 6, and in West Cutting. Many must be attributed to structures of some substance but no spatial patternings are discernible. There are no apparent morphological differences between the ungrouped postholes and those allocated to suggested buildings.

Apart from Late Bronze Age pottery, VCP sherds were found in two postholes, F173 and F208. A radiocarbon date of 843–777 cal BC was obtained for posthole F25 in South Cutting. A Neolithic axe fragment in F200 (Fig 42.2) and two quernstone fragments (in F56 and F229) were found as components of posthole packing. Finally, an iron blade and strip were found in the fill of F5 (Fig 36.4 and 8), and a stone lid in F231.

As noted above, F256 and F265 seem to form a pair of postholes replaced by F258 and F261. The latter two postholes contained pottery, with a sherd of VCP in F258.

Fig 27 Outer Ward: West Cutting under excavation, view east (Photo P Hough)

The overlying layers in the Outer Ward contained a number of objects of prehistoric date. These included copper alloy bracelets (Fig 34.2–3) and a horse harness link (Fig 34.4); a glass bead (Fig 44.2); two shale rings (Fig 43.5–6); four clay loomweights (Fig 52.6–8) and a possible pedestal (Fig 52.9); and a quernstone (Fig 41.1), a stone spindlewhorl (Fig 42.9), and two jet/cannel coal beads (Fig 42.15–16), amongst other stone items (Table 21).

The Lower Green (Fig 3)

Small-scale excavations by the modern gatehouse at the foot of Beeston crag encountered a layer of sand above natural, containing Late Bronze Age pottery. This was overlain by a sandy soil with further prehistoric material including Iron Age VCP sherds. A possible feature or an erosion gully running downslope, as well as two possible postpits, were noted. Forty metres to the south, prehistoric pottery, with VCP sherds preponderant, was found in salvage work during a watching brief. The evidence suggests prehistoric occupation here and the amount of VCP may be significant.

Period 4: Romano-British to the thirteenth century

At the Outer Gateway, the trackways of Period 3B, and the later southern terminal of the ditch, were sealed beneath a layer of dark soil with charcoal, 234 (Fig 19, Section 6). This layer was recorded running downslope, almost from the scarp edge, for 14m, spread across the Period 3 trackway over a width of 6m. In addition it sealed the ditch terminals F186 and F490 and the postholes F539 and F567. Further down, layer 446 represented an intermittent continuation of 234. Layer 234 was examined in the field by Richard Macphail who suggested (p 84) that it might represent a hillwash layer or a trampled layer marking an entranceway. He noted too that it overlay a truncated surface.

Prehistoric pottery was found in 234, ranging in date from Neolithic to Iron Age. The rarer later Iron Age Fabric 26, also noted in ditch F490, was represented. In addition a sherd of Romano-British pottery was found. A radiocarbon determination on charcoal within layer 234 (HAR-6504) gave a date of 405–270 cal BC.

Elsewhere deposits of sand, stone, and brash were recorded and, in addition, a number of large boulders. In illustrated sections these suggested Period 4 layers can be noted overlying ditch F185 (Fig 20, Section 10, layers 296, 298, 299, and 306) and forming the layers overlying the Period 3 postholes in the south-eastern part of the site (Fig 20, Section 9 and Fig 19, Section 8, layers 443 and 444). Boulders were encountered below the steepest scarp sections both north and south of layer 234. Downslope in Section 6 (Fig 19), layer 446, the equivalent of 234, was overlain by layers 426 and 428 apparently the same as 444 and 443 respectively.

To the rear of the Period 3B rampart a uniform deposit of sand and stone (828) was recorded which may be a hillwash deposit (Fig 18, Section 4).

Layer 234 directly underlay the Period 5 medieval trackway, suggesting that an entranceway from low ground on to the hill was constantly maintained here throughout the early historic and early medieval periods. The presence of the Roman sherd, the composition of the layer, its very mixed cultural content, and the truncation of the surface below, all suggest that it represents a hillwash deposit dating from the early historic period following the disuse of the Iron Age hillfort. The layer must represent both a trackway and occupation debris from within the defences washed out through the entrance. The other erosion deposits to north and south are likely to indicate a continuing episode of decay and collapse of the Period 2 and 3 defences.

At Tower 7, ditch F1000 (Fig 21) lay beneath a deep layer of sand and rubble with sand and fine pebble lenses, 1007. This may represent a succession of erosion deposits over a long period. Part of the composition of the layer may well derive from the Period 2 and 3 defences located at the scarp edge above. A stabilisation of hillside erosion may be indicated by the overlying soil layer 1006. The Period 4 layers here were the subject of study by Richard Macphail and Ken Whittaker (p 84). A radiocarbon determination of 673–892 cal AD (HAR 8101) was found from the soil layer 1006 (p 85).

Nine sherds of Romano-British pottery (Table M24, M1:E9) and two brooches (Fig 37) were found in Period 4 and later layers at the Outer Gateway and Outer Ward. The pottery assemblage included five second-century samian sherds, all except one abraded.

At the Lower Green excavations (Fig 3), the prehistoric levels were sealed by an overall layer of irregular stones and pebbles, which was compacted in places, and associated with Romano-British building materials. Finds of Romano-British pottery from the second to fourth centuries were associated (M1:E9–14). The evidence seems to represent a yard related to nearby buildings, or perhaps a trackway within a settlement.

3 The finds

The Beeston Castle Bronze Age metalwork and its significance

by Stuart Needham

Introduction

The excavations yielded a good number of objects of copper alloy of which nine are diagnostic Bronze Age types. To these may be added a tenth piece found by a metal detector user previously. These have all been catalogued. The undiagnostic metalwork obviously presents more problems in deciding which were relevant to Bronze Age activity. At the Outer Gateway, where a good stratigraphy was recorded, two fragments seem to belong to Bronze Age or immediately post-Bronze Age contexts, and these have been included in the catalogue. In the Outer Ward areas the copper alloy material came from topsoil, or, in a few cases, from features (Table 12). The features are rarely unequivocally dated and are thought to include many of post-Bronze Age date (p 35). In view of these difficulties full catalogue entries have not been provided except for two pieces: one (no 14) has a composition matching the Late Bronze Age objects and the other (no 13), although possibly not contemporary, has a distinctive ingot form worthy of description. In the discussion, however, it is argued on circumstantial evidence that some of the undiagnostic material could belong to the Late Bronze Age activity. This material is covered in Appendix 1 (M1:B6–8).

Classification of the axes

The scheme employed in this report develops that first created for the Petters hoard (Needham 1986; 1990). There, four broad classes of socketed axe, all previously recognised, were labelled Classes A–D. Two of these occur in the Beeston assemblage along with a fifth class, here labelled E.

Ribbed socketed axes (Classes B and E: Figs 30–2)

The majority of the socketed axes from Beeston Castle are ribbed forms with three roughly vertical ribs descending from the lower of two horizontal mouth mouldings (Figs 30.1, 2; 31.5, 6; 32.9; and 33.7). These fall into two groups. Two of the complete examples correspond in all respects to the group defined elsewhere as Class B (Needham 1986, 42–3; 1990, 32), which is well distributed in the Midlands and southern England. The broken axe (Fig 33.7) should also belong to this class. The other three ribbed axes differ, however, in having a body which is more squat with sides that expand more rapidly from below the mouth mouldings. The latter difference is well illustrated by a certain metrical value which has been calculated for all the Beeston axes (Table 13). The squat class is termed Class E for convenience, but the extent to which it merges into Class B in one

Table 12 Outer Ward: Copper alloy objects

	Features	Topsoil
Diagnostic LBA types		
Axes	1	3
Knife	—	1
Spearhead	—	1
Sword	—	1
Total	1	6
Undiagnostic pieces		
Lumps	12	14
Ingot	1	—
Thin wire	—	6
Plate/sheet/strip	2	2
Others	—	6
Total	15	28

direction and classic Yorkshire type axes in another remains to be resolved through wider studies. The general proportions of Class E have much in common with Yorkshire axes, especially perhaps the axe illustrated in Figure 31.5.

Although some examples among the corpus of Yorkshire type axes published recently by Schmidt and Burgess (1981) are very similar to Beeston Class E axes, the majority differ in having very widely spaced ribs, the two outer ribs lying virtually along the body angles. This is perhaps the classic trait distinguishing Yorkshire axes from all other ribbed forms, and again the axe illustrated as Figure 31.5 is closest in this respect.

Axes which are closely similar to the Beeston Class E examples are classified by Schmidt and Burgess (1981) not only within their Yorkshire type (eg nos 1429, 1444, 1447, 1517, and 1521), but in two cases within their Welby type (nos 1339 and 1342), which otherwise contains axes attributable to Class B. This highlights the potential problem of gradation from one regional stylistic preference to another and deserves fuller investigation, as was indeed acknowledged by Schmidt and Burgess (1981, 223).

A distribution map for Yorkshire axes across Britain as a whole was last published by Burgess and Miket (1976, 6, fig 2). The definition is presumably the same as that employed by Schmidt and Burgess (1981), the distribution thus encompassing a number of Class E-like variants. Even so the Midlands, with the exception of Lincolnshire, are astonishingly empty of finds and the Beeston Castle examples therefore are noteworthy additions.

Table 13 Relative body expansion of ribbed socketed axes (in mm)

Axe	W1	W2	LB	$\frac{W2-W1}{LB}$	Class
1	24.5	31	50	0.13	B
6	26.5	34.5	60	0.13	B
2	25	43.5	70	0.26	E (unfinished)
5	29	38.5	45	0.21	E
9	26	34	40	0.20	E

W1 width of face immediately below lower mouth moulding
W2 width of face at lowest point before any hammer working
LB length of body between W1 and W2

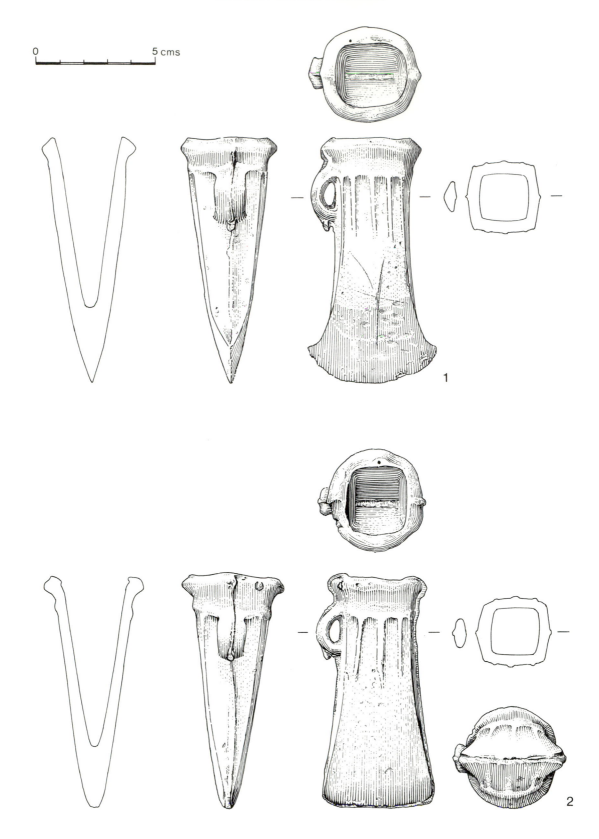

Fig 30 The socketed axes from the Late Bronze Age rampart; scale 2:3

Only one axe amongst the Cheshire finds published by Davey and Forster seems likely to conform to Class E, that from Byley (1975, no 86). A further axe from Congleton (not the hoard) is uncertain because it is poorly recorded (ibid, no 88). Similarly Class B axes appear to be infrequent in Cheshire despite their relatively widespread distribution in the Midlands as a whole. Just two Cheshire examples are known (ibid, nos 121, 129), one being in the important local hoard of Congleton, which appears to be a personal set of equipment dating to the Ewart Park phase.

In fact the dating of both kinds of ribbed axe present at Beeston Castle is well established in the Ewart Park phase *c* 900–700 BC.

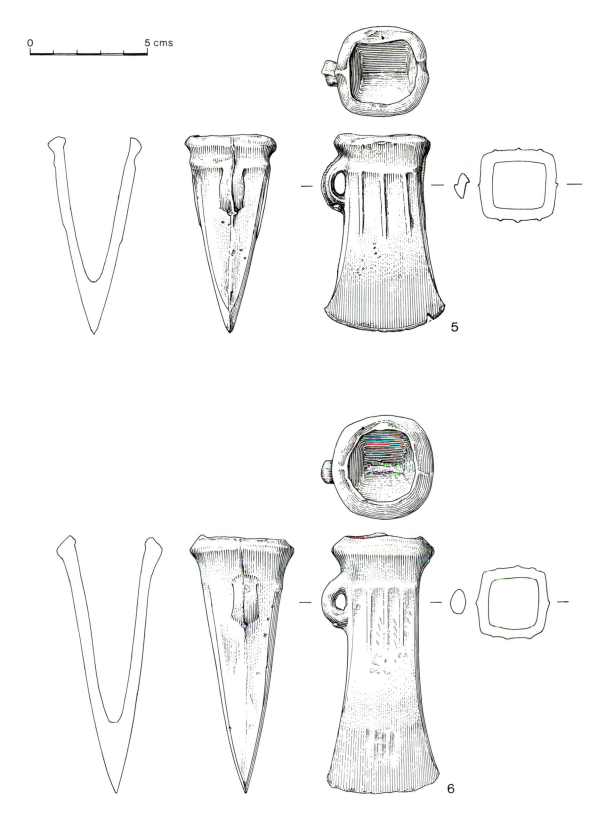

Fig 31 Two socketed axes from the Outer Ward, South Cutting; scale 2:3

The faceted axe (Fig 32.8, Class D)

Faceted axes of the long slender proportions that are primarily a feature of the British series have been grouped as Class D elsewhere (Needham 1986; 1990, 41). Needless to say there is considerable stylistic variation within this class and Schmidt and Burgess have attempted to express this variation by defining three variants within their type Meldreth (equivalent to Class D) in dealing with the northern British material (1981, nos 1212–1252).

Specific features of the Beeston faceted axe are the duodecimally faceted body, deep collar, and groove-defined mouth moulding. The first feature is quite exceptional since these axes almost invariably have an octagonal section. A rare duodecimally faceted axe is one from the Thames (British Museum 1864.5–11.4). The deep collar is a well-known feature and seems to have a specifically northern emphasis. Small bead mouldings (the lower mouth moulding) at the base of such a collar are recurrent throughout the series and the enhancement by bordering grooves on the Beeston piece can be seen to relate to a variety of fine groove/rib combinations erratically present (eg Schmidt and Burgess 1981, nos 1231, 1235, 1236, and 1244).

The very fine finish received by the Beeston Class D axe is typical of the class. The careful removal of casting flashes, which is far more consistently done than on any contemporary axe type, suggests a more prestigious role.

The socketed knife (Fig 33.10)

The noteworthy features of the socketed knife are its fluted blade, straight socket/blade junction, and near rectangular socket section. The straight socket junction places this example, along with the vast majority of British finds, in Hodges' Thorndon type (1956, 38). This terminology however, masks some heterogeneity in the group as acknowledged by Burgess (1982, 38–9). He ascribes knives with fluted blades such as the Beeston example to a type Hammersmith, but has not taken socket sections into account in his classification. The rectangular form of the Beeston example is rather unusual but is occasionally matched on the general type, eg in the Grays Thurrock hoard, Essex (O'Connor 1980, fig 56.4). A few socketed knives seem to match the example from Beeston Castle in all essential aspects of morphology; one such example comes from further south in the West Midlands, at Lyonshall in Herefordshire (National Bronze Index, British Museum). In fact few socketed knives are known from the West Midlands and the Welsh Marches. A large specimen, again with fluted blade, comes from close to Beeston at Hordley, Shropshire (NBI).

The sword blade (Fig 33.11)

Little can be said about the sword blade fragment which is not very diagnostic. The blade section is most commonly encountered on Ewart type swords and given the associations at Beeston Castle this is perhaps the most likely origin.

The spearhead (Fig 33.12)

The Beeston Castle spearhead is relatively short and squat in proportions. Ehrenberg (1977, 15) has described such weapons as 'short stumpy spearheads', defining them metrically as shorter than 100mm, with a maximum blade width about one third of the length. The Beeston Castle specimen certainly fits these criteria and also has the typically wide mouth. Although these may represent just one end of the large spectrum of shapes and sizes associated with plain peghole spearheads, it does seem possible, especially looking at the standardisation achieved in some groups (eg Blackmoor: Colquhoun 1979, fig 4.4), that this was conceptualised as a specific type in the Late Bronze Age,

perhaps with a specific functional role. Only large-scale metrical analysis can test whether these constitute a definite sub-population.

The short stumpy type seems to have emerged within the Wilburton metalworking tradition to become frequent in Ewart contexts (Colquhoun 1979, 106).

Technology of axe casting

There is one noteworthy technological point to be made about the axes of Classes B and E. Where loops survive they have, in four cases out of five, a small spur projecting from the underside. Parallel examples of this feature can be found elsewhere, though often the spur has been virtually removed. Its occurrence can be explained by reference to bronze moulds for casting ribbed axes. Such moulds often have an elongated cavity alongside but separate from the axe matrix (eg at Brough on Humber, Briggs *et al* 1987, 19, fig 6; at Washingborough, Davey 1973, 90, no 216; and at Heathery Burn, Britton 1968, no 71). This cavity or 'overflow' chamber descends from the underneath of the loop where an extremely narrow gate would allow molten metal to pass through it from the main mould cavity. Strictly speaking this is not an overflow since it would begin to fill before the axe casting itself was complete. Its function instead appears to have been to ensure the successful casting of the loop. It is possible that experience taught Late Bronze Age smiths that loops were prone to be miscast if the passage of molten metal around the mould cavity resulted in a pocket of gas being trapped in the void for the loop. Normally gases might not have escaped quickly enough to allow the molten metal to take up the loop matrix fully. By adding the side chamber the metalworkers avoided this risk, yet still checked the amount of metal that could escape the main mould and be wasted. The constriction at the entrance to the side chamber would readily allow gas out but would severely arrest the flow of metal, thereby preventing much from escaping before local cooling took place to solidify the metal. If the mould assembly and the molten metal became too hot, so that the melt continued to flow through the constriction, then the side chamber would fill but no further loss from the matrix cavity would occur. The smith would therefore be sure of obtaining a full casting of the axe by simply ensuring there was a little extra in the melt, as would have been standard practice in any case. When the casting was extracted any metal formed in the overflow chamber would be snapped off the axe in the same way as the casting jet, and later returned to the melting pot.

Dating of the Bronze Age metalwork

In dating Bronze Age metalwork we are normally dependent on conventional typological dating. The Ewart phase attribution for the Beeston diagnostic finds would place them at c 900–700 BC in calendar years. The radiocarbon dates from Beeston itself, and from a direct association with a Class B axe from the Breiddin hillfort, broadly confirm rather than refine this dating. One radiocarbon measurement is on burnt timbers associated with the Period 2B Late Bronze Age rampart: 2860±80 BP (HAR-4405). The two-sigma range cali-

Fig 32 Socketed axes from the Outer Ward: West Cutting (8) and pre-excavation find South Cutting area (9); scale 2:3

brates to the span 1300–840 cal BC. Although mainly earlier than the accepted dating of the Ewart phase, this span could easily be accounted for if the sample represents timber lacing of the rampart, which might be expected to make use of mature timber. The determinations for the Period 3B rampart, although wide-ranging,

are argued to centre on the fourth century BC (p 86) well after Bronze Age metalworking ceased.

A number of other Late Bronze Age sites producing Ewart metalwork have also yielded radiocarbon results, but the only direct association relevant here is the measurement on part of the wooden haft from a Class

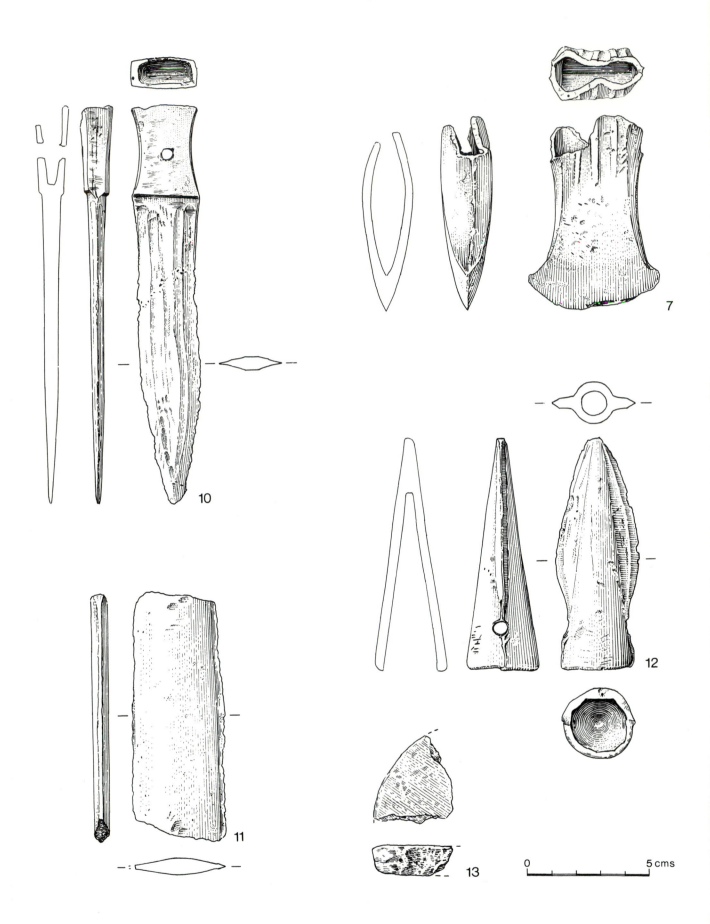

Fig 33 Bronzes from the Outer Ward: socketed knife from West Cutting (10), scrapped axe fragment (7), scrapped sword blade fragment (11) and spearhead (12) from South Cutting, bronze ingot fragment (13) from East Cutting B; scale 2:3

B socketed axe from the Breiddin excavations (Musson 1991). The result of 2704±50 BP (BM-798) calibrates at two sigma to 1020–790 cal BC. This would seem to point to an early rather than late date within the currency of Ewart types.

Conclusions from the analyses
by Duncan Hook and Stuart Needham

It was possible for Duncan Hook (Department of Scientific Research, British Museum) to analyse all of the ten diagnostic Bronze Age pieces by atomic absorption spectrophotometry (Appendix 2, M1:B9–C1). The compositions show a fair degree of homogeneity both in the trace element levels present and in the amount of added lead and tin. They are all leaded tin bronzes, although one piece has an unusually low value for lead (no 9). These results suggest that all the pieces in the group could be made from metal from one source or, perhaps more likely, from a regional pool of metal in circulation where repeated recycling and mixing had created a homogeneous composition.

Of the six undiagnostic bronzes analysed quantitatively only one has a composition which closely corresponds to the above group (no 14). This piece at least can be regarded as related to Late Bronze Age metalworking. Four other lumps have distinct compositions which are again fairly well clustered (M1:B13–14). These fragments are tin bronzes without any deliberate lead additive, giving another distinction.

Two main options present themselves for the explanation of this second composition group. If they represent residues from casting and/or recycling operations, then they would be the residues of a tin bronze working tradition. Numerous analyses to date suggest that in the Late Bronze Age bronze metalwork systematically included lead in greater or lesser quantity. As casting residues, therefore, these fragments would probably belong to another period. We should not, however, completely rule out the possibility that these pieces result instead from some intermediate process in Late Bronze Age metalworking. These small lumps would, in this model, have to be considered as representing previously unused metal at some intermediate stage prior to its addition to recycled material in the Late Bronze Age. In this case its different impurity suite would have modified that of the recycled stock according to the relative proportions mixed. However, it might be difficult to accept these small amorphous lumps of alloyed tin bronze either as freshly smelted metal (ie prills) or as residues from the refining of the intermediate alloy, rather than as general casting waste. On balance therefore it would seem most likely that they are residues of another period.

The ingot fragment (no 13) was shown to have a composition which is distinct from both groups.

Fifteen smaller fragments of metalwork, mainly from the Outer Ward, were analysed qualitatively by X-ray fluorescence. Only two (nos 3 and 4) were shown to be leaded bronzes, both having come from stratified positions within the rampart sequence at the Outer Gateway indicative of a Late Bronze Age or earliest Iron Age date.

The significance of the assemblage

The Late Bronze Age metalwork assemblage at Beeston Castle would appear to be unusual in the frequency of complete implements. Although the associations at the site suggest in general terms a settlement context, it is difficult to find parallels with assemblages from excavated settlements of the same period.

The distribution and specific contexts of the Beeston Castle metalwork are central to its interpretation. The finds come from two excavated areas which lie 130m apart. At the Outer Gateway, two complete axes (Fig 30.1 and 2) lay within the body of material interpreted as the first phase of a rampart sequence (Period 2B). They were 4m apart and can be regarded as separate finds. Two more pieces (nos 3 and 4) may be relevant to this phase in view of their stratification only a little higher in the Period 3A rampart; neither is diagnostic and both are small pieces, but they are leaded tin bronzes typical of the Late Bronze Age, and may have originated from the suggested Period 2B metalworking area (p 24). Copper alloy material stratified in the rearward platform (and not covered here) might include further fragments residual from the Late Bronze Age activity.

The majority of the Bronze Age metalwork comes instead, however, from the Outer Ward, having been retrieved from all trenches (Fig 21). The metalwork was widely dispersed, most pieces coming from the topsoil and just one (Fig 31.6) from a subsoil feature.

Before discussion is taken any further it is necessary to address the question of how much of the undiagnostic metalwork and clay refractory debris should be regarded as contemporary with the Late Bronze Age bronzes. The contexts are generally unhelpful, having little by way of independently datable material in association. Unfortunately the refractories are not diagnostic, but their general character and the technology employed are in keeping with a Bronze Age rather than later date. For the small nondescript metalwork the best evidence available is probably that of composition. Analysis suggests that little of it relates clearly to the Late Bronze Age artefacts (only one of the five quantitatively analysed lumps). Nevertheless, taking into account also the two large bronzes which had been scrapped (Fig 33.7 and 11), there is evidence that some metalworking took place in the Outer Ward area during the Late Bronze Age.

The Late Bronze Age assemblage at Beeston Castle does not conform to the character of Middle and Late Bronze Age assemblages typical of settlement debris; in particular there are no small tools, personal implements, or small fragments of larger implements, and few if any ornamental fittings (although there is a possible pin shank fragment). That this is not due to a regional difference is suggested by the assemblage excavated at the Breiddin hillfort, Powys, which represents a classic range dominated by pins, rings, studs, etc (Coombs 1991). It seems possible that the difference may be explained in terms of the excavated area of the Outer Ward being a specialised metalworking area during the Late Bronze Age. The domestic debris (eg pottery) could relate to the day-to-day needs of the metalworkers themselves, or have spread laterally from adjacent residence units. The presence of a concentration of clay refractories in the South Cutting supports this interpretation; that material would have a low survival rate if subjected to weathering, trampling, or processes of physical dispersal for any length of time. The clay refractories are likely therefore to be close to the area of use, ie casting, and to represent terminal phases of activity after which they were worked into the soil profile by natural processes. Two of the larger bronzes (Fig 33.7 and 11) had been scrapped and were presumably destined for the melting pot. The others may represent a mixture of worn objects intended for recycling, newly made objects, and tools in general use by the metalworkers.

It is possible that these large bronzes, which would be expected only occasionally to have accidentally escaped the recycling routine, were actually deposited as a hoard. There is no compelling evidence that they constitute a dispersed hoard, however, and it would seem just as likely that they are a genuine scatter or 'Area Find' as defined in Needham *et al* (1985, vi). They may represent a sequence of losses over some time or instead belong mainly to an abandonment horizon.

Although the occurrence of material relating to metalworking is coming to be expected on excavated Late Bronze Age sites, the Beeston assemblage may have more specific connotations. On some sites metallurgical debris is represented as diffuse 'background noise' amongst domestic rubbish. Occasionally discrete dumps of clay refractories have been found, suggesting metalworking nearby, but such dumps have tended to be the sole evidence found for metalworking (Dainton, Devon being an exception). At Beeston, the interpretation offered above suggests that the trenches in the Outer Ward were located at an area that was primarily concerned with metalworking at some stage in the Ewart Park phase. It has not been possible to suggest such a specialised area on a Late Bronze Age site to date, although a scatter of Late Bronze Age metalwork from inside South Cadbury hillfort, Somerset, is described as coming from a 'furnace area' (Alcock 1971, 5). At Runnymede Bridge one group of bronzes may relate to a short-lived phase of scrapping preparatory to recycling, and a similarly restricted horizon is suggested by the distribution of metalworking debris in the large ditch at Petters (O'Connell 1986). Even at Petters the relevant remains may be secondary rubbish rather than in primary locations.

If metalworking was an important activity on the Beeston Castle hilltop, then the choice of a freshly cast and largely unfettled axe for incorporation in the contemporary Period 2B rampart assumes added significance. It is clear that this axe could not have been lost whilst in use and the coincidence of two axes lying just 4m apart at essentially the same stratigraphic horizon also militates against the suggestion of accidental loss. The axes lay within the body of the earliest rampart and seem best interpreted as deliberate incorporations, perhaps as foundation deposits. In such a context the symbolism of a newly cast axe may have been deemed important.

Another point to make in the context of metallurgical activity is that sources of copper ore are known at the foot of the hill itself and at the nearby Peckforton hills.

These were worked in the nineteenth century and Tylecote has already speculated that they may have been exploited in the Bronze Age (1987, 29). The general area of the Peckforton hills has yielded a small cluster of Middle to Late Bronze Age metalwork, both bronze and gold, including two hoards to the south of Beeston (Longley 1987, 94, fig 17 upper).

Catalogue

(Throughout the catalogue L = length, W = width, B = breadth, D = depth, Wt = weight, Dm = diameter, and Th = thickness)

1   Socketed axe, Class B (Fig 30). Mostly retaining mottled blackish/dark green patina; scattered lighter green pockmarks and small corrosion lumps, especially towards cutting edge. Intact and fairly sharp parts of cutting edge are interspersed with corrosion damage. Extensive hammer rippling over bottom 30mm of blade, but no defined bevel line at top. Hammering has created well-expanded blade tips with slight side hollows and slight kinks in line of body angles. Numerous fine grinding marks run longitudinally on faces. Side flashes survive as low stumps intermittently hammer flattened, except for a more protuberant thin web above loop and a spur projecting from underside of loop. Flash and feeder stumps well removed from mouth. Body angles crisp with very light beadings along their upper halves. Three stouter ribs descend vertically from horizontal rib moulding below a pronounced upper mouth moulding of near biconical form. Socket tapers to narrow rectangular end. Loop broad with isosceles section. L 102.5mm; W cutting edge 53.0mm; W mouth 41.7mm; B mouth 39.0mm; max B loop 12.4mm; D socket 70mm; Wt 288.4g. AM Lab no 840299, OG 641, Period 2B rampart.

2   Socketed axe, Class E (Fig 30). Patchy surface of dull green, yellowish brown, pinkish spots, and brighter greens. Last mainly associated with flaking of very thin surface layer. Some undulations and 'dimpling' of surface is likely to represent original as-cast form. Cutting edge in totally blunt as-cast state with casting flash still present, but probably hammered over; also minimal hammering of adjacent surfaces has created small facets. Much but not all of side flashes partially reduced by cutting/hammering. Projecting spur from underside of loop. Mouth flash and feeder stumps fully and neatly removed. Casting defect in form of a double notch into upper mouth moulding.

Very pronounced biconical upper mouth moulding with rib moulding below. From the latter descend three vertical ribs which are neither especially straight nor evenly spaced. Fairly angular body angles, especially crisp towards cutting edge. Body cast with marked flare and minimally concave sides. Loop broad with flattened oval section. Socket tapers to thin wedge end. L 97.0mm; W cutting edge 46.1mm; W mouth 41.0mm; B mouth 42.0mm; max B loop 12.0mm; D socket 71.0mm; Wt 299.2g. AM Lab no 852661, OG 676, Period 2B rampart.

3 Shank fragment (not illustrated). Patches of yellowy-green patina, badly flaked to dry light green surface; generally fragile.

Probably of circular section with curve towards one broken end. Could belong, for example, to pin shank, thick wire bracelet, or rivet. Extant L 12.5mm; max Dm 3.3mm; Wt 0.3g. AM Lab no 844288, OG 674, Period 3A rampart.

4 Blob of copper alloy (not illustrated). Small knobbly lump with much of surface flaked away. Max dimension 4.7mm; Wt 0.06g. AM Lab no 844294, OG 637, Period 3A rampart.

5 Socketed axe, Class E (Fig 31). Very dark green patina, part flaked thinly to green dry surface and much speckle-pocked to similar surface. One blade tip slightly chipped due to corrosion, rest of cutting edge intact and sharp being backed by narrow (1–2mm) and steep bevel carrying concentric grinding marks. Hints of hammer marks up to 25mm above edge, but no defined bevel. Blade tips only modestly expanded with no development of hollows. Several small dimples in surfaces are possible casting defects, as also is rounded notch in mouth top on one side. Casting flash removed to broad, low stump on lower sides, but fairly prominent higher and incorporating stump of a spur on underside of loop. Two halves of loop either side of flash are mismatched, giving dislocated lenticular section, but whole of body shows good valve matching. Feeders and flash round mouth virtually wholly removed, final hammering having then created some facets. Upper mouth moulding sub-biconical, lower one rib-like and supporting three prominent vertical ribs, fairly evenly and widely spaced. Body cast with moderate flare and with somewhat round body angles. Socket tapers to flattish rectangular end. L 84.0mm; W cutting edge 51.5mm; W mouth 41.2mm; B mouth 38.7mm; max B loop 10.3mm; D socket 62.0mm; Wt 238.3g. AM Lab no 810415, OW 145, fill of F50, Period 2B.

6 Socketed axe, Class B (Fig 31). Grey-green patina broken by pocking to light green dry surfaces. Short stretches of cutting edge intact and sharp, but most, including both blade tips, is corrosion-chipped, probably since excavation. Bands of fine grinding marks run parallel to cutting edge, whilst hammering probably extended higher up blade; this caused slight change in line and crispness of body angles as well as small blade tip expansion and associated hollows. Probable as-cast dimpling on upper body surfaces. Casting flash removed on lower sides, leaving only a ghost, and reduced to low stump above, at least partly by hammering; stump of projecting spur on underside of loop; stump of mouth flash round inner edge of socket mouth with feeder base above either face; a punched bevel encircled this flash.

Good angular body angles. Three vertical ribs, not quite evenly spaced, descend from slight step defining the base of moulding, which expands trumpet-like to biconical upper mouth. Loop roughly oval sectioned. Socket tapers to thin wedge end. L 109.0mm; extant W cutting edge 48.6mm; W mouth 43.0mm; B mouth 44.4mm; max B loop 11.0mm; D socket 79.0mm; Wt 307.1g. AM Lab no 819159 OW 226, Period 9.

7 Socketed axe, blade half, Class B (Fig 33). Green patina much broken by pocking to dry light green surface, especially towards cutting edge. Signs of hammer marks associated with crushing of body at the break, thus certainly scrapped. The lower parts of three vertical ribs on either face are disfigured by this damage. Many minor dents and scratches over body. Blade tips well expanded thus having created blade tip hollows. Some evidence of hammer marks survives on steepish edge bevel despite corrosion; bevel not crisply defined at top. Low, rounded stumps of casting flashes on sides. Cutting edge damaged by corrosion, but rough furrow in central part may be due to original flaw. Socket ends in sharp wedge form. Body angles fairly angular. Extant L 79.5mm; W cutting edge 52.6mm; D socket 65.0mm; Wt 134.1g. AM Lab no 819160, OW 180, Period 9.

8 Socketed axe, Class D (Fig 32). Mottled blackish green/milky green patina, areas broken by speckled mini-pocking to light green surface, especially close to cutting edge. Both tips of latter are corrosion chipped, but remainder is intact with sharp, acute edge. Band of grinding marks (up to 10mm broad) concentric with edge, and diffuse hammer marks extending to about 25mm up the blade. Body very well polished but diffuse traces of longitudinal grinding marks along facets. Casting flashes extremely well removed leaving traces only in loop angles, and, much flattened, at points around mouth top.

Upper mouth moulding virtually flat-topped with fairly angular profile; concave underside has obtuse break of angle before reaching lower moulding. The latter would originally (as-cast) have been a small step, thus overall a trumpet moulding; however a bead- or rib-moulding effect has been created in post-cast working by punching two horizontal grooves, one at the step, one higher. In a few places punch strokes have not held the line thus spoiling otherwise neatly executed grooves.

Loop with D section, body with symmetrical duodecimal section. Blade tips expand abruptly. Socket tapers to flattish rectangular end. L 113.0mm; extant W cutting edge 44.0mm; W mouth 33.0mm; B mouth 31.5mm; max B loop 6.0mm; D socket 83mm; Wt 154.7g. AM Lab no 865095, OW 557, Period 9.

9 Socketed axe, Class E (Fig 32). Remnants of green patina much disfigured by pocking to dry green surface. Some light file marks across central rib of one face. Small fragments of patina close to cutting edge suggest concentric grinding marks; edge itself broadly intact, but blunt, probably due to corrosion and subsequent damage. Moderate blade tip expansion occurs below a defined curved bevel about 18mm above edge; no associated blade tip hollowing. Perforation high in side wall has rounded edges – almost certainly an original casting defect. Low, thin stump of casting flashes on sides, but very little left on mouth top.

Upper mouth moulding with rather changeable profile, rounded to sub-biconical. Lower moulding survives as slight bump only, as do three widely spaced ribs. Body angles fairly angular. Loop with thin lenticular or D-section. Socket tapers to very thin rectangular end. Body profile slightly hollowed between rib ends and edge bevel. L 85.5mm; extant W cutting edge 49.5mm; W mouth 40.0mm; B mouth 36.5mm; max B loop 9.0mm; D socket 68mm; Wt 160.1g. AM Lab no 794742, pre-excavation chance find, more or less from centre of South Cutting.

10 Socketed knife (Fig 33). Mottled green/blackish green patina with only limited pocking. Large stretches of cutting edge including tip are ragged from corrosion chipping; upper parts only are intact and sharp, being backed by very narrow secondary bevels (< 1mm). Breakage on one face at mouth probably ancient. Hammer rippling, including rounded and elongated indentations, covers much of blade surfaces and gives wavering facet junctions. Dense band of fine grinding marks across both faces at top of blade immediately under socket. Similar copious transverse grinding marks cover whole socket surface, on the sides crossing slight vestiges of the reduced casting flashes. Some lipping round inside of pegholes due to punching from outside.

Socket has flat top and evenly waisted body terminating in near straight, abrupt step to blade. Internal socket tapers to flat, thin rectangular end. Blade had slight constriction before swelling to maximum girth, this shape being reflected by the central of five longitudinal facets.

Wood fragments were retrieved from the socket during conservation. Extant L 159.5mm; W mouth 26.4mm; W shoulders 27.2mm; min intact blade W 23.0mm; max extant blade W 24.0mm; extant B mouth 12.5mm; B socket end 9.4mm; Th blade top 7.0mm; D socket 33.0mm; Wt 88.8g. AM Lab no 865088, OW 522, Period 9.

11 Sword blade fragment (Fig 33). Slightly greyish-green patina broken by scattered pocks to lighter green dry surface. Virtually all of cutting edges blunted to greater or lesser extent by fresh corrosion chipping; one very short stretch is just about intact with sharp edge thinned by slightly hollowed edge bevels. Small clusters of hammer marks lie on midrib alongside both breaks, though on one face only.

Broad convex-sectioned midrib with slight flanking hollowing inside bevels. Distance between edge bevels narrows steadily towards one break, indicating the fragment is likely to originate from gently tapering part of blade. Extant L 100.5mm; max extant W 37.7mm; max Th 6.2mm; Wt 103.3g. AM Lab no 819161, OW 158, Period 9.

12 Socketed spearhead (Fig 33). Dark green-brown patina largely intact. Blade edge damaged by fresh corrosion chips in several places including tip. Rest of edges possibly intact, but they are rounded rather than sharp. Neat concave edge bevels follow blade outline. Casting flashes have been left rather prominent on socket.

Leaf-shaped blade. Near circular socket/midrib section tapering quickly from squat socket. Socket has small circular flattish end. Extant L 94.0mm; W mouth 29.5mm; B mouth 28.8mm; max W blade 33.5mm; D socket 70.5mm; Wt 72.8g. AM Lab no 801508, OW 10, Period 9.

13 Ingot fragment (Fig 33). Green patina intact. Original edge an even convex curve and one angle rounded to give a plano-convex profile. Original surfaces are slightly uneven and may include some small hammer indentations. Extant radius 30.0mm; W 39mm; max Th 12.7mm; Wt 55.1g. AM Lab no 865100, OW posthole F285, Period 3.

14 Lump (not illustrated). Small fragments of green patina but most flaked to a powdery light green surface. Broadly wedge-shaped piece, probably broken at the thicker end; tapers a little to other, rounded end; roughly oval section. Possibly part of a thick tang or punch. L 13.3mm; W 12.0mm; Th 7.7mm; Wt 4.5g. AM Lab no 865129, OW posthole F264, Period 3.

Iron Age copper alloy objects (Figs 34 & 35)
by Jennifer Foster

1 Rim for leather vessel (Fig 34)

(*Note by Peter Ellis:* (a), (b), (c), and (d) were found in 1984 at the Outer Gateway west of the curtain wall in the Period 2B layer 860. Their position was recorded three-dimensionally and indicates that they in fact belong with (e), (f), and (g) found the season before in the Period 3 layer 833 filling pit F831.)

(a) Half of an oval rim, probably from a leather vessel discussed below. Made of beaten bronze, the rim consists of a double plate riveted to the leather with three carefully planished disguised rivets. On the outer surface the rivet heads are almost impossible to see. Decorated with two incised lines, one below the rim, the other following the gently curving lower edge. On the inner surface beating marks can just be seen; on the outer surface, where it is finished to a mirror-like surface, there are none. Broken at both ends. The leather would have been thick (3mm); a few fragments remain inside the rim. AM Lab nos 852657 and 852658.

(b), (c), and (d) Three fragments representing the other side of the rim. They mirror exactly the curve, shape, and rivets of (a). This suggests that the diameter is not distorted and that the original object was oval in shape, not circular. None of the pieces joins.

(b) No edges. Part of outer face of binding with upper line of decoration, lower line broken off. Rivet 4mm long is planished as in (a). AM Lab no 844290.

(c) Internal face of binding, one rivet. AM Lab no 852659.

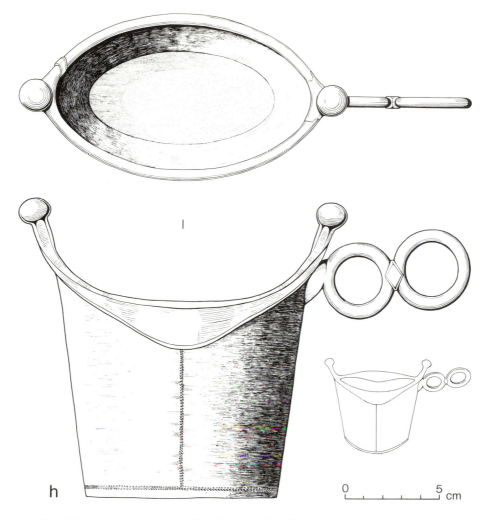

Fig 34 Iron Age copper alloy objects: reconstruction of leather vessel; scale 1:2

(d) Top of rim, outer edge has upper line of decoration. Edge on inside face. AM Lab no 852660.

(e) Extension of rim which rises up into a domed knob (knob A). The knob is of cast bronze and was cast onto the beaten rim. It is just possible to see the joins on the inside of the rim. The knob is of a slightly different colour than the rim, owing to the different composition of the pieces (see below). The rim is decorated with two incised lines (a), with the upper line of decoration rising up into a point beside the knob, while the lower line ceases below it. Here the bronze was carefully filed flat; this was the area covered by the handle (g). The decoration was evidently done after the knob had been cast onto the rim. Diameter of knob 15mm. AM Lab nos 844291, 844293, and 844295.

(f) Knob B from the other side of the vessel matches knob A exactly except that the area under the knob has been finished for display; there was no handle on this side. It has the same diameter (15mm) as knob A and was similarly cast on to the beaten rim. On one side this join subsequently cracked and has been supported by a bracket (decorated with two incised lines) and a rivet, not as well disguised as the original rivets. The other arm has also been broken, and this looks worn. It is possible that the vessel was used in

a fragmentary condition. The knob also is corroded. AM Lab no 844287.

(g) Cast handle in the form of two joined circles with a diamond between them. Beautifully made and finished. The handle is the blue-green bronze of knobs A and B. It was at a steep angle to the rim (see reconstruction, Fig 35) and would have borne the not inconsiderable weight of the vessel; the outer circle is slightly damaged in consequence. The fitting plate is also damaged on the lower edge. D inner circle 39mm, outer circle 41mm, one of rivets 7mm; D rivet heads 3.5mm. AM Lab no 844289.

(h) Reconstruction of the vessel (Fig 35). Pieces (a) to (g) are almost certainly from a single object, the rim and fittings of a leather vessel. The rim plates were made first, by beating from a low-tin sheet bronze. Radiography by Gerry McDonnell indicates that the ends of the rim plates were then flattened and the knobs cast on. The handle was the last piece of the vessel to be added, fitting the rim of the vessel, below knob A, snugly without solder by means of a convex oval plate, the underside of which still bears the scratches where it was filed to fit against knob A. The area of bronze below knob A was also carefully filed flat to accommodate the handle. There is a casting flaw here, which would have been covered by the

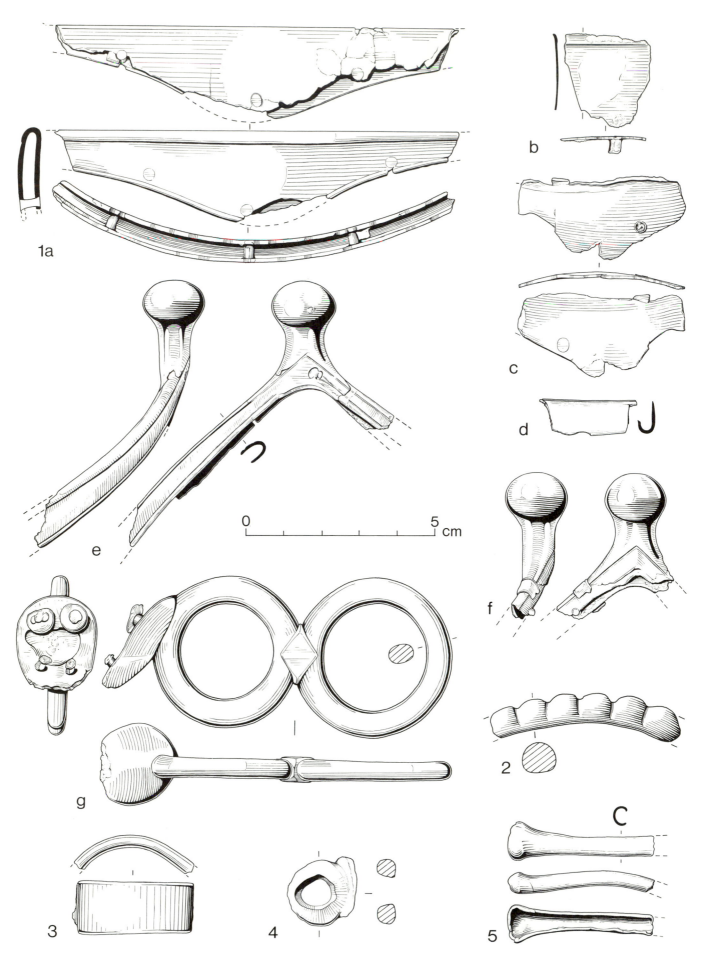

Fig 35 Iron Age copper alloy objects: fragments of rim of leather vessel (1) , bracelet fragments (2–3) , horse harness link (4), binding strip (5); scale 1:1

handle plate. The handle was riveted on to the leather with four rivets, which, like the rivets on the rim, have been so well planished that they are almost impossible to see on the outer surfaces, although they are now a slightly different colour owing to differential composition. After the handle was attached, the rim plate was decorated with a double incised line, and the rim then riveted to the leather vessel. The leather must have overlapped where it joined, but there is no sign from the remaining bronze pieces where this was. The vessel was oval in shape, rather than round, approximately 135mm long internally and 75mm across. The depth is difficult to estimate, although a plausible reconstruction, as shown here, indicates a depth of *c* 130mm. The capacity would be a little over 1 pint (0.5 litres), and it was probably designed as a drinking vessel. It is not possible to say, of course, whether the vessel was flat-bottomed or rounded; although later Iron Age drinking tankards were flat-bottomed (Corcoran 1952) they were of wood rather than leather.

One of the interesting aspects of the bronze fittings is the careful choice of alloys, evident in the different colours between the beaten bronze rim, which is a yellow-green, and the cast knobs and handle, which are blue-green in colour. Knob A is composed of a leaded high-tin bronze (Gerry McDonnell, SEM analysis, M1:C2–5), chosen specially for its properties in casting: the presence of lead would increase the fluidity of the metal and it would be liquid at a lower temperature than unleaded bronze. However, the subsequent alloy is more brittle and would not be suitable for beaten sheet bronze, like that used for the vessel's rim: this is of a low-tin bronze (SEM analysis, M1:C2–5). The difference in colour between the two alloys was probably not noticeable when the object was made.

This is a rare and beautiful vessel made by a highly accomplished craftsman. It is very well finished, down to the last rivet. It would have been greatly prized during use, and was carefully mended when it cracked. It was probably secreted in F831 either with an intention to retrieve it at a future date, or as a final resting place for a ritual object.

2 Cast copper alloy bracelet/armlet segment decorated with round knobs, broken at both ends. D-shaped section. Badly corroded and worn. There are a few knobbed bracelets/arm rings from Britain, most of which were found in the Arras graves in Yorkshire (Stead 1979, 72–7). This fragment is unusual in that there is generally a gap or ridge between the knobs. Continental parallels suggest that the type lasted from the Late Hallstatt into the La Tène period. Cunliffe suggests (1974, 146–7) that all the British knobbed bracelets were imported from France and Switzerland. L 50mm. AM Lab no 731 852, OG Tower 5, SGT 5, Period 9.

3 Undecorated cast bracelet fragment broken at both ends, at one end with force. Ovoid section. Diameter distorted. L 30m. AM Lab no 865093, OW 543, Period 9.

4 Cast horse harness link, broken at the collar. Ovoid

hole probably extenuated by wear: most links of this type have circular holes (eg Cunliffe 1974, fig 10.5). L 17mm. AM Lab no 819098, OW 166, Period 9.

5 U-shaped section binding strip with splayed terminal, other end broken. Stress cracks at terminal, due probably to beating during production (Tylecote 1962). A very similar piece from Danebury, described as possible scabbard binding, was not later than 100BC (Cunliffe 1984b, 342, Fig 1.49). L 37.5mm. AM Lab no 830461, OG 443, Period 4.

6 Domed weight with tapering central hole. Distorted on one side probably due to casting fault. Worn. This is not pre-Roman in date and could be post-medieval. D 11mm. AM Lab no 865087, OW 522, Period 9.

Iron objects (Fig 36)
by Ian Stead

1 The upper part of the blade and lower part of the tang of a dagger. The fragment is 112mm long, of which the blade is 76mm at one side and 82mm at the other (the shoulders are not level). The shoulders slope from the thin rectangular-section tang (7 × 3mm) to a maximum width of 42mm. From there the blade tapers sharply to about 33mm and then maintains that width. Several La Tène I dagger sheaths are flared at the mouth to take blades of this shape (e.g. Jope 1961, nos 16, 21, and 25). AM Lab no 844352, OG 854, Period 3A.

2 Spear- or javelin-head. L. 111mm. It has a pronounced midrib that tapers from the socket and a single large perforation (10 × 9mm) at one side. Inside the socket are traces of the mineral-preserved wood of the shaft, to which the head has been attached by an iron rivet. Spearheads with perforated blades are known from the continent, usually in La Tène II contexts (Brunaux and Rapin 1988, 126), but they seem to be much larger than the Beeston Castle specimen. There is a close parallel, but longer (200mm), from Roodstown, Co Louth (Raftery 1983, no 285), and one with two perforations, from Broomlee Lough, Northumberland (Manning 1976, no 19). AM Lab no 835039, OG 311, Period 7.

3 Socketed tool, with curved blade slightly expanded from the socket. Perhaps a somewhat delicate adze rather than a chisel. AM Lab no 852646, OG 862, Period 3B.

4 Small curved blade with a short tang. Perhaps a razor. L 81mm. There are similar examples from All Cannings Cross (Cunnington 1923, 126, pl 21.11) and Gussage All Saints (Wainwright 1979, 104, fig 80.1104) but the type continued into Roman times (cf Manning 1985, type 23, especially Q.66 and 67, from Hod Hill). AM Lab no 811921, OW 28 in posthole F5, Period 3.

5 Swan-neck pin with broken head (indicating it could have been a ring-headed pin). L 85mm. For the type see Dunning 1934. A copper alloy ring-headed pin

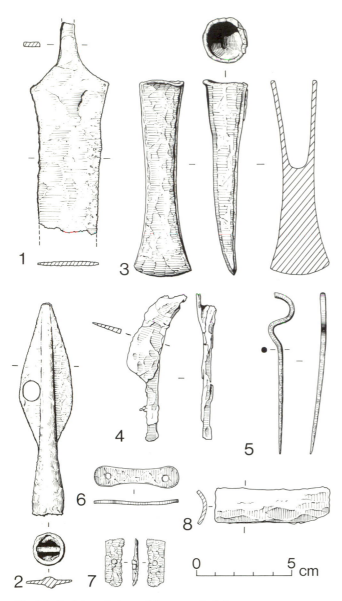

Fig 36 Prehistoric iron objects; scale 1:2

was found in a Late Bronze Age context at Runnymede Bridge (probably seventh century BC, S Needham, pers comm) so iron examples might occur as early as iron was used in this country. They are well known from Iron Age settlements such as Gussage All Saints (Wainwright 1979, figs 80.1081 and 80.1103) and All Cannings Cross (Cunnington 1923, 129, pl 21.2–4) – where there is also an iron swan-neck pin (ibid, pl 21.1). AM Lab no 852640, OG 860, Period 3A.

6 Strip with rounded ends, perforated at each end for a nail or rivet. Perhaps a repair strip. L 46mm. AM Lab no 852643, OG 862, Period 3B.

7 Broken strip with remains of four copper alloy rivets. L 25mm. AM Lab no 852644, OG 860, Period 3A.

8 Thin strip, curved in section and curved along its length, as if a segment from a hoop (eg a nave-hoop – but it is very thin for that). AM Lab no 811920, OW 28 in posthole F5, Period 3.

The Romano-British brooches (Fig 37)
by Sarnia Butcher

The full report on two brooches is in microfiche (M1:C6–7). In brief they are:

1 Trumpet brooch, first to second century AD, probably made in the north-west part of the province. Outer Gateway, Period 9.

2 Enamelled brooch, second century AD. Outer Ward, Period 9.

The metalworking evidence
by Hilary Howard

(*Note:* The following report is based on Chapter III.5 of Hilary Howard's PhD thesis (Howard 1983). The report describes the material found in the Outer Ward in 1980. Metalworking evidence from later excavations is described in an appendix (p 56). The analytical results, including fabric descriptions, are available in the microfiche (M1:C8–11).

Illustrated fragments (Fig 38)

Outer Ward

1 Crucible; Fabric 1. OW 20, Period 9.

2 Crucible; Fabric 2. OW 7, Period 9.

3 Crucible; Fabric 2. OW 7, Period 9.

4 Crucible; body, Fabric 2, and upper relining, Fabric 1. OW 19, Period 9.

5 Mould; inner valve for socket or ferrule, Fabric 3. OW 3, Period 9.

6 Mould possibly for sword; inner valve, Fabric 3, and outer wrap, Fabric 4. OW 19, Period 9.

7 Mould for sword; inner valve, Fabric 3. OW 19, Period 9.

Outer Gateway

8 Crucible/furnace lining. OG 618, Period 3A.

9 Crucible with slag adhering. OG 618, Period 3A.

10 Mould; two curving grooves. OG 353, Period 7.

Discussion

Metalworking debris recovered during the excavation of the Outer Ward area in 1980 comprised some 20 fragments of bivalve clay moulds and five crucible sherds (including Fig 38.1–4). The mould fragments are generally poorly preserved, but parts of matrices for

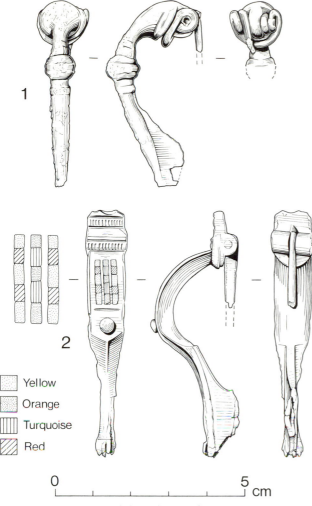

1

2

Yellow
Orange
Turquoise
Red

0 5 cm

Fig 37 Romano-British brooches; scale 1:1

able. Most moulds are too abraded for identification of the range of implements cast, and the lack of stratigraphic relationships precludes any suggestion of separate casting phases. A measure of technological information was obtained from fabric analysis (different clay preparation and slightly different inclusion suites for inner and outer mould components), but at this stage no distinct groups can be defined on mineralogical grounds.

While all the mould fragments at Beeston could conceivably be derived from a single casting episode, the crucible evidence suggests a longer period of activity. Two crucible fragments were identified with inclusions differing from the moulds. Variations in grain size, range, and matrix density show that at least three and possibly five vessels are represented. The use of an organic crucible paste is unique in British Bronze Age contexts, and illustrates the individuality of smithing groups during this period. Whilst it is possible that the Beeston smiths added charcoal or other organic material to a ferruginous clay, it is equally likely that naturally carboniferous clays such as those occurring in abundance at Bunbury may have been deliberately selected for crucible making. The relining of one organic and sand-tempered crucible sherd (Fig 38.4) with the more siliceous carbon-free material is especially interesting, and suggests the concurrent use of two distinct pastes for crucible production by the Beeston smiths. X-ray fluorescence detected trace amounts of lead in two samples of Fabric 2, and a little tin in the relined fragment (presumably in the relining layer) but the amounts detected were very small and near the detection limits for the machine used (J Bayley, pers comm). Although it would be unwise to deduce that the selection of different crucible pastes was related to the composition of the metal to be melted, the possibility cannot be entirely discounted.

The individual requirements of Bronze Age crucible and mould makers are emphasised when the Beeston refractory fabrics are compared with those of the various pottery groups from the site (Table 22). Unlike the pottery no rock fragments are present in the Beeston

casting swords (Fig 38.6 and 7) and a socket or ferrule (Fig 38.5) were tentatively identified.

The small collection of refractories from Beeston is extremely difficult to interpret. Although a bivalve technology and the presence of spearhead and ferrule matrices point to a Late Bronze Age date, little more can be inferred from the mould evidence at present avail-

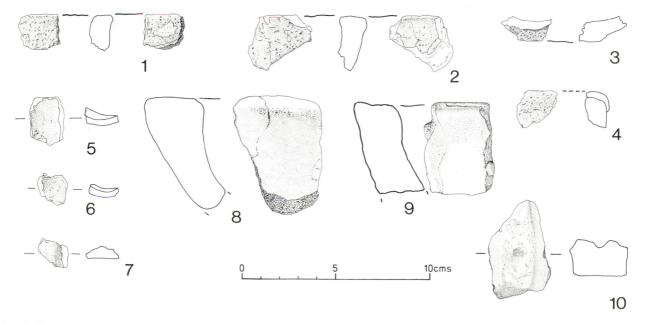

1

2

3

5

6

8

9

4

7

0 5 10cms

10

Fig 38 Refractory debris; scale 1:2

refractories which, with the exception of the organic-rich crucible sherds, consist exclusively of sand, sandstone, a little quartzite, and moderately micaceous or non-micaceous clay. Raw material studies have shown that all these refractory ingredients could be obtained with ease in the vicinity of Beeston crag. Although the deposits exploited cannot be identified with certainty, close matches between clays and refractories have been made. It is clear that, as at other bronze production sites of this period, the Bronze Age smiths at Beeston were familiar with the range of locally available materials, and were able to adapt these materials to meet their own stringent requirements.

Appendix
by Peter Ellis and Cathy Royle

Further fragments of moulds and crucibles were identified in later excavations at the Outer Gateway. In addition, during the course of the analysis of the prehistoric pottery, a group of sherds with slag adhering was isolated. This additional refractory debris was macroscopically identified and no thin sectioning or X-ray fluorescence analysis has been undertaken. While the pieces are visually similar to those assessed by Hilary Howard it was thought preferable not to assign them to the fabric groups outlined above.

The five crucible fragments included one piece and joining sherds from the Period 3A rampart (Fig 38.8 and 9). An inner valve mould fragment was noted in a Period 7 layer (Fig 38.10). There were also four sherds with slag adhering.

The distribution of the Outer Ward find spots (Fig 22) strongly suggests a centre of metalworking located near the South Cutting, since the amount of refractory debris found in the East and West Cuttings is small in comparison. Within the South Cutting the finds are concentrated in the southern area, suggesting the focus of activity lay there or nearby.

A second concentration of metalworking debris find spots is to the north of the prehistoric entranceway, and is principally located in the Period 3A rampart. In addition, soil analysis of these rampart layers (p 83) suggested furnace debris and waste from high temperature fires. The position of this material must suggest that it was already waste at the time of the construction of the rampart. The rampart components must presumably have been gathered from close at hand and thus a second metalworking location can be postulated in Period 2B just inside the enclosure entranceway.

The condition of the moulds does not, unfortunately, allow comparisons between the examples from the two separate find locations. In view of the arguments outlined above for long-standing production, it is likely that the two identified metalworking locations were not contemporary.

The flint
by Rebecca Smart

A total of 862 flint pieces were recovered from the excavations, of which the majority (671) came from the Outer Ward (Tables M14 and M16, M1:C13–14); almost all the remainder derived from the Outer Gateway (Tables M17 and M18, M1:D1). The collection can be considered as wholly residual. The full report is available in the microfiche (M1:C12–D1). A list of the illustrated pieces and the discussion is presented here. Flakes of rock crystal are the subject of a separate report (M1:D6).

The illustrated flint tools (Figs 39 & 40)

1 Microlith; narrow blade, steep backing, retouch on upper half of both ends; Mesolithic. OW 652 posthole F175, Period 2.

2 Blade; use on left side has caused flaking, on poor-quality flint; Mesolithic. OW 73, Period 9.

3 Blade; evidence of use on right edge, on fine banded chert; Mesolithic. OW 543, Period 9.

4 Blade; retouch left edge, patina broken by retouch, bulb snapped off at later date; Mesolithic. OW 543, Period 9.

5 Microlith; steep retouch on left side partially removing bulb, evidence of use right edge; Mesolithic. OW 612, Period 9.

6 Arrowhead, leaf-shaped; broken, tip snapped off at bulb end, very thin in section with minimal retouch on bulb side, on good chalk flint; Early Neolithic. OW 161, Period 9.

7 Arrowhead, leaf-shaped; delicate retouch all round, blunted in places; Early Neolithic. OW 7, Period 9.

8 Arrowhead, leaf-shaped; fine pressure flaking; Early Neolithic. OW 543, Period 9.

9 Arrowhead, leaf-shaped; very delicate, heavy light grey patina; Early Neolithic. OW 612, Period 9.

10 Blade, ?small knife; delicate pressure flaking on both edges, on good chalk flint; Late Neolithic/Early Bronze Age. OW 154, Period 9.

11 Knife or scraper; delicate pressure flaking, very steep angle of retouch; Late Neolithic/Early Bronze Age. OW 557, Period 9.

12 Knife or blade; retouch left side, generally rounded by use with a slight gloss, right edge steep blunting retouch; Late Neolithic/Early Bronze Age. OW 10, Period 9.

13 Knife; delicate retouch both edges and bottom, slight gloss runs parallel to right edge on bulb side, slight use along edges with much heavier use at tip where slightly rounded; Late Neolithic/Early Bronze Age. OW 10, Period 9.

14 Scraper; delicate retouch, very slight stepping due to use. OW 19, Period 9.

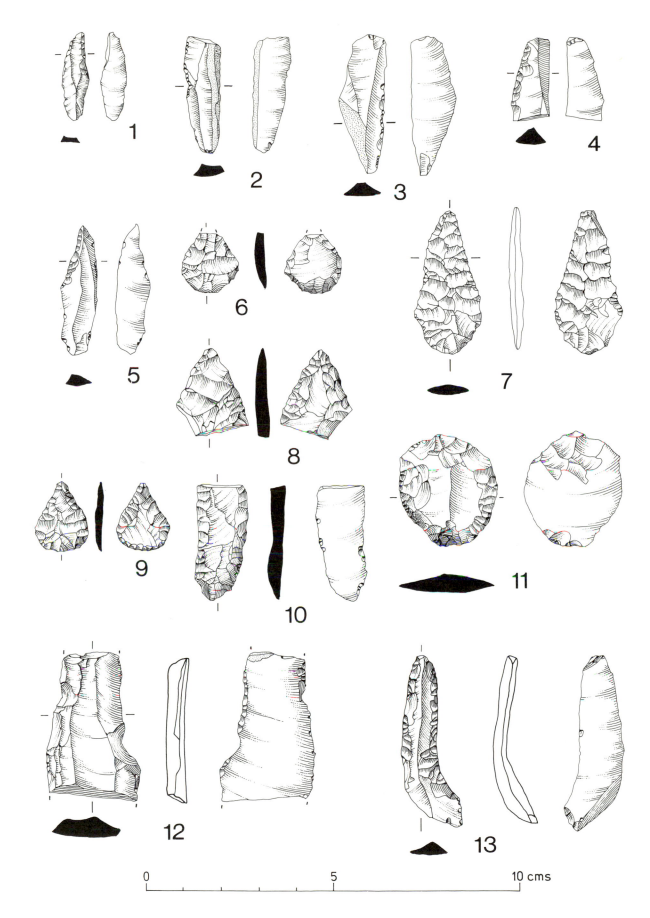

Fig 39 Flint implements; scale 1:1

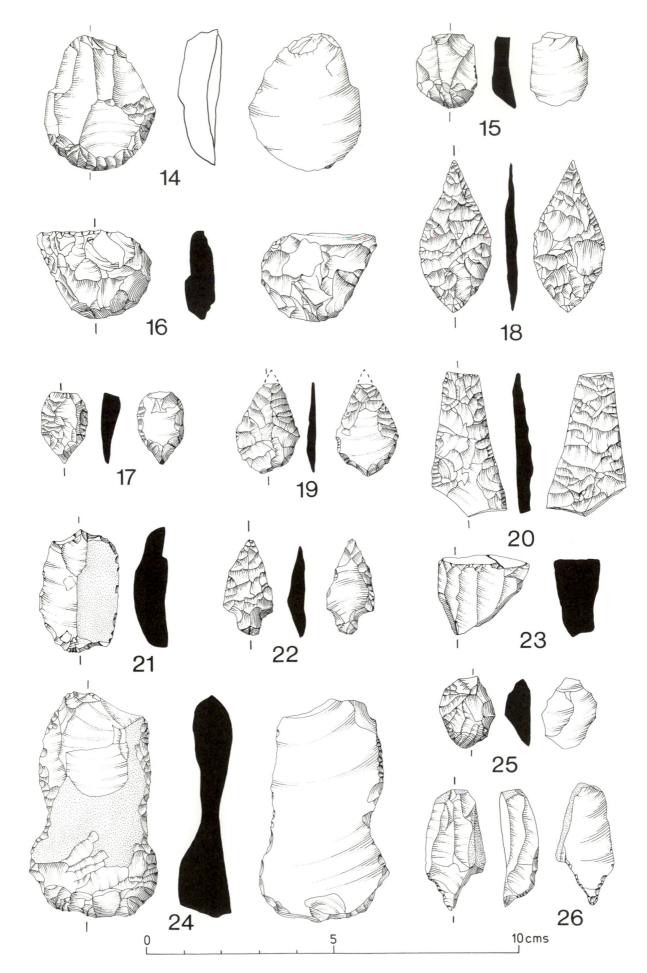

Fig 40 Flint implements; scale 1:1

15 Scraper; some cortex remaining, delicate retouch at end, on good chalk flint. OW 211, Period 5.

16 Scraper, short end; light thermal fracturing occurred after retouch, possible crude attempts to reshape scraping edge from bulb side, no gloss. OW 7, Period 9.

17 Point (not an awl); delicate retouch both sides, pressure flaking on top side (ventral). OW 543, Period 9.

18 Arrowhead, leaf-shaped; fine delicate retouch, on good grey flint; Early Neolithic. OG 656, Period 2B.

19 Arrowhead, leaf-shaped; broken at tip; Early Neolithic. OG 676, Period 2B.

20 Arrowhead, ?barbed and tanged; broken, fine delicate pressure flaking, on light grey good flint. OG 657, Period 3A.

21 Scraper, double end; very heavily burnt, some damage on bulb side. OG 831, Period 3B.

22 Arrowhead, tanged; most of the retouch on one side only resulting in a thick section. OG 349, Period 6.

23 Core fragment; four clear blade-like negative facets, on poor quality red chert, probably from local boulder clays. OG 823, Period 5.

24 Scraper, large end; retouch along all edges with evidence of heavy use. OG 804, Period 5.

25 Scraper, small; fine delicate retouch, on mottled grey good flint. OG 284, Period 9.

26 Awl; light retouch on dark grey good flint. LG 2, Period 9.

Discussion

The only local flint source is from the boulder clay covering much of the Cheshire plain (Fig 2). This contains many erratics, including flint probably derived from Northern Ireland or submarine chalk outcrops in the Irish Sea (Poole and Whiteman 1966, 61). The quality of the boulder clay flint is generally poor, being coarse in texture and difficult to work. There is little evidence that it was extensively used at Beeston. Most of the flint raw material is of good quality and must have been imported into the area, possibly from Yorkshire or north Lincolnshire.

The imported flint is unlikely to have travelled in its natural nodule form but more likely as prepared cores or flake blanks, as attested in south-west England (Coles 1978, 118; Grinsell 1985). The low proportions of primary and secondary flakes (Table M15, M1:C13) support this hypothesis, while the handful of rejuvenation flakes and core fragments indicates the presence of cores (Fig 40.23). The scarcity of good flint probably led to the reuse of any sizeable pieces of flint such as cores, explaining the fragmentary nature of the few surviving examples.

Dating of the collection is extremely difficult. A wide time span is probably involved. There are too few complete flakes or whole cores to give even a loose date to the debitage. The datable Mesolithic material comprises the two microliths (Fig 39.1 and 5), the worked blades (Fig 39.3 and 4), and the blade scraper end (Fig 39.2). Of the 11 whole or fragmentary arrowheads, 5 are clearly leaf-shaped and are Neolithic (Figs 39.6–9; 40.18 and 19). A Beaker or Early Bronze Age presence is suggested by the tanged arrowhead (Fig 40.22) and by the knives (Fig 39.10–13). The remaining tools, comprising scrapers (eg Fig 40.14–16, 21, 24, and 25), awls (eg Fig 40.26), points (eg Fig 40.17), arrowheads (eg Fig 40.20), and retouchers, and the miscellaneous worked flints are difficult to date and could well cover more than one period. Since arrowheads are by their nature easily lost, the Beeston examples may be chance losses and not necessarily connected with the flint collection as a whole.

Pottery and metalwork found at Beeston indicates a Late Bronze Age date for an episode of site use. However the Beeston flints, by comparison with the small number of flint assemblages from other Late Bronze Age sites (Micheldever Wood, Hampshire: Fasham and Ross 1978; Shearplace Hill, Dorset: Rahtz and ApSimon 1962), include a larger number of knives, and many of the scrapers have fine retouch rather than the coarse retouch noted at the above sites. However, the lack of comparable flint assemblages in the area make any detailed conclusions extremely difficult.

The non-flint lithic finds
by Don Henson and Linda Hurcombe

A condensed report is available in microfiche (M1:D2–5) and the full report is in the archive. The illustrated pieces and a discussion of the assemblage are presented here.

The illustrated pieces (Figs 41 & 42)

1 Saddle quern, lower stone; sandstone. OW, East Cutting A.

Table 19 Stone objects: composition by type of the assemblage

Querns	Axes	Whetstones	Pestle stones	Hammerstones	Rubbing stones	Spindlewhorls	Lids	Pot-boilers	Other
14	3	17	36	7	17	6	25	109	162

0 ⎣ ⎸ ⎸ ⎸ ⎸ ⎸ ⎦ 6 cms

Fig 41 Quernstone; scale 1:4

2 Neolithic axe, butt fragment. OW, F200, West Cutting.

3 Neolithic axe, butt fragment. OG.

4 Whetstone; fine green sandstone. Period 3A rampart.

5 Whetstone; basalt. Period 3A rampart.

6 Whetstone; green vesicular lava. OG, Period 5.

7 Spindlewhorl or weight; fine micaceous sandstone. Period 3A rampart

8 Perforated disc; fine micaceous sandstone. Period 3A rampart.

9 Spindlewhorl; Passage Beds stone. OW, East Cutting A.

10 Spindlewhorl or bead; fine green sandstone. OG.

11 Loomweight; Passage Beds stone. OG.

12 Disc; micaceous Passage Beds stone. Period 3A rampart.

13 Disc; micaceous Passage Beds stone. Period 3B rampart.

14 Disc; micaceous Passage Beds stone; 3B rampart

15 Bead; jet or cannel coal. OW, South Cutting.

16 Bead; jet or cannel coal. OW, South Cutting.

17 Hone, ?post-medieval; black mudstone. OG.

Table 20 Stone objects, Outer Gateway rampart layers

Period	Querns	Whet-stones	Pestle stones	Hammer-stones	Rubbing stones	Spindle-whorls	Lids	Total
2B	—	—	—	1	—	—	—	1
3A	1	2	13	2	1	2	9	30
3B	—	—	5	1	1	—	3	10
Total	1	2	18	4	2	2	12	41

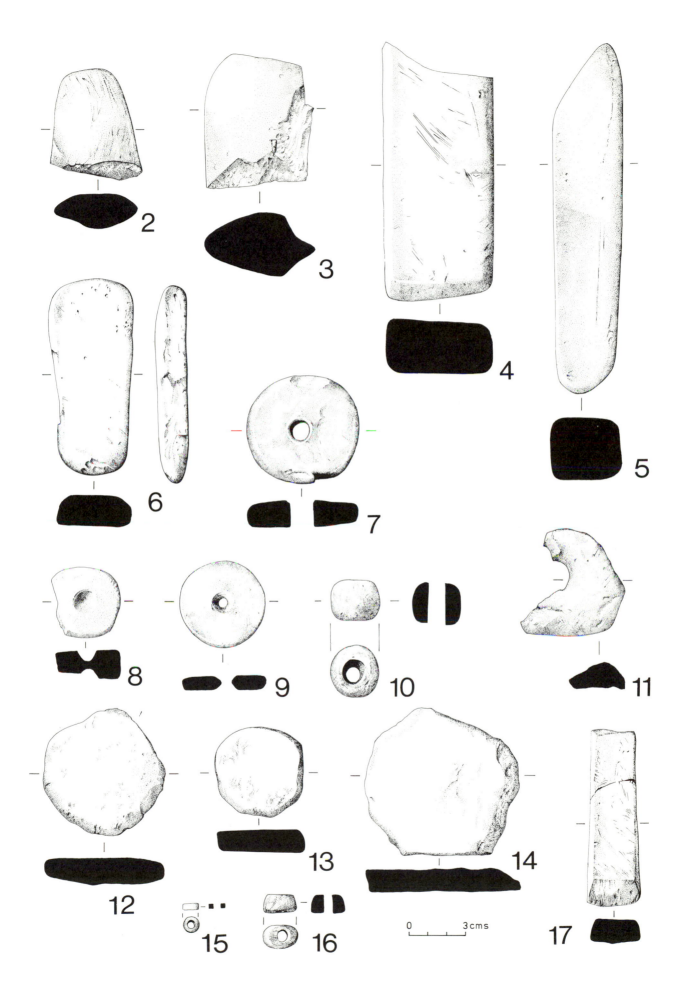

Fig 42 Stone objects; scale 1:2

Table 21 Stone objects, Outer Ward

Period	Querns	Axes	Whet-stones	Pestle stones	Hammer-stones	Rubbing stones	Spindle-whorls	Lids	Pot-boilers	Miscellaneous	Total
3 postholes	3	1	1	—	—	2	—	1	—	—	8
later layers	6	—	8	10	3	6	3	9	98	8	151
Total	9	1	9	10	3	8	3	10	98	8	159

Discussion

A wide range of stone types was found (Table 19). Study of the assemblage suggested that the lithic resources were exploited with an awareness of the different properties of the stones. Preferred raw materials, both quarried and obtainable as surface finds, were clear. Sandstone Conglomerate was used for the querns; Passage Beds stone for querns, discs, and rubbing stones; quartzite pebbles for the pounding and crushing pestle stones; green siltstone for whetstones and rubbing stones; igneous erratics also for rubbing and abrasion stones. Field survey of the locally available stone sources suggested that over 80% of the stone examined could have been obtained from quarrying in the vicinity of Beeston crag. The remaining material, although of a foreign origin, could well have come from locally found glacial erratics. Although there is little evidence to distinguish imported material, the use of non-local flint raw material (p 59) indicates that some stone was brought from considerable distances.

Wear patterns on the utility stones were closely studied and the evidence in the majority of cases suggests the use of each stone for a special function. These functional aspects can only be guessed at. Some uses are generally indicated, as, for instance, corn grinding by the querns, and the working of wool or other fibres by the spindlewhorls. In addition stones seem to have been involved with heating, and for working metal and other stones (whetstones). The pestles and rubbing stones could have been used for producing fine sand for crucibles and for other activities associated with metalworking, or for preparing pottery temper. Other possibilities are food and herb preparation, and working on skins. Other stone categories suggest the use of discs as lids or counters. Of interest is the group of 31 stones from seven different categories which are likely to represent a Late Bronze Age assemblage collected in the Early Iron Age Period 3A rampart layers, and these must represent debris from a working area nearby (Table 20). The presence of a quern fragment, and of the spindlewhorls, indicates corn grinding and weaving at Beeston in the Late Bronze Age. The Outer Ward, however, produced the majority of stone finds (Table 21).

The objects of shale (Fig 43)
by Angela Bliss

Discussion

Six different rings are presented of which at least four were originally of sufficient diameter to have been worn as bracelets, armlets, or anklets. Analysis of the rings by X-ray fluorescence by Michael Heyworth at the Ancient

Monuments Laboratory, English Heritage and by Gill Spencer at the Research Laboratory for Archaeology and the History of Art, Oxford has shown that they are not of jet. Therefore they are probably of shale. It remains possible that other non-jet materials, such as cannel coal or lignite, are represented.

Two of the rings, 1 and 2, are from the pre-Iron Age Period 2B rampart and a third, 3, is from the Early Iron Age Period 3A rampart. The date of the rings suggests that they were hand-cut rather than lathe-turned. Although 1 and 3 are eroded and decayed, the rings are finely worked and regularly made with smooth edges and parallel faces. Ring 2 is so well finished as to be almost indistinguishable from later lathe-turned rings. The grooves on its inner face may represent tooling marks.

The evidence from the later Bronze Age/Early Iron Age site of Eldon's Seat, Dorset suggests that neither section shape nor size have either a regional or chronological significance (Cunliffe and Phillipson 1968, 226). The fine finishing of the rings is interesting and can be paralleled by other examples from the later Bronze Age hillforts such as Thwing and Grimthorpe, both in East Yorkshire (Manby 1980, 320–1; Stead 1968, fig 10.1–3). Other examples of well-made jet/shale rings are known from a number of sites including Heathery Burn Cave (Britton 1968), Fengate (Pryor 1980, fig 13.6), and the later Bronze Age/Early Iron Age site at Staple Howe (Brewster 1963, figs 66.1–3).

The three remaining rings were unstratified and were found above the hillfort rampart (4) and in the Outer Ward (5 and 6). The crudeness of the hand-worked decoration on 6 stands in marked contrast to the fine finishing of the ring, which is so highly smoothed and polished as to look like jet. It may be that the decoration represents secondary working of inferior craftsmanship which took place away from the original site of manufacture, especially in view of the lack of parallels.

There is no evidence to suggest that the rings were worked on site. Their visual differences suggest more than one source. With the exception of ring 5, which is of brown shale, they are all of black shale. Only ring 6 breaks with a conchoidal fracture and can take a high polish. Ring 5 has a higher iron content and ring 2 has a higher copper content (M Heyworth, pers comm). This may well be explained by different material types or different sources, although copper concentrations can also be affected by deposition conditions (Pollard *et al* 1981).

There are few known Bronze Age shale-working sites. At Eldon's Seat, Dorset, shale ring working is associated with the initial occupation (Cunliffe and Phillipson 1968). Early Bronze Age working of cannel

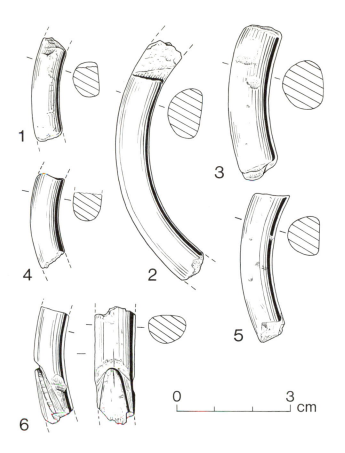

Fig 43 Shale rings; scale 1:1

coal is known in Derbyshire at Swine Sty (Machin 1971 and 1975) and Totley Moor (Radley 1969). At Barnby Howes, East Cleveland, craftsmen worked 'jet' ornaments (Ashbee and ApSimon 1958, 20–1). Many sites in the Pennines have produced undated, isolated finds of partially worked shale rings (Beswick 1975, 209), which may suggest that working sites are in fact quite numerous. Although the Pennines are a nearby location of attested prehistoric shale-working there is not sufficient evidence at present to suggest that they are the source of the Beeston rings.

Catalogue

(D=diameter, L=length, W=width)

1   Fragment of an undecorated ring of D-shaped section. The surface is heavily weathered but the inner and outer edges appear smooth and parallel. OG 879, Period 2B.

2   Part of an undecorated ring of D-shaped section. All the surfaces are finely smoothed and burnished. The inner surface bears many irregular and shallow circumferential and oblique grooves and the upper and lower surfaces bear irregular, slightly incised lines. D *c* 70mm, OG 641, Period 2B.

3   Part of an undecorated ring of rounded D-shaped section, now laminated into two pieces. The surface is heavily weathered but vertical cuts and a deep transverse groove are visible on the lower/upper sur-

face. The inner and outer edges are quite smooth and appear to be parallel. D *c* 85mm, OG 872, Period 3A.

4   Horizontally sheared fragment of an undecorated ring of uncertain- (oval?-) shaped section, which is highly convex on the inner surface. The surfaces have a smooth finish, although the extant edge shows pitting in some places. OG 806, Period 9.

5   Part of an undecorated ring of D-shaped section. The surfaces are regular and finely smoothed. The outer surface bears many irregular cuts which are also visible on the inner surface together with circumferential striations. The inner and outer edges are parallel. D *c* 80mm, OW 838, Period 9.

6   Part of a ring of D-shaped section with grooved decoration on its upper edge, the original form of which is not known as the ring is broken at this point. The extant decoration consists of a 'tongue' of a similar width to the ring created by a wide and deeply cut curved groove. The groove is crudely cut and the 'tongue' bears knife cuts along one edge. The other surfaces are highly smoothed and polished and bear lightly incised lines. The inner and outer edges are parallel. D *c* 80mm, OW 557, Period 9.

The prehistoric beads (Fig 44)
by Peter Ellis (based on notes by Margaret Guido)

1   Fragments of an amber bead. IW A1, Period 9.

2   Dark blue glass with white decoration. Iron Age Oldbury type, second/first century BC (Guido 1978, 56). OW 543, Period 9.

The prehistoric pottery
by Cathy Royle and Ann Woodward

Introduction

The prehistoric assemblage from the excavations at Beeston Castle consists of many small fragments of irregularly fired, hand-made vessels. With few exceptions they are tempered with large angular crushed rock fragments of glacial drift derivation. The bulk of the

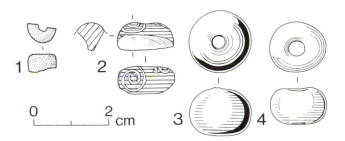

Fig 44 Prehistoric (1–2) and post-medieval (3–4) glass beads; scale 1:1

material is of Late Bronze Age date, but a small proportion of the assemblage extends the date range from the
Early or Middle Neolithic to the Iron Age. Because the
pottery fragments are generally very small (only two
nearly complete vessels could be reconstructed), a
study of the material leans heavily on fabric analysis
rather than a comparison of forms. In total 1140 sherds
were analysed, a further 1765 pieces being either fired
clay or sherds too small for fabric analysis. The following report analyses the assemblage under the following
headings: raw materials, technology, forms, decoration,
function, exchange, analysis, and cultural affinities.

Raw materials

In 1981 Elaine Morris began petrological analysis on the
Beeston Castle material and identified (in an archive
report) eight fabric types (Fabrics 1–8) and two fired
clay types (Fabrics A and B). After further excavation
up to 1985, the present authors continued this work,
fitting the newly excavated material into these eight
fabric types where possible and identifying macroscopically a further 18 types (Fabrics 9–26), the
petrological analysis being carried out by Agostino Fa-
varo.

Brief descriptions of each fabric type are contained
in microfiche (M1:D7–13); more detailed petrological
descriptions are contained in the archive reports.

Table 22   Prehistoric pottery: source and date of fabrics (listed in chronological order)

Fabric	Date	% by weight	Source of raw materials
10	Early/Middle Neolithic	0.1	glacial drift of Cheshire/Shropshire basin
11	Early/Middle Neolithic	0.1	glacial drift of Cheshire/Shropshire basin
12	Early/Middle Neolithic	0.2	glacial drift of Cheshire/Shropshire basin
13	?Late Neolithic	0.5	glacial drift of Cheshire/Shropshire basin
14	Late neolithic/Early Bronze Age (Beaker)	0.1	glacial drift of Cheshire/Shropshire basin
15	?Late Neolithic/Early Bronze Age (Beaker)	0.7	glacial drift of Cheshire/Shropshire basin
16	Early Bronze Age	0.8	glacial drift of Cheshire/Shropshire basin
17	Early Bronze Age	0.6	glacial drift of Cheshire/Shropshire basin
18	?Early Bronze Age	1.2	glacial drift of Cheshire/Shropshire basin
21	?Middle Bronze Age	0.2	glacial drift of Cheshire/Shropshire basin
19	?	0.9	glacial drift of Cheshire/Shropshire basin
20	?	0.004	not known
2	Late Bronze Age	52.2	glacial drift around Beeston Castle
3	Late Bronze Age	1.6	glacial drift of Cheshire/Shropshire basin
4	Late Bronze Age	1.9	glacial drift around Beeston Castle
5	Late Bronze Age	1.3	glacial drift around Beeston Castle
6	Late Bronze Age	0.2	Wrekin Hill, Shropshire, or glacial drift deposit consisting of rhyolites only
7	Late Bronze Age	4.3	glacial drift of Cheshire/Shropshire basin
8	Late Bronze Age	3.9	glacial drift of Cheshire/Shropshire basin
9	Late Bronze Age	18.1	glacial drift of Cheshire/Shropshire basin
22	Late Bronze Age	1.8	glacial drift of Cheshire/Shropshire basin
23	Late Bronze Age	1.1	glacial drift of Cheshire/Shropshire basin
24	Late Bronze Age	1.3	glacial drift of Cheshire/Shropshire basin
25	Late Bronze Age	0.3	glacial drift of Cheshire/Shropshire basin
1	Iron Age	6.3	south-east Cheshire, Middlewich/Nantwich area
26	Iron Age	0.1	glacial drift of Cheshire/Shropshire basin
Fired clay			
A	—	—	local clay source near Beeston Castle
B	—	—	local clay source near Beeston Castle

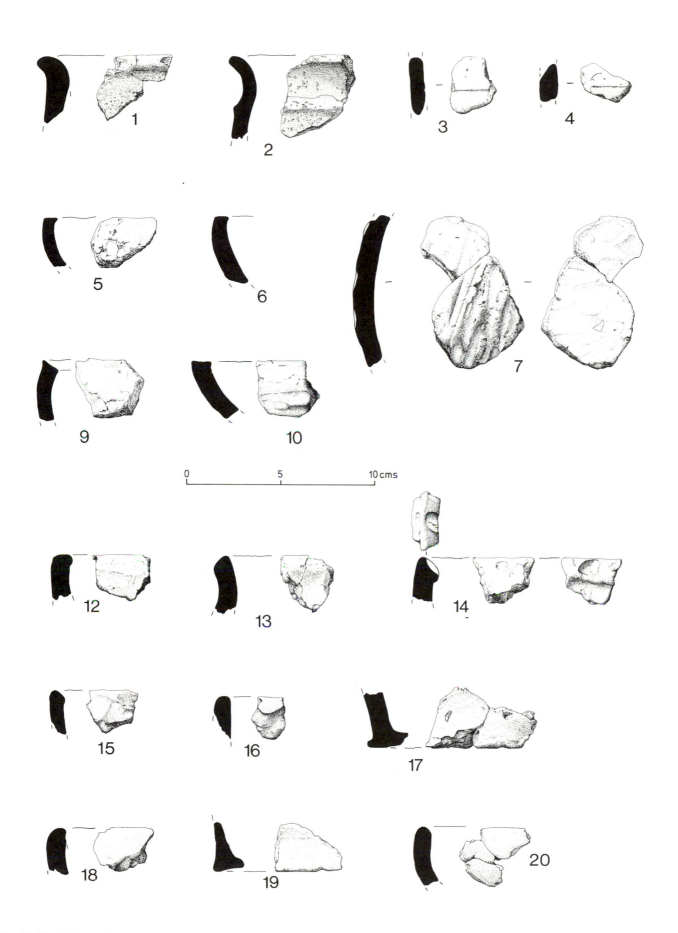

Fig 45 Neolithic and Early Bronze Age pottery; scale 1:2

Sources of clay and temper

After a survey of some of the worldwide ethnographic literature of pottery making, Arnold (1981) was able to conclude that 29% of communities obtain their potting clay at a distance of 1km or less, and 82% from less than 7km away. As for the pottery temper, 52% obtained this from up to 1km distant, and 96% from up to 8km.

In the area around Beeston Castle, Hilary Howard (M1:C8–11 and Howard 1983) carried out a raw material sampling programme as part of her study of the mould and crucible fragments. Eleven sites up to 6km away were sampled, and all could have provided material for either moulds or crucibles. Fired Clay A is similar to the mould fabrics, and the clay matrix to the pottery Fabric 4.

For unspecialised functions, such as hearth or wattle and daub construction, the nearest clay sources will usually suffice since no specific qualities other than plasticity are required. Clays are readily available in the Beeston Castle area, so the community there would not have needed to venture very far afield for supplies. The proportions, shapes, and size range of the quartz grains, and the micaceous and iron-rich clay matrix of Fired Clay B, are all similar to Fabrics 1, 2, 3, 4, 5, 7, and 8.

The crushed angular rock fragments used as temper for most of the fabrics can all be found in the glacial drift deposits of boulder clays and Lake District and Scottish erratics in the Cheshire/Shropshire basin. This again implies a close local source for pottery made of these fabrics. Fabric 6 may have a more precise source for its raw materials. According to Elaine Morris its very dense clay matrix and rhyolite inclusions originated from a nearby quartz-free clay source, either an outcrop of rhyolite, such as The Wrekin in Shropshire (Earp and Hains 1971, 16) or from a glacial drift deposit consisting only of rhyolites. Beeston Castle Fabric 6 is identical to Wrekin fabric 2.

The source of Fabric 1, the Cheshire stony-tempered VCP, is easier to pinpoint. Morris's work (1985, 366) has shown that the likeliest area for the production of Cheshire stony VCP is south-eastern Cheshire, in particular the area from Middlewich to Nantwich.

The occurrence of the various fabrics by weight, and summaries of the dating and sources, are shown in Table 22.

Technology

The prehistoric pottery types from Beeston Castle (with the possible exception of Fabric 26) are hand-made. Large angular rock fragments are added to sandy clays to prevent the pots shrinking too much while drying. Some fabrics only have sand as a temper (Fabrics 15, 18, and 24), while Fabric 20 appears to contain fossil shell fragments. Fabric 26 is vesicular, due to the leaching out of its original organic or calcareous inclusions.

It was anticipated that the vessels would have been formed by starting with a flat round slab of clay for the base, and then building the sides up with coils or collars of clay. This does indeed seem to be the case. Although some vessels are constructed with deliberately protruding feet, at least one was so irregular that it was likely to have been very roughly formed from the original flat base, the coils for the vessel sides perhaps having a smaller circumference. Coil building is indicated by several sherds which have broken along the line of construction, resulting in a smooth, regularly concave or convex break surface (eg Fig 46.27, OW 18, Period 9). This is presumably due to the new coil being placed on the previous one, and the join being smoothed over in a downward direction on both the inside and the outside. At least one Early Bronze Age sherd (not illustrated) seems to show evidence of the collar method of construction, where deeper bands of clay are joined together by smoothing the join upwards on the outside and downwards on the inside (or vice versa).

Several base sherds have a very gritty appearance on the bottom, probably resulting from being stood on deposits of crushed angular rock fragments used for temper, when the clay was still soft. On the base of one vessel (Fig 48.42, OG 674, Period 3A), two curving grooves may indicate that the vessel was removed from its place of manufacture by using a cord or wire. Figure 50.77 (LG 14, Period 9), a Fabric 1 VCP base, may exhibit the same feature.

Most of the vessels are irregularly fired, causing variations in the colours of outer and inner surfaces, as well as core areas. These colours can vary within fabric types and even within vessels themselves. Generally the pottery is quite hard, although Fabrics 7 and 10 are often crumbly. The finer, sandy fabrics tend to be more evenly fired. Pottery Fabrics 1–26 are all anisotropic (ie fired below c 800° C), with the exception of two Fabric 2 vessels (Fig 46.26 and 27, OW 18, Period 9) which were isotropic (ie fired above c 800° C). Although not joining, these two sherds may derive from a single vessel. Both had an extremely iron-rich coating applied to the exterior surface, which, when fired, resulted in a bright orange-red exterior contrasting with a light grey core and interior. Six other sherds, also of Fabric 2, possessed similar iron-rich coatings.

Forms

Neolithic and earlier Bronze Age pottery

Amongst the large assemblage of Late Bronze Age/Early Iron Age pottery it was possible to isolate a small but significant series of sherds belonging to earlier ceramic styles. These sherds accounted for 5.4% of the total assemblage by weight (see Table 22). They belonged to various Neolithic or Bronze Age traditions and the diagnostic sherds are described below. Most are illustrated in Figure 45, and their decorative features are described here.

Neolithic (Fig 45)

1   Plain, slightly everted rim sherd from a bowl of the Grimston series, Fabric 10. OG 503, Period 3B, and OG 535, Period 2A.

2   Everted rim and neck from a plain wide-mouthed carinated bowl of the Grimston series, Fabric 12. OG 505, Period 1.

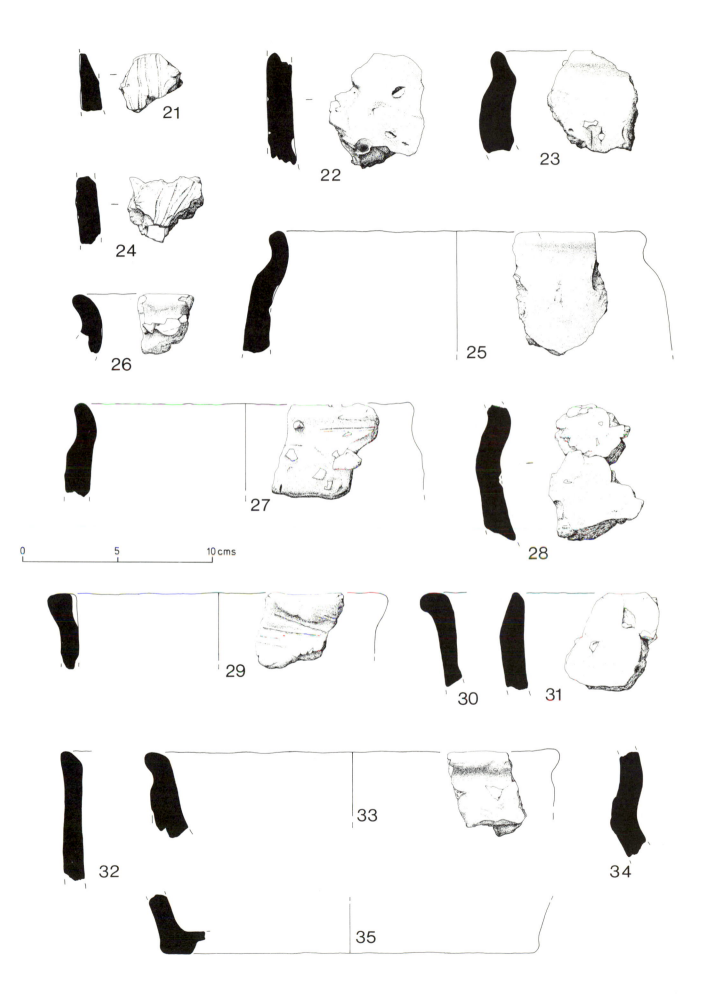

Fig 46 Late Bronze Age pottery: Fabric 2; scale 1:2

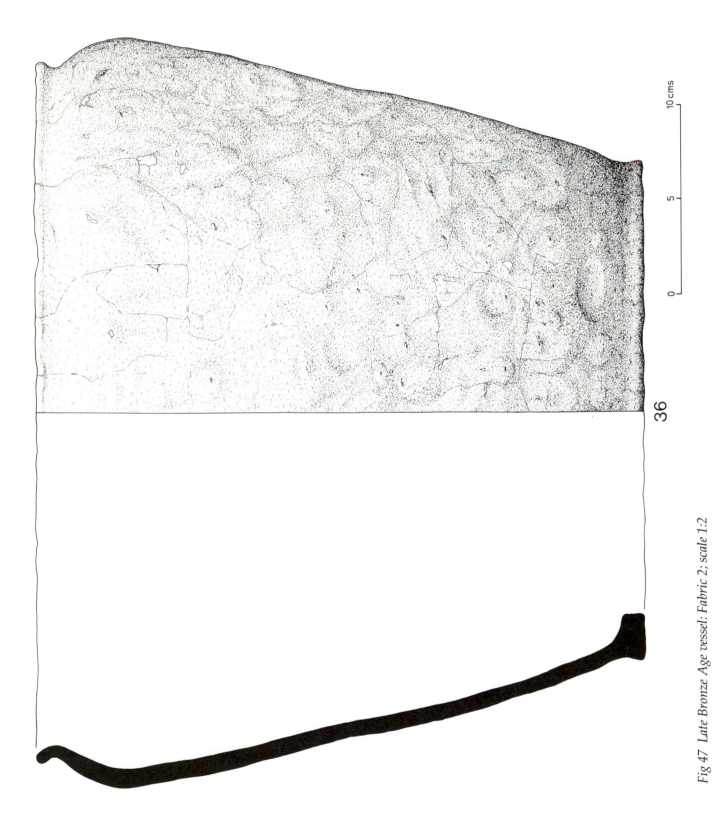

36

10 cms

5

0

Fig 47 Late Bronze Age vessel: Fabric 2; scale 1:2

Beaker and related wares

3 Wall sherd decorated with one incised horizontal line, very worn, Beaker, Fabric 14. OW 612, Period 9.

4 Wall sherd decorated with very worn incised lines; one broken horizontal line and other faint traces, Fabric 14. OW 612, Period 9.

5 Flat-topped rim sherd from a plain round-bodied bowl, Fabric 15. OG 854, Period 3A.

6 Flat-topped rim sherd from a larger bowl, Fabric 15. OG 860, Period 3A.

7 Joining wall sherds from a round-bodied vessel, irregular fingertip smears and grooves on exterior surface, rough fingertip smoothing on interior; rusticated ware, Fabric 15. OG 877, Period 3A.

8 Plain, thin rim sherd, Beaker, Fabric 18. OW 790, posthole F235, Period 3 (not illustrated).

9 Rim sherd from a bowl with internal rim bevel, Fabric 18. OG 860, Period 3A.

10 Flat-topped rim from a bowl, traces of rustication on exterior surface, Fabric 18. OG 860, Period 3A.

Early Bronze Age

11 Plain wall sherd broken at coil join, Urn, Fabric 17. OW 277, Period 9 (not illustrated).

12 Plain flat-topped rim sherd, Urn, Fabric 17. OW 543, Period 9.

13 Plain rim and part of concave collar from a Collared Urn, Fabric 17. OW 543, Period 9.

14 Rim sherd with fingertip impressions on the internal bevel, the bevel formed by folding the rim inwards; Collared Urn or Food Vessel (globular bowl type), Fabric 18. OW 218, Period 9.

15 Plain rim sherd with internal bevel, Urn or accessory vessel, Fabric 18. OW 543, Period 9.

16 Plain simple rim sherd, Fabric 18. OW 612, Period 9.

17 Two joining fragments of externally expanded base angle, Urn, Fabric 16. OG 886, Period 3A.

18 Plain simple rim sherd, Urn, Fabric 17. OG 674, Period 3A.

19 Simple base angle, Urn, Fabric 17. OG 832, Period 3B.

20 Plain rim from a round-bodied vessel, ?accessory cup, Fabric 18. OG 637, Period 3A.

Late Bronze Age and Iron Age (Figs 46–48)

Due to the fragmentary nature of the prehistoric ceramic material from Beeston Castle it was only possible to reconstruct the complete profiles of two vessels: a slack-shouldered, bucket-shaped jar with everted rim (Fig 47.36, OG 642, Period 3B) and a barrel-shaped jar (Fig 49.54, OW 838, Period 9). Any discussion of vessel forms based on the remaining rim sherds must therefore be viewed with caution. Base sherds are generally uninformative, being either plain or having a slightly protruding foot. The base angle is nearly always about 15° from the vertical. Because of the small size of most of the sherds any estimation of rim or base diameter is likely to be unreliable. The majority of rim sherds appear to represent less than 10%, and often less than 5%, of their vessel circumference. The angles of rim, especially the simple rounded or flattened rims of barrel-shaped jars, are also difficult to determine.

With such coarse domestic material a description of each rim shape would be of little value. In some cases one rim sherd may have differing profiles along its length. However, with a few exceptions the Late Bronze Age material can be divided into two main vessel categories: slack-shouldered jars with everted rims, and barrel-shaped jars.

The slack-shouldered jars with upright or everted rims have a rim diameter of between 180 and 220mm with the exception of the large reconstructed vessel (Fig 47.36) which has a rim diameter of *c* 290mm. Three shoulder sherds of this vessel type were also recovered. The wall thickness is generally 100–130mm thick. With one exception (Fig 48.47, Fabric 6, OW 19, Period 9) all recognisable rim sherds from this vessel category are of Fabric 2, and it is this vessel form which exhibits the iron-rich exterior coating (Fig 46.27, OW 18, Period 9).

In their various forms fragments of barrel-shaped jars constitute the majority of rim sherds recovered. There appear to be several versions of rim profile, but all represent variations on the same general theme:

(a) rounded (Figs 46.26 and 27, OW 18, Period 9; 47.36, OG 642, Period 3B);

(b) flattened (Figs 46.29, OW 522, Period 9; 48.39, OG 872, Period 3A, 43, OW 838, Period 9, 48, OW 557, Period 9, and 51, OW 612, Period 9; 49.57, OW 27, Period 9 and 60, OW 166, Period 9);

(c) internally-bevelled (Figs 46.32, OW 612, Period 9; 48.37, OG 355, Period 3B and 52, OG 101, Period 7);

(d) straight (Figs 48.39, OG 872, Period 3A; 49.54, OW 838, Period 9 and 59, OW 557, Period 9);

(e) inturned (Figs 48.45, OG 92, Period 7, 49, OG 616, Period 3B, and 53, OG 933, Period 3A; 49.58, OW 838, Period 9);

(f) tapering (Figs 46.31, OW 557, Period 9; 48.44, OG 67, Period 9; 49.61, OW 557, Period 9 and 62, OW 277, Period 9).

The rim diameters of these vessels range from *c* 180–260mm and the thickness of the vessel wall is between 90 and 130mm. Only one complete profile from this vessel category was reconstructed (Fig 49.54, OW 838,

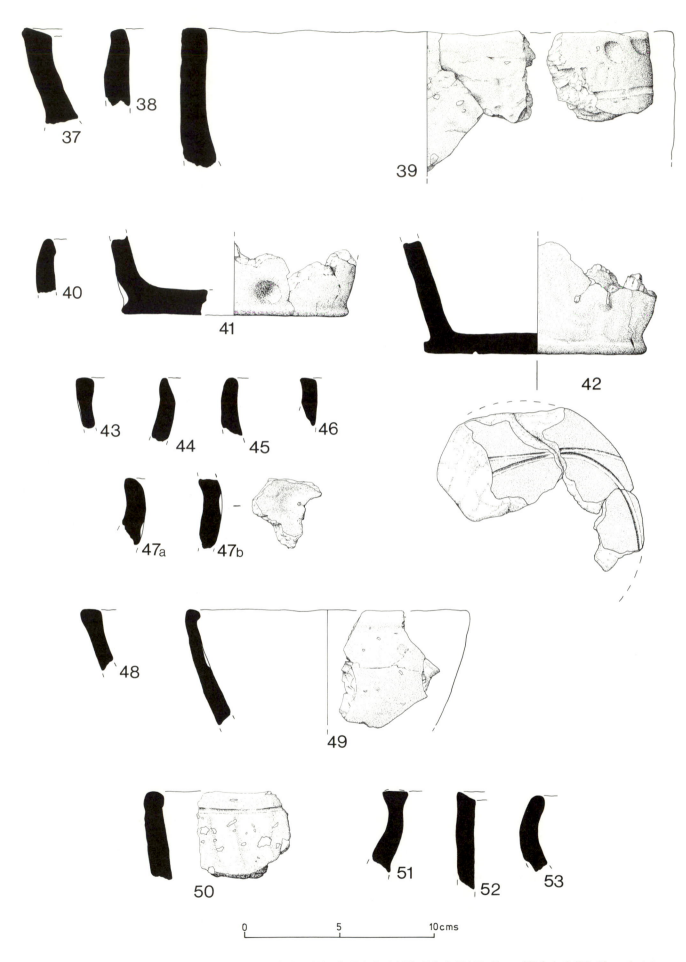

Fig 48 Late Bronze Age pottery: Fabric 2 (37–42), Fabric 4 (43–6), Fabric 6 (47), Fabric 7 (48–9), and Fabric 8 (50–3); scale 1:2

Period 9) but enough survived to estimate a rim diameter of 260mm, a base diameter of 195mm, and a volume of over 1.2m^3. Again, with few exceptions, most of these rim sherds are of Fabric 2.

Of other vessel types represented, one shoulder sherd comes from a thick-walled jar with a raised horizontal cordon. This sherd (Fig 46.34, OW 612, Period 9) joins a neck sherd (not illustrated) which shares the same find number as a rim sherd and a base sherd, all apparently of the same fabric, although there is some doubt as to whether these sherds are from the same vessel. The rim sherd has a flattened top, slightly sharper on the inside (or outside) edge and curves inwards (or outwards). The base has a fairly sharp protruding foot.

Alongside these coarse wares are a few sherds in Fabrics 23, 24, and 25, which are sandier and finer (especially Fabric 24) and can be seen as fine ware versions of the two main vessel types. One unusual find is that of a miniature vessel (Fig 49.62, OW 277, Period 9), presumably used as a cup, which looks like a bucket-shaped or globular jar with a delicately made, everted rim, and which has a rim diameter of c 80–100mm. The fine ware examples of barrel-shaped urns (eg Fig 49.59, OW 557, Period 9) exhibit the same variety as the coarse wares.

An unusual rim sherd in Fabric 23 is illustrated in Figure 49.58 (OW 838, Period 9). The vessel wall thickens at the shoulder and curves fairly sharply inwards, retaining this extra thickness all the way to the rounded rim. The fabric is hard and sandy, with no large inclusions, and the sherd may be from a bucket-shaped urn with a hooked rim, the only one of its kind in the Beeston assemblage. The vessel wall is 110mm thick, and the estimated rim diameter is 180mm.

Flat-rimmed bowls occur mainly in the Late Neolithic and Early Bronze Age material, but one rim sherd, possibly from a deeper bowl or a globular pot, was found in the Outer Ward (Fig 49.57, OW 277, Period 9). The body of the sherd is c 100mm thick and curves gently inwards, finishing in a flat-topped rim with an exterior lip. Another sherd in the same fabric (Fabric 23) may be of a similar form, although the rim appears more upright and has both an internal and external lip to its flat top. It is also possible that the Fabric 24 decorated sherd (Fig 49.60, OW 166, Period 9), with slashes on the flat rim, is from a flat-rimmed bowl, as it has an internal lip, but the sherd is badly damaged and the description is a tentative one.

Only one sherd of fine ware shows signs of burnishing. This is illustrated in Figure 49.63 (OG 674, Period 3A), an expanded, flat-topped or internally-bevelled rim from a thin-walled, wide-mouthed vessel. The reddish-brown coloured sherd is burnished on the exterior and the rim edge only. Like the coarse wares, all these sherds of fine wares are from hand-made vessels.

A rim sherd from a sharply carinated, thin-walled vessel was described by Morris as being similar to a situlate vessel from Mam Tor (Barrett 1979, fig 19.4). If this is correct, and if such situlate vessels are supposed to be ceramic imitations of bronze buckets which first appeared in the eighth century BC, then a post-eighth century date for this vessel would seem reasonable. However, the sherd seems just as likely to be similar in form to the rim of a globular pot, also from Mam Tor

(Barrett 1979, fig 27.5), and since it bears certain similarities to a rim from a slack-shouldered jar (not illustrated), it may be safer to regard it as another representation of this vessel form.

Iron Age (Figs 49 and 50)

Cheshire stony VCP

Most of the Cheshire stony VCP (Fabric 1) recovered from Beeston Castle is in small pieces, since the fabric is often ill-fired and soft and crumbles easily. The majority of the rim sherds and the most informative of the base sherds are illustrated. One rim sherd from the early excavations (OW 18, Period 9, sherd 570) was described by Morris as being a simple, flared shape with a flat, smoothed top rising from a constricted neck. Rim sherds recovered later are all slightly different, but essentially simple (Fig 50.66). They may be flat-topped or rounded and similar to VCP rims from Fisherwick (Banks and Morris 1979, fig 14). The bases tend to be quite thick. One (Fig 50.74, OW 557, Period 9) is a simple base rising at c 25° from the vertical, while three others (including Fig 50.75, OW 612, Period 9 and 77, LG 14, Period 9) seem to be parts of very large protruding feet. The sherd from the Lower Green (Fig 50.77) appears to have an especially pronounced foot and it may be similar to the base of a putative reconstruction of a stony VCP container from Fisherwick (ibid). With the material available from Beeston it is impossible to reconstruct a profile of a VCP container, but similar material from other sites indicates that such containers were tall and flared, with small, flat bases of up to 170mm diameter and rims of up to 250mm diameter.

As noted below (p 74), the occurrence of Fabric 1 pottery beneath the Period 3A rampart suggests a currency for Middlewich/Nantwich VCP from the Early Iron Age.

Fabric 19

The handful of sherds of Fabric 19 are sandy and organic-tempered, two of them being from bases with an extremely small diameter (Fig 50.78, OW 877, fill of posthole F268, Period 3 and 79, OW 612, Period 9). The form of the base is unusual as it is extremely thick (c 30mm) and small (60/80mm diameter) and flares out at c 40° from the vertical before curving upwards again. The exterior of the larger sherds shows very rough smoothing marks. The date and function of these sherds are not clear; they do not appear to be Droitwich VCP (E Morris, pers comm).

Fabric 26

Of the vesicular, organic-tempered Iron Age pottery there are only two sherds, both rims, from two different vessels. One (fig 49.65, OG 234, Period 4) has a sharp reversed-'S' profile leading to a flat rim with an interior lip. The vessel wall is 60mm thick and the estimated rim diameter is 180mm. The second rim sherd (not illustrated) is simpler in profile, slightly everted, with an estimated rim diameter of 160mm. The vessel wall is 90mm thick.

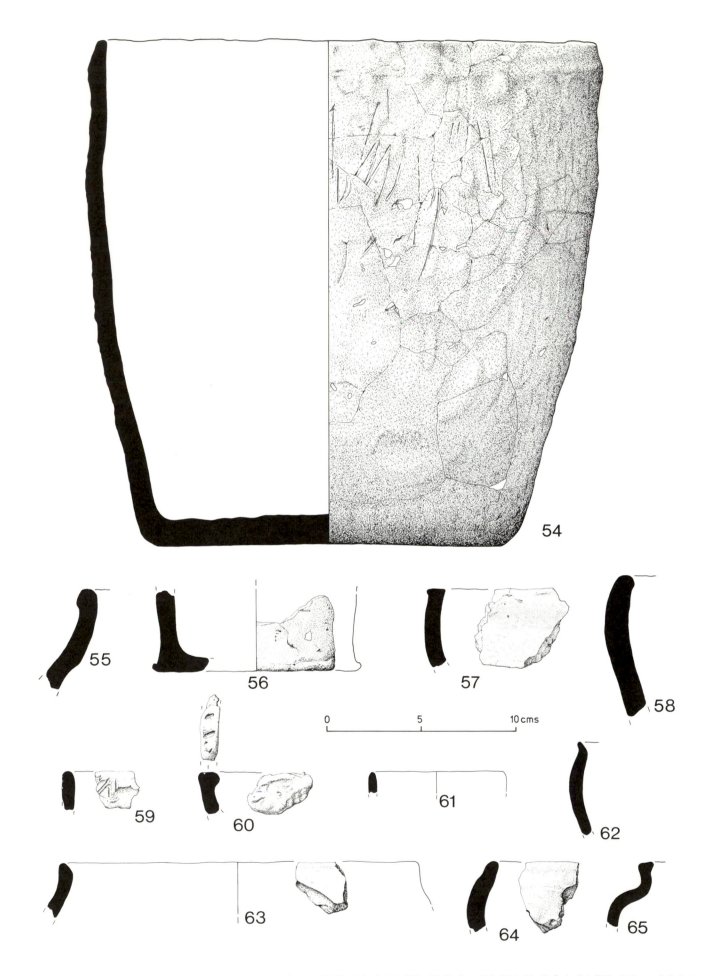

Fig 49 Late Bronze Age and Iron Age pottery: Fabric 9 (54), Fabric 22 (55–6), Fabric 23 (57–8), Fabric 24 (59–64), and Fabric 26 (65); scale 1:2

Decoration

Out of *c* 2500 sherds, of which only *c* 1100 were large enough to record and classify according to fabric type, only eight sherds of Late Bronze Age date show any signs of decoration. The decorated earlier pottery has been described above (p 66).

As might be expected, fingertip and fingernail impressions occur on sherds of Late Bronze Age date. A possible shoulder sherd of Fabric 7 (not illustrated) exhibits a deep fingertip impression on its exterior, but a similar impression on its interior may mean that it is due to clumsy shaping of the pot rather than deliberate decoration. One large Fabric 2 body sherd (Fig 46.22, OW 612, Period 9) has irregular fingernail impressions on the exterior, which do not seem to indicate any particular pattern. Another Fabric 2 sherd, a slightly everted rim from a slack-shouldered jar (Fig 46.23, OW 73, Period 9) appears to have a horizontal row of fingernail impressions just below the shoulder of the vessel.

Three sherds, again of Late Bronze Age date, a Fabric 24 rim (Fig 49.59, OW 557, Period 9) and two Fabric 2 body sherds (Fig 46.21, OW 612, Period 9 and 24, OW 105, Period 9), have shallow, roughly vertical grooves on their exterior surface. These may be decorative grooves made by lightly brushing the soft clay with twigs or something similar.

Only one rim sherd in Fabric 24 shows parallel, diagonal slashing on its flattened, inturned rim (Fig 49.60, OW 166, Period 9) and only one (possibly from a neckless, barrel-shaped jar) shows a single horizontal incised line about 10mm below its flattened rim. This sherd (Fig 48.50, OW 166, Period 9) also has a very wide, shallow, vertical groove on the exterior, probably the result of smoothing the clay when building up the sides.

In addition to these decorated sherds, the vessels with an iron-rich exterior coating, described earlier (p 66), could also be viewed as decorated. The applied haematite-rich slip turns a bright orange-red on firing, contrasting with the pale grey of the core area and interior surface. This treatment is rare, and is applied only to coarse Fabric 2 types, including at least one slack-shouldered jar.

Function

Some idea of the functions of the prehistoric pottery at Beeston Castle may be gained by a study of both the vessel forms and fabrics. The large vessels of coarse fabric, such as the two reconstructed vessels (Figs 47.36, OG 642, Period 3B and 49.54, OW 838, Period 9), are likely to have been used as cooking or storage jars, the latter having a calculated volume of over $1.2m^3$, whereas the bowls of finer fabric (Figs 48.49, OG 616, Period 3B and 49.61, OW 557, Period 9) may have been used for serving or eating. The vessels with an iron-rich coating, although of coarse fabric, may also have been considered as part of the 'fine ware' assemblage. The vessel illustrated in Figure 49.62 (OW 277, Period 9) is in a class of its own, a miniature version of a slack-shouldered jar, which, with a rim diameter of *c* 80–100mm, is more like a small cup, with a very delicate rim. It could also perhaps have been a 'demonstration model', a child's plaything, or a small drinking cup.

Fabric 1 has a special function, as it denotes the Cheshire briquetage, used for drying salt produced in the Middlewich/Nantwich area, and for transporting it to sites in the general area of the northern Welsh Marches.

Some sherds have a black, crusty, 'sooty' coating on them which flakes off easily. It was interesting to note that of the 56 sherds with 'sooting', all the body or base sherds showed it only on the interior, while rim sherds showed it on combinations of interior, rim edge, and exterior, as if this 'sooting' was some decayed residue of the original contents of the vessel. Blackening due to sooty fires or matter acquired in a post-depositional phase would surely have resulted in this black residue also being on the exterior of body sherds and break surfaces respectively.

Unfortunately no single vessel form dominates the range of sherds exhibiting 'sooting'. As to the fabrics, 31 of the sherds are of Fabric 2; 7 are of Fabric 8; and Fabrics 3, 5, 7, 11, 16, 18, 22, 23, and 25 all include one or two sooted sherds each. The fabric types are not significant as they simply reflect the rough proportions of these fabrics in the assemblage as a whole. The distribution of these sherds will be discussed later.

In addition, dark horizontal bands appear on some vessels, usually the slack-shouldered jars with everted rims, along the rim edge and on the start of the shoulder. Sometimes there is a lighter-coloured gap in between them. This may be a result of sooting from fires, where the most protruding part of the vessel catches the rising smoke. Perhaps the paler band in between is the result of protection by a strap wrapped around the neck of the vessel to suspend it over a fire for cooking.

Exchange

The presence of Cheshire stony VCP at Beeston Castle indicates the existence of at least one trade network in which the site was involved. Salt was evidently transported to Beeston from the Nantwich/Middlewich area from the Early Iron Age, and Beeston Castle may well have become involved later in an extended distribution chain. Whether the site developed a controlling role within the network is not yet clear.

A trading link with people further south may be indicated by the appearance of Fabric 6 at Beeston. The source of this fabric, identical to Wrekin fabric 2, is likely to be The Wrekin or the area around the hill. Only nine sherds of Fabric 6 have been recovered at Beeston Castle and it seems likely that they represent evidence of one or two vessels containing a special substance transported from the Wrekin area to Beeston. It may be significant that the only Fabric 6 rim sherd appears to be from a slack-shouldered jar with everted rim, a container which could easily be sealed by tying down a cloth over its mouth and under the rim.

Analysis

First it is necessary to deal with some general types of analysis which proved to have negative results.

For the Outer Ward, features with prehistoric pottery were plotted and colour-coded by fabric type. It was hoped that sets of postholes containing potsherds of the same fabric might reveal the existence of structures.

Only 68 of the features contained pottery, however, and no structures were apparent; there was no significance in the distribution of rim forms within these features. No conclusions could be drawn from the distribution of features with early pottery in them, some features having both Early Bronze Age pottery and Cheshire stony VCP.

In addition, all the spot finds were plotted by fabric type, and again there was no apparent significance in the distribution, although in general sherds tended to cluster near features. There was no specific area in the Outer Ward producing a higher concentration of VCP, so it was not possible to see one area set aside for the breaking up of VCP containers and the distribution of salt. Interestingly, the Lower Green area, although producing few potsherds, had a relatively high proportion of VCP, seven out of the 12 sherds being of Fabric 1.

Metalwork, loomweights, spindlewhorls, and 'sooted' potsherds were all plotted to see if they represented areas of specialisation, but with little result. All these different categories of finds were well spread over a general area, and although there seems to be more material in the South Cutting, this may be because the area lay away from the footpath, and therefore suffered less erosion. The junction of West, South, and East Cutting A produced little material but this may reflect post-medieval terracing.

A study of fabrics, forms, and distribution of prehistoric pottery at Beeston Castle prompts the suggestion of four theories of possible activity:

(1) that the prehistoric site has been more or less continuously utilised from the Early/Middle Neolithic to the Iron Age;

(2) that although pottery from most periods exists, the bulk of the prehistoric pottery from Beeston Castle is Late Bronze Age in date, and the site was almost completely aceramic from the Early Iron Age;

(3) that Cheshire stony VCP and its contents appear to have been in use from the Early Iron Age;

(4) that trade was carried out with at least one site to the south as well as with the salt-producing site or sites to the east.

These four theories will now be considered in turn.

(1) Continuous utilisation

As can be seen in Table 22, most periods from the Early/Middle Neolithic are represented by finds of pottery at Beeston Castle. The percentages of the total assemblage weight are given for each fabric type, showing that the Late Bronze Age period is by far the best represented.

(2) Aceramic Iron Age

There are five instances of sherds joining between contexts of the Period 3B rampart and the earlier 3A rampart; one instance of sherds joining between the Period 3B rampart and the occupation level behind the Period 2B rampart; and one instance of sherds joining

between the Period 3A rampart and the Period 2B levels. There is no difference between the phases in terms of fabrics or forms used, so the prehistoric material (other than VCP and the Neolithic and Early Bronze Age material) may be seen as one homogeneous assemblage of Late Bronze Age ceramics, which are found in all the rampart phases, with no new fabrics or forms appearing in successive phases. Since 42 sherds occur in Period 2B contexts, 84 in 3A and 3B rampart layers, and only 34 in post-rampart contexts, it is reasonable to assume that the material is residual from at least as early as the construction date of the Period 3B rampart. A higher proportion of material in each rampart make-up could be expected since the occupation levels behind the line of the defences would have been dug through to provide material for building up the rampart. Either the same occupation layers were dug into on each occasion of rampart construction, or the latest rampart incorporated material it disturbed in the earlier ramparts. The dearth of pottery in post-rampart 3B layers contrasts with the 40 sherds of VCP.

The same picture is provided by the comparative absence of pottery from the Period 3 postholes in the Outer Ward and, with the exception of three sherds, one Late Iron Age in date, from the fills and recuttings of the defensive ditch, apparently first cut in Period 3A.

For these reasons it is clear that Beeston Castle was aceramic from the Iron Age onwards, except for VCP and a few possibly imported pieces of Fabric 26. This situation is paralleled elsewhere in the region (Morris 1985, 368).

(3) Cheshire stony VCP

Although the VCP sherds occur predominantly in contexts later than the Period 3B rampart, the presence of three sherds beneath the Early Iron Age platform to the rear of the 3A rampart, and four in the body of the rampart, must suggest the use of VCP containers earlier than or contemporary with the 3A rampart, and certainly prior to the Middle Iron Age rampart dated by radiocarbon to around 400 bc.

(4) Trade

Trade with the salt-producing area of Nantwich/Middlewich is now indicated by the appearance of Cheshire stony VCP at several sites in the northern Welsh Marches including Beeston. As indicated above, sherds of Fabric 6 (Wrekin fabric 2) may indicate a trade in other materials too. It would be interesting to discover whether pottery fabrics identical to Wrekin fabric 2 occur at other sites in the region.

Cultural affinities

Neolithic, Beaker, and Early/Middle Bronze Age

The earlier prehistoric ceramic assemblage from Beeston Castle provides a welcome addition to the corpus of Neolithic and Early Bronze Age pottery known to have been found in Cheshire. A map of all such finds known to the authors is shown in Fig 51, and a catalogue of the mapped items appears in the microfiche (Table

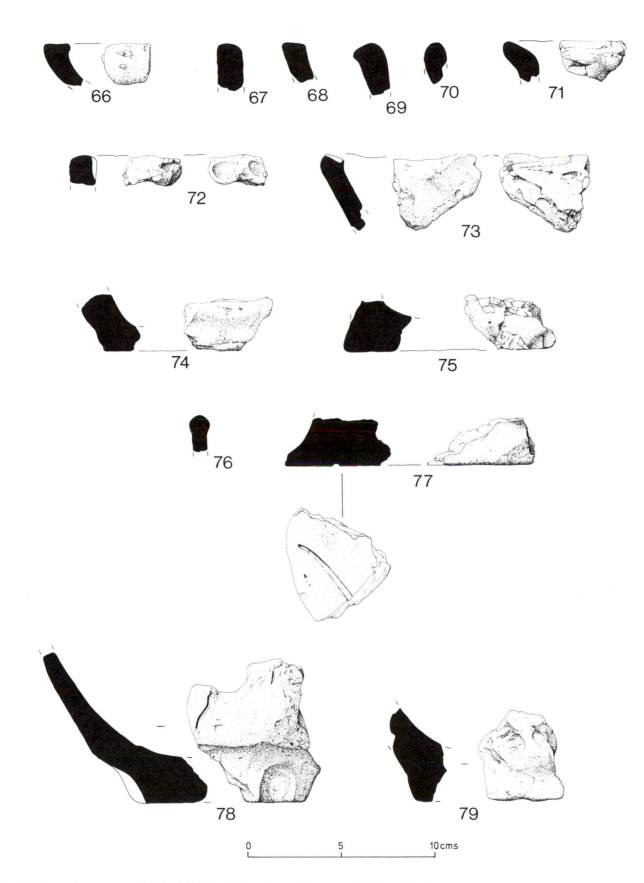

Fig 50 Iron Age pottery: Fabric 1 (66–79) Very Coarse Pottery or VCP; scale 1:2

M23, M1:E1–8). The main sources used are the Victoria County History of Cheshire, vol I (Longley 1987), Longworth's catalogue of Collared Urns (Longworth 1984), and the county Sites and Monuments Record (information kindly provided by Richard Turner). The fabrics of the vessels and fragments, now housed in the Grosvenor Museum Chester, were identified macroscopically by Catherine Royle.

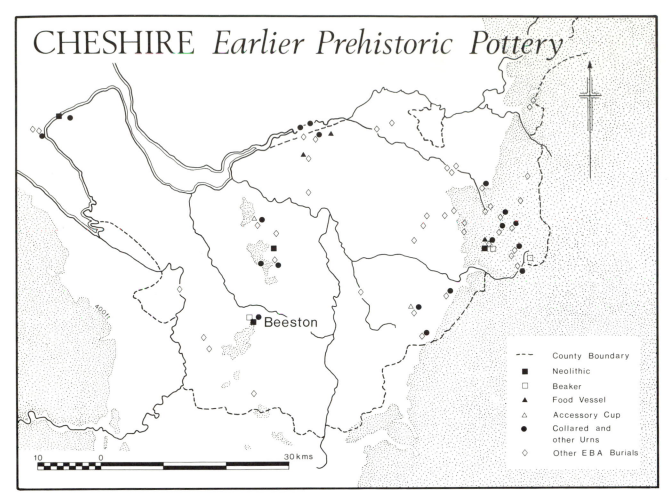

CHESHIRE *Earlier Prehistoric Pottery*

Beeston

	County Boundary
■	Neolithic
□	Beaker
▲	Food Vessel
△	Accessory Cup
●	Collared and other Urns
◇	Other E B A Burials

10   0   30 kms

Fig 51 Distribution of Neolithic and Bronze Age pottery in the region; scale as shown

The earlier Neolithic Grimston bowl sherds from Beeston Castle cannot be matched elsewhere in the county. The only Neolithic sherds previously known in Cheshire are of the Peterborough tradition, with the addition of one possible Grooved Ware vessel from Delamere. These would date from the Late Neolithic period; the nearest earlier Neolithic parallels for the Beeston Castle pieces come from Aston-on-Trent, Astonhill, and Green Low, Aldwark, all in Derbyshire (Vine 1982, 321). The gritted, hard-fired fabrics with their smooth, almost burnished surfaces can be matched at the Breiddin, Powys, where a rim sherd and carinated wall fragments suggest an open Neolithic bowl shape (C Musson, pers comm). At Sharpstones Hill, Shropshire, black, hand-made pottery has also been described as being typical of the Neolithic period (E Morris, pers comm). Here the temper was of crushed quartz pebbles, whereas at Beeston Castle Fabric 12 contained clasts of granite. Further quartz-tempered wares were identified at Willington, Derbyshire, where Grimston-style bowls were represented, as at Beeston Castle, by rim fragments from plain carinated bowls (Manby 1979, figs 58.14 and 58.15).

Beaker fine wares are not well represented in Cheshire. The decorated sherds from Beeston Castle are matched only by one complete vessel, the step 6 Beaker from Garnsworth (Longley 1987, fig 11.2), and by the bowl fragments found at Highfield Lane East, Winwick (Freke 1991, fig 10.5). The fabrics of the Beeston Castle

sherds contained quartz sand and granite and are matched by the fabric of the Winwick bowl, although the clasts in that vessel were rhyolite or tuff. The coarse surface-smeared bowls, with their fine sandy fabrics, have been ascribed, somewhat tentatively, to the Beaker rusticated tradition. The closest parallels may be found at Swarkestone, Derbyshire, where fingernail rusticated coarse vessels were recovered in association with a roughly grooved cordoned Beaker (Vine 1982, 331 and 333). Most of the Early Bronze Age sherds derive probably from Collared Urns or accessory cups. These classes of pottery are well represented in Cheshire (Fig 51). The simple rims, rims with internal bevel, concave necks and simple or expanded bases all may be paralleled amongst the urns known from elsewhere in the county (Longley 1987, figs 10–12). The tempers used in the vessels represented at Beeston Castle include quartz sand, granite, rhyolite, and basalt, and all the fabrics are characterised by a soapy texture. This texture and variety of clast types are all found amongst the other Collared Urns known from the county, with the addition of grog, limestone, andesites, and a possible example of organic temper indicated by voids. All these tempering agents would have been available locally, either in clay deposits or derived from specially selected glacial erratics. A few sherds tempered with densely distributed medium granite clasts may have been of Middle Bronze Age date but no diagnostic items were present.

The map (Fig 51) shows that most earlier prehistoric pottery derives from the areas of higher ground, and indeed the vessels have been recovered mainly from round barrows. These monuments have survived best on the more elevated and marginal land, but a scatter of unidentified urns, many recorded before the twentieth century, also occupies the lower ground. This evidence, together with that of the distribution of metalwork (Longley 1987, fig 17), indicates that the landscape was exploited fully during the Bronze Age period. Whether the Beeston Castle sherds derive from one or more destroyed round barrows, or from an occupation site, is considered in Chapter 4.

Late Bronze Age

As described above, the bulk of the prehistoric pottery from Beeston Castle appears to be a plain ware assemblage comprising slack-shouldered jars, barrel-shaped jars, and a few possible flat-rimmed, lipped bowls, typical of the Late Bronze Age. Other sites in the north and north-west which have produced similar assemblages to the Beeston material include: Mam Tor, Derbyshire; Ball Cross Farm, Derbyshire; Sharpstones Hill, Site A, Shropshire; Moel y Gaer, Rhosesmor, Flintshire; Willington, Derbyshire; The Wrekin, Shropshire; Castle Ditch, Eddisbury, Cheshire; Castle Hill, Almondbury, Yorkshire; and the Breiddin, Powys. Except where specifically mentioned, all fabrics are different to the Beeston material, one of the characteristics of this pottery being its use of local raw materials.

Large, barrel-shaped vessels with everted rims, similar to the Beeston Castle examples occurred at Mam Tor (Barrett 1979), Ball Cross Farm (Stanley 1954), Sharpstones Hill, Site A (E Morris, pers comm), Moel y Gaer (Guilbert 1976), Willington (Elsdon 1979), the Wrekin (Stanford 1984), and the Breiddin (C Musson pers comm). Mam Tor produced a range of coarse and finely made jars, and at Ball Cross Farm, although few rim sherds are illustrated in the report, they seem to come from simple, barrel-shaped jars, or jars with slightly everted rims. According to an archive report by Elaine Morris, the majority of the pottery from Sharpstones Hill, Site A, is hand-made and tempered with local inclusions of crushed basaltic rock, or granite and rhyolite from glacial drift deposits. The vessel forms (barrel-shaped jars or slack-shouldered/situlate jars), and the absence of Middle/Late Iron Age pottery, suggest that the occupation represented by this assemblage is likely to be of Late Bronze Age or Early Iron Age date. The pottery from Moel y Gaer is described as being coarse, heavily gritted, and having slack profiles with slightly everted or flat-topped rims, which indicates another similar assemblage.

Excavations at Willington produced a large, well-stratified collection of Early Iron Age pottery. This was divided into six main categories, two of which, the large slack-shouldered jars with upright or slightly everted rims, and the barrel-shaped or straight-sided jars and bowls, can be paralleled in the Beeston Castle assemblage. At Willington, the slack-shouldered jars fall mainly into the category of material for which a date of late eighth to early seventh century bc is assumed. The barrel-shaped jars, on the other hand, appear to have a much longer life, being dominant in a later phase (dated fourth to second century bc) as well as in the Early Iron Age phase of occupation.

Although in the small published corpus of rim sherds from The Wrekin no direct parallels for the Beeston material could be found, the necked jars and barrel-shaped jars, generally of Late Bronze Age/Early Iron Age date, appear again. Similar rims to the Wrekin sherds appear at the Breiddin (Stanford 1984).

Since Castle Ditch, Eddisbury, is one of the closest hillfort sites to Beeston Castle, it would be interesting to compare the ceramic assemblages. However, the material from Castle Ditch is no longer available, and the only description is of a hard-fired, sandy-buff ware forming the rim and sides of a high-shouldered, flat-rimmed cooking pot (Varley 1952, 17). Apparently the same type of material or vessel was found at Maiden Castle, Bickerton (Varley 1935, 1936), and was thought to be of Iron Age date. According to Varley the closest parallel site to Castle Ditch is the hillfort on Almondbury Hill, Yorkshire. His support for this comes from a plain, vesicular, grey-buff sherd from a round high-shouldered cooking pot of Iron Age date (Varley 1952, 53). In his 1976 report Varley gave the vessel forms from Castle Hill, Almondbury (round-shouldered jars with straight or everted rims) an Early Iron Age date (Varley 1976, 407, fig 7.1 and 7).

Like the Beeston rim sherds the rims from vessels at the Breiddin are sometimes rounded, but more usually they are flattened or internally bevelled; barrel-shaped, conical, or situlate jars seem to dominate the assemblage. The date given for the Bronze Age settlement at the Breiddin is c eighth century bc.

As at Beeston Castle, vessel bases from the other assemblages are generally simple and flat, occasionally having a slight protruding foot. The covering of finely crushed stone on the underside of base sherds mentioned elsewhere occurs at the Breiddin also.

Although slack-shouldered jars with everted rims and barrel-shaped jars dominate the Beeston assemblage, there are a few flat-rimmed lipped bowls. Plain bowls also occur at Mam Tor, and at the Breiddin a few rims may belong to open bowls.

Certain decorative motifs used at Beeston Castle also occur at some of these other sites. At Mam Tor five sherds from a large barrel-shaped vessel with everted rim showed a red coating on their exterior surfaces (like the iron-rich coating on Fig 46.27, OW 18, Period 9) although the raised arcs of circles on this vessel do not appear at Beeston (Coombs and Thompson 1979, fig 23.1). One vessel, in the common jar form, from the Wrekin also displays an iron-rich, thick slip or coating on the exterior surface.

The most common form of impressed decoration, as might be expected, is executed by fingertip or fingernail. At Mam Tor decoration is restricted to the kind of impressions that sometimes appear on the shoulder of a vessel (Barrett 1979), and at Moel y Gaer decoration is again limited to fingertip or fingernail impressions, and an Early Iron Age date is suggested (Guilbert 1976). One or two fingermarks or nail impressions are visible on the Breiddin material, but these may be unintentional. Decoration is also rare on the Willington material, where it consists of fingertip marks on the rim or shoulder and light brushing in the earlier phase, and deep random slashing or light vertical brushing in the later phase. Light vertical brushing (possibly with twigs) may be in evidence on, for example, Figure 46.24 (OW 105, Period 9). Some sherds from the Breiddin also have been brushed or wiped.

One sherd from Beeston Castle (Fig 49.60, OW 166, Period 9) displays a series of parallel, evenly spaced, diagonal slashes on the flat top of the rim. Although the rim shape is different, a rim with similar incised decoration occurs at Ball Cross Farm (Stanley 1954, fig 3.12).

A vessel from the Breiddin, a sloping-shouldered jar with an upright rim, has a raised horizontal cordon on its shoulder, and this is paralleled at Beeston (Fig 46.34, OW 612, Period 9). The vessel profiles appear to be similar, and the bases both have a slightly out-turned foot.

Perhaps the most interesting aspect of the Wrekin material is that two of the five fabric types identified by Elaine Morris are similar to fabrics from Beeston Castle (Morris 1984). As mentioned earlier (p 66), Beeston Castle Fabric 6 is identical to Wrekin fabric 2 (the rhyolite-tempered fabric), the source of the rhyolite possibly being the Wrekin hill itself. Beeston Castle Fabrics 7 and 8 (granite and rhyolite-tempered) are almost indistinguishable from each other and both have some similarities with Wrekin fabric 3. The only decoration on the Wrekin pottery is fingertip impressions just below the rim.

Excavations at the defended hilltop settlement of the Breiddin, Powys, in the central Welsh borderland, produced a large body of prehistoric ceramic material. The fabric shows variations in texture and temper, and, as with the Beeston pottery, firing conditions are inconsistent. The anisotropic clay matrix contains angular crushed rock fragments, probably of local origin, and these can be very coarse, up to 10mm or more across. One fabric, though, may indicate a non-local source for pottery production. This is the Breiddin fabric 5, a rhyolite-tempered fabric with dolerite (Morris, archive report). The closest likely sources for these rock clasts are the glacial deposits of the Cheshire Plain. Although rare at the Breiddin, it is a variation of this fabric type which is so abundant at Beeston Castle (Fabric 2). One sampled sherd from the Breiddin, according to the archive report by Elaine Morris, is from a context dated to 710 ± 80 bc. The forms of the vessels are generally similar too, although again diagnostic sherds are often small and rim angles and diameters can be difficult to estimate. The average rim diameter is 200–250mm reducing to 130–180mm at the base, and the thickness of the vessel wall is usually c 10mm.

Iron Age

During the Iron Age two main salt-producing centres provided and distributed salt to sites in western Britain: Droitwich and a site in Cheshire. The distribution of salt from the two centres can be mapped by the occurrence of the two different container fabrics used exclusively at each site (Morris 1985).

At Beeston Castle it is the Cheshire stony VCP which is found. The previously earliest dated sherds of Cheshire stony VCP away from the production site is at the Wrekin, where two sherds come from a posthole with a radiocarbon date of 390 ± 70 bc. Other sites, the Breiddin, Collfryn, and Fisherwick (Morris 1985), also indicate that Cheshire stony VCP was principally current in the Middle or Late Iron Age. Although at Beeston Castle an earlier date of occurrence can now be suggested, the bulk of the material clearly postdates the Period 3B rampart.

No comparative material was seen to match the two Fabric 26 rim sherds from Beeston Castle (Fig 49.65, OG 234, Period 4).

Clay objects (Fig 52)
by Cathy Royle and Ann Woodward

Description and provenance

A small collection of fired clay objects, mainly loomweight and spindlewhorl fragments, came from the excavations at both the Outer Gateway and the Outer Ward. Three spindlewhorl fragments were found in the Period 3A rampart layer 637. Two of the three (Fig 52.1 and not illustrated) are between 11 and 13mm thick, have an estimated diameter of 30–32mm, and estimated total weights of 11.4g and 12.9g. The fabric is a fine, slightly sandy, fired clay. The third fragment (Fig 52.2) is only tentatively described as a spindlewhorl as it is larger than the other two fragments but too small to be a loomweight. Three loomweight fragments came from Period 3A layers at the rear of the rampart. Two (Fig 52.3 and 5) were of a fairly fine, hard, fired sandy clay fabric and came from layers 864 and 854, the former exhibiting a flat base and smooth rounded sides. The third (Fig 52.4) was of a different fabric, a coarse, sandy, possibly unfired clay. Its diameter is approximately 110mm and the central hole has an estimated diameter of 17mm. Because it is so coarsely made its shape is difficult to determine, but it may have been bun-shaped or cylindrical. The weight of the recovered fragments (found in layer 860) of this loomweight total 419g.

A prehistoric date is clearly indicated for the Outer Gateway pieces, and their position in the the Period 3A rampart suggests a Late Bronze Age context in line with the other material scraped up in the Early Iron Age defences. The four loomweight fragments (Fig 52.6–8 and not illustrated) from the Outer Ward may also be of Late Bronze Age date. These are all of a fine, sandy, fired clay fabric similar to the Outer Gateway examples. Because of the small size of the fragments no reliable reconstruction of their shape can be attempted although a bun or cylinder shape is suggested. Two were found in South Cutting and two in East Cutting A.

One other fired clay object was recovered (Fig 52.9). It came from the South Cutting and, like the loomweights, was of a sandy fabric. It appears to be complete and may be some sort of plinth or pedestal. None of the Outer Ward pieces was found in a prehistoric context.

Discussion

Cylindrical or bun-shaped clay loomweights occur commonly on occupation sites of the later Bronze Age in southern England. Cylinders of similar size to those from Beeston have been found at Trevisker, Cornwall

(ApSimon and Greenfield 1972, fig 24.A1) and Itford Hill, Sussex (Burstow and Holleyman 1957, fig 25), while that from Thorny Down, Wilts (Stone 1941, fig 8) is about half the size. At Shearplace Hill, Dorset a series of bun-shaped weights varied in diameter from 60–106mm (Rahtz and ApSimon 1962, fig 22.1–3). Fragments of cylindrical weights also came from Late Bronze Age sites in Surrey (Kingston, Farnham, and Carshalton), as well as from Knights Farm Site 2 in the Kennet valley. Again the size range matched that of the example from Beeston (Bradley *et al* 1980, fig 37).

Spindlewhorls are less common on Bronze Age sites in the south, but the Beeston items may be matched at Weston Wood, Surrey and at Plumpton Plain Site B, Sussex, where nine examples displayed 'shapes varying between cylindrical, biconical and roughly spheroidal with a tendency towards becoming biconical' (Holleyman and Curwen 1935, figs 18–36).

Insect attack in charcoal
by the late Maureen Girling

Charcoal representing upright structural timbers (F621 and F624) of the Period 3B Iron Age rampart at the Outer Gateway was examined for possible insect attack, in addition to species identification and radiocarbon determinations. A further example from the Period 4 layer 323 was also examined. The charcoal showed clear evidence of beetle attack in the form of larval borings and flight holes indicating that the wood was subject to insect infestation. These signs have survived burning and charring.

Fifteen samples were examined (tabulated in Girling 1985). Although it was not possible to reach a definite conclusion the signs of infestation were most likely caused by *Anobium* sp. ('woodworm' or 'furniture

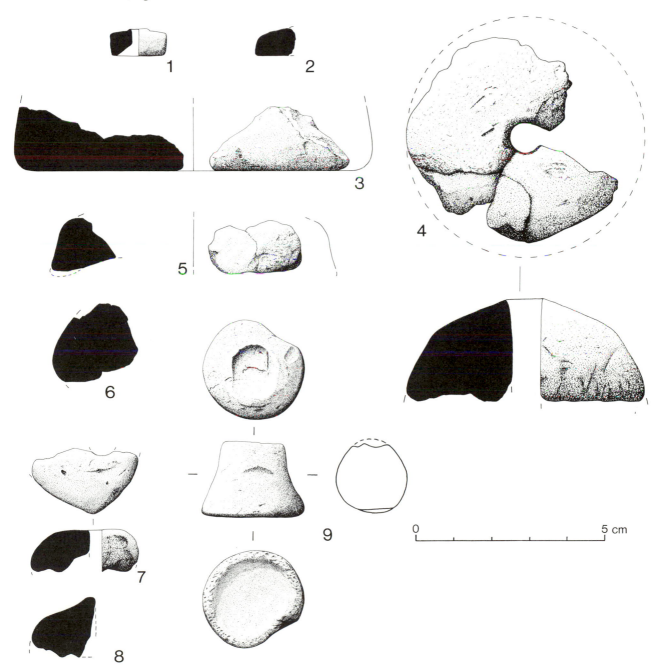

Fig 52 Objects of baked clay; scale 1:1, except 1 and 2, which are 1:2

beetle') and by *Xestobium rufovillosum* ('deathwatch beetle'). In addition to insect borings, it was possible to identify galleries, a possible brood chamber, and frass (the remains of wood after it has passed through the larval gut).

The charred plant remains from prehistoric contexts
by Glynis Jones and Richard Moss

The relationship of crop compositions to Period 3 buildings and Period 2 pit groups (M1:F1–3), together with Tables M25–M32 (M1:F5–M2:C14) and Figures M54–M61 (M2:D1–E2), are available in the microfiche. A methodological outline, details of the species represented, analysis of the samples, interpretation of the evidence, and conclusions are presented here.

Methods

Between 1980 and 1985 *c* 800 soil samples (typically of 40 litres each) were collected from postholes, pits, and layers in the Outer Ward and from postholes and layers of the overlying Period 3A platform inside the Outer Gateway. Postpipes and packings were sampled separately where they could be distinguished. The samples were processed for the recovery of charred plant remains by flotation and subsequent wet sieving using a 125 micron mesh to collect the flot and a 600 micron mesh to collect the heavy residue. Samples collected before 1985 were sorted without further sieving or subsampling. For samples collected in 1985, both flot and residue were subsequently dry sieved using a 1mm mesh and the >1mm fractions of *c* 250 samples were randomly subsampled (using a sample splitter) and sorted (at ×10 and ×20 magnification) for charred plant remains.

High priority was given to the sorting of samples from prehistoric postholes and pits in the Outer Ward as these contexts were relatively undisturbed and most likely to reflect the functions of buildings and areas; 170 samples were sorted from these negative features (15 samples from post-medieval features were also sorted but not submitted for identification). Lower priority was given to layers in the Outer Ward as these were all very disturbed; a small number of samples (15) were sorted to establish whether the plant remains differed markedly from those in the postholes and pits. Low priority was also given to samples from the Outer Gateway as the layers forming the platform had all been redeposited from higher up the slope and are therefore stratigraphically uncertain; 50 samples were sorted in order to compare the species represented with those from the Outer Ward. The data presented here are based on samples from the East and West Cuttings of the Outer Ward – samples from the South Cutting were rejected (p 81).

Plant remains were identified by comparison with fresh material using magnifications of ×8 to ×40.

Species represented

The main crop species represented were the glume wheats, emmer (*Triticum dicoccum* Schübl) and spelt (*T. spelta* L.). The charred grains of these two species are difficult to distinguish but the glume bases (chaff) are more distinctive. Characteristic grains and glume bases of both species were present though many fell into an indeterminate category. Emmer and spelt, in varying proportions, together dominate all samples. Given the secondary depositional context of the samples (see below), however, and the presence of cereal grains not identified to species, it is not possible to determine whether spelt and emmer were grown together as a maslin or were cultivated separately and became mixed post-depositionally.

Grains of barley were also frequently encountered. All those that could be determined were of the hulled variety and the presence of twisted grains indicated the six-row species (*Hordeum vulgare* L.) though many of the grains were indeterminate. (Grains of two-row barley are all straight whereas two thirds of the grains from six-row barley are twisted.) There were also occasional rachis internodes (chaff) of six-row barley and a few grains of the free-threshing bread wheat (*T. aestivum* L.) in some samples. Both barley and bread wheat are represented as only minor components of samples and so may simply have been contaminants of emmer/spelt crops and not cultivated in their own right.

Grains of oat (*Avena* sp.) were also present in many samples but it is not possible to distinguish wild from cultivated species on the basis of grains. Some oat floret bases (chaff) were recovered and most of these were from wild species (*A. fatua* or *A. ludoviciana*); a few could have been from either *A. ludoviciana* or one of the cultivated species (*A. sativa* or *A. strigosa*).

Elsewhere in Britain, on the evidence currently available, emmer is the predominant wheat in the Neolithic, giving way to spelt by the Iron Age (M Jones 1981; Greig 1991), but retaining its importance in parts of highland northern Britain (van der Veen 1992). Six-row barley is documented throughout this time (M Jones 1981; Greig 1991). Closer to Beeston, the Iron Age sites of the Breiddin (Hillman, 1991) and Collfryn (Jones and Milles 1989) in north Wales have produced very similar crop assemblages dominated by emmer and spelt.

Of the wild species represented a few were probably collected, eg hazelnut (*Corylus avellana*), blackberry/raspberry/dewberry (*Rubus* sp.), sloe/cherry/plum (*Prunus* sp.), and elder (*Sambucus nigra*). The vast majority of the 'wild' species, however, probably grew as weeds of the cereal crops.

The species represented in the >1mm flots and heavy residues include some indicative of damp conditions (eg *Polygonum persicaria* – persicaria, *P. lapathifolium* – pale persicaria, *Galium palustre* – marsh bedstraw, *Eleocharis palustris/uniglumis* – spike rush, and probably *Carex* spp. – sedges). If these species were weeds of crops this implies that cultivation was not restricted to the steep and freely draining hill of Beeston crag itself. Suitably damp conditions would have been available within close proximity of the site. More detailed consideration of weed ecology as an indicator of where the cereals may have been grown would require sorting of the <1mm fractions (where for example any seeds of the acid loving *Rumex acetosella* – sheep's sorrel, should be found). This laborious task has not yet been undertaken because the uncertainty surrounding both the degree of contemporaneity and the absolute date(s) of the plant remains would seriously reduce the value of any positive results.

Analysis of samples

General

Samples from layers in the Outer Ward produced very few charred plant remains compared to the majority of those from the postholes and pits, though the range of species was similar. In the light of evidence for erosion (p 83), it seems likely that the sparse plant remains in these layers were derived from disturbance of the postholes and pits rather than the reverse.

The range of species represented in samples from the Outer Gateway was similar to that from the Outer Ward but the quantity of material was again low.

Actual densities of plant material (number of items per litre of soil) were not calculated, as, for postholes and pits at least, it was thought these were most likely to reflect the depth of the feature in relation to any layer or layers from which the plant remains were derived (see below).

Outer Ward pits and postholes

Choice of samples

The range of species represented is very similar for all the postholes and pits in the Outer Ward. Such differences as occur are in the relative proportions of species and of grains to glume bases. Samples with 100 or more cereal items were therefore selected for further analysis as these would provide reasonably reliable estimates of relative proportions. Re-sorting of 25 flots from samples collected in 1980 and 1981 from South Cutting showed that significant quantities of glume bases had been overlooked, probably because of the difficulty of sorting large quantities of unsubsampled, unsieved flot. Unfortunately the heavy residues from these samples could no longer be located for re-sorting and so their further analysis had to be abandoned as reliable estimates of the relative proportions of grain to glume bases could not be calculated. Material selected for analysis comprised over 100 samples with 100 or more cereal items (totalling c 60,000 cereal items) from the East and West Cuttings (collected in 1985). The identifications for these samples are tabulated in Tables M25–M32 (M1:F5–M2:C14), and the proportions of the major crop components plotted on site plans in Figures M54–61 (M2:D1–E2).

Assessment of recovery method

It is immediately apparent from Tables M25–M28 that the ratio of emmer and spelt grains to glume bases is consistently high in the flots, whereas in the heavy residues it is consistently low. Clearly a processing method which relied on flotation alone would have failed to recover most of the glume bases and grossly distorted the ratio of grains to glume bases in most samples. The great majority of hazelnut shell fragments were also recovered from the heavy residues. The decision to use a system which included wet sieving as well as flotation, and the considerable time spent sorting plant remains from the heavy residues, were amply rewarded in terms of the quality of retrieval.

Crop compositions

The majority of samples produced emmer/spelt grains and glume bases in more or less equal proportions – the approximate proportion in which they are represented in the wheat ear. (An ear of emmer or spelt is composed of a number of spikelets, each usually with two grains tightly enveloped by two glumes or husks.) The most likely explanation for this ratio of grains to glume bases is therefore that, at the time of charring, the grains were still enclosed by glumes – in other words they were in the form of whole spikelets or ears which then disintegrated (as they commonly do) on charring. Indeed, intact spikelets were found in some samples. The proportions of emmer to spelt spikelets vary considerably from sample to sample.

Some samples had a rather higher ratio of spelt/emmer grains to glume bases and a similar imbalance is possible in many samples where indeterminate wheat and cereal grains were common. Grain-rich samples may simply reflect the differential destruction of glume bases under certain charring conditions (Boardman and Jones 1990). Conversely several samples which were richer in glume bases cannot easily be accounted for by differential destruction. Straw nodes which would usually be removed at an early stage of cleaning were infrequent but they do not survive charring as well as grains and glume bases (ibid).

Although crop species other than emmer and spelt contributed relatively little to the overall composition of samples, barley was rather more common in East Cutting A.

Weed seeds were rare compared with cereal grains, even allowing for the fact that the <1mm flots and heavy residues have not yet been sorted. This suggests that the crops had been cleaned of weeds, perhaps by sieving, before they were charred. Thus it seems likely that the wheat was in the form of disarticulated spikelets rather than whole ears, unless the ears had been harvested by plucking, leaving most of the weeds in the field. The proportion of weed seeds in samples rich in glume bases was not unusually high, suggesting that these samples do not reflect the admixture of crop cleanings.

The relationship of crop compositions to Period 3 buildings and Period 2 pit groups is discussed in the microfiche (M1:F1–3).

Interpretation

Interpretation of the data presented in microfiche is complicated by the need to use the composition of the plant samples as evidence both for the nature of the activities from which they are derived and for the relative date of their deposition. This is necessary because the plant remains have been recovered from at least secondary depositional contexts, in postholes and pits which are themselves not securely dated. Thus similarity of composition in adjacent features may help to identify groups of contemporary features and, if the discard of the plant remains can be assigned to the usage or abandonment of buildings, may throw some light on their function.

All the plant material has been preserved by charring and so was probably burnt accidentally, during storage or food preparation, or deliberately, through use of discarded crop processing residues as fuel (Hillman 1981). Emmer and spelt spikelets predominated in the majority of samples, as described above, and these normally would have been dehusked to release the grain as required for food preparation. They are unlikely therefore to have been deliberately burnt while still whole. It is more likely that they were accidentally burnt either when in store (glume wheats are best stored as whole spikelets since in this state they are relatively protected from fungal and insect attack – ibid) or while being parched (the parching of spikelets makes them easier to dehusk – ibid). If these finds of spikelets are the result of accidents to a valued resource rather than deliberate burning of unwanted waste, it is probable that they represent one or two major charring episodes rather than frequent minor incidents.

If most of the plant remains recovered do result from one or two accidents, it is perhaps surprising that they are dispersed over so wide an area (at least the full length of the East and West Cuttings and probably into the South Cutting as well – there were abundant cereal remains in the South Cutting but whether in the form of spikelets it is not possible to establish). Unless the plant remains were dispersed laterally after charring, their distribution would seem to imply either parching in bulk or, more probably, a large storage complex. Either way, this suggests activity above the domestic level. Even if the plant remains were charred in numerous small accidents, this suggestion is still plausible, as storage or parching are the only activities positively attested in this extensive area of the site.

What would be the date of this complex? Samples from the packing of postpits should have been deposited when the various buildings were constructed. The soil filling the spaces between the stones packing the postpit is most likely derived from the pit dug to erect the post, and the plant material could therefore be derived from the surface or from a buried layer or layers cut through by the pit. Thus the plant material could immediately predate the construction of the building (ie be broadly contemporary with the construction), could predate it by some length of time, or could be of mixed date.

Where postpipes and packing from the same posthole can be distinguished, the composition of plant remains in each tends to be very similar (Figs M54–M61, M2:D1–E2). This suggests that the earth fill in the post packings (containing charred plant remains) fell or filtered into the postpipes when the posts were removed or as they decayed. Plant remains from the postpipes therefore also apparently date to the construction phase of the various buildings, or earlier, and their composition cannot shed any light on the function of the buildings. Undifferentiated fills of postpits presumably contain plant material from both packing and pipe, but, since the source of the plant material is probably the same for both, deposition again dates to the construc-

tion phase. Plant remains from other pits probably entered after these features had served their primary purpose and could again be derived either from the surface or from a buried layer. Unfortunately erosion has been widespread in this area so that ancient layers – surface or buried – have not survived (p 83).

If the plant remains entered the various features from surface deposits, more or less contemporary with the cutting of the features, then the similarity of composition between features of very different date is irreconcilable with the suggestion of charring in just one or two major accidents. Even if charring took place in several minor accidents, however, the similar composition of some neighbouring features of different date would demand that emmer and spelt were burnt in the same proportions and in the same spot over a long period of time. Derivation from a surface layer, therefore, would imply that the proposed relative chronology of features is flawed, and that most features are in fact contemporary with each other.

Alternatively the plant remains may be derived from a layer buried before the majority of features were cut (ie during or before the Late Bronze Age/Early Iron Age). Any such layer must have been eroded or dug away after the majority of the features were filled up. This explanation is rather complex but is compatible with the evidence in two respects: first, with the suggested phasing of features, and, secondly, with the fact that position in the excavated area is as good a guide to crop composition as either date of deposition or membership of a particular building.

Thus the date of primary deposition of the charred plant remains is uncertain, but must be earlier than the secondary deposition in Late Bronze Age/Early Iron Age pits. The only certain way of dating this activity would be to date the plant remains themselves. This would also resolve the question of whether or not all the plant material is contemporary and which, if any, of the construction periods it is associated with. The existence of a storage complex or of large-scale processing at any time in the pre-Roman period is, of course, of the utmost importance.

Conclusions

The study raises some important points with regard both to archaeobotanical methodology and to the nature of the prehistoric settlement at Beeston and its relationship with the surrounding countryside. An observation of methodological importance is that large numbers of glume bases and hazelnut shell fragments failed to float and were recovered from the heavy residues. This emphasises the need for methods of recovery which incorporate sieving of material that sinks (eg French 1971, Kenward et al 1980, Badham and Jones 1983) and for an efficient programme of subsampling to streamline the laborious but essential task of sorting the resulting flots and heavy residues.

As regards the status of the prehistoric settlement at Beeston, the suggestion of a pre-Roman storage or parching complex raises the possibility that the site served some sort of central place role. At the Iron Age hillfort of Danebury in Hampshire, Martin Jones has argued for the communal dehusking of cereals, grown within a wide hinterland (M Jones 1984, 1985). In the Thames valley the same author has also suggested a distinction among minor settlements between those which produced and those which consumed cereals (M Jones 1985).

Further excavation and archaeobotanical study is clearly desirable, first, in other parts of the settlement, to determine whether grain dehusking took place on a large scale or domestic scale and whether grain was also stored on a domestic level; and, second, at other sites in the area, to ascertain whether movements of grain can be detected, such as have been suggested in southern England – in this context, the existing <1mm flots and heavy residues from Beeston should be examined to determine whether they contain weed seeds indicative of particular habitats. The third, and of course most urgent, avenue for future research is direct radiocarbon dating of the Beeston plant remains themselves, to test the suggestion that they are the result of just one or two major charring episodes, to determine when these took place, and so to allow plant usage at Beeston to be viewed in the context of a regional network of contemporaneous and economically interdependent sites.

The soils and pollen
by Richard Macphail

Introduction

Excavations by Peter Hough in the Outer Ward, at the Outer Gateway, and below Tower 7 were the subject of a number of soil reports by the author (Macphail 1980, 1981a, 1981b, 1983, 1984, and 1987). Study of a pollen sequence below Tower 7 was undertaken by Ken Whittaker (Whittaker undated) and is discussed in Macphail 1987. The following is a summary of the main findings and conclusions of these reports.

Environmental studies at Beeston have been limited by a combination of erosion within the Outer Ward and lack of soil stability along the steep slopes at the Outer Gateway. Hence, although truncated soils, colluvial, and occupational sediments readily occur, well-sealed *in situ* buried soils are rare. In addition, sediments at the site were not generally suitable for fossil pollen studies, both because of instability and because of their highly oxidised nature and induced high pH around the Gateway. The sediments are naturally acid, but medieval use of mortar has superimposed alkaline conditions upon them. It was therefore encouraging to find a series of ditch fills sealed by a soil dump below Tower 7, which contained good quantities of pollen. This sequence was investigated by Ken Whittaker, and two levels were dated by radiocarbon assays. The soils examined at the different excavation sites have been analysed, described, and classified following the criteria laid down by Avery and Bascomb (1974), Hodgson (1974), and Avery (1980) respectively. In particular the 1985 rampart profile east of the curtain wall was additionally studied by thin section analysis of the Ah/occupation and the Bs/Bs(t) layers (Bullock *et al* 1985; Courty *et al* 1989).

The Outer Ward

The site is characterised by a humo-ferric podzol. This soil contains weakly formed Bh and Bs horizons, and also the eluvial Ea horizon is only partly leached. The shallow nature of the Ah and eluvial horizons suggests that the soil may well have been affected by erosion, and is indicative of the soil being truncated. The present-day ease with which the soil is disturbed and eroded, and the particular slope unit position of the soil in question, are further indications of erosion processes applying in the past.

The Outer Gateway ramparts

Three areas were examined, the deposits beneath and east of Tower 5 in 1981/2, and the rampart layers north of the gateway, east and west of the curtain wall, in 1983 and 1985. Analysis of the bank layers at Tower 5 suggested that the soils were already strongly podzolised at the period of embankment (Fig 18, Section 3). Layers of grey sand (164 and 159, Period 3A) may relate to heaping up of Ea horizon material from local humo-ferric podzols on to a soil already truncated as far as the Ea horizon (layers 324 and 160, Period 2B). Later work to the north of the entrance indicated that the truncated humo-ferric podzol layers forming the rampart there were in all ways comparable to the rampart material at Tower 5 (Fig 18, Section 5). The lowest bleached sand deposits probably relate to prehistoric strongly leached sand forming a cover to the eroded parent material. A phase of anthropogenic activity gave rise to the charcoal rich 'burned bleached sand' (layer 669, Period 2A). A later phase of colluvial sand produced the 2b Ea horizon, which was stable enough to allow organic matter laminations to form prior to the next on-site phase, the dumping of reddish brown heterogeneous loamy sand (layer 641, Period 2B). This phase was again succeeded by colluviation or dumping of leached sands (layer 637, Period 3A), in the upper part of which a podzol Ah horizon developed prior to the latest (Middle Iron Age) phase of rampart construction using stone revetting. The very loose nature of these soils combined with the natural slope beneath may indicate the need for revetting and for dumps of more cohesive sand.

West of the curtain wall the deposits were similar (Fig 18, Sections 1 and 4). Soil micromorphology indicated that the Ah horizon (layer 872, Period 3A) could be divided into two major components: natural and anthropogenic. The natural elements were bleached (leached) sand grains and amorphous organic matter infills and coatings normal for Ah horizons. Frequently however this material was affected by human activity and contamination. These included charcoal and phytoliths (from grass/cereals), dusty clay coatings relating to trampling, and rare amorphous infills common in occupation sediments and resulting from organic waste. There was also evidence of the employment of fires of a higher temperature than necessary for purely domestic needs. One suggestion is that the heavily burnt deposits are redeposited fragments of hearths scraped up for rampart construction, and possibly related to metallurgy in view of the presence of metalwork and moulds. Again there was evidence of a diffuse junction between the lower relic subsoil (layer 884, Period 2B) and the overlying podzolic sands of the platform.

The Outer Gateway approaches

A colluvial sand (layer 432), brown in colour, stoneless, and approximately 0.4–0.5m thick, was of the same grain size as the sands upslope (Fig 19, Section 6). Coarse layering throughout its depth strongly suggested that it was colluvial, and associated finds suggested a prehistoric date. There was no evidence of a wind-blown origin, and it seemed probable that the deposit was concentrated in its down-valley position as the result of anthropogenic soil disturbance upslope. At its surface there was evidence of a deeply truncated soil with only the base of a Bs horizon preserved. This was overlain in part by a dark soil layer (234, Period 4), which was not a topsoil or buried soil. Layer 234 may be seen either as a soil bed base for the overlying cobbles (layer 235, Period 5), or as the result of a combination of trample of people and stock at an entrance area, and the erosion and mixing, through access use, of the Ah and loose Ea horizon deriving from the layers below. Elsewhere on the slopes in front of the gateway a solifluction deposit containing many small boulders was noted which may well have come downslope along the line of the entrance.

The prehistoric ditch below Tower 7 (Fig 21)

Dating

The ditch, F1000, is considered to be prehistoric on the grounds of its relationship to ditch F185 at the gateway and to the later Civil War ditch, F1001. The radiocarbon dates for the ditch section are: layer 1014, 2b Ah, 791–410 cal BC, and layer 1006, the humic A horizon, 673–892 cal AD (HAR-8102 and HAR-8101 respectively). Radiocarbon soil dates have to be carefully interpreted, more so than charcoal dates. Normally a correction date in excess of a millennium is applied to radiocarbon dates from buried soil A horizons (Macphail 1987, 360). However the correction applies to topsoils formed *in situ* over many thousands of years, and this is not so in the case of the two Beeston sediments. The length of time over which the soil formed in each case therefore needs to be decided. In the case of the b Ah horizon above the ditch fill, field analysis showed it to be a moderately deeply formed mature topsoil over a weakly developed B(s) horizon. It therefore seems to have had plenty of time to form residual organic matter, so the radiocarbon age may suggest that it was quite recently buried (even though some fine charcoal was present), or that the date is unreliable. The Civil War ditch F1001 provides an archaeological *terminus ante quem* for the deposit. In contrast, the lower buried humic horizon (2b Ah) appeared as a narrower and more humic band that was less like a slowly developed topsoil than a moderately rapid accumulation of organic matter in fine material concentrating in the damp bottom of the ditch. The date can more satisfactorily be considered as a 'peat' date than a soil date, and the ditch is therefore accepted to be Early Iron Age.

Soil pollen

The pollen sequence of 31 levels was carried out by Ken Whittaker (unpublished report in archive) under the supervision of N Balaam, and a pollen diagram of four zones was produced. The more organic levels were sampled at 40mm intervals, the less organic at 100mm intervals, and a total pollen sum of 500 grains at each level (excluding *Alnus* and spores) was counted. A summary relating to the interpretation and dating of the ditch is presented.

In pollen zone 1 both the primary mineral fill (layer 1014, 2b B) and the humic band (layer 1012, 2b Ah) contain high arboreal pollen ratios, primarily consisting of *Quercus* (oak) and *Corylus* (hazel). Other woodland elements are present, including *Ilex* (holly), *Betula* (birch), *Alnus* (alder), and *Tilia* (lime). The non-arboreal pollen component consists primarily of *Gramineae* (grasses) and *Pteridium* (bracken). Cereal pollen and weed species associated with agriculture are also present. The data suggest that the Early Iron Age ditch was cut in a wooded environment, although open areas for agriculture were probably contemporary with the occupation of the site.

Pollen zone 2 occurs in sands probably eroded from the Late Bronze Age and Iron Age ramparts (layer 1007), so that problems of differential preservation and residuality have to be considered. All that may be said from the pollen is that the environment probably became increasingly open. This suggestion may be supported by local evidence, since palaeomagnetic and pollen data from the nearby Peckforton Mere indicates a primary peak of erosion related to intensified agriculture, possibly during late prehistory or the early historic period (Oldfield *et al* 1985, 38–40), although there has been no absolute dating.

The more recent history of the crag, as represented by soil pollen in the mature soil profile (layer 1006) above the ditch fill (pollen zone 3), indicates that the area became rewooded first with *Betula* and *Quercus*, then by *Alnus* and *Corylus*. The modern soil pollen (pollen zone 4, layer 1003) reflects the open nature of the present vegetation.

Discussion

Beeston crag is composed of coarse Permo-Triassic sediments, such as the Keuper Sandstone, Keuper Sandstone Conglomerate, and Bunter Upper Mottled Sandstone. These freely draining deposits have given rise to humo-ferric podzols of the Delamere Soil Series (Furness 1978), and typical brown sands, within the Bridgnorth Soil Association (Ragg *et al* 1983). The development of these soils is now examined.

Firstly periglacial deposits have been suspected on the site including probable solifluction gravels at the Outer Gateway, and microfabric analysis has confirmed that soils developed under a periglacial environment were present. During the Flandrian, primary soil formation appears to have been brown sand development in the sandstone parent material as it continued to weather (Avery 1980). It is evident that the brown sand soil progressively acidified, developing into a podzol. Although the soil pollen data are not

Table 33 The radiocarbon dates

Harwell number	Date BP	+/–	Calibrated date range, 1 standard deviation	Site/context/period
HAR 4401	2620	90	843 – 777 cal BC	OW posthole F25 Period 3
HAR 4402	2380	100	760 – 390 cal BC	OG posthole F213 Period 3B
HAR 4405	2860	80	1160 – 920 cal BC	OG 160 Period 2B rampart
HAR 4406	2280	80	402 – 234 cal BC	OW posthole F29 Period 3
HAR 5609	2400	70	757 – 397 cal BC	OG 376 Period 3B rampart
HAR 5610	1890	120	30 cal BC–250 cal AD	OG 375 Period 3B rampart
HAR 6459	2480	100	800 – 400 cal BC	OG 323 Period 4
HAR 6461	5330	110	4340–4003 cal BC	OG 542 Period 1
HAR 6462	5140	90	4036–3816 cal BC	OG ditch fill F490 Period 3B
HAR 6464	2300	80	405 – 258 cal BC	OG F621 Period 3B rampart
HAR 6465	2430	70	765 – 402 cal BC	OG F624 Period 3B rampart
HAR 6468	2290	70	402 – 257 cal BC	OG F621 Period 3B rampart
HAR 6469	2370	80	752 – 390 cal BC	OG F621 Period 3B rampart
HAR 6503	2350	70	487 – 387 cal BC	OG F621 Period 3B rampart
HAR 6504	2310	70	405 – 270 cal BC	OG 234 Period 4
HAR 8101	1230	90	673 – 892 cal AD	OG 1006 Period 4
HAR 8102	2480	70	791 – 410 cal BC	OG ditch F1000 Period 3A

tightly dated, it can be inferred that the soils at Beeston Castle developed under a mixed oak woodland, which was still extant into the Late Bronze Age. It is probable that the podzolisation evidenced beneath the Iron Age rampart had developed in the first place under a mixed oak woodland cover. Such development without full forest clearance and the impact of heathland vegetation is well documented, for example at Caesars Camp, Kent (Cornwall 1958; Dimbleby 1962), and the chemical mechanisms are understood (Davies 1970; Mokma and Buurman 1982). It would appear that the initial prehistoric defences were provided in an environment of mixed oak woodland with local clearance, and where cultivation of cereals and patches of waste ground are suggested.

The soil pollen suggests that the site became increasingly open in later prehistory, but abandonment of the area after Iron Age occupation led to the crag becoming increasingly rewooded. This may also be inferred to be the case in the area as a whole from the sedimentary record at Peckforton Mere (Oldfield *et al* 1985, 38–40), and Beeston crag was probably wooded when it was fortified in the 1220s.

The radiocarbon and archaeomagnetic dating results
by Peter Ellis

Seventeen radiocarbon dates were obtained from samples of wood and charcoal, and from charcoal-rich silts. In addition an archaeomagnetic date was obtained for burnt stones in the Iron Age rampart. The radiocarbon dating results are tabulated (Table 33) and discussed below, while the archaeomagnetic data follows.

Archaeomagnetic dating
by Tony Clark

Four blocks of burnt sandstone in the Iron Age rampart were orientated by the archaeologists, using the disc method with a magnetic compass, and were sent to the Ancient Monuments Laboratory. Measurements on subsamples showed that two of these were closely similar and fitted on to the Iron Age part of the reference curve, from which it was deduced that they were probably undisturbed, while the other two readings gave very aberrant results, indicating movement since heating. The date obtained from the first two blocks was 360–240 cal BC and 400–200 cal BC at 1 and 2 standard deviations respectively (AML ref 873704–5). A description of the techniques used, and measurement data for these samples, are given in Clark *et al* (1988).

Discussion

A single date was obtained from the Period 1 Neolithic occupation area (HAR-6461). The sample came from fragments of charcoal in layer 542. As will be argued below, the date from a nearby sample (HAR-6462) may represent a further Period 1 date from disturbed material.

HAR-4405, from charcoal lying on the surface of the 2B rampart, gave a date centred on the turn of the second and first millennia BC. As noted by Stuart Needham (p 45), this may be mature wood from earlier than a rampart construction date, which is better suggested by the two Ewart Park bronzes thought to be foundation deposits. At the two-sigma range the date calibrates to 1300–840 cal BC. While it can be argued that the timber was felled earlier or was reused, this remains a problematic date.

A number of dates were obtained from the charred post remains on the Period 3B rampart. These may be secondary to the initial rampart construction. The two massive timbers F621 and F624 yielded four samples

(HAR-6464, 6468, 6469, and 6503) and one (HAR-6465) sample respectively. A further date came from an associated displaced fragment of wood (HAR-5609 from layer 376). An aberrant date in the Roman period came from another displaced fragment (HAR-5610 from layer 375). Although these six dates (disregarding HAR-5610) provide a wide-spanning date range from 765–257 cal BC at one standard deviation, they must reflect the position of the dates on the ambiguous Iron Age section of the calibration curve, rather than a widely disparate group of features from different rampart phases. On calibration, the dates fall into two overlapping blocks, one earlier (HAR-6459, 6465, and 6469) and one later (HAR-6464, 6468, and 6503). Of the two rampart postholes, F621 provided dates from both groups, while F624 gave the earliest date of the group. The actual difference of 140 radiocarbon years between all the samples is likely to indicate that the dates are all much closer, and may come from a single episode. A date in the fourth century BC may be suggested. The archaeomagnetic dates discussed above could possibly be associated with an initial process of vitrification prior to the establishment of the timber structure, but seem more likely to represent a later episode of burning.

An associated date (HAR-4402) came from posthole F213 south of the entrance. This feature may have been for a revetting post at the front of the rampart, but the slopes here are very steep and the stratigraphy confused.

Of the two samples from the prehistoric ditch below the defences, HAR-6462 came from layer 546 in the Period 3A ditch F490. The presence of Iron Age pottery in the same layer provides the dating evidence for the filling of this ditch, and the sampled charcoal must have derived originally from the Neolithic horizon to the east, dated by HAR-6461, as material eroded into the ditch. The sample from below Tower 7 (HAR-8102 from layer 1014, the primary ditch fill of F1000) is discussed in more detail by Richard Macphail (p 84), who suggests that the date is acceptable without the usual correction for radiocarbon soil dates. The ditch may then be dated either to the Late Bronze Age/Early Iron Age or to the

Iron Age if the date is grouped with the Period 3B rampart dates discussed above.

Layer 234, from which HAR-6504 came, is argued to be a Period 4 deposit representing both hillwash and a trampled surface overlying the Iron Age entrance track. The layer contained Romano-British pottery, and the sample date may indicate the presence of timber fragments from the period 3B rampart upslope. A further Period 4 sample came from layer 1006 sealing ditch F1000 below Tower 7 (HAR-8101). This date is also discussed by Richard Macphail who casts doubt on its reliability (p 84). However, a date in the late first millennium AD may be correct for a stabilising soil established after a long period of erosion following the abandonment of the hillfort. A final Period 4 sample, HAR-6459, derived from displaced wood beneath collapsed rampart stone downslope from the scarp edge.

At the Outer Ward samples were obtained from two postholes both in South Cutting, HAR-4401 from F25, and HAR-4406 from F29. The difficulties of dating the Outer Ward postholes are discussed below. The radiocarbon dates suggest both Bronze Age and Iron Age occupation. The date for F25 is significantly earlier than the Outer Gateway group.

The dates provide a useful framework for the Iron Age defences, with the single Period 2B date supporting other dating evidence to suggest that the defensive sequence commenced in the Late Bronze Age. The two Neolithic dates from the slopes below the plateau confirm the pottery evidence from this area, while the Outer Ward posthole dates make it clear that the posthole data are not all contemporary and that occupation there was long-standing.

The radiocarbon dating was undertaken at the Harwell Laboratory and was facilitated by Jill Walker. The scientific dating programme was organised successively by Tony Clark and David Haddon Reece at the Ancient Monuments Laboratory. Calibration was undertaken by David Jordan of the Archaeometry Section of the Ancient Monuments Laboratory using the calibration curves of Stuiver and Pearson (1986) and Pearson and Stuiver (1986).

4 Discussion of the prehistoric and Roman evidence

by Peter Ellis

The Neolithic and Early/Middle Bronze Age data

The pre-Late Bronze Age features found at Beeston were few, comprising a possible Neolithic burnt structure, a pit from the Outer Gateway excavations, and a few possible postholes from the Outer Ward. The Period 2A line of postholes and the linear slot from the Outer Ward and the Outer Gateway may be any date from Neolithic to Late Bronze Age. By contrast to the small number of features, the finds present a more detailed picture. The handful of microliths in the flint assemblage may indicate use of the hill in the Mesolithic period. Subsequently the presence of three, or possibly four, different Neolithic pottery fabrics suggests more than the passing use attested by the flint arrowheads. At the Outer Ward, concentrations of flint flakes may indicate areas of activity. Occupation therefore appears to have been widespread, and there are hints of complexity.

The radiocarbon dates of 4340–4003 cal BC and 4036–3816 cal BC, associated with the burnt area at the Outer Gateway, accord well with other dating evidence from close by. Pollen data from the area north of Beeston suggest that an initial clearance phase here, presumably associated with farming, did not occur until the end of the third millennium. Radiocarbon dates from the post-glacial pollen site of Hatchmere suggest uncalibrated dates between 5269 and 4692 BP (Switsur and West 1975a, 39; 1975b, 303), and the pollen profile here is in accord with those from Flaxmere and Abbots Mere. At Flaxmere there followed phases of forest regeneration; of flooding, possibly towards the end of the second millennium; and finally of renewed clearance activity coinciding with the arrival of the Romans although this area may have been affected by swamps and meres in the early post-glacial periods.

In the earlier Bronze Age six sherds from urns and four probable flint knives, both artefact types often found in barrow contexts, suggest the presence of burials on the crag, and the hypothesised round barrows could well be associated with a community. Contemporary occupation may be attested by the finds of pottery from later layers at the entranceway. The clay sources of the Neolithic and Bronze Age fabrics are suggested to be the drift deposits of the Cheshire Plain (Table 22). The flints found during the excavations tend to support the pottery evidence by indicating a succession of differing occupations and activities. The flint raw material was most likely brought to the area from the east coast, suggesting wide regional contacts in addition to use of the hill over a long period (p 59).

Unlike other parts of the British Isles there is little air photographic information for the area. The distribution of earlier prehistoric pottery suggests that sites are concentrated on and around the sandstone outcrops (Fig 51; Table M23, M1:E1–8); but this may only reflect the zones less damaged by subsequent land-use, rather than occupation foci. With the extent and complexity of prehistoric land-use exhibited elsewhere it would seem best to assume the same degree of occupation in the fertile Cheshire Plain, and thus to see the Neolithic and Bronze Age evidence at Beeston in the framework of a well-utilised region.

The defences (Fig 62)

Period 2A

The enclosure sequence at Beeston Castle appears to begin in the later Bronze Age, with the possible palisade postholes and slots from the Outer Gateway and Outer Ward. Other early hilltop definitions have been noted at, for example, Castle Ditch, Eddisbury where a trench was found (Varley 1952, 34); at the Breiddin where a double line of postholes reinforced a bank (Musson 1976, 296); and at Oswestry, Shropshire (Varley 1948).

Period 2B

The subsequent defences are represented by a slight bank on the scarp edge. It is possible to interpret the crossways timbers as lacing within a rampart or as the remains of a timber superstructure on a levelled platform. The difference in the finds associated with layers above and below the timbers suggests two separate defensive processes. A similar division of the early deposits was noted at the Breiddin (Musson 1976, 297).

Apart from the outlines of carbonised wood there were no definite indications of the nature of the Period 2B defences. A number of discontinuities in plan and section may represent postpits but cannot be placed in a coherent plan. To the rear of the defences the scatter of postholes and spread of occupation debris suggest that they came to a simple entrance with no inturning. The evidence suggests that there was no accompanying ditch.

The two copper alloy axes of the Ewart Park tradition, located beneath the timber frame and near to the entrance, may be a deliberate deposition marking the significance of the site and its defences (p 48). The choice of metalwork may have a connection with the function and status of the site, and indicate one of its most valued attributes. Finds of metalworking debris in the Period 3A defences and the Outer Ward demonstrate that smiths worked at the site. Pottery in the bank may be associated with similar pottery from The Wrekin (Fabrics 7 and 8), and with a rare pottery fabric found at the Breiddin (Fabric 2).

Period 3A

The subsequent slight overlying bank is argued to represent a new episode of defensive work because of the presence of a wider range of pottery fabrics, and of metalworking debris. These components are paralleled

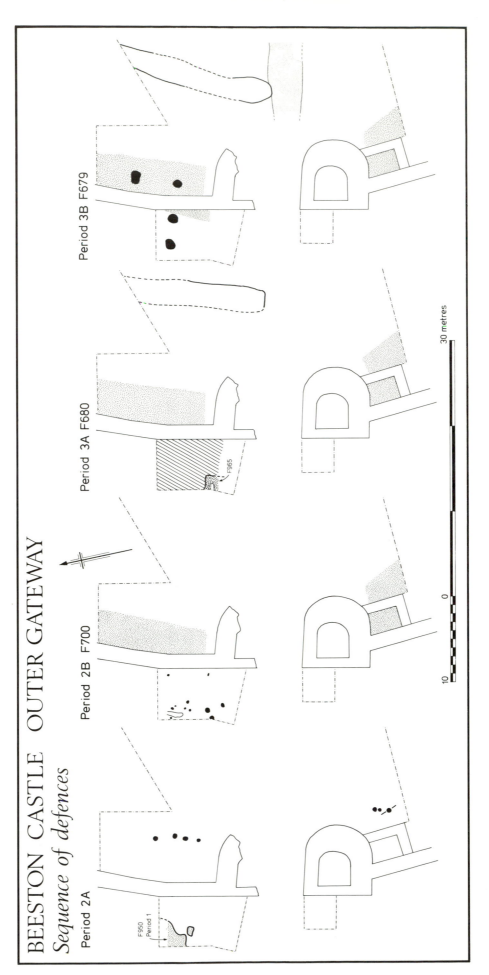

BEESTON CASTLE OUTER GATEWAY
Sequence of defences

Period 2A

Period 2B F700

Period 3A F680

Period 3B F679

F950
Period 1

F965

10   0   30 metres

Fig 62 *Outer Gateway: sequence of defences, Periods 2A to 3B; scale as shown*

by the material found in the sloping layers to the west at the entranceway, and it is argued that bank and platform are contemporary. The later rampart has removed any evidence for the nature of the bank. A steep-sided ditch was cut in this period below the rampart, defining what may have been a narrow entrance passage. The layers to the rear of the rampart must represent special provision at the entrance. Inturned entrance banks either side of a narrow passage are present nearby at Castle Ditch, Eddisbury (Varley 1952, fig 4), and are common in the Marches (Savory 1976, fig 8). At Beeston, the finding of the cache of slingstones supports the interpretation of these entrances as twin fighting platforms at the entrance. A parallel to the slingstone cache is provided by a group of 500 egg-sized stones at Crickley Hill (Dixon forthcoming). The evidence suggests a later alteration in the form of the stone spread and the possible hearth and charcoal spread, and these may represent surviving elements of a guard chamber as at Eddisbury, where the provision of stone guard chambers was secondary (Varley 1952, 29), and at a number of sites to the west (Savory 1976, fig 8).

Period 3B

The stylistic change in rampart construction is marked by the use of stone rubble rather than sand as the core of a timber framework. There appears to have been an initial, trenched front and rear boulder revetment. It is a pity that these features cannot be more definitely identified and presented, since there seem to be no parallels in the literature for the foundation trenches (Avery 1976, 12). The boulder revetment may have been carried upward as a drystone wall, since there could not have been more than two courses at the most of the massive boulders noted at the gateway. Within the rubble core there is marked evidence for cellular construction, and these differing infills may represent all that remains of a timber box frame. Two very large vertical posts were found, one of oak and one of ash, and must represent some upper timber palisade on top of the stone rampart. The associated postholes to the rear are secondary, and may well indicate a timber structure associated with an entranceway, possibly the north side of a walkway across the entrance. Later, they appear to have been deliberately removed and their postpits backfilled.

That there may have been vitrified sections of the rampart elsewhere is attested by the finds of heavily burnt and vitrified material spread throughout the excavated sites (M3:G5). However, at the excavated points the evidence is not clear. Burnt stones appear to belong discretely to the boxed areas as though they were already burnt when placed there rather than fired *in situ*. The area of vitrification is very small. However any argument that already burnt material was introduced to the rampart is contradicted by the archaeomagnetic date suggesting that burning was contemporary with or followed construction.

The hillfort rampart was firmly recognised only to the north of the gateway. Further south there are merely stone layers above the earlier rampart in positions suggesting parallels with the stratigraphy further to the north, but no evidence of the boulder footings. It may be that the Iron Age defences ran to the west of the excavated area more or less along the line of the curtain wall. Further south again at Tower 7 the cutting beneath the tower floor appeared to expose the front of the early rampart but with little evidence of the Iron Age defences. It is possible that the boulder revetting discussed above was confined to the entranceway.

An entranceway is clearly defined by the terminal of the north ditch. The southern continuation of the ditch was not located north of the exposure below Tower 7, and must have been obliterated by later ditches in the Outer Gateway excavation. Differing trackway elements were located, including the marks of an apparent timber corduroy at the junction of ditch and track, and evidence for patching and repair where the stone surface had been worn or eroded.

With the exception of the possible palisade posts at the south-western edge of the Outer Ward, there is no evidence of prehistoric defences on the north, south, or west sides of the plateau. Although it is possible to argue that at all periods the enclosure defences were confined to the east side, cutting off the promontory otherwise protected by sharp natural slopes, it would seem more likely that, at least in the Iron Age, the hillfort was enclosed by artificial defences. Only at the Inner Ward are the natural slopes sharp enough to provide an effective obstacle, and even at the small nearby site of Helsby (Forde-Johnston 1962, fig 2) there are additional defences on the cliff side. Until excavation took place at Beeston in 1981 there were no ground indications of prehistoric defences anywhere, and it may be that parts of a complete circuit remain to be found. It is clear on the ground, however, that any such circuit could only have had a ditch on the east side.

Dating

While the Period 2B radiocarbon date suggests a construction date at the turn of the second and first millennia BC, it is possible that the bronzes and the Late Bronze Age pottery fabrics offer a more realistic date. The dated timber could have been felled some time before its use, or have been reused. The continuance of Period 2B until the Iron Age may be suggested by the increased number of pottery fabrics found in the open area to the rear of the rampart at the gateway.

The Period 3A defences are argued to contain almost wholly residual pottery, the exception being the sherds of VCP found in the rampart and to its rear at the base of the additional platform. Further support for an early Iron Age date is provided by the finds of ironwork in layers forming the upper platform at the rear of the rampart. The provision of a ditch is likely to have taken place at the same time as attention to the entrance defile, and thus the ditch with its radiocarbon date of 791–410 cal BC below Tower 7 is also taken as an indicator of date.

Period 3B seems to be well dated by the group of radiocarbon dates from the timber posts on top of the stone bank, by the archaeomagnetic date from *in situ* burning, and by the further sherds of VCP found in and behind the rampart. The single sherd of Iron Age pottery in the ditch fill below the defences also supports the suggested dating. The closure of the sequence appears to have occurred before the Roman conquest. It is possible that the hillfort came to a sudden end, as may well be witnessed by the failure to retrieve the bronze and leather vessel (Fig 34.1) from its hiding place behind the rampart. The small quantity of Period 4 Romano-British finds do not indicate reuse of the hillfort, although the Roman period radiocarbon date (HAR-5610) from an apparent Period 3B rampart layer raises this possibility.

Occupation and utilisation

There is a wealth of evidence for Late Bronze Age and Iron Age occupation in the form of long-lived defences, a range of pottery and other finds, wide-ranging radiocarbon dates, and the possibility of major crop storage and metalworking centres located on the same site at different periods. All demonstrate that a considerable period of complex occupation is represented at Beeston. The evidence of the crucibles (p 55) suggests an understanding of the potential of the clays of the area, with the consequent accumulation of technical knowledge and the establishment of a tradition. From this, too, long-standing residence at Beeston may be argued. There is Late Bronze Age pottery distributed over the excavated areas, and some of the fabrics indicate wide contacts. Other indicators of Late Bronze Age/Early Iron Age occupation are the pottery vessels and the shale rings. Food preparation is witnessed by the finds of quernstones and utility stones in the 3A rampart and in the packing of three later postholes in the Outer Ward.

The metalworking evidence (p 48) strongly suggests the actual site of a Late Bronze Age production centre, which would have been accompanied by structures for the workers and for the production process. Apart from the composition of the metal assemblage itself, a key argument is the finding of fragile crucibles and moulds indicating both a primary place of deposition, and little subsequent disturbance. The pottery and domestic debris seem likely to be associated. A link with the Late Bronze Age rampart is provided by the axes probably placed in the bank as foundation deposits.

However, the complex of postholes at the Outer Ward was without any evidence of accompanying occupation levels, exterior surfaces, or working areas, and an association with metalworking can only be inferred. The chronological position of the suggested circular structures is not clear. The plant remains evidence suggests that there may have been a widespread buried soil. Denudation and consequent loss of stratified deposits must be suspected in the Outer Ward areas since the prehistoric period. Evidence for major structures, founded in deeper subsoils than survive today, may well have been lost, while the survival only of features cut into bedrock may present a distorted picture. A further distortion, in this case to the dating evidence, arises from the absence of Iron Age pottery in the region.

The crop remains evidence suggested that crop processing at Beeston predated the pits of Period 2 and the postholes of Period 3. The homogeneity of the remains present in all the features examined suggested that the material arrived in the features from a pre-existing layer or layers. From the perspective of the crop remains, the Outer Ward structures may represent a rebuilding of storage and accommodation facilities immediately following a disastrous fire. The date of this event would be indicated by radiocarbon dating of the plant remains themselves, but, whatever its date, it is clear that the existence of large-scale storage facilities should be envisaged, together with areas for processing and parching the grain.

The data, although exceptionally rich for a prehistoric upland site, are to some extent contradictory. It is possible to suggest two alternative sequences, the first involving a crop storage complex followed by metalworking and widespread occupation, both located in the Late Bronze Age, and the second involving Late Bronze Age metalworking succeeded by an Iron Age crop storage complex and associated or later occupation.

Beeston Castle in its regional and national context

The identification of a hitherto unknown Iron Age hillfort is a rarity given modern survey and air reconnaissance. To find a new hillfort preceded by a much rarer Bronze Age defended enclosure is even more surprising, and Beeston can now be added to the lists of both Bronze Age and Iron Age defended sites.

In its local context Beeston can be seen as part of a group of defended prehistoric sites located on the ridge of higher ground running from the Mersey estuary in the north to the Malpas Peckforton ridge in the south, and clearly intended to exploit the plain on either side. These sites have been surveyed and discussed by Forde-Johnston, who pointed out that all except Eddisbury shared the common attribute of a use of natural features such as steep cliffs, as at Helsby, Woodhouses, Kelsborrow, and Maiden Castle, and a river or lake, as at Bradley and Oakmere (Forde-Johnston 1962, 34). By comparison Beeston is very much larger than all except Eddisbury. It is tempting to regard the small, heavily defended sites at Helsby, Oakmere, Kelsborrow, Maiden Castle, and Bradley as possible Early Iron Age defended sites, to which may be added the unfinished fort at Woodhouses. These sites may then be seen as a relatively short-lived group owing their existence and characteristics to the special circumstances of the Early Iron Age (cf Cunliffe 1984a, 20).

Setting this group on one side, Beeston and Eddisbury may be seen as the key sites of the area, representing large Iron Age developed hillforts. At Beeston there were Early Iron Age and Late Bronze Age antecedents, with a possible primary palisade. Eddisbury, too, may have pre-Iron Age origins. There is evidence of a palisade, and subsequently of two prehistoric phases, according to the excavator (Varley 1952, 49), or three according to other scholars (Cotton 1954, 61; Forde-Johnston 1962, 38). Features of interest at Eddisbury included an inturned entrance and a possible guard chamber, and the parallels with Beeston have been discussed above. The pottery assemblage, although not available for study, may contain Late Bronze Age/Early Iron Age material (p 77).

In a wider context the new evidence from Beeston demonstrates that metalwork was produced on the site. Its use as foundation deposits in the Late Bronze Age defences demonstrates its importance. If the crop storage complex can be shown to be Late Bronze Age, perhaps preceding the metalworking, it will represent the first such evidence for large-scale crop storage in Britain at that time. It was only detectable at Beeston because the complex was destroyed in a major conflagration. If it can be placed after metalworking ceased, and prior to the Outer Ward suggested buildings, it may then be hypothesised that the Period 2B to 3A transition was marked by the closure of the metalworking site, and by the exploitation of the agricultural potential of the area. The degree of agricultural expropriation may be in part witnessed by the emphasis on defence shown by the ditch and the fighting platform, although presumably this must also reflect competition with other sites.

Iron Age occupation on the Cheshire Plain should be similar to that in neighbouring areas such as the upper Severn valley in Shropshire (Carver 1991a). Aerial survey of both lowland and upland areas to the south and west of Cheshire has recorded the cropmark evidence of Iron Age/Romano-British landscapes comprising widespread field systems and numerous enclosure sites and farmsteads of a wide morphological range (Whimster 1989). Consideration of the excavation and air photographic evidence in Shropshire has shown that it does not fall easily into a division of sites into either hillforts or lowland farms, and a complex settlement hierarchy has been suggested (Carver 1991b, 4). Although the social structures involved, as they emerge from future research, are unlikely to be simple ones, the hillforts would presumably have dominated the settlement hierarchy. Some control of agricultural produce is already suspected at hillfort sites; it may also be the case that Beeston with other major hillforts in the Welsh marches exercised some control over the production and distribution of salt. At Beeston, the Cheshire stony-tempered VCP fabric used as a salt container appears at an earlier date than previously recognised, first occurring at the same time as Droitwich VCP (Morris 1985).

The nature of the impact of Rome on the Iron Age landscape of the region, outside the towns and forts, is virtually unknown. The number of surviving cropmark sites demonstrates the potential for future work (Jones 1975; Ellis *et al* forthcoming). Although the Romano-British evidence at Beeston is slight, it does not suggest any occupation or reoccupation of the hillfort area. However, there were some indications of Iron Age/Romano-British continuity at the possible settlement at the Lower Green, although the nature of the site was ill-defined by the excavations.

Excavation of the Beeston sites had to surmount the problems presented by erosion and the superimposition of the great medieval castle gatehouse and curtain wall. Nevertheless the excavations have produced a body of data to be added to the known evidence for Bronze Age and Iron Age defended sites, and have demonstrated a new hilltop site to be added to the increasing number where long-lived prehistoric occupation is suspected at different periods since the Mesolithic.

PART II MEDIEVAL AND POST-MEDIEVAL

The main events in the medieval and post-medieval sequence at the different excavation sites are presented in Table 34.

5 The castle: history and structure

by Laurence Keen

The historical and documentary background

The construction of Beeston Castle was started by Ranulf, the sixth Earl of Chester. The early history of the castle cannot be understood without an examination of the history of the earldom and its relationship with the Welsh principalities.

The earldom owed its origin to the Mercian revolt of 1069 and the threat of Anglo-Welsh resistance to William the Conqueror. William had given the city of Chester and the county to Gerbod the Fleming. Gerbod soon withdrew to the Continent and William made his follower, Hugh of Avranches, earl in 1071 (Orderic Vitalis, ii, 260; iii, 216–17). The earldom then consisted of Cheshire, Flintshire, and much of Denbighshire. Earl Hugh died in 1101. He was succeeded by his son Richard, who drowned in the Channel together with the Crown Prince, when, on 25 November 1120, the White Ship foundered.

The power of the earldom extended far beyond the bounds of Cheshire, with possessions in Lincolnshire and eastern England, and as far south as Wiltshire and Gloucestershire. The earls also had extensive interests in Normandy. From the Domesday Survey it can be seen that most of the earl's English income was derived not from his 48 manors in Cheshire but from his other estates. The earl's military resources showed the same picture: two-thirds of his service was provided by fiefs outside Cheshire, with no more than 80 knights from Cheshire.

On Earl Richard's death, his possessions and title passed to his cousin, Ranulf Meschin, whose mother was a daughter of Richard, Duke of Normandy. From Earl Ranulf I the earldom passed in 1129 to his son, Ranulf de Gernons (Ranulf II), and then, in 1153, to his grandson Hugh (II) of Cyfeiliog. On Hugh's death in 1181 the inheritance passed to his son Ranulf de Blundeville (Ranulf III), a minor.

Earl Ranulf II seems to have placed little emphasis on conquest in Wales; rather, by a policy of marriage alliances with Welsh dynasties, he enlisted Welsh support for his ambitions in England. During the reign of Henry II, because Chester was not an English base against Wales, Henry relied on alliances with Welsh princes to reduce the power of the Earl of Chester. When Earl Hugh rose in rebellion against Henry in 1173, David, son of Owain Gwynedd, and Rhys ap Gruffydd supported the king to help defeat the revolt (for further discussion see Barraclough 1951, on which these paragraphs are based).

The earldom was weakened by forfeiture (1174–7) following Earl Hugh's revolt, and by the minority of Earl Ranulf III (White 1976). Ranulf III was knighted by Henry II in 1188. In the same year he married Constance, daughter and heiress of Conan, Duke of Brittany, and widow of Geoffrey, the king's third son. The earl's interests were centred on his own possessions in Normandy and those of his wife. The loss of Normandy in 1204, therefore, naturally focused Ranulf's energies on English politics. The new Welsh ruler, Llywelyn ab Iorwerth of Gwynedd, had married King John's illegitimate daughter Joan. By his treaty with John against the Scots in 1209 he had allied himself to the English cause. But a break came in 1210 and John gathered a large army at Chester in 1211 against Llywelyn, who was demoralised by John's campaigns, based on much experience and knowledge of the country. Llywelyn allied himself with the baronial party against King John and further established his position by marrying his daughter Gwladus to Reginald de Braose. Earl Ranulf and Llywelyn were on opposite sides. Ranulf had advanced his claim to the Perfeddwlad in 1210, built a castle at Holywell, and rebuilt the castle at Degannwy (Alcock 1967). Between 1212 and 1218 Llywelyn was in confrontation with the Marcher lords in the South West and South East, where he exploited his opportunities. But it was from Chester that the greatest threat to his principality came. Llywelyn re-

Table 34 The medieval and post-medieval sequence: location and period of the main events

	Inner Ward	*Outer Gateway*	*Outer Ward*
Period;	inner ditch; castle buildings	entranceway; castle buildings	—
Period 6	—	Tower 5; pits	—
Period 7	Civil War occupation; demolition	Civil War occupation; ditch and outer bank	?terraces
Period 8	—	gatehouse reoccupation; demolition	—
Period 9	—	—	quarrying; Bunbury Fair

alised that his position depended not only on military strength but on coming to terms with the Marcher lords. In 1218 he made peace with Ranulf, and two years later confirmed the alliance by meeting the earl on his return from crusade. Finally in 1222 he sealed the friendship with the marriage of his daughter, Helen, to the earl's heir and nephew, John le Scot. Llywelyn now had a powerful ally at court, and a friendly neighbour on his eastern border (Davies 1987, 241, 248).

Ranulf's entente with Llywelyn established the earldom's security from Welsh advances, and consolidated his position in English politics. He was among King John's most powerful supporters. The singular status and independence of Cheshire at this time is illustrated by the need for Cheshire to obtain a separate charter of liberties from its earl (Barraclough 1951, 37).

After John's death in 1216, during the minority of Henry III, Earl Ranulf exercised a major political role. Following his return from the Holy Land in 1220 his power decreased. The uneasy relationship with Hubert de Burgh, justiciar, no doubt led Ranulf to make sure that Llywelyn was an ally. After his confrontation with Hubert de Burgh and the king's party, Ranulf was forced to give up the castles of Shrewsbury, Bridgnorth, and Lancaster in 1223.

'The source of his strength lay not in Chester, but in the immense territorial power he had built up … across the length and breadth of central England' (Barraclough 1951, 34). John granted him the honour of Leicester in 1215, the honour of Lancaster in 1216, and in 1217 he was created Earl of Lincoln. He 'added office to office and lordship to lordship, reaching southwards into Staffordshire and Leicestershire and eastwards to the Lincoln coast' (ibid). He took part in the battle of Lincoln, was commander-in-chief in the French campaign of 1231, a crusader who led the capture of the Egyptian fortress of Damietta, and one of two Englishmen whose deeds are mentioned in *The Vision of William concerning Piers the Plowman*:

Ich can nouht parfytliche my *pater-noster*, as the
prest hit seggeth
Ich can rymes of Robin Hode, and of Randolf, erl
of Chestre,
Ac of oure lord ne of oure lady, the lest that eure
was maked.

(Skeat 1886, 167)

'Ranulf III impressed contemporaries and posterity not because he ruled a "palatinate" in Chester, but as a man of affairs, a statesman, a crusader and a stalwart soldier' (Barraclough 1951, 34).

Earl Ranulf's position was secure enough for him to go on the crusade of 1218 (Christie 1886, 50). He returned to England in 1220 and arrived at Chester on 16 August to be received 'with great honour by the clergy and people' (ibid). In 1226 the local annalist records that, first, Ranulf levied a tax, and, second, began to build Beeston Castle (ibid, 52–4). Some historians have interpreted the tax as linked particularly to Beeston (for instance Ridgway and Cathcart King 1959, 3). But Ranulf Higden, a monk of Chester, records for the year 1220 Earl Ranulf's return from the Holy Land and the building of castles at Chartley, Staffordshire, and Bees-

ton, and the Cistercian Abbey of Dieulacres, Staffordshire, all paid for by a tax throughout his lands (Lumby 1882, 198). There is every reason to suppose that the earl started building a third castle, at Bolingbroke, Lincolnshire, at the same time (Thompson 1966, Drewitt 1976).

Ranulf had founded the Abbey of Dieulacres in 1214. To his new foundation he transferred the monks of Poulton Abbey, Cheshire, which was too exposed to the Welsh (*Mon Angl*, v, 626). On his death at Wallingford in October 1232 his body was buried in Chester, and his heart at Dieulacres.

After the earl's death his widely-spread possessions were divided between his four sisters and their descendants. His nephew, John le Scot, representing the eldest co-heir, was given the earldom of Chester. Eales has stressed that a key point, not taken up by biographical studies of Ranulf, is the fact that the issue of his succession, important because of the sheer scale of his possessions, must have caused the earl great concern for many years before his death. The speed of the succession and the scale of the potential legal complications which were swept aside, give the impression of a settlement planned long before Ranulf's death. The county of Cheshire does not seem to have been taken into the king's hands at any time in 1232 (see Eales 1986 for a full discussion of Earl Ranulf's ingenuity in securing the succession).

In contrast, when Ranulf's nephew, Earl John, died in June 1237, Henry III almost immediately appropriated the earl's possessions and gave orders to Henry de Audley about the custody of the castles of Chester and Beeston. Crossbows and other weapons found in the castles were handed over (*CPR 1232–47*, 184–5 (6 June), 188 (22 June); *CR 1234-37*, 538–9 (22 June)). John de Lacy, Earl of Lincoln, was appointed *custos* of the county and of Chester and Beeston Castles on 10 July (*CPR 1232–47*, 189).

In 1238 the constable of Beeston Castle was instructed to hand over the eyrie of falcons to Thomas de Herlham, for the king's use (*CR 1237–42*, 43). The king's concern for the last earl's castles is well demonstrated in the Pipe Rolls. Allowances were paid for two knights and 30 serjeants for castle-guard at Beeston between August 1237 and August 1238 (Stewart-Brown 1938, 36). The wells were attended to, a cable bought for one well, and buildings repaired during the same period (ibid, 38). One hundred pigs were salted and sold and 20 were sent to Beeston (Stewart-Brown 1938, 39). On 25 January 1238/9 instructions were given for the well to be repaired, and a bucket with a good rope to be found for the well. Orders were given on 18 May 1239 for the walls to be taken care of, a cable bought for a well, and the houses of the castle to be repaired. Francus de Brene, constable, was instructed to have a rope to draw the water suitable for the well of the castle on 3 June (*CLibR 1226–40*, 310, 383, 388). The Pipe Roll account for August 1238 to August 1239 includes 12d spent *de novo cremento de uno domo extra castellum de Rupe*, and 34s 8d for one cable, suitable for drawing water, for the well (Stewart-Brown 1938, 42, 45).

To what extent Earl Ranulf's design for Beeston Castle, incomplete at his death, had been realised by his nephew, can only be a matter of speculation, as there are no documents comparable to those which exist for the period when the castle belonged to the Crown. These show clearly that during the reign of Henry III substantial works were carried out. In November 1241, John Lestrange, justiciar of Chester and *custos* of the castles of Chester, Beeston, and Halton, received 1000 marks from the Irish Treasury, of which 250 went towards the fortification of Beeston and Rhuddlan Castles (*CPR 1232–47*, 267). For this period the Pipe Rolls contain details of payments to the constable of Beeston Castle, and John Lestrange is paid for his services (Stewart-Brown 1938, 58–60, 67).

Between Christmas 1241 and Christmas 1242, John Lestrange accounted for much expenditure connected with the Welsh rebellion. A total of £410 12d was spent on strengthening the castles of Beeston and Rhuddlan (Stewart-Brown 1938, 71), while £8 17s 10½d went to the repair of buildings at Chester, Beeston, and Shotwick Castles (ibid, 73). Payments were made also to knights, mounted serjeants, foot-serjeants, and crossbowmen garrisoning Beeston and Rhuddlan Castles (ibid, 72; *CPR 1232–47*, 278 [16 March 1242]). The constable of Beeston Castle was paid livery at 11½d a day in 1241 (*CLibR 1240–45*, 20, 59).

Lestrange remained as justiciar until August 1245, the year in which, in October, he was replaced by John de Grey. Lestrange's accounts end when the king visited Chester in August 1245 for the campaign against the Welsh. Knights and serjeants detained at Beeston and Rhuddlan Castles in 1242 were paid an unspecified sum, which, with the cost of finishing two turrets at Beeston Castle, amounted to a total of £242 17s 10½d (Stewart-Brown 1938, 77). In the accounts for 1241–2 a list of general repairs refers to work at Chester, Beeston, Shotwick, and Frodsham Castles (ibid, 78).

Lestrange's *remanent* (residual account) of his 1242–5 Cheshire account was not submitted until 1252–3; it deals mostly with Welsh affairs but includes a reference to all the king's hostages being removed from Chester Castle to Beeston in 1245 (ibid, 79; *CR 1242–47*, 327–8). On 6 February 1246, the justiciar was instructed that the hostages and prisoners in the king's prison in Beeston Castle were 'to have such liveries as they used to have in the time of John Lestrange' (*CLibR 1245–51*, 25).

In de Grey's account for 30 October 1245 to 30 October 1247, £20 was spent on repairing buildings in Chester and Beeston Castles, and a total sum of £10 was paid to chaplains for two years' duties (1245–6, 1246–7) in the chapels in the two castles (Stewart-Brown 1938, 89; *CLibR 1245–51*, 29). In the account for 30 October 1247 to 2 July 1250 the chaplain and chapel at Beeston are mentioned again. Repairs to buildings in Chester and Beeston Castles amounted to £10 in 1247–8 (Stewart-Brown 1938, 94). Further repairs to the two castles, mentioned in the same account, cost 50s in the first quarter of 1247–8, and 48s 2½d in 1250 (ibid, 94–5). Beeston Castle's continuing use as a prison is shown in 1249, when 12s was spent on carrying Welsh hostages and a man named Philip Calston from Chester to Beeston (*CLibR 1245–51*, 246 (25 July)).

On 14 February 1253/4, Henry III gave his eldest son, Edward, later Edward I, Cheshire and the Welsh lands, with all the castles and towns (*CPR 1247–58*, 270, 272, 285, 365). Prince Edward was created Earl of Chester. The king's gift was to descend to the earl's heirs and never to be separated from the Crown. This gift set the scene which was to last until after the end of the Middle Ages. From now on either the king or the heir-apparent controlled Cheshire (Booth 1981, 50).

The prince was abroad until November 1254, so the judiciar, Alan de la Zouche, was ordered to give full seisin. It was not until 17 July 1256 that the prince visited Chester, and the nobles of Cheshire and the men of north Wales paid him homage and fealty. Zouche remained as judiciar until Michaelmas 1255, when Gilbert Talbot was appointed. On 26 September 1255, Zouche was instructed to hand over all supplies and arms in the castles of Chester, Beeston, Diserth, and Deganwy (Stewart-Brown 1938, 106; *CR 1254–56*, 134).

On account of disturbances in the Welsh marches Zouche was sent to preserve the peace in 1262: on 25 December, Thomas de Orreby, justiciar of Chester, was commanded to deliver the castle of Chester, Beeston, and Shotwick (*CPR 1258–66*, 238).

There are no Pipe Roll accounts for the period 1254–70 because the revenues of Cheshire and the north Wales lands belonged to the prince and not to the king.

Beeston Castle had a part to play in the civil wars of the 1260s between Henry III and Simon de Montfort, Earl of Leicester. Under the terms of the peace made after de Montfort's success at the Battle of Lewes in May 1264, Prince Edward and his cousin Henry of Almain were made hostage. Edward was confined in Dover, Wallingford, and then in the Earl of Leicester's castle of Kenilworth. On 24 December the tenants of the shire, castle, and honour of Cheshire, were ordered to serve the Earl of Leicester as they used to serve the last earl of the old line, Ranulf de Blundeville. Prince Edward's confinement ended on 8 March 1265, but he continued to be deprived of the county of Cheshire. On 28 May Edward was able to escape. Mustering the support of Roger Mortimer, the Earl of Gloucester, and other nobles, he assembled an army. Worcester surrendered to him, and on 29 June he took Gloucester. After success against his opponents at Kenilworth on 31 July, he intercepted Simon de Montfort's army at Evesham on 4 August, where he was victorious: de Montfort was slain along with his son Henry and many others; Humphrey de Bohun, the younger, was wounded and died at Beeston Castle in October.

After his victory at Evesham, Edward moved north. He took with him to Beeston Castle prisoners captured by his supporters, James de Audley and Urian de Saint Pierre. Chester Castle, which had not been taken, surrendered.

The Benedictine abbey of St Werburgh, Chester, had not been affected by the political conflicts. In 1264 a row of houses belonging to the abbey was demolished to allow the construction of a ditch around the city as a protection against 'the barons or the Welsh' (Burne 1962, 34). On 14 August 1265 Simon de Whitechurch, Abbot of St Werburgh, went to Beeston Castle to see Prince Edward. The abbot had been admitted by Simon de Montfort, not by the prince, who was the abbey's patron. 'Contrary to the hopes of many, the Lord Edward, urged by divine inspiration, received the abbot with clemency' (Christie 1886, 94–6).

Edward succeeded to the throne in November 1272, but did not return to England until August 1274. It is significant that Llywelyn ap Gruffydd ignored the summons to attend the coronation on 19 August; nor did he comply with the summons to meet the king at Shrewsbury in November. Edward I went to Chester in September 1275 to meet Llywelyn, who refused to come to him. He also failed to attend the following parliament.

In the autumn of 1276 the king was at Gloucester and Evesham taking measures against the Welsh. In November he sent knights into the Marches to keep order, and on 12 November it was agreed 'that the king should make war on the Welsh with the force of the kingdom' (*Foedera*, I, ii, 535). On 17 November the king decided to go against Llywelyn as a 'rebel and a disturber of his peace' (*CR 1272–9*, 359–60). It was not until November 1277 that Llywelyn submitted at Rhuddlan and finally did homage. During the military campaigns of 1277 against the Welsh, and those of 1282–3 and 1294–5, the building of ten new castles in Wales and four new 'lordship' castles took place, as well as additional building at three existing Welsh castles and work at several border castles (Hewitt 1929, 78–81; Colvin 1963, i, 293–408; Morgan 1987). Chester was of the greatest importance as a base for the military campaign and as the centre for the co-ordination of personnel, provisions, and building materials in a castle-building programme of enormous scale.

Beeston Castle's strategic position, and what little administrative role it had had previously, became of minor relevance now that the power-base was firmly centred in Chester; Edward's new castles became the bases for military campaigns against the Welsh. This is not to say that Beeston Castle remained ungarrisoned or the buildings neglected. The Pipe Roll for July 1270 to Michaelmas 1274 records the payment of 100s to John Arneway, a well-known Chester merchant, for cloth taken for the use of the serjeants in Chester and Beeston Castles (Stewart-Brown 1938, 109). Subsequent accounts submitted for the years to 1302 contain regular payments to the justiciar for the custody of Beeston Castle (ibid, 119, 123, 129, 155, 167, 175, 182).

In 1275–76 provision was made for men-at-arms in the Marches and for Chester and Beeston Castles (ibid, 125), and in 1287–8 and 1288–9 a total of £8 4s 11½d was spent on repairs to Beeston Castle for work ordered on 16 November 1288 (ibid, 167; *CR 1279–88*, 521).

On 7 February 1300/1 Edward I created his son, the future King Edward II, Prince of Wales and Earl of Chester. In April 1301 the prince appointed William of Melton his first chamberlain. Melton's accounts, and those of his successors to 1360, have been published (Stewart-Brown 1910; 1938 Appendix). In Melton's account for September 1303 to September 1304 an expenditure of £109 2s 4½d is entered for works at Beeston Castle.

The three towers in the Inner Ward were repaired, steps, galleries, doors, windows, and a new bridge were made, the walls of the three towers were raised and crenellated 'because they formerly had high wooden surfaces, and now they are made level', and a 'great massive stone wall', 34ft high, 7ft thick, and 20ft long, was made before the new bridge to receive it. Masonry work was carried out to the gate of the 'Dungon', hinges, hooks, locks, and keys made for the great gate,

and doors and windows for the three towers. The use of the word 'Dungon' here is of interest: it is applied to the whole of the Inner Ward, in the same way that the term was used at Degannwy Castle in 1250 (Colvin 1963, ii, 625).

The works were carried out, under the general direction of Master Richard the Engineer, by Master Hugh of Dymock, master carpenter, and Master Warin, master mason. Roger le Belgeter made the bolsters for supporting the bridge, with 22lb of brass which had been bought for him; iron, steel, and coals were provided for the smith.

Timber was brought from the forest of Delamere. Lead trimmings from the great tower of Flint Castle, and lead from Northop, were carried to Chester Castle, where the lead was founded into sheets, along with other lead bought for Jordan of Bradford and Benedict of Staundon. Brother Thomas le Plummer, a monk of Combermere, was chief plumber – a fascinating reference to the use of monastic labour. Brother Thomas spent 145 days fixing the lead on the roofs of the three towers, with nails on a bed of sand, to prevent the wooden boards from rotting (Salzman 1967, 265–6). Madoc le Quarreour 'and his fellow' pointed the masonry; lime and timber boards were brought from Chester, and a cable from Flint. Women were paid for carrying water from one furlong away – a surprising item, since water should have been available from the castle wells.

Ithel, the smith, and his assistant were paid for making masonry tools. Soap and grease were bought for the machines used to draw and raise timber, and ropes for raising the timber and drawing the drawbridge (Stewart-Brown 1910, 42–44).

In the following year, under the direction of Master Robert of Glasson, the outer gate was repaired at the cost of £14 6s 3d (Colvin 1963, ii, 560).

Edward II become king in 1307. His immediate problems with the barons, led by Thomas, Earl of Lancaster, may have been the reason for an assessment of the condition of the royal castles. The houses and towers at Beeston were mended and repaired in 1312–13 by Robert the carpenter of Kyngislegh (Kingsley) and William the plumber, at a cost of 45s 7½d (Stewart-Brown 1910, 81).

The Earl of Lancaster's threats to Edward were no doubt the reason why the castle at Beeston was garrisoned between 20 May and 20 July 1313 by Sir Ralph de Vernon, with two esquires, and six bowmen; Ralph and his esquires were paid 3s a day, and his bowmen 4d (ibid). This temporary garrison put the castle in a state of defence against raiding parties. The arrangement may be compared with the instructions given in 1318 by the Earl of Lancaster to the constable of his castle at Bolingbroke, Lincolnshire: the constable had to choose 12 or more tenants to act as a temporary garrison; only authorised men were to be given access and the drawbridges were to be raised and the gates closed by day and by night (M W Thompson 1965). The Earl of Lancaster's rebellion in 1332 ended with his trial at Pontefract and his beheading on 23 March. The keeper of the castle was ordered on 13 April 1322 to remove the garrison of men 'put therein by reason of the late disturbances in the realm and to keep the castle in the same way as before the disturbances'. Victuals were to be kept safely, and those that would not keep were to be sold (*CR 1318–23*, 437).

The chamberlain of Chester was instructed on 2 March 1326 to cover the towers of Beeston Castle; the wells and peels (courtyards) at Beeston and at the castles of Chester, Flint, and Rhuddlan were to be cleansed, at a cost not exceeding £140 (*CR 1323–27*, 450). What works were actually carried out cannot now be determined. In 1324–5 £15 3s 93/4d was spent on 'divers works' carried out by Hugh of Peck and Walter of Hereford, masons (£4), Master Richard of Legh, carpenter (£4), and Robert of Huxelegh (£7 3s 93/4d) (Stewart-Brown 1910, 96–7). Additional works to the 'houses, chambers, turrets and other buildings in the king's castles of Chester, Beeston, Flint and Rhuddlan' were ordered on 18 May 1328 (*CR 1327–30*, 288).

The justice and chamberlain of Chester were instructed, on 6 February 1331, to inspect the castle and determine what repairs were required and the cost of them (*CR 1330–33*, 186).

The castle was surveyed when Edward III's eldest son was created Earl of Chester in 1333. It was reported that the castle was 'well and surely sited on a rocky eminence, and very well enclosed'; no repairs were recommended (Colvin 1963, ii, 560).

A constable (William Carey), watchman, and janitor were paid £10 in 1347–8 (Stewart-Brown 1910, 123). In 1359–60 £51 12s 51/2d was spent on carpentry works in repairing the castle, and in carriage of timber from Peckforton Park. Masons, quarriers, and other workmen, and cement, iron, and steel cost £34 10s 21/2d. Alan of Maurdyn, plumber, was paid 7d a day – a total of £7 18s 8d – for 272 days spent roofing the tower of the castle with lead, and Richard del Flynt, Alan's servant, 49s 4d for 37 weeks work at 16d a week. A workman helping Alan, and nails and tin, cost 46s 7d. Thomas le Smith of Denbigh was paid 33s 6d for making four locks for the gate (Stewart-Brown 1910, 271–2). Repairs were continued in 1361–2: £11 14s 7d was paid to masons, quarrymen, and other workers, and mortar, iron, and board were bought (Booth and Carr 1991, 34.4).

Richard II (1377–99), having no heir, retained the earldom of Chester for himself. He made it a principality in 1398. Richard continued to appoint a constable for Beeston Castle, along with a janitor; in 1395 Henry Champneys was appointed constable (Ormerod 1881, ii, 274). In May 1399 Richard went to Chester before setting sail from Milford to Ireland, to avenge the death of the Earl of March in the previous September, carrying with him his regalia and treasure. Some of the treasure, however, is said to have been sent from Chester for safe-keeping in other castles in the area. This rumour may be relevant to Beeston, as the following account makes clear.

Following Henry of Lancaster's landing in Yorkshire in early July, and his march on Bristol, Richard sailed to Milford and made his way to north Wales. Henry reached Chester on 9 August. Richard arrived at Conway, to find himself hemmed in. Resigning the crown, he was taken to Flint, where Henry met him on 19 August. Richard was then taken to Chester before his journey to London and the Tower.

Not only Chester but many other castles were taken by Henry, and many men were killed and their goods confiscated, according to the Kirkstall Chronicle (Clarke 1931, 133). 'Vessels and many other goods found in water cisterns' and 'other secret places' were seized (Adam of Usk, quoted in Thompson 1904, 26). The Dieulacres Chronicle, a local text, adds that Henry seized treasure and other valuables that had been buried (Clark and Galbraith 1930, 172).

These events were described and published in 1631 by John Stow: he states that Beeston Castle, six (actually ten) miles from Chester, was surrendered without resistance, although of great strength, garrisoned with 100 men, and provisioned for a five-year siege. Stow adds that Henry found there coin to the value of 100,000 marks, and other jewels 'which Richard caused to be kept' worth twice that sum, 'all of which Duke Henry took with him' (Stow 1631, 321). C A R Radford has drawn the author's attention to a seventeenth-century manuscript volume in the British Library (Harley 2111), apparently compiled in Cheshire c 1640, containing accounts of local interest in Chester and Cheshire. The volume relates the same story as Stow, but with additional material from another source not mentioned by Stow. It is possible that Stow was using this other source for his account (Radford, pers comm). The story should not be dismissed as a later elaboration of the events recorded in the Kirkstall and Dieulacres Chronicles, and by Adam of Usk, since the story appears in much the same form in a fourteenth-century poem by Jean Creton (Webb 1824, 122–4, 345–6).

Creton had been on Richard's expedition to Ireland and went with the Earl of Salisbury to Conway, but was not with the king from the time Richard left Ireland until he arrived at Flint (Clarke and Galbraith 1930, 138–9). Creton's account, however, differs from Stow in the identification of the castle:

A vj. mile de la ville y avoit
un autre fort, que hoult on appelloit
Sur une roche moult hault assis estoit.

[Six miles from the town there was another castle, called Holt, set on a very high, rather narrow rock.]

Since the descriptive parts of these lines and the comment, in later lines, that '*ansi faut pas our pas aller a pie amont*' [so it was necessary to go on foot, step by step, to the summit], are more applicable to Beeston than to Holt, it is very probable that Creton confused Holt (*hoult*) with Beeston's medieval name – *castellum de Rupe*. The references to Beeston in Stow and the British Library manuscript reinforce the view that Creton's identification was wrong. Nevertheless, Creton's account shows that the story of a large amount of money and valuables was current when he was writing his poem. The various accounts of this story had led to much effort being expended in clearing the well in Beeston Castle's Inner Ward in the hope of finding Richard's treasure (see p 104 below). Similar efforts have been made at Holt.

Expenditure on the castle under Richard II amounted to no more than a few shillings a year, and in the fifteenth century the castle appears to have been rather neglected (Colvin 1963, ii, 560). It was not abandoned, however, since janitors, porters, or keepers were appointed regularly during the fifteenth century. Richard, Duke of York, had the castle and manor included in the lands and possessions of the earldom of Chester in 1460. Thomas Colbrand was appointed keeper of Beeston at the beginning of the reign of Henry VII, but was still asking for wages and arrears in 1502 (Driver 1971, 54). By the early sixteenth century the castle was ruinous (Leland 1548, quoted in Ormerod 1882, ii, 275).

The manor of Peckforton, which included Beeston Castle, was sold by the Crown to Hugh Beeston in 1602 for £2,500 (Mostyn Estate Records no 4270). Prior to this the estate had been leased to members of the Beeston family.

The will of Sir Hugh Beeston, dated 16 January 1626, refers to his two poor kinsmen, George and Richard Beeston, who were living in the castle, and requests that they be maintained in the 'house room and easements and commodities' that they 'hold and occupy within the walls', or be rehoused elsewhere (Mostyn Estate Records no 8847).

A late sixteenth-century account of the castle describes the Inner Ward, 'with a Goodly strong Gatehouse, and a strong Wall, with other Buildings; which when they flourished, were a convenient Habitation for any great Personage', and the outer 'Wall, furnished with Turrets' and 'first a fair Gate' (Erdeswicke 1717, no page).

When the Civil War broke out, Cheshire was divided. Chester was a royal base, but the towns in the east of the county were held by the Parliamentarians. The importance of Beeston Castle was recognised by both sides, since it controlled a number of lines of communication and, from its commanding position, the movement of troops could be seen easily.

The castle, with 'much wealth and other goods of the gentry and other neighbours brought thither for safety', was occupied on 20 February 1643 by the Parliamentary forces under Sir William Brereton, and garrisoned with between 200 and 300 men (Hall 1889, 38). At this time Brereton 'caused the breeches to be made up with mud walls, the well of the outer ward to be cleansed, and a few rooms erected' (Dore 1965–6, 104; see also Dore 1984 and 1990).

Following the arrival of part of the royal army from Ireland at the end of November, Brereton's headquarters at Nantwich were captured. Just before dawn on 13 December, Captain Sandford, of the Royalist army from Ireland, with eight firelocks, entered 'the upper ward of Beeston Castle by a byeway'. Captain Steele, Parliamentary governor of the castle, who had 60 men against Sandford's eight, received Sandford in 'his lodging in the lower ward', and after dinner agreed to surrender the castle – perhaps because additional Royalist troops were outside the main gate – and, with his soldiers, was allowed 'to depart with their colours and arms' to Nantwich. All the stores and ammunitions, and the large quantity of private goods in the castle, were left in the care of the Royalist force (Hall 1889, 91–2).

Brereton's forces besieged the castle again in November 1644. After a successful Royalist attack on a detachment of 26 Parliamentarians in a house nearby, the Parliamentary siege of the castle grew closer and large forces were concentrated on it. Brereton reported that 'We have almost finished a mount before Beeston Castle gate, which is encompassed with a strong, deep trench. This will command and keep them in the castle, so that they dare not issue out in strong parties to annoy the country or bring in provision' (Morris 1923, 84; Dore 1984, 370).

The siege works, including 'good buildings' on the mound, were only just completed in May 1645 (Hall 1889, 169). But by the summer the castle had been restocked and Brereton's earthworks thrown down (ibid, 169–70). In early August the surrounding ditch had been dug again, and another strong fort was erected, within musket shot of the gate to the outer ward, containing 100 men, and stocked with provisions and ammunitions (Hall 1889, 180).

After the defeat of the king at Rowton Heath, Beeston Castle was surrendered on 15 November 1645. Captain Vallett and 56 men were allowed to march out under safe conduct (Hall 1889, 188–9). At the time of the surrender the garrison had almost no provisions. The governor's horse was so weak from lack of fodder that it could hardly carry him out of the castle. 'Theire was neither meate, Ale nor Beere found in the castle, save only a peece of Turkey pye, Twoe Bisketts, a lyve Peacock and a peahen' (Hall 1889, 189).

On the day after the surrender Brereton ordered provisions and ammunitions to be removed from the fort outside the gate into the castle, and the fort and all siege works to be pulled down (Dore 1965–6, 116). Chester fell on 3 February 1646.

The Parliamentarians issued warrants to the constables of Bunbury, Tarporley, Wrenbury, and Acton for the 'pulling down and defacing' of Beeston. This was carried out before Whitsun: 'Onelie the Gatehowse in the lower warde and parte of some Towers in the heigher warde, weire lefte standings, which scythens are pulled downs and utterlie defaced' (Hall 1889, 206–7).

After the Civil War the castle remained in much the same state as it is today. In the eighteenth century it was a favourite subject for engravings and paintings. In 1703 George Walley is recorded as renting and living in a 'house and close by the castle gate' (Mostyn Estate Records no 6085). The only activity recorded at the castle is stone quarrying: a stone quarry in the Outer Ward is documented in the eighteenth century (Mostyn Estate Records no 6089). A 'horse causeway' mentioned in 1722 may be associated with quarrying work. In 1759 workmen were paid for stone quarrying, gunpowder was purchased, and a blacksmith employed (Mostyn Estate Records no 5385). Quarrying continued in the nineteenth century (CRO DTW Acc 2477 for 1868).

The ownership of the castle passed, by marriage, to Sir Thomas Mostyn of Mostyn Hall, Flintshire (Clwyd) in the eighteenth century. In 1840 the estate was purchased by John, first Lord Tollemache. Between 1844 and 1850 he commissioned Salvin to build Peckforton Castle, a medieval castle in its arrangements, but without so many of a medieval castle's inconveniences. His new castle was clearly designed to complement Beeston Castle on the outcrop of rock nearby. Some of Beeston Castle's walls were repaired and a skimpy gatehouse, medieval only in its plan, was built at the road entrance, to control those who came to the hill for picnics, to see the kangaroos, which were run on Beeston crag by the Tollemaches, or to visit the Bunbury Fair.

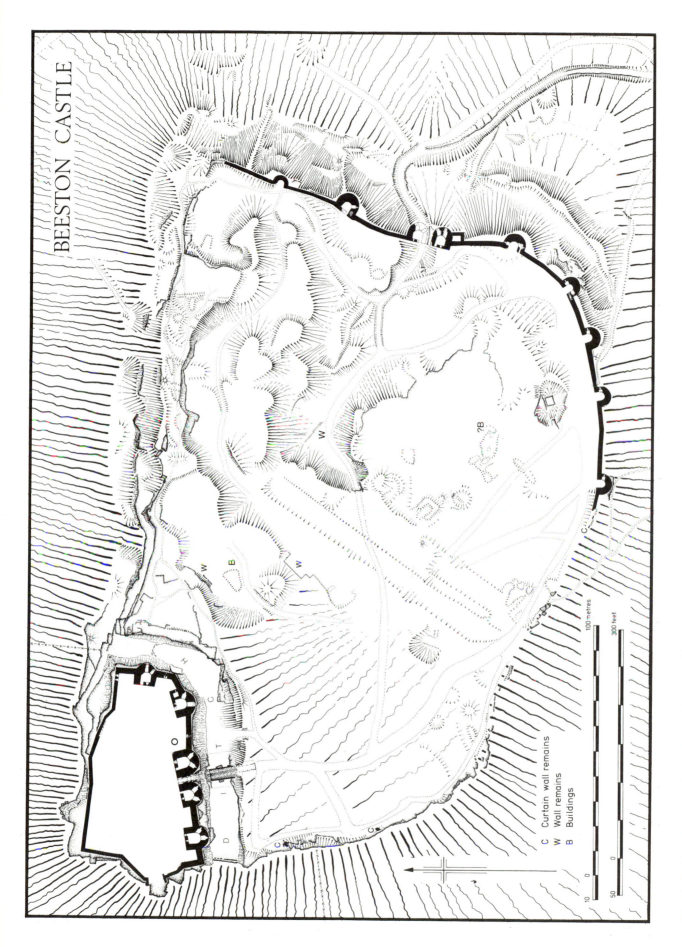

BEESTON CASTLE

C   Curtain wall remains
W   Wall remains
B   Buildings

100 metres

300 feet

Fig 63 Beeston Castle: hachure plan of hilltop and hill slopes; scale 1:1500

Beeston Castle was taken into guardianship by the Ministry of Works in 1959. The archaeological excavations reported in this volume were carried out, on the one hand to make the Inner Ward safer for visitors and, on the other, with those on the Outer Gate, to make the surviving structure more intelligible to the general public, by exposing more of the medieval building.

Architectural description

'A place well guarded by walls of a great compass, by a great number of its towers, and by a mountain of very steep ascent', so William Camden (1551–1623) described the castle. *Castellum de Rupe*, the Castle of the Rock, was the name used consistently during the Middle Ages. Its defences used the natural strength of the prominent and dramatic rock outcrop to maximum advantage (Fig 63). From every direction the long-distance view of the castle shows the rocky hill and defences in stark outline. At close quarters the defences appear more formidable than they actually are because of the sloping ground in front of them. The towers look higher from the outside than they are internally: a deception achieved by the fact that the lower ground to the front and the lower parts of the most of the towers form a revetment to the solid ground behind (Fig 64).

The castle was planned in two parts: an Inner Bailey sited on the highest point, with a high, precipitous, natural defence to the north and a rock-cut ditch to the south; and an Outer Bailey with walls, towers, and a gatehouse, following the contours. The Outer Bailey encloses a very large area (Fig 63), so large that its defences must have been dictated by the existing defences of the Iron Age hillfort, which it was thought prudent to take into account. Not to have done so, and to have constructed a smaller Outer Bailey, would have left the prehistoric defences for the use of any assailant. The plan of Beeston Castle, therefore, was influenced by existing earthworks and by the topography. It may be compared with Chartley Castle, Staffordshire, where the layout of Ranulf's stone castle was dictated by the plan of the existing motte and bailey: here the motte was utilised to accommodate a circular keep and a gatehouse, towers, and curtain wall constructed on top of the earlier earthworks. At Ranulf's third castle at Bolingbroke, Lincolnshire, on the other hand, there were no earlier features to determine the castle plan.

Although Beeston Castle was never completed fully to its original plan – the absence of large halls, kitchens, stables, etc is particularly notable – it nevertheless was provided with a completed outer defence and Inner Ward, its military strength lying in two massive gatehouses and curtain wall towers. Even in this state of construction the castle was a striking symbol of lordship, dominating the surrounding countryside.

Fig 64 Inner Ward: gatehouse towers, view north-east (Photo H Hawley)

Despite the absence of many of the buildings necessary for the castle to function as an administrative centre and residence, enough accommodation was provided, by small halls and chambers in the gatehouses and by chambers in at least two of the towers in the Inner Ward, for the basic requirements of the constable, who was most likely to have been in residence for long periods, and of the visiting earl, his officials, and guests.

The castle is constructed of local stone quarried on site: grey Keuper Sandstone, mainly from the ditch in front of the Inner Ward, and the underlying red Upper Bunter sandstone. The only dressed and finely tooled stone was that needed, for example, to construct gateways, doorways, and windows. All the walls of the castle were built of hewn stone with rough vertical faces, the courses of masonry being levelled up with small stones. The unexceptional quality of the construction, however, would perhaps have been hidden by external rendering of lime mortar, or by limewash.

The Inner Ward (Fig 3)

Gatehouse and entrance

The wide, flat-bottomed ditch surrounding the Inner Ward on the south was the quarry for most of the stone for the Inner Ward: wedge-holes for extracting the stone are to be seen in many places along both faces of the ditch.

The gatehouse was reached by a stone causeway, 4.7m wide, which stops short of the main gateway. The great difference in levels between the ground of the Outer Ward and the gatehouse means that the top of the causeway had a steep ramp. The gap between the causeway and entrance passage was spanned by a drawbridge. Accounts show that the bridge and causeway were built in 1303–4 (p 96). However, there is now no evidence for a drawbridge and it is difficult to see how one would have functioned. Furthermore, the present dimensions of the causeway do not correspond with those given in the medieval accounts (Hough 1978; Weaver 1987). Encased by the causeway and projecting from it on the west side is a roughly shaped pillar of natural stone 4m high. This was no doubt the intermediate support for the timber bridge which was replaced by the causeway.

The modern footbridge has been constructed slightly above the medieval ground level of the gatehouse passage, which has been severely reduced towards the ditch, either deliberately or by erosion. Until recently access was gained by nineteenth-century rock-cut steps from the top of the filling in the ditch.

A pointed arch with two plain square orders leads to the gate passage between two half-round gatehouse towers (the East and West Gatehouse Towers). In front of the arch there was a two-leafed gate. The position of the iron crooks upon which the gate was hung is indicated by irregular recesses on either side; the grooves for the crooks are visible on the lower surfaces of the recesses on the west side. The flat outer surface of the second order of the arch served as a rebate for the gate when closed, and indicates that the gate opened outwards. On either side of the archway are the holes for a drawbar to secure the gate. Beyond the drawbar holes

Fig 65 Inner Ward: gateway, view south (Photo L Keen)

is a portcullis slot, visible in the side walls and in the solid masonry above. Further into the passage, originally covered by the wooden floor of the chamber above, its width increases with a rebate: two recesses, one on either side, once contained the iron crooks for a second gate, the leaves folding back against the walls of the widened passage. The inner gate passage arch is pointed and, like the outer, has two plain square orders (Fig 65).

There is no access from the gate passage to the towers on either side: doorways to these are in the rear wall of the gatehouse, which is constructed directly on natural rock cut down to create a more level surface. The doorway to the West Gatehouse Tower has a pointed arch with chamfered arrises. On the east side two holes in the door rebate mark the position of iron crooks. On the west side there is a groove for the door latch, and to the west of the doorway there is a square-headed window with a deep external chamfer and internal splay. In the sill there are two square holes, set diagonally, for iron bars; curiously there are no similar holes in the jambs or head. As the stonework does not follow the adjacent courses the window is probably a fourteenth-century insertion. In the outer wall of the tower are two vaulted embrasures with narrow arrow-loops with cross-slits and fishtail bases covering the ditch and entrance causeway. To support the wooden floor of the room above there are six plain corbels: one in each corner on the north, three over the east embrasure, one over the west embrasure, and one midway on the straight west wall.

A hole between the two embrasures at the level of the springing of the embrasure vaulting probably marks the position of another corbel to carry a wall-post.

Less survives of the East Gatehouse Tower: almost all of the east side has been demolished. In the rear wall both jambs of the doorway remain, with one hole for an iron door-crook on the west side. In the south wall are remains of two embrasures. The greater part of the eastern one has gone; its western part survives with part of the vault and the fishtail base and side with a cross-slit of the arrow-loop. The western embrasure is complete, but the arrow-loop contains blocking, presumably dating to the Civil War. A window in the rear wall, in a position similar to that in the West Gatehouse Tower, may be assumed.

Traces of the original medieval lime mortar survive on parts of the walls. Three plain corbels to support the wooden floor above survive over the western embrasure, and between the two embrasures, at the level of the vault springing, there is another corbel for a wall-post: this arrangement is the same as in the West Gatehouse Tower.

The second stage of the gatehouse, in contrast to the grey stone of the towers and passage below, is built mainly of red sandstone. Access to this level was through a doorway in the north wall of the West Gatehouse Tower, approached originally by an external wooden stair. The doorway has chamfered arrises; an angle on the chamfer suggests that it was pointed like the doorway to the tower below. There are two holes for iron door-crooks in the west rebate. The room reached through this door occupied both towers and the area above the passage, with walls set back from the wall-faces of the ground floor. This chamber had a wooden floor supported by the corbels in the towers below. The front walls of the towers are solid; the only surviving evidence for windows is one in the north, rear wall over the east wall of the west tower. This is square-headed and has a deep external chamfer. Square sockets in the lintel indicate the position of three vertical iron bars. Internally the window splay has a segmental arch above and a seat with undercut chamfers on either side. This window, like that on the ground floor which it matches in style, is an insertion.

In the front wall over the passage, which contains the portcullis slot, are two square holes: these served to hold timbers locking the portcullis in position when raised. There are now no clues to suggest how the portcullis was lifted. It could have been raised by ropes running through pulleys fixed in the ceiling of the first floor chamber, or by a windlass located on the first floor or in the storey above. In the west wall of the West Gatehouse Tower a passage leads to a blocked doorway giving access to the curtain wall-walk; the doorway is clearly visible on the external face. From a door in the north-west corner of the West Gatehouse Tower, one jamb of which survives, a flight of nine steps rises over the passage to the wall above. A single corbel in the north wall, larger than those supporting the first floor, indicates the position of the floor of the storey above. Another corbel half-way up the corner, at the junction of the East Gatehouse Tower with the flat front wall above the gatehouse passage, marks the position of a wall-post supporting the upper floor.

The gatehouse now consists of two stages. It is uncertain if the surviving staircase from the first floor gave access to another storey, or to the roof and battlements. The accommodation in this extra floor would have added to that provided by the room on the first floor of the gatehouse, and by the chambers on the first floors of the South-West and South-East Towers. It is reasonable to suggest that the accommodation provided here may have been used by the constable.

The masonry work on the gate, mentioned in the building accounts for 1303–4, cannot be identified with any certainty. It is unlikely to have consisted of making provision for the portcullis, since the portcullis slot is an integral part of the structure and there are no indications that it was an insertion. Windows are referred to in the accounts, and as those in the back wall of the gatehouse are insertions in the original fabric they could perhaps belong to the work carried out at this time.

South-West Tower and Curtain Wall

Three steps, two of stone and the third rock-cut, lead from the doorway down to the floor level inside the tower (Fig 74); the door jambs have chamfered arrises. The rock-cut step and the natural stone floor showed distinct traces of chisel marks after the tower had been excavated (Fig 75). A drawbar hole, going 0.98m back into the wall, is visible in the west door rebate. Below it is a recess for a post-medieval door-lock. In the east door rebate is the recess for the lower iron door-crook. There is a square-headed window with deep external chamfer in the back wall: it has square socket holes for iron bars, two on the sill and two on each jamb. Two small holes on the east jamb, one with part of the iron crook and its lead fixing still present, indicate that the window had a wooden shutter. In the south wall, facing south and south-east to cover the causeway and ditch, are the remains of two embrasures. The fishtail base of the arrow-loop in the south-east embrasure survives. The roughly mortared interior walls were exposed after the tower was excavated: on the east wall of the entrance a builder's vertical marking-out line for the internal face of the rear wall was visible. Three corbels to support the wooden floor above survive in the west wall. Excavation showed that the first floor chamber was plastered and had a fireplace: a blackened fireplace lintel with a chamfered rear face to the flue showed that the fireplace was 1.37m wide. The fireplace and chimney were probably constructed in the west wall. This is the only indication of a heated chamber in the Inner Ward. Indeed there is no evidence for others elsewhere in the castle. The wall-walk from the first floor of the gatehouse would have given access to this heated chamber, which must have been of some importance. If the accommodation in the gatehouse was for the use of the constable, this chamber may have provided separate private quarters. To the east of the tower the height of the curtain wall has been much reduced. It survives to parapet level on the west where one side of a merlon is visible.

To the north of the south-west corner of the ward two round-headed arches carry the curtain wall over two rock fissures (Fig 76, Section 9). These may have been intended for latrine chutes from a building in the south-

Fig 66 Inner Ward: F70 in area W, view north; scale in feet (Photo L Keen)

west corner which was never constructed. The wall built behind the curtain wall here is later in date (F17; Figs 80 and 82). The west curtain wall is interrupted by a substantial gap, where the natural rock forms a ledge overhanging the cliff below. This 'Pulpit Rock' has lost any medieval masonry that may have existed. It is the obvious location for the eyries of falcons recorded in the thirteenth century.

Prior to excavation a levelled area in the north-west corner suggested that a large building might once have been here. This possibility is strengthened by the tusks of masonry 7m to the east of the north-west corner: the tusks are of grey stone in contrast to the red sandstone blocks below. No evidence was found in the excavation for any structure in this position. Between points 18m and 25m from the north-west corner a section of repaired wall is apparent externally: this was confirmed by excavation (F70; Figs 66, 67, and 72). A few metres west of the north-east corner are the remains of two single-light windows in the curtain wall. The west window has an internal rebate to take a wooden shutter. The windows suggested the presence of a building but excavation failed to establish any evidence for it.

East Tower

This tower has a rounded external face like all the other towers in the castle. However, it differs from them in its internal plan: the internal face has three straight sections of wall instead of a curve. The threshold of the doorway is slightly above the level of the floor. Both the threshold and the jambs have a chamfered arris. In the south door rebate there is a drawbar hole and above it a latch groove. On the north a recess for the lower iron door-crook was revealed during excavation. In the rear wall the square-headed window is narrower than those in the other towers in the Inner Ward. Externally it has a deep chamfer, though not as deep as those in the windows of the gatehouse and South-West Tower. There is a small square socket in the sill and lintel and two sockets in each jamb for iron bars. The window splay is covered internally by a rounded arch. In the outer wall are the remains of two embrasures, one facing east, the other south-east. Although almost all of the arrow-loops have gone the fishtail bottom of both loops survives in each embrasure. Two joist holes and a single corbel in the north-west corner indicate a wooden floor

to the chamber above. There are slight indications that the walls were plastered.

Between the East and South-East Towers the battlements survive in a good state: the only place in the castle where they are so well preserved. The parapet is built mainly of red sandstone in contrast to the grey stone below. Four merlons survive. Cut into the wall-walk and going beneath the parapet are six roughly square channels to take the wooden beams for hoarding (a wooden covered gallery attached to the curtain wall and projecting over the ground below). South of the East Tower is a blocked opening with a large lintel (F45; Fig 80) which is probably a Civil War gunport.

South-East Tower and garderobe

In the rear wall of the tower one door jamb with external chamfered arris survives on the west side. Inside the doorway is an iron-stained groove for an iron door-crook. To the east are one jamb and sill of a square-headed window with a deep external chamfer and internal splay. There is one small square socket in the sill and two sockets in the jamb for iron bars. As in the other towers there are two embrasures, one facing south, the other south-east. The one on the west side, which faces south, has remains of stone paving: that on

Fig 67 Inner Ward: F70 in area W, view west; scale in feet (Photo L Keen)

the east, after excavation, had a plastered floor. The latter embrasure is largely intact and its vaulting remains. One side of the arrow-loop with a cross-slit survives. There is a rounded corbel in the north-east corner and a line of joist holes. In the thickness of the east wall there is a garderobe pit. Access to the garderobe was from the first floor, along a passage in the thickness of the east wall. Joist holes for the floor of the garderobe are visible and show that the wooden latrine seat was against the north wall. It may be inferred that the garderobe also served the stage above. The garderobe pit is as deep as the surviving masonry. At ground level outside the tower on the east is a narrow outlet passing through the east wall to the garderobe pit.

A second blocked opening (F86; Fig 80), between the South-East Tower and the East Gatehouse Tower, is probably a Civil War gunport.

The well (Fig 72)

In 1794 the well was said to be filled to within 90 yards (82m) of the top, and to be 160 yards (146m) deep. The well was almost completely cleared out to a depth of 366ft (111.93m) in 1842. At the same time a protective stone coping was built around the top. Later the well-head was covered by a stone hut to stop visitors throwing material down the shaft. The well has been explored on two occasions: between January 1935 and April 1936, and in 1976.

In 1935 the depth of the well was said to be 110yd (100.1m). Medieval masonry was noted to a depth of about 200ft (61m). It is recorded that below the masonry the shaft, 6–7ft (1.82–2.13m) wide, was cut through solid dark red sandstone. Three openings in the sides of the shaft were recorded. There are conflicting measurements for the position of the openings above the top of the infilling. Approximate depths below the top of the well are, probably, the first at 260ft (79.2m), the second at 290ft (88.4m), and the third at 327ft (99.19m). The first opening, at compass bearing 50° magnetic east of south, was found to be 11ft (3.35m) high, tapering from 3ft (0.92m) beneath a large semicircular arch to 18in (0.45m) at the base. The opening was recessed 3ft 6in (1.06m). At 6ft (1.83m) above the base of the opening there was a 4ft (1.22m) deep shelf, with headroom of 5ft 4in (1.62m). Beyond the 4ft (1.22m) deep entrance passage a tunnel had been cut for about 30ft (9.14m) on an approximate compass bearing of 92° magnetic west of south. Near the end of the explored length of the tunnel, holes for poles were noticed near roof height. This passage is probably the one explored in 1842. It was then said to be 60ft (18.28m) in length, with a draught strong enough to blow out candles. The second opening was 3ft (0.91m) wide and 6–7ft (1.83–2.13m) high. It gave access to a passage cut into the rock for 8ft 6in (2.59m). The third opening was a rectangular shaft 5ft 6in (1.67m) high, 2ft 6in (0.76m) wide, and 12ft (3.65m) long, cut on compass bearing 170° magnetic. Slots were observed on both sides of the entrance (Beeston Field Centre MS; *Cheshire Life*, October 1937, 16–17 and November 1937, 7–9; Dalton 1794; le Saxon 1895; Jones 1897).

The interpretation of these three features is difficult. The change in direction in the highest, from the entrance to the tunnel, and its length, suggest that it may have been intended for a salley-port. A fissure in the roof of the tunnel, recorded by the explorers, may have been the reason why the tunnelling was abandoned.

A further 15 tons of spoil were removed but the shaft became waterlogged and in January 1936 excavation was abandoned at a depth of 339ft (103.2m). The abortive 1976 explorations focused more on the possibility of rock-cut chambers just below the surface (*Cheshire Life*, January 1978). The motivation for the explorations in the well appeared to have been the search for the treasure supposedly hidden in Beeston Castle by Richard II and the hope of finding underground passages from the Inner Ward to the plain below.

The Outer Ward, curtain wall, and Outer Gatehouse (Figs 3 and 63)

All the curtain wall towers, with the exception of Tower 2, have semicircular external front faces and no stone rear walls. Towers 2, 6, and 7 show evidence of steps up to the wall-walk. Evidence in Towers 6 and 7 shows that all the towers must have had timber floors. Structural details suggest that the towers were built prior to the construction of the linking curtain wall. Although there is no evidence surviving to demonstrate the fact, all the curtain wall towers must have had at least one storey above the level of the battlements: this is amply demonstrated in castles where towers survive to a greater extent. The extra storey provided, on the one hand, the facility to cover the adjacent battlements if these were taken by attackers and, on the other, additional accommodation. Embrasures with arrow-loops were constructed in the bottom stage of each tower; their number and direction were determined by the slope of the ground on which the towers were built.

Tower 1

Only the semicircular ground plan survives of this tower, which is much smaller than others along the curtain wall. The masonry projects very slightly (0.25m) from the back of the curtain wall, which extends 17m to the north; traces of the wall can be seen for a further 9m. A rock outcrop, exposed in the quarry to the west, forms the north-east corner of the Outer Ward. Westwards, quarries have left a narrow ridge of stone which probably represents the line of the curtain wall enclosing the Outer Ward on the north.

Tower 2

The tower sits awkwardly in the curtain wall: to the south-west the wall kinks to reduce the wall thickness from 2.3m to about 1.8m. Access to the tower, which had a solid stone rear wall, would have been through a doorway on the south side. To the north of where the doorway would have been is one jamb of a window in the rear wall. The sloping ground to the south is covered by a south-facing embrasure. It has springers for the vault and evidence of repairs. In the side walls of the tower are remains of two sets of steps giving access to the first floor; four steps remain in the south wall and two in the north. On the south side one step provides access to the curtain wall-walk between Towers 2 and 3. There is no trace of joists for the wooden floor, only a wide, elliptical internal sill on the east side for joists to rest on. Two stones project from the north external face of the tower; their east faces are 0.9m from the junction of the tower with the curtain wall. This indicates that the curtain wall was intended to be built further forward than the place in which it was subsequently constructed. A straight joint is visible in the curtain wall to the south, at a point 6m north of Tower 3. The joint is particularly noticeable since, to the north, there is a predominance of red sandstone.

Tower 3

Towers 3 and 4 are the north and south towers of the Outer Gatehouse (Fig 79). Most of Tower 3 has been completely demolished (Fig 68). In the solid stone rear wall, which continues the line of the internal face of the curtain wall, are the remains of a window with internal splays and a sloping base. The sill has a chamfered arris and three very eroded sockets for bars. Nothing remains of the doorway. In the north part of the tower one side of the north, east-facing embrasure survives. Two half-rounded corbels to support a wooden first floor are visible in the north wall. The foundations of the front of the tower have been destroyed below the original internal floor level; the plan is now marked out by a new external face (dated 1989) using old stones. The portcullis slot in the south wall is not original and is a stone found during the excavations.

Gate passage

The only details of the passage are the features remaining in the north wall of Tower 4. Here part of the portcullis slot survives to a height of 1.15m (Fig 19, Section 6; Fig 79). A square hole, 0.26m deep and 0.9m forward of the portcullis slot, is for securing the outer gate, which must have opened outwards like the outer gate of the Inner Ward Gatehouse. There are no signs to indicate the position of the iron crooks to carry the gate.

Tower 4 (Fig 79)

The walls survive to their highest point where Tower 5 abuts the south wall (Figs 68 and 69). In the rounded front wall are two embrasures, one pointing ahead (east), the other in a more south-easterly direction. In each case only the floor and one side of the embrasure survives. No corbels or joist holes survive in the well-preserved south wall: there is no indication of a sill. In the solid rear wall of the tower the southern splay of a window survives. North of the window is a doorway with chamfered arrises on the jambs. In the top surface of the remains of the northern jamb is a slot for an iron door-crook. The south-west back corner of the tower is 1.98m back from the rear face of the curtain wall.

Apart from the corbels in Tower 3 there is no evidence for the upper parts of the gatehouse. From the surviving details of the gatehouse of the Inner Ward it may be assumed that there was originally a first floor chamber or hall occupying the space over the two towers and the gate passage. Access to it was either

Fig 68 Outer Gateway: gatehouse and curtain wall, view south (Photo P Hough)

Fig 69 Outer Gateway: Tower 5, view north (Photo P Hough)

joist holes in the south internal face. This stage was lit by a narrow, single-light, vertical opening in the east wall with a long thin lintel. Internally there is an offset on the east wall at the level of the first floor joist holes: there is another slight offset just below the second floor joist holes. Externally there is an offset at second floor level on the south and east faces, and a chamfered offset on the east face at basement floor level.

For both the first and second floors there are latrines in recesses within the thickness of the south wall. That for the first floor has a lintel supported by corbels, and that for the floor above has a lintel consisting of a single slab resting on the side walls of the recess. There is carbon blackening on the side and rear walls of the latter. The shaft from the second floor latrine is located to the east of the shaft from the first floor one. Both shafts terminate in square openings with sloping sills at the base of the south wall, just above the turf.

There is no precise dating for the construction of this tower: the archaeological evidence suggests a medieval date. Its purpose was clearly to provide extra accommodation with latrines for the gatehouse. The basement, originally unlit, may well have been used for storage. It is, however, the only secure place which now survives. Since the evidence in the Inner Ward demonstrates that all the ground floor doors of the towers and gatehouse could be secured by drawbars on the inside – the same arrangement no doubt existed in the Outer Gatehouse and Tower 2 – none of these could have been used for the custody of the prisoners known to have been kept at Beeston. The basement of Tower 5, therefore, may be considered as a possible candidate for the place where prisoners were housed.

Tower 6

This is the most unusual of the towers on the outer curtain wall. On the north and south sides are vaulted embrasures with arrow-loops covering the adjacent stretches of curtain wall. Both arrow-loops have square lintels. A narrow passage in the south wall of the tower, reached from the outside, led originally to a staircase giving access to the first floor. The staircase was built over the southern embrasure: massive stone lintels of the roof survive and its southern wall curves anti-clockwise. One of the lintels serves as part of one tread of a flight of steps leading up to the wall-walk on the south. The east wall of the passage survives as do the remains of three other steps. At the top of the steps is a thin red sandstone slab placed vertically and slotted into a grooved stone on the south side. Behind this slab is another step and, visible only in plan, the east side of a passage narrower than the passage for the flight of steps to the north, the inserted vertical slab is an alteration. The timber first floor is indicated by four joist holes in the south wall of the tower. There is no evidence to suggest whether or not the back of the tower was enclosed; if it was, timber was undoubtedly used. The upper floor perhaps had an embrasure facing outwards, to complement the embrasures covering the curtain wall.

The curtain wall to the south has been breached and repaired between points 10 and 12m south of this tower. This gap is shown on the 1874 Ordnance Survey map.

from an external staircase or directly from the wall-walks of the adjacent curtain walls. The height of Tower 5, built against Tower 4, suggests that the Outer Gatehouse may have had three, or even four stages.

Tower 5

This square tower, a later addition to the outer defences, was built by constructing two walls in the angle of curtain wall and the south face of Tower 4 (Fig 69). As the result of settling, the joints between the tower and the walls of the curtain and Tower 4 are quite wide. In comparison with the other masonry of the castle, the masonry in this tower is poor, with haphazard use of roughly dressed large and small stones. The basement had a flagstone floor revealed during excavation (Fig 89). This floor level was approximately at the same level as the floor of the second stage in the adjacent gatehouse tower: the present gravel surface is well below the level of the original flags. The basement was originally unlit: later a crudely constructed small window was cut through one of the two latrine shafts in the south wall. There are no indications of a door into this basement stage, so access was probably by a ladder from the floor above. Five joist holes are visible in the east wall. Corresponding joist holes were cut into the outer face of the medieval curtain to support a timber first floor. This stage is lit on the east side by a narrow, rectangular, square-headed window with an internal splay. The floor above had a timber floor with joists: there are five

Six metres south of the tower there is a drain passing through the curtain wall.

Tower 7 (Fig 21)

Two embrasures with arrow-loops are sited on either side of the tower. The west embrasure has a roof of pitched stone with a slightly lower arch with small stones cut into the springers over the entrance. There is a stone lintel over the arrow-loop which has been partially blocked by two large stone blocks. The pitched-stone roof of the embrasure in the east wall is shallower than that in the west. Two courses of sandstone blocks have been inserted into the base of the arrow-loop.

A door jamb for an inward-opening door survives at the level of the wall-walk on the east side of the tower. The adjacent parapet survives to a height of 1.53m. On the west side a flight of five steps leads up to a narrow doorway, the jambs of which survive; another four steps lead up to the wall-walk. On the east side, at first floor level, there are remains of another flight of steps and the east wall of the staircase passage, leading up to the battlements of the tower. Five joist holes in the south wall indicate a timbered first floor; the joists and floor would have cut across the top of both embrasures. At first floor level the south face is intact and has no embrasure. The back of the tower is open. No evidence for a back wall was found during excavation. Large stones projecting from both the east and west external faces of the tower are tusks placed ready for the construction of the adjacent stretches of curtain wall The tower is built directly on to rock, and a V-shaped marking-out notch is visible in front of the south wall.

Tower 8

An embrasure with arrow-loop is located on the east side of the tower, as are the embrasures of the remaining Towers 9 and 10. This arrangement was necessitated by the steeply rising ground to the west, and ensured that the arrow-loops covered the ground sloping downhill to the east. It may be assumed that embrasures in the upper stages covered the rising ground to the west and the ground to the south, in front of the towers. The embrasure has a pitched-stone roof with a pronounced inverted V. On the north side of the embrasure is a recess with a massive stone lintel. The junctions with the curtain walls on both east and west sides demonstrate the tower was constructed before the curtain wall. The tower has an open back. There are no surviving details of the first floor.

Tower 9

The foundations are built directly on to a rock platform with a V-shaped marking-out notch in front of the front wall. The embrasure in the east wall is in a poor state of preservation. The south internal face is angled, while the north face appears to have been straight. All traces of the arrow-loop have disappeared. Three joist holes to support the timber first floor are visible in the front wall of the tower. The tower is open-backed. It would seem from the surviving stonework in the back of the side walls of the tower that the curtain wall was built after the tower.

Tower 10

Like Towers 7, 8, and 9, the foundations are built directly on natural rock with a small marking-out notch. There is an embrasure in the east wall and both straight sides survive. Several courses of the arrow-loop remain with a fishtail base. The tower is open-backed.

For the next 20m there are surface indications of the stonework of the curtain wall. The spacing of the surviving towers to the east suggests that there must have been at least another five towers in the curtain wall. At the extreme north-west corner of the Outer Ward there is a solitary piece of masonry, only 1.5m high externally, with a right angle (Figs 70 and 86). It may reasonably be suggested that this is the masonry of another tower.

The Outer Ward well (Fig 63)

Lying in a rock-cut hollow the well is now almost completely filled in. It is undoubtedly one of the wells referred to in the medieval accounts. It was cleared and brought back into use in the Civil War (Dore 1965–6, 104). William Webbe recorded its depth as 240ft (73m). The quarrying marks on the sides of the hollow are characteristically post-medieval and suggest that the hollow may have been enlarged in the Civil War.

Fig 70 Outer Ward: curtain wall F90, area P, view north; scale in feet (Photo L Keen)

6 The excavations

by Peter Ellis

Period 5: medieval

Inner Ward (Figs 71 and 72)

Excavations in the Inner Ditch (Hough 1978) showed that the vertical-sided ditch cutting was carried right through to the north and west sides, with a pinnacle of rock acting as an initial bridge support. Construction of the Inner Ward on the summit of the crag would have been preceded by the excavation of the Inner Ditch for stone to provide building materials. The Inner Ward data is presented first from the gatehouse, then from the remainder of the southern side, and finally from the west, north, and eastern excavations.

The East Gatehouse Tower walls were constructed directly on to bedrock, with no evidence of foundation trenches (Fig 73, Section 6). The semi-circular south wall rested on an offset. A layer of concreted mortar, EGT 6, overlay the offset, and was sealed by a mortared rubble floor, EGT 4. Layer 6 may represent a mortar mixing level, F59, during construction of the tower.

In contrast some ground preparation was necessary to provide the footings for the West Gatehouse Tower (Fig 73, Section 7). Here the tower area now lies *c* 1m below the bedrock surface immediately to the north of the tower. It would seem that some clearance of unstable rock had taken place before a firm base was found for the footings. The south wall footings were carried up to ground level. The interior was then infilled with layers of sand, rubble, and small stones, containing charcoal and mortar (WGT 25, 38, 39, 41, 42, 44, and 45). A floor of mortar and stone, WGT 16, sealed these layers at the level of the threshold, just below wall offsets marking the commencement of the above-ground tower structure.

On the exterior, examination of the north face of the Inner Ditch below the tower suggested that the tower footings are at the same level as inside. The buttressing noted below this level appeared to have been added subsequently (Fig 64).

Foundation trenches, F35, F62, and F63, were recorded in area N to accommodate the footings of the curtain wall west of the gateway and of the South-West Tower. F35 and F62 represented the curtain wall footing trenches, and F63 the trench for the west wall of the South-West Tower. The remaining foundation trenches for the South-West Tower had been cleared as gullies in a later period. A concreted layer of mortar, F34, was also recorded, and may represent the remains of another mortar mixing area during the construction phase. Only to the rear of the West Gatehouse Tower and between the gatehouse and the South-West Tower did medieval levels survive, represented by layers of compacted sand and stone.

The initial construction process for the South-West Tower involved the cutting back of the Inner Ditch face to form a ledge, F82, 2.75m below ground level (Fig 73,

Section 8). The semi-circular south wall footings must then have been constructed freestanding, with backfill layers of sand and silt, SWT 7, 14, and 15, between the rear of the footings and the rock face (Fig 74). Presumably loose rock had been cleared back to provide a solid base for the walls; chisel marks were clear on the rock face itself (Fig 75). The base of this cut lay some 2.5m higher than the outside base of the wall to the south, where the tower footings were brought up by a series of four offsets to a point more or less level with bedrock on the interior of the wall. On the interior the footings displayed further offsets below the interior floor level.

A pit, F21, was excavated into the upper part of the backfilling behind the footings, SWT 7, and layers of sand and stone, interleaved with charcoal deposits, were noted in its base, SWT 9–13 (Fig 73, Section 8). The pit was then partly filled by and sealed beneath a layer of soil, SWT 5/8, in turn underlying a mortar and sandstone floor level, SWT 4, covering most of the interior of the tower. There was no subsidence in the floor, and the pit had evidently been carefully levelled. An offset was located above the floor level on the south wall. The coincidence between the back of the ledge and the interior line of the curtain wall suggests that F82 may have continued beyond the tower limits to the east and west, but this could not be tested by excavation. A possible interpretation might be that construction of the curtain wall and tower footings was not immediately followed by the above-ground structure.

To the east of the gate tower, further medieval features were revealed in addition to the well. Deep cuts, F84, into the rock east and west of the well, F85, may be associated with its construction. Overlying the Period 4 sand were medieval levels of soil and stone cut by a short section of unmortared wall, F7, and a semicircle of similarly unmortared stones, F11. A rectangular cut into bedrock, F10, was also noted. The curtain wall is pierced by a drain outflow, F86, in this area. This may have been a medieval provision, but any interior features associated with the drain must have been removed subsequently.

F7 may represent the remains of a structure, and F11 an associated oven. A rough shelter in the angle of tower and curtain wall is possible, perhaps marking a temporary building during a construction phase.

Further east there was no evidence of foundation trenches for the South-East Tower, where the walls were laid directly on to bedrock (Fig 78, Section 5). An apparently natural step downward lay beneath the north wall of the tower, and a natural rock fissure was also recorded. A layer of plaster, SET 5, represented the medieval floor.

The garderobe pit and its drain on the east side of the tower were found to have been blocked with a silt layer suggesting a deposit of cess. An unsuccessful attempt to unblock the drain was represented by a cut into the silt. This was sealed directly beneath tumbled masonry and may date to the later medieval or Civil War periods.

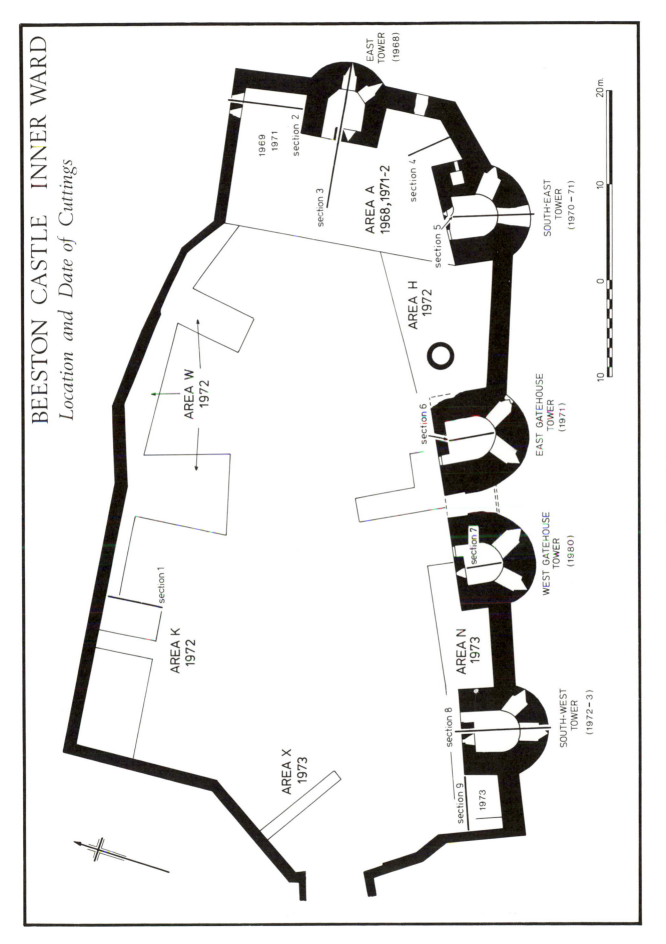

BEESTON CASTLE INNER WARD
Location and Date of Cuttings

EAST TOWER (1968)

1969
1971

section 2

section 3

AREA A 1968, 1971–2

section 4

section 5

SOUTH-EAST TOWER (1970–71)

AREA H 1972

AREA W 1972

section 6

EAST GATEHOUSE TOWER (1971)

section 1

AREA K 1972

section 7

WEST GATEHOUSE TOWER (1980)

AREA N 1973

AREA X 1973

section 8

section 9

1973

SOUTH-WEST TOWER (1972–3)

20 m.

10

0

10

10

Fig 71 Inner Ward: location of sections, date and location of excavation cuttings; scale 1:400

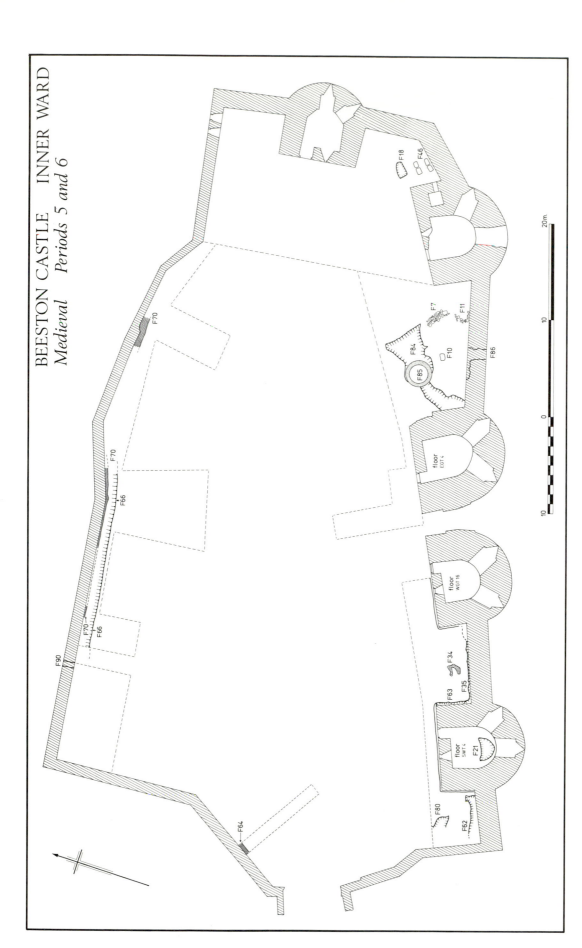

Fig 72 Inner Ward: Periods 5 and 6; scale 1:400

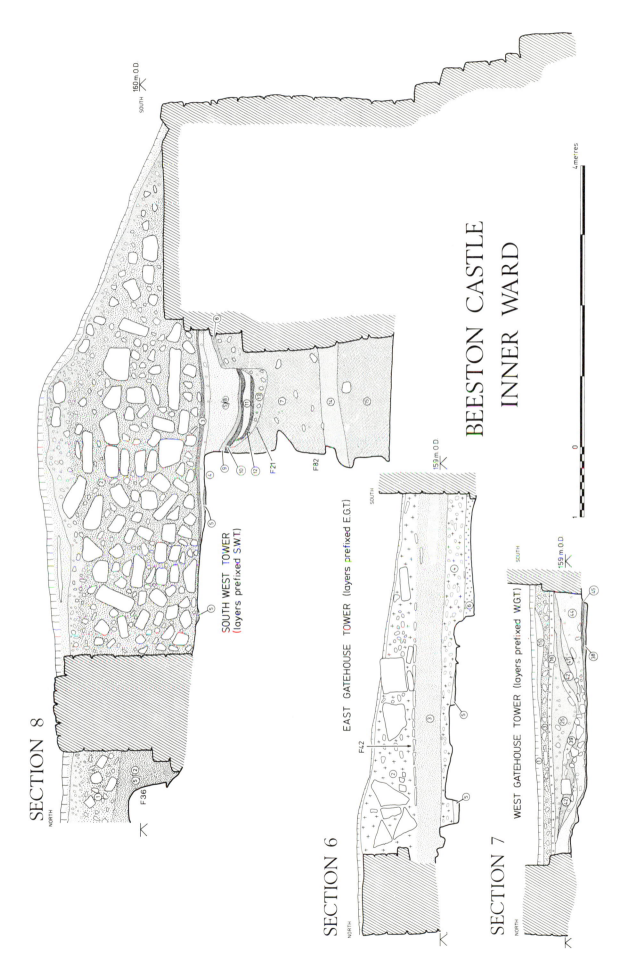

Fig 73 Inner Ward: sections 6, 7, and 8 (reversed); scale 1:50

Fig 74 Inner Ward: interior of South-West Tower, view east; scale in feet (Photo L Keen)

The west and north curtain walls of the Inner Ward were about half the thickness of the south and east walls against the inner side of the Inner Ditch. Examination of the curtain wall in area N, north of the south-west corner of the Inner Ward, showed the wall supported on two relieving arches, 5m north of the corner (Fig 76, Section 9), carrying the wall over two natural fissures in the rock. On the interior, a pit, F80, was recorded filled with layers of sand and soil, N 23–6, N 28–32. It is possible that this represents an abortive attempt to cut a drain or garderobe chute through to a point beneath the relieving arches.

Further north the curtain wall was seen in areas X and K to rest on an offset (F64 in area X, F70 in area K: Fig 77, Section 1). In area K, excavation of the foundation trench was terminated 1.4m beneath the natural rock level, without locating its full depth. It may be presumed that extensive ground preparation work preceded the wall construction, as below the South-West Tower. The curtain wall footings would have been built freestanding on a prepared ledge of solid rock, with backfill layers of silt, K 3, and soil with stone, K 5, behind the foundations. A drain, F90, was noted 10.5m east of the north-east corner, cutting beneath the wall, and this may be a medieval feature. Along the north curtain the offset continued to the east of area K. In the eastern part of area W it widened to a maximum of 0.83m at a point where the wall crossed a sharp rise in the level of bedrock (Figs 66 and 67). East of this point the medieval wall survived only in the form of a patchy rubble and mortar layer beneath the subsequently re-built wall.

In the east part of the castle, excavation showed no evidence of foundation trenches for the curtain wall (Fig 77, Sections 2 and 4). The East Tower was similarly constructed directly onto bedrock with the exception of a trench, F44, cut into a discontinuity in the bedrock (Fig 78, Section 3). Here a rubble backfill layer, A 14, was noted.

In area A, probable medieval layers survived against the north and east walls. These were represented by layers of plaster and mortar, A 15, soil and stone, A 16, and by mortar and rubble deposits, A 8, 9, 9a, 9b, and 10 (Fig 77, Sections 2 and 4). In the area between the East and South-East Towers, a sealing humic layer was noted, A 7. It is possible that these layers represent a deliberate levelling at the foot of the curtain wall, or construction debris. In the south-east angle they sealed a slight hollow, F18, cutting through the Period 4 sand into bedrock, while, to the south, four stones, F46, were located at the level of A 10. These appeared to form a solid, level base to take the weight of some object above ground level.

Foundation trenches were, therefore, only provided at points of unstable bedrock. Deep foundations were clear on the north curtain wall and at the South-West Tower and, to a lesser extent, at the West Gatehouse Tower. The latter two bedrock defects must have become apparent during excavation of the Inner Ditch. Slighter foundation trenches were noted for the curtain wall west of the gateway, as far as the south-west corner. Elsewhere the walls were placed directly on to bedrock.

Internal floors of mortar and stone were noted in both gatehouse towers and in the South-West Tower. A floor of plaster was recorded in the South-East Tower.

The absence of any alterations or additions to the floors, and the lack of occupation levels, suggests that they were maintained in readiness for the defence of the Castle. Elsewhere there is no evidence as to the function and use of the different parts of the Inner Ward, and it is likely that the main living quarters were on the first floor of the gatehouse and of the other towers. Only the stone pads in the south-east corner hint at use of the exterior. The slight structures and possible hearth by the well may be attributed to a building phase, as too may the mortar spreads, and the pit in the east side of the Ward.

An upper fill of F63, the foundation trench for the west wall of the South-West Tower, contained a Henry III Long Cross penny, struck in the late 1260s and lost before 1279. An unworn halfpenny of Edward I, deposited *c* 1280–1300, was found in the upper fill of the north wall foundation trench in area W. A Henry III Short Cross penny, lost before 1247, was found in a Period 9 layer (p 132, coins 2–4).

Medieval pottery was found in the construction trenches for the curtain wall in areas N (Fig 123.1, 2, 7, 14) and K, and for the South-West Tower. A large pottery group was found beneath the floor of the South-West Tower in F21 and overlying layers (Figs 123.5, 6, 10, 13; 124.24, 30; 125.36, 49, 50; 127.93, 97; 128.117, 134). Sherds of the later thirteenth-century Fabric F were found in the north wall and South-West Tower trenches, and in layers overlying F21 but beneath the floor of the South-West Tower (Fig 123.9). Other sherds of diagnostic later pottery were found in the medieval layers abutting the east curtain wall. However, this pottery was quantitatively overshadowed by pottery of secure thirteenth-century date (Figs 123.3–5, 17; 124.22, 23, 32,

33; 125.41, 51; 126.53, 57; 127.94, 100; 128.110, 125, 129, 130, 136, 137; and 129.147).

The coin and pottery evidence suggests a later date for the South-West Tower and the north curtain wall than for the initial building phase. The coins provide *termini post quem* in the later thirteenth century. The construction sequence evidence for the South-West Tower would certainly be compatible with a later date for the tower than for the rest of the south side, as would the spread of sherds from vessels found beneath the tower floor (M3:A9).

Other finds were few. A lead disc (Fig 104.94) and an ivory die (Fig 106.19) were found in layer N 6, and three arrowheads (Fig 108.16–18), and, presumably intrusive, a fragment of shot header in layer N 4. A possible chest handle (Fig 98.123) and a silver tag-end (Fig 103.84) were found in area H, while a ceramic marble (Fig 107.25), possibly post-medieval and intrusive, was located in the west wall foundation trench in area K. Finally an iron buckle (Fig 97.95) was found in SWT 8 beneath the floor of the South-West Tower.

There were few secure occupation layers. How much can be made of this in terms of assessing the extent of use of the castle is not clear. The post-depositional movement of the pottery (M3:A8) suggests that the Inner Ward was kept relatively clean. However finds of medieval material in later contexts from the Inner Ward and Inner Ditch are few. The absence of interior features, apart from those associated with construction work, suggests that the use of Beeston Castle was limited. However, the medieval finds hint at items of high quality, while the animal bones from the medieval levels suggest a varied diet (Table M59, M3:G1)).

Outer Gateway (Fig 79)

A trackway layer of orange gravel, F235, kerbed in places, was recorded over an east–west length of 26m, with a maximum surviving width of 7m (Fig 19, Section 6, and Fig 79). The layer narrowed within its kerb to coincide with the later gatehouse entrance, and widened out downslope before dividing into two tracks, one running north-east and the other south-east. Kerbing was noted on the north side and possible remnants may be indicated by F418 at the point of bifurcation (Fig 19, Section 6). The trackway overlay the Period 4 layer 234 and, at the gateway, was seen to underlie the footings of Tower 4 (Fig 19, Section 6). To the east F235 overlay gravel and stone layers (403, 404, and 409), possibly successive road surfacings. The southern trackway eastward was cut by later features.

The evidence suggests that an initial route was formed prior to the construction of the gate towers, giving access on to the hill plateau and thence to the Inner Ward and the construction work there.

At the gateway, foundation trenches, F603 and F604, only slightly wider than tower and wall footings, were noted on the north side of Tower 3, and to the east of the curtain wall. The wider foundation trench north of the change of alignment in the curtain wall is a later Period 9 cutting. By contrast the construction trench west of Tower 3, F822, was 2m wider than the wall, and turned east apparently to align with the north wall of

Fig 75 Inner Ward: chisel marks on rock in South-West Tower; scale 1 foot (Photo L Keen)

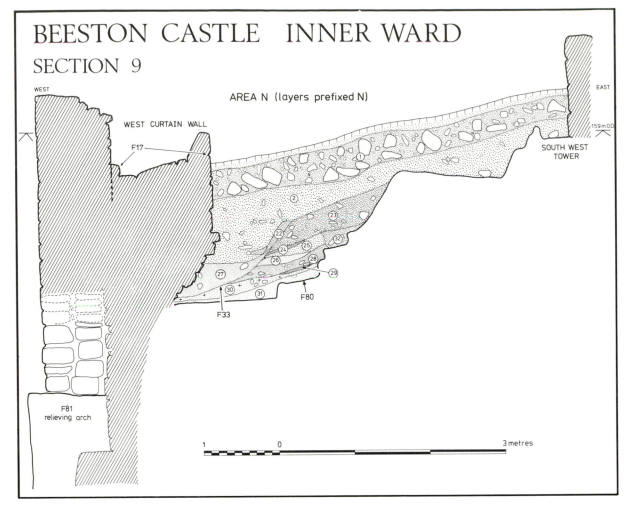

Fig 76 Inner Ward: section 9 (reversed); scale 1:50

the tower and trench F603. The curtain wall trench to the north, F813, was narrower than F822, and, within 3m of the tower, was confined to the width of the wall footings. Both trenches were cut to a similar depth. No trenches were noted within the tower.

While the plan of the foundation trenches west of the tower suggests that its construction was conceived as a separate unit with a large foundation trench specifically for its construction, the fills of tower and curtain foundation trenches could not be distinguished. The size of the construction trench west of Tower 3, and the absence of a similar-sized cutting west of Tower 4, may perhaps indicate that larger gateway towers were initially intended but abandoned with the construction of Tower 3.

A construction trench, F211, on the outer, east, side of the south gate tower, Tower 4, was recorded running to the south. The trench widened to 0.4m within Tower 5, cutting the prehistoric ramparts. No construction trench was definitely noted on the west side, but it is possible that the trench lay below layers 42 and 43 (Fig 19, Section 7). South of Tower 4, the curtain wall trench, F917, within the later square tower (Tower 5), was 1.7m wide and at least 1.5m deep, cutting through the prehistoric rampart layers (Fig 18, Section 3). The fills of F211 and F917 could not be distinguished, and the evidence suggests that they were open at the same time.

Within Tower 4, a number of layers were en-

countered beneath Period 7 occupation levels (Fig 19, Section 7). Above bedrock, the edge of which was seen here to turn to the west, a layer of sand with some charcoal inclusions, 156, lay beneath a layer of sand and rubble, 154. Above 154 and directly beneath the Period 7 floors was a layer of sand and rubble containing angular stone chippings, 116. There was no evidence of a foundation trench on the east side of the east wall of the tower, and it is probable that the level within the tower was raised by deposition of material within the already constructed drum tower footings. While the layers beneath represent this infilling, layer 116 may have served as a working level for the construction of the upper parts of the tower. There was no evidence of the original floor, nor of medieval occupation levels attributable to Periods 5 or 6. The evidence suggesting that the plan of Tower 4 was totally excavated to bedrock may indicate the same for Tower 3.

The tower and curtain wall footings were seen, where exposed, to be of coursed rubble, resting on large sandstone boulders north of Tower 3, and below the north wall of Tower 4 (Fig 18, Section 2; Fig 19, Section 6). These stones may be the inner revetment of the Period 3B defences, taken by the medieval builders to provide a sufficiently firm base for their walls. At the entranceway the large projecting stone beneath Tower 4 (Fig 19, Section 6) may, alternatively, represent a definition of the medieval entranceway, F235. Within

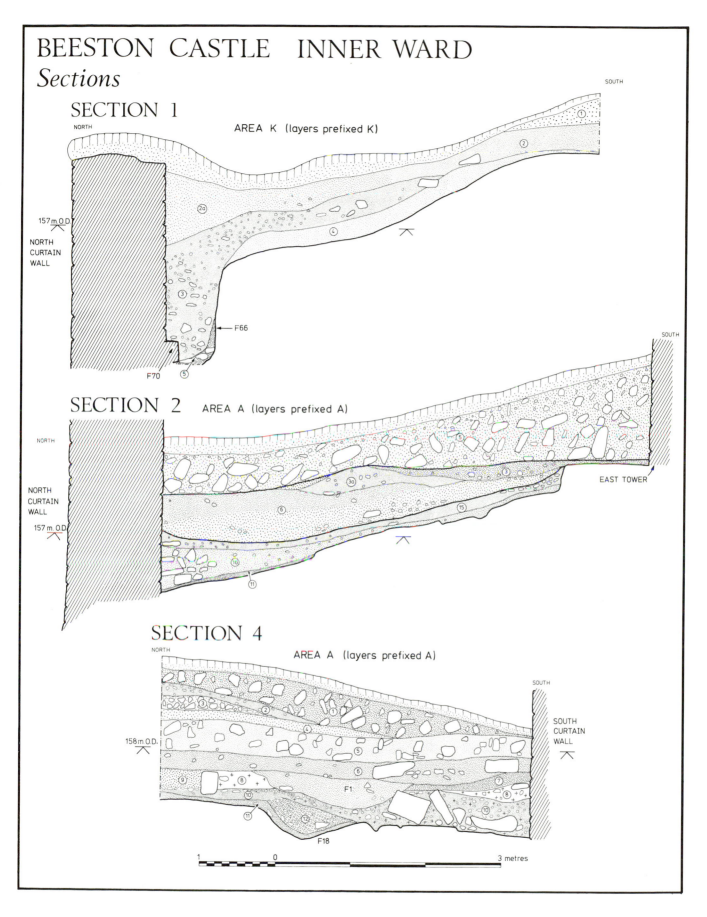

Fig 77 Inner Ward: sections 1, 2, and 4; scale 1:50

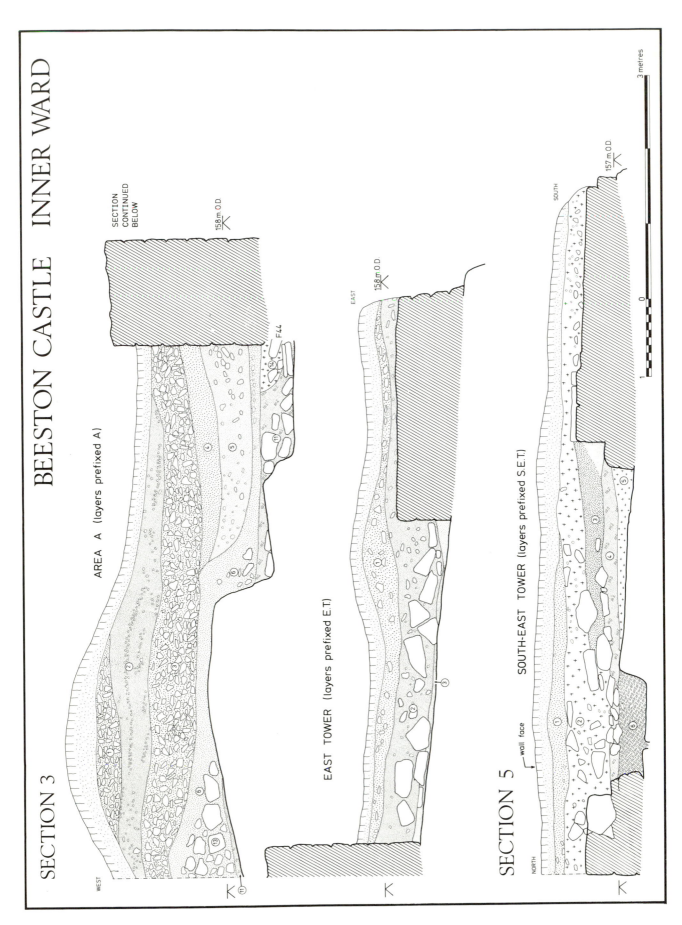

BEESTON CASTLE INNER WARD

SECTION 3

AREA A (layers prefixed A)

EAST TOWER (layers prefixed E.T.)

SECTION 5

SOUTH-EAST TOWER (layers prefixed S.E.T.)

Fig 78 Inner Ward: sections 3 (reversed) and 5; scale 1:50

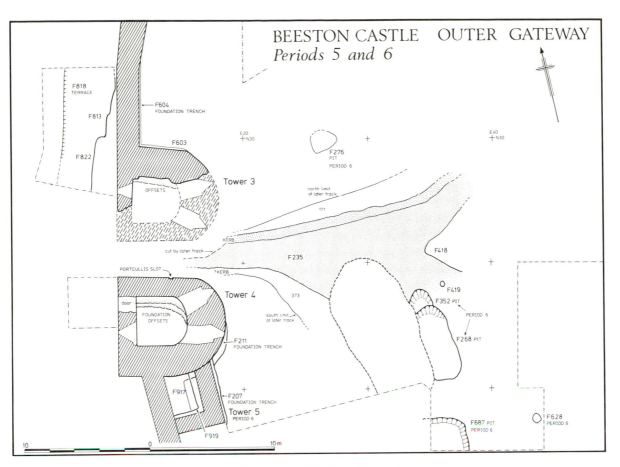

Fig 79 Outer Gateway: gatehouse and curtain wall, view south (Photo P Hough)

both gatehouse towers was evidence of offset foundation courses. Their position must indicate a response to the sharp fall in the bedrock noted within Tower 4 and probable within Tower 3. Further offsets were recorded on the east side of the curtain wall north of the gateway. These ran on beneath the slight change in the wall alignment to the north constructed in Period 9.

At Tower 7 the lowest layers beneath the tower floor are interpreted as possibly representing elements of the prehistoric defences (p 29); and it is suggested that the cut down the face of layers 17 and 22 (Fig 21) may indicate the site of the Period 3B boulder revetment. The surface of layers 10, 20, and 21 seemed to represent a compacted floor level, and spreads of charcoal were recorded, perhaps from hearths.

At area P to the south of the Inner Ward (Fig 3), excavations by Laurence Keen revealed a surviving fragment of the Outer Ward curtain wall (Figs 70 and 86). The stump of wall, F90, may represent the position of a tower. Erosion of the scarp edge in this area would have removed evidence of the curtain wall itself.

While the construction sequence could not be determined from the surviving archaeological evidence, the size and layout of the construction trench to the rear of the north gatehouse tower suggest that work focused initially on the gateway, and that perhaps the planned size of the gate towers was reduced. The similarity between the backfilling layers in tower and curtain wall foundation trenches, both north and south of the gateway, indicates that construction of gatehouse and curtain was contemporary.

Within the curtain wall on the north side a possibly boulder-revetted sloping terrace, F818, was noted. This was 4m wide and ran parallel to the wall (Figs 79 and 18, Section 1). An unmetalled track along the back of the curtain wall may be indicated.

Medieval pottery was found in the backfill layers in Tower 4 and in F822, the Tower 3 trench (Fig 123.11 and 12). Amongst a large group of pottery was a single sherd of the later thirteenth-century Fabric F, found in F822. Medieval coins (p 132, nos 1, 5–8), one of John and the remainder of Edward I, were found in post-medieval layers.

The trackway, F235, was overlain by deposits of rubble, 261, within which surfaces could be recognised at different levels. Layer 261 underlay an intermittent surface of cobbles, F271. To the south these levels were continued beyond the southern limit marked by F235, with trampled surfaces and a layer of cobbling, 373, corresponding to F271. At the entranceway F235 was overlain by a further layer of stone and rubble, 263, marking a sharp change in gradient. In places the surface of both 263 and F271 was marked by a layer of brown soil and worn stones.

This further trackway level was subsequently raised by the addition of a rubble layer, 171. A differentiation was noted in this layer between levels of voided rubble and more compacted soil-packed stones, and the latter levels were taken to represent further trackway surfaces. At the gateway a layer of fine metalling, 227, was noted. Layer 171 spread further north than the initial trackway F235, and to the south was defined by a stony bank overlying layer 373.

These successive layers combined both trackway surfaces and layers clearly intended to raise the entranceway levels. The gradient of the final layer, 227, related both to the base of the portcullis slot, and thus a levelled area within the gateway towers, and to a mark scored on the side of the large boulder underlying the southern gate tower (Fig 19, Section 6).

Finds of medieval pottery were made in a number of trackway layers (Figs 126.70; 127.92; 128.119) together with a few, presumably intrusive, sherds of post-medieval pottery in upper levels. Amongst thirteenth-century fabrics a single sherd from a Fabric F vessel (Fig 128.119) was found in a layer equivalent to 171.

Following the construction of the gateway, the track may have run up to a gate at the rear of the gate towers before later deposits brought the trackway up to an access, on a level gradient, beyond a portcullis entrance at the front of the towers. During this process it seems that make-up layers extended southward beyond the original route and that, at an early stage, cobbled surfaces ran directly to the gateway from the south-east. The Fabric F vessel sherds found in the foundation trench of Tower 3 and in the trackway may indicate that the provision of the gateway and the raised access was contemporary, and occurred in the later thirteenth century.

Further excavation on a small scale took place to the north (Fig 3, Cuttings A, B, and C). A trackway was visible on the ground running from the Outer Gateway area along the hill contours to the north. This was sectioned by three trenches, in all of which some evidence was found of levelling on the eastern downslope side, together with wheel ruts 1m apart. With the exception of a single post-medieval sherd overlying the track, no indications of date were found. This trackway seems to represent the route continuing northward associated with the entranceway layer F235, and its subsequent alterations, while the southern route noted within the excavation would represent the route towards Beeston village and the main thoroughfares.

Period 6: Later medieval

Outer Gateway (Fig 79)

A garderobe tower (Tower 5), of later medieval character, was added within the angle of Tower 4 and the curtain wall on the outside of the circuit (Fig 69). Its foundation trench, F207 and F919, cut the foundation trenches of Tower 4 and the curtain wall to the south, and cut through the prehistoric rampart layers (Fig 18, Section 3). The trench was located at the same construction level as that for the curtain wall, but may have postdated rubble layers, 898–900, banked against the curtain wall. Both the trench and the rubble layers were sealed beneath a deposit of dark soil, 897, in turn underlying layers of mortar and rubble, 895 and 894. A layer of sand and mortar, 893, spread across the interior of the tower, may represent the make-up levels for contemporary occupation.

The rubble layers banked against the curtain wall may be interpreted as deposits accumulated in Period 5 prior to the construction of Tower 5. Subsequently the interior levels were raised by infilling before a floor level was established, although no medieval layers were noted above layer 893.

The function of the tower is indicated by two garderobe chutes from the first and second floors, and these must relate to accommodation on the upper gate tower floors. Access to the lower floor of Tower 5 was from the upper levels and there were no window lights. The room may well have been used as the prison suggested by the documents (p 212).

A continued maintenance of entranceways must be assumed in Period 6. Although all the medieval entranceway evidence has been described under Period 5, it is possible that some of the upper resurfacings should be attributed to Period 6. There is, however, evidence, discussed below, that the southern routes went out of use, and that Period 6 access was directly from the east or north-east. The indications are that less importance was attached to access to the castle in the later medieval period and thus remetallings are unlikely.

Three quarry pits or an interrupted ditch were recorded in the south part of the excavation. These features would have terminated traffic on the southern Period 5 access routes. F352 was concave-profiled and filled with voided rubble. It was cut by a second pit, F268, 6m long and at least 2.5m wide, with vertical eastern and southern sides, and a flat base (Fig 19, Section 8). The west side was cut by a Period 7 ditch. F268 was filled with layers of sand and voided rubble. A large boulder overlay and had partly sunk into the upper fills to the south. The pit was separated by a 2m-wide area of unexcavated bedrock from a second pit-like feature, F687, which was only partially excavated, its upper fills comprising layers of sand and stone.

These pits cut the Period 4 erosion deposits as well as the Period 5 trackways F235, F271, and layer 171. A possibly stone-packed posthole, F419, was located at the same horizon to the north-east, and a second possible rock-cut postpit, F628, was noted to the south-east.

The backfills of F352 and F268 suggest that these features may represent quarries refilled with unused material from stone, shaped and split at the quarry site. The position of the pits lay partly across the line of the early entrance route F235 and must thus mark its partial disuse. The posthole, F419, placed directly in the centre of the earlier Period 5 route may represent an associated feature, perhaps a crane placement.

To the north of the entrance route a further large pit, F276, was recorded (Fig 20, Section 11). Its north side had been truncated by the later Period 9 entranceway and it may represent a pit on the same scale as those to the south, although its sloping sides suggest a smaller feature. Backfilled layers of sand and rubble, 176 and 237, were recorded.

None of the medieval pottery associated with the construction of Tower 5 was diagnostic. The medieval pottery in the fills of F268 was, however, more instructive. Amongst sherds of vessels in earlier pottery fabrics (Figs 124.21; 126.77–9; 127.82, 83, 88, and 92) were two Fabric F vessels (Fig 128.118 and 120), and a jug (Fig 128.122) in the late medieval Fabric G. Post-medieval finds in an upper layer, 312, must be intrusive.

The position of these pits, partly across the medieval entrance, demonstrates a lack of importance attached to the castle entranceways at the time of their digging in the later medieval period. The additional garderobe tower, Tower 5, may therefore belong to an earlier period of activity. The paucity of later medieval pottery

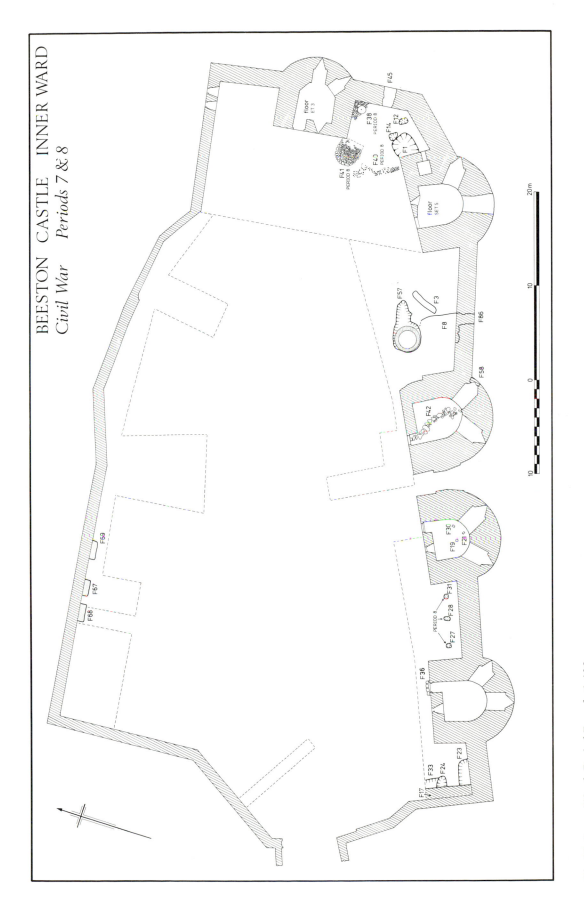

BEESTON CASTLE INNER WARD
Civil War   Periods 7 & 8

Fig 80 Inner Ward: Period 7; scale 1:400

Fig 81 Inner Ward: West Gatehouse Tower, view north (Photo P Hough)

and coins in the overall finds assemblages from all periods suggests that there was little later medieval occupation of the castle buildings.

Period 7: Civil War

Inner Ward (Fig 80)

The Period 7 evidence from the Inner Ward is presented in a clockwise sequence starting at the gatehouse.

A layer of soil and stone, EGT 3, was recorded in the ground floor room of the East Gatehouse Tower directly overlying the Period 5 floor (Fig 73, Section 6). Outside the rear of the tower a cobbled surface occupied the same horizon as a layer of rubble, F42, inside the tower. F42 overlay EGT 3 and appeared to represent a rough stone spread thrown down at the entranceway and across the room. The blocking of the east arrow-loop probably belongs to this phase. In the West Gatehouse Tower a dump of fine sand and stone in the north-west corner overlay the medieval floor, which was cut by three rectangular postholes, F19, F21, and F30 (Fig 81). A circular postpipe was noted on the north side of F19 and it was clear that prior to decay the post had sloped to the north.

The medieval floor of the South-West Tower was overlain by a thin layer of soil trample, SWT 3, containing fragments of wall plaster (Fig 73, Section 8). The north foundation trench of the tower, F36, appeared to have been cleared and used as a gully judging from the

post-medieval clay pipes and pottery in the backfill.

North of the south-west corner the west curtain wall had been strengthened. The additional wall, F17, more than doubled the width of the wall. It continued for 8m north of the south-west corner, and its south end abutted the south curtain wall (Figs 82 and 76, Section 9). Its foundation trench, F33, cut the suggested medieval pit, F80, and the south curtain wall foundation trench, F62. Subsequently F33 was cut by two pits, F23 and F24, alongside the newly emplaced wall.

On the north side of the Inner Ward three graves, F67,

Fig 82 Inner Ward: curtain wall strengthening F17 in area N, view west; scale in feet (Photo H Hawley)

F68, and F69, were excavated alongside the curtain wall in area K. Grave F67 was 1.85m long and 0.66m wide, F68 was 1.8m long and 0.63m wide, and F69 was 1.9m long, 0.65m wide, and c 0.5m deep (Fig 83). All three burials were supine and were aligned with their heads to the west. A later disturbance had removed the skull from F68. This latter and the burial in F69 were laid out with their hands crossed over the pelvis. Coffin nails were recorded in F67 and F69. The level from which the graves were excavated was not clear. All three burials represented young adult males (M3:F9–11; Table M58, M3:F9). A shallow pit was located to the west.

In the East Tower a layer of clay, ET 3, may represent a floor provided in this phase (Fig 78, Section 3), while in the enclosed space between the South-East and the East Tower, a group of features were recorded which postdated the medieval layer A 7. A large shallow pit, F1, appeared to be associated with two small pits F12 and F14 (Fig 77, Section 4). F1 was filled with mortar and soil, and F12 and F14 with charcoal, soil, and clay. These features were sealed beneath a layer of soil, A 6, and may have a relationship with F45, the aperture in the east curtain wall suggested to represent a Civil War gunport (p 103).

In the South-East Tower an accumulation of soil and silt, SET 4, was recorded overlying the medieval floor (Fig 78, Section 5).

East of the gateway a large pit, F57, filled with mortar and rubble was excavated at the wellhead. The uniformity of the fill suggested that backfilling had occurred relatively soon after its cutting. The cut was irregular with a maximum depth of 2.04m. The relationship between F57 and a further feature, F8, was not clear. F8 had removed the upper surface of bedrock from the east side of the gate tower to west of the well, and had also destroyed the presumably medieval drain associated with the Period 5 culvert. A soil-marked linear feature, F3, was recorded.

All these features and levels relate to the Civil War occupation, with the possible exception of the additional walling at the south end of the west curtain wall, which may be late medieval. The function of F17 is unclear: it may be all that was completed of an intended strengthening of the wall circuit on the west and north sides.

The Civil War occupants used the medieval floor surfaces within the tower ground floor rooms. In the East Gatehouse Tower some 0.4m of material accumulated prior to the rough flagstone path laid across the floor. The blocking of the arrow-loop indicates that these apertures no longer had a function, presumably being too small for matchlock use. In the opposite gatehouse room the postpits are paralleled by similar features at the Outer Gateway. From the angle noted for one of the posts some kind of stand may be envisaged.

In the angle between East and South-East Towers the group of pits may be associated with the gunport. Later features here are discussed under Period 8, and a roof is suggested under Period 8 which may be of earlier, Civil War date.

Two Nuremberg jettons and a James I farthing were found in the pit F1 in area A, while a forged James I farthing and a Charles I farthing were found in the East Gatehouse Tower in layer EGT 3 (p 132, nos 14, 16, 20–2). Mid-seventeenth-century clay pipes were found

in F1, EGT 3, and, in large numbers, in the South-East Tower (SET 4, Figs 119.39, 120.43). Other equally closely dated pipes came from the South-West Tower, SWT 3, and from F36 to its north (Fig 120.40), as well as from pits F23 and F24 in area N (M2:G3).

Sherds of 72 post-medieval pottery vessels were found in a number of Period 7 layers, with particularly large groups from area A at the east end of the ward, area N in the south-west, the East Gatehouse Tower, and the South-East Tower (Figs 130.1–9; 133.63–5; 135.88–90; 137.109). Comparatively little pottery was found in the South-West Tower and the West Gatehouse Tower, and none in the East Tower. It is possible to contrast the assemblage here with that from the Outer Gateway, and to suggest that the more circumscribed range of forms represents the use of pottery for storage or indicates the better quality of pottery used by officers (Table M56, M3:D2).

Other finds (p 134) came principally from within the towers. In the East Gatehouse Tower these comprised a door bolt (Fig 93.62), a bone pin or parchment pricker (Fig 106.14), an ivory peg (Fig 106.15), and a copper alloy book-clasp (Fig 101.41). From the South-East Tower came a number of spurs (Figs 112.3, 4; 113.5–8; 115.30, 31), two horseshoes (Fig 99.130 and 131), a bone handle (Fig 106.13), a boot heel (Fig 97.99), and an iron plate (Fig 94.41). The handle of a glass vessel was also

Fig 83 Inner Ward: burial F69, view west; scale in feet (Photo L Keen)

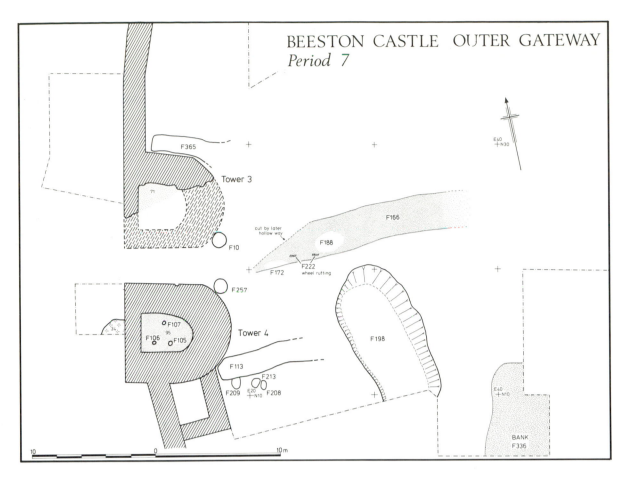

Fig 84 Outer Gateway: Period 7; scale 1:300

found here (Fig 116.32). In the South-West Tower a buckle (Fig 97.93), a ring (Fig 101.37), a marble (Fig 107.26), and fragments from lead shot moulds (not illustrated) were found. Further finds came from the east end of the ward, and included four bindings (Fig 102.61–4), a belt hook (Fig 102.69), and a needle (Fig 103.75) from the pit F1. Other layers here produced a lock hasp, a padlock key, and a chest key (Figs 96.74 and 75; 102.71), a buckle plate and a medieval buckle (Fig 100.10 and 13), arrowheads (Fig 108.12 and 13), shears blades (Fig 93.18 and 19), and a hinge (Fig 94.37). From the area of the well came two knives (Fig 93.16 and 17), an iron tool (Fig 95.55), and a bone offcut (Fig 107.22).

These finds represent intensive use of the Inner Ward during the Civil War. There are some indications that the ground floors of the towers were used for storage. The South-East Tower assemblage may indicate an equipment store, and layer EGT 3 may be the result of constant use and trample. Occupation would have been on the upper floors. Amongst the pottery assemblage storage and drinking vessels were common, as well as some bowls. Finds in the South-West Tower and in later layers suggest the production of shot. The possible gunports show that the defenders were prepared to abandon the lengthy outer curtain and concentrate their resources in the Inner Ward. The burials were located away from the main occupation areas, and may represent Royalist casualties of the siege.

Outer Gateway (Fig 84)

Within the south tower, Tower 4, a compact level of sand and stone, 95, was located overlying the Period 5 layer 116 (Fig 19, Section 7). Three stone-packed postholes, F105–7, were cut from this layer. All were square or rectangular placements with stone packing in a rectangular pit. Groups of stakeholes, generally 0.2m in diameter and 0.4m deep, appeared to be associated. They comprised 26 separate features, one group clustered between F105 and F106, with a stakehole cutting the backfill of F105, and a second group toward the doorway. Three further stakeholes lay to the east of F107. Layer 95 lay just below the level of the lower offset on the north side of the tower, and the 0.1m-high face of the upper offset was plastered in places. This level lay 0.5m below the door threshold to the west.

The stone-packed postholes may represent some kind of subdivision of the lower gatehouse room. The stakeholes appear to be more temporary; none occur toward the centre of the room and the majority lie within the zone marked by the postholes. They may represent the position of working areas or equipment storage placements which were regularly altered. The medieval floor levels must have been deliberately lowered, taking the new floor level below the door threshold, possibly to maximise the storage facilities offered by the room.

In a second phase the floor was raised by the addition of a make-up level of sand and rubble, 77, overlain by a spread of burnt material, 86. This in turn underlay a floor of compacted grey brown sand, 76. Layer 76 comprised successive trampled layers containing much occupation debris. On this surface a burnt area was located to the north, overlying the lower offset of the medieval footings. Extensive scorching was also noted on the northern wall-face of the room. A change in function in the second phase is indicated, with the renewed floors and the hearth showing intensive use.

Outside the tower to the west were interleaved layers of coal, ash, and gravel, 42 and 43. Over these was evidence of make-up layers of sand and clay, 39 and 35, underlying a level of mortar, 34, which may represent the floor of a structure on the same level as the entrance door to Tower 4. A test pit at the south-west corner of Tower 4 located a layer of paving at the level of layer 34, further attesting structures or yards to the rear of the tower.

In Tower 3 little survived the Period 9 demolition. However, a level of sand and mortar, 71, possibly a floor level, just below the medieval offset in the north wall footings, presents enough similarities to the Tower 4 evidence to suggest that the sequence in Tower 3 may have been similar, and that the floor levels in both towers were initially lowered.

Further south in Tower 7, post-medieval finds in layer 8 suggested its deposition in Period 7. Both the floor level and the area to the rear of the tower had been raised to form a level 0.75m above the medieval surface (Fig 21).

A substantial pit, F257, located on the south side of the entrance between the two gate towers, was paralleled by a second pit, F10, which had been heavily truncated by the Period 9 entranceway. The surviving part of F10 below bedrock was sufficient to indicate a similar diameter to F257. F10 would have been sited against the north gate tower, complementing F257 to the south, and both may represent the positions of posts forming a gateway structure. Although, in the context of the castle structure, the pits seem a relatively unsophisticated approach towards the provision of a gateway, they are very large and would have held substantial uprights. The renewed gateway must indicate that the portcullis had long gone out of use and could not be refurbished.

Layers associated with the early post-medieval entrance can be identified overlying the medieval entranceway surface, 171. F166 comprised a relatively complete stretch of over 15m of cobbled surface. Two depressions, probably eroded potholes (F172 and F188 filled with 174 and 84 respectively), were noted in the surface cutting through 166 into the medieval surfaces (Fig 19, Section 6). Wheel rutting, F222, was recorded in two places running to the entrance, where a layer of compacted soil and rubble, 89, was located.

From the entranceway the track ran to the north of the medieval line and this route seemed to be initiated in Period 7. In addition there was a suggestion of an additional route to the north of F166, with cobbling and trampled layers overlying zones of rubble and a dump of flat stones.

On either side of the entrance were two ditches, F113 and F365, running east from the castle walls and dying out downslope. Two postholes F208 and F209 were recorded, with F209 cut by F113. The ditches may represent clearance channels to carry water away from the

Fig 85 Outer Gateway: Period 7 ditch F198, view east (Photo P Hough)

tower bases, or possibly preliminary work for an abandoned defence protecting the entrance.

Earlier entrances were blocked to the south by the cutting of a flat-based ditch F198 (Fig 85). The ditch cut the fills of the Period 6 pits to the east (Fig 19, Section 8), and the upper medieval road layer 171. It terminated to the north in a line just to the north of the south side of the gateway. A vertical face to the west enhanced the steepness of the hillside.

To the east a bank of voided rubble was deposited on the Period 4 erosion deposits. The bank, F336, comprising layers 337 and 335, terminated northward within the excavation although a later cutting may have removed part of its terminal (Fig 20, Section 9; Fig 19, Section 8). Southward F336 survived as a feature visible on the ground, and could be traced to the south-east corner of the hillside (Fig 63).

Interpretation of the bank and ditch is aided by the location of similar features 60m to the south below Tower 7 (Fig 21), where a slightly wider (5m as opposed to 4m), flat-based cutting, F1001, terminated to the west in a vertical face. The ditch here was clearly related to a bank, F1002, the southern counterpart of F336. Bank and ditch thus represent a defensive feature. This interpretation is complicated if a comparison is made between the two profiles across bank and ditch at the Outer Gateway and at Tower 7. The profile of F1001 shows a lower base level to the east, together with a possible recutting line in the fills 1015. There is a marked similarity with the complete profile of F198 and F268 at the Outer Gateway. It is possible to suggest a primary ditch and bank with a recutting westward and presumably a refurbishment of the bank. If this is so, then the Period 6 pits should be allocated to Period 7.

The fills of ditch F198 must belong to a post-Civil War infilling. They comprised base layers of sand and rubble together with charcoal and dark soil deposits deriving from the Period 4 erosion layer 234, overlain by layers of voided rubble, 101 and 108, and further deposits of sand and stone. Medieval pottery was found in the base fills of F198, while pottery, clay pipes, and other finds of the Civil War period, discussed in more detail below, were not located below layer 108. It would appear that medieval deposits were initially backfilled into the ditch. The fills of sand and voided rubble continued above the inner lip upslope to the west. A more secure post-medieval date for the ditch was provided by finds, again discussed below, in the primary fills of F1001 and in the bank F336.

Other post-Civil War demolition evidence has been included in Period 7. Layers of stone rubble and soil (51 and 54), up to 0.4m thick, in which dressed stones were incorporated, sealed the trackway, F166, the gatepost pit, F257, and the ditches, F113 and F365.

Plentiful and consistent dating evidence for Period 7 at the Outer Gateway was provided by coins, clay pipes, pottery, and other finds.

Two James I coins, a penny and a half groat, were found in F365 in front of Tower 3. A Nuremberg jetton, a further James I half groat, and a forged Charles I 20 pence piece were found in F105.

Seventeenth-century clay pipes were found in a number of contexts. From the floor levels of Tower 4 came a large mid-seventeenth-century assemblage, mostly from the upper floor layer 76, although the fill of posthole F106, from the earlier phase, contained a single, probably seventeenth-century stem. A small number of seventeenth-century pipes were found in upper layers of the ditch F198, while mid-seventeenth-century pipes were found in the base fill of its counterpart below Tower 7, F1001. Postholes F208 and F257 produced seventeenth-century pipes, as did the ditches either side of the entrance, F113 and F365 (Figs 117.7, 10; 119.33). Other layers with mid-seventeenth-century pipes were found to the west of Tower 4 (Fig 119.31), and forming the entrance trackway (Fig 119.38), the latter including F166. Finally the demolition layers in front of the gateway yielded a large mid-seventeenth-century group (Figs 117.3, 8; 118.16 and 17).

Post-medieval pottery of the same date was found in the gateway pits F10 and F257; in the upper fills of F198, and layers forming the bank F336; in trenches F113 and F365; and in posthole F208. Of the layers within Tower 4, layer 76 contained a large pottery group, while sherds were also found in the fill of one of the stakeholes and in posthole F105. A further large assemblage was found in layers to the rear of Tower 4 (Figs 130.10, 11; 131; 132; 133.43–62; 134; 135.82–7, 91–7; 136; 137.105–8, 110–25; 138).

Numerous small finds came from these horizons. Inside Tower 4 layer 77 produced a fragment of vessel glass (Fig 116.19), while from layers to the rear of the tower came an iron rod (Fig 98.111), a powder pan pin (Fig 108.24), a jaw screw from a gun (Fig 108.26), and window leads (not illustrated). Trackway layers in front of the gatehouse produced a padlock key (Fig 96.66) and a fragment of plate in iron (Fig 98.100), a medieval buckle (Fig 100.2), a fitting (Fig 100.16), a strap ornament (Fig 100.19), and a bell in copper alloy (Fig 101.50), and a lead rod (Fig 109.34). Musket balls, one impacted, were also found here. From an upper layer in Tower 5 came a medieval iron knife (Fig 93.3), and from the postpit F257, an iron buckle (Fig 97.88). Finds from the two ditches on either side of the gateway comprised, from F113, an iron spout (Fig 98.109), a medieval belt ornament (Fig 100.18), and a stud in copper alloy (Fig 101.53), four window leads (not illustrated), a powder pan cover (Fig 108.21), a powder flask nozzle (Fig 109.39), and two glass fragments from beakers (Fig 116.13 and 15). From F365 on the other side of the gateway came a scissors handle (Fig 95.42), a lock and keyhole plate (Fig 96.64 and 65), and a buckle (Fig 97.77), all of iron. From the west side of Tower 3 came a knife fragment (Fig 98.101) and a binding strap (Fig 98.108) in iron, and late medieval copper alloy strap ornaments (Fig 100.21–6). The fills of ditch F198 contained an iron padlock key (Fig 96.67) and buckle (Fig 97.76), and a medieval copper alloy buckle (Fig 100.3). An iron possible candlestick fragment (Fig 98.107) and a silver object (Fig 103.83) were found further down the slope.

The post-Civil War layers in front of the gateway (51, 54, and 60) produced a large assemblage. Iron objects comprised knives (Fig 93.2, 4–7, 9), a chain (Fig 94.20), a spatula (Fig 95.43), a small spud (Fig 95.44), a hoe (Fig 95.46), a candlestick fragment (Fig 96.57), a padlock bolt (Fig 96.63), a buckle (Fig 97.77), plates, probably from a chest (Fig 97.78 and 79), a weight (Fig 98.102), a spout

(Fig 98.103), plate fragments (Fig 98.104 and 105), a strip (Fig 98.106), a binding strap (Fig 98.110), an arrowhead (Fig 108.7), and a gun scourer (Fig 108.29). Copper alloy objects comprised a gilt buckle which perhaps came from the same mould as one found at Leicester and had probably belonged to an officer (Fig 100.1), medieval strap ornaments (Fig 100.15, 17, and 20), a ring (Fig 101.32), a pin (Fig 101.42), a lace tag-end (Fig 101.51), and a fragment of binding (Fig 101.52). Other objects comprised a lead bar (Fig 104.87) and rod (Fig 109.35), window leads (not illustrated), and two bone knife handles (Fig 106.2 and 4). Vessel glass fragments were found from a possible wine glass (Fig 116.2), a beaker (116.17), and an apothecary's flask (Fig 116.30). Sixteen musket balls, four impacted, came from these layers, as did many of the numerous fragments of the jack of plates (Figs 110–11). Eleven spurs were found (Figs

112.2; 113.14–17; 114.26–7; 115.32–4 and 37) and a stud attachment for a spur leather (no 37).

The Civil War evidence from the Outer Gateway indicates intensive use and remodellings of the lower room in Tower 4, and the use of the area outside the tower to the west. In Tower 3, a floor at the same level as that in Tower 4 suggests similar contemporary use. Entranceways were renewed and, in part, relocated to run north of a stretch of ditch and outer bank, the ditch provided with a deliberate flat base and vertical wall accentuating the steepness of the hillslope. Other slighter ditches were recorded at the entranceway, as was evidence for a massive timber gateway. Finds of pottery and especially clay pipes provide a secure date in the mid-seventeenth century.

Other clearly military changes are recorded for the castle fabric on the outer circuit. The widening of arrow-

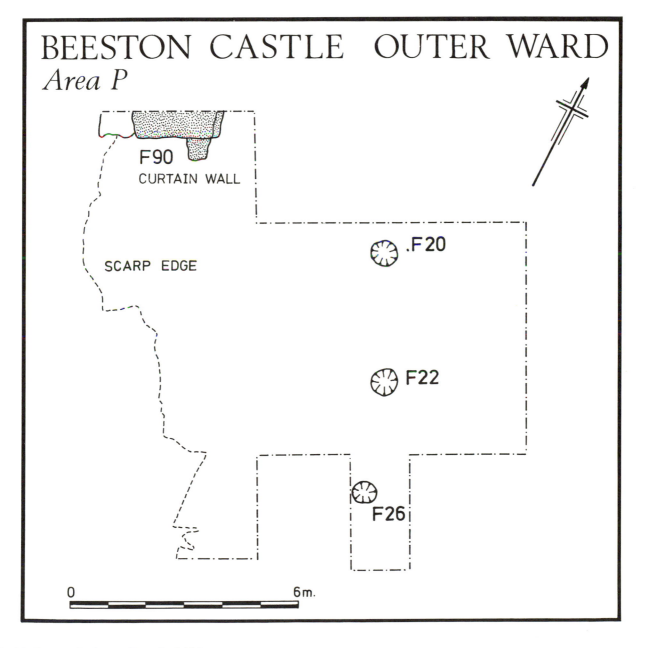

Fig 86 Outer Ward: area P; scale 1:100

loops in Towers 8 and 9 may have been intended to accommodate flintlock guns. In contrast to the gateway evidence the floor in Tower 7 was raised.

All the earlier post-medieval evidence at the Outer Gateway can be assigned to the Civil War. Unlike the Inner Ward towers, the Outer Gateway tower deposits were not immediately sealed by demolition material. However, the deposits containing building stone in front of the gateway may indicate some demolition following the cessation of hostilities. It is in these deposits that the bulk of the finds were made, indicating a wholesale clearance of the gateway buildings. Later activity further redistributed some of this Civil War material into later Period 8 and 9 contexts.

The finds attest the scale of the occupation, and provide a picture of the non-perishable material required to equip and maintain the military presence. While there was a strong military element provided by the armour, musket balls, guns, and the evidence for lead shot, whether in the form of runners or window leads, the remaining material, leaving aside the handful of medieval objects, indicates the range of items required for day-to-day needs. The clothing accessories, glass vessels, pottery containers, clay tobacco pipes, and eating utensils, together with the tools, locks, keys, candlesticks, and building fittings, demonstrate the range of surviving material from the two-year reoccupation of the castle.

Outer Ward (Fig 92)

The terraces apparent on the plateau (Fig 63), although clearly the site of Period 9 activity, may have been constructed at an earlier date. The topographical evidence suggests that the terracing was already in existence at the time extensive quarrying began, since the two principal quarry areas appear to respect the northern end of the long terrace.

The levelling comprised one long terrace, 110m by 7.5m, with a second terrace, measuring 50m by 13m, sited below the main terrace to the south-east. These areas were partly examined by the excavations. The upper terrace was cut by East Cutting A and South Cutting, while the lower terrace terminated in the south part of South Cutting. A stone-sided and capped drain, F74 and F153, was recorded running along the rear of the main terrace. The drain joined a second, similar drain, F152, set at right angles and running downslope to the east. A ditch, F43, to the south of the South Cutting may represent a further element of the drainage scheme, possibly the robbed-out line of a drain similar to F74. In East Cutting A a short section of coursed stone walling, F227, was found, aligned to the terracing and presumably associated.

It is possible that Civil War features are represented, with drained terraces forming levelled areas for the temporary accommodation of soldiers. The section of walling may represent the remains of more permanent structures erected here. Finds of seventeenth-century pottery and clay pipes were largely confined to the area of East Cutting A, where a Charles I penny was also found. These finds derived from overall layers which also contained Period 9 finds. The recovery of six mus-

ketballs suggests some Civil War use. Amongst the other finds, items of Civil War date comprised hinges and straps (Fig 94.34–6), a key (Fig 96.69), a dress fastening hook (Fig 97.97), stirrups (Fig 99.124 and 125), and a powder flask nozzle and four powder holder caps (Fig 109.38, 42, 43, and not illustrated).

A line of three postholes in area P (Figs 3 and 86) has been discussed already in a prehistoric context (p 21). They could represent Civil War-period blocking of breaches in the medieval curtain.

Period 8: Late seventeenth century

Inner Ward (Fig 80)

Rubble spreads overlying the floors and occupation levels in the ground floor tower rooms are likely to have resulted from demolition soon after the raising of the siege, since there are no sealed items suggesting later use (Figs 73 and 78). However, two groups of features outside the towers suggest some activity later than the mid-seventeenth century.

At the south-east corner of the Inner Ward some occupation took place between the East and South-East Towers. Here three features were set into the Period 7 layer A 6. A linear spread of bricks covered by a layer of yellow mortar, F40, ran north from the back of the South-East Tower. It is possible that a slight wall footing is represented. At the north end of F40 a D-shaped stone hearth, F41, abutted the south-west corner of the East Tower (Fig 87). The sides were well constructed of dressed stones set in yellow clay, and contained a spread of randomly placed rubble. The straight side was stained red by heat and an area of burnt clay was recorded. To the east, in the angle of the East Tower and the curtain wall, a pair of millstones had been set into a rubble base, F38 (Fig 88), and these formed the base for a chevron-shaped brick setting, F39. A layer of charcoal was apparent under the bricks, and F38 may in its earlier phase have been a hearth.

Notches cut into the south-east corner of the East Tower and the north-west corner of the South-West Tower may be associated. They may have supported a

Fig 87 Inner Ward: F41 in area A, view north; scale in feet (Photo L Keen)

Fig 88 Inner Ward: F38 in area A; scale in feet (Photo by H Hawley)

roof joist, and indicate a temporary use of a sheltered part of the castle, perhaps during the slighting process. Rainford style clay pipes suggesting the presence of demolition gangs were found in this area (M2:G3). However, later activities, perhaps the provision of a shelter during quarrying or shepherding work on the hill, also provide likely contexts.

There was no dating evidence to distinguish this phase of activity from the Period 7 evidence. The bricks in the upper part of F39 were of a more recent type than those in F40. All these features were directly buried by spoil from the well excavations of 1842 and must have been clear on the surface at that time.

Between the West Gatehouse Tower and the South-West Tower, a line of three rectangular postpits was recorded, F27, F28, and F31. The stratigraphic position of these was not clear, and they appeared in excavation to have been cut from the Period 5 level. However, F31 contained the stump of a wooden post, indicating a more recent origin. It is possible that another shelter against the curtain wall, during or following the slighting of the castle towers, is represented. Rainford style pipes were again found in this area.

Outer Gateway (Fig 89)

At the castle entrance a revetted track and steps were cut into the Period 7 layers of rubble in front of the gateway (Fig 90). The new entranceway was formed of earth, rubble, and stones, 82, acting as a make-up layer for a pathway surface, 52 and 64 (Fig 19, Section 6). These levels were confined to north and south by dry-stone walls, F83, revetting banks of light red rubble. The walls were constructed in part with reused building stones, including a door jamb fragment. The trackway terminated east of the gateway at the lowest of a flight of four steps, F111, built on to an area of rubble, 110, similar to the side banks. Building stones were again reused in the steps. The southern revetment wall crossed the infilled northern terminal of the Period 7 ditch F198.

The track was traced for 5m, and was then lost until a layer of metalling seen in section, F238, represented its continuation eastward (Figs 19, Section 6 and 20,

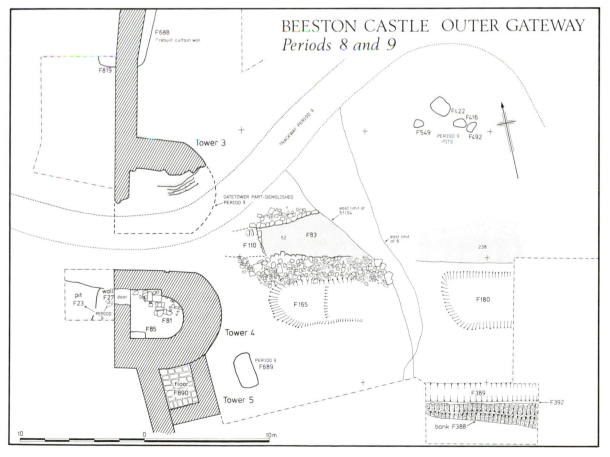

Fig 89 Outer Gateway: Periods 8 and 9; scale 1:300

Fig 90 Outer Gateway: Period 8 entrance path and steps, view east (Photo P Hough)

Section 9). To the south of the entranceway a hollow, F165, 3.7m wide and 0.3m deep, appeared to represent a westward continuation of a further hollow, F180 (Fig 20, Section 9), filled with soil and stone, 387. Further south a bank, F388, was recorded crossing the Period 7 Civil War bank, with a drystone revetment, F392, and a ditch, F389, on its north side. This bank could be traced on the ground running east–west for over 20m.

These features may be contemporary, and represent not only an access to the gateway, but also an element of landscaping and drainage on the steep hillslopes to the south. Other earthworks may have existed to the north, but have been destroyed by the later entrance. The revetted bank and ditch to the south may represent a field boundary bank, paralleled by a similar bank north of Tower 1 (Fig 63).

The new approach to the castle suggests a private and domestic occupation of the castle, rather than an access to the hill plateau. There was clearly no way on to the hill here for wheeled vehicles. The occupation evidence is limited to the remains of flagstone floors, F81 and F890, within Towers 4 and 5. Some stones of F81 were heat-cracked and may have formed the base for a hearth (Fig 19, Section 7; Fig 91). In Tower 5 a group of make up layers were provided beneath a well-laid stone floor, F890 (Fig 18, Section 3). In Tower 3 a layer of flat stones may indicate the remains of a further flagstone floor.

A build-up of soil in the revetted way, and the partial collapse of the drystone walling, indicated the decay of the access route prior to its abandonment, the latter

attested by the deposition of a deep layer of soil and stone, 6, emplaced over the earlier entranceway features. The layer may be associated with the cutting of a new access route on to the hill plateau, curving northward to give a gentle gradient before following the former entrance route at the gateway. Tower 3 was largely demolished to accommodate the new route.

Finds from these Period 8 levels comprised further large assemblages of Civil War period clay pipes, pottery, and other finds. However, a late seventeenth- or early eighteenth-century date for Period 8 was afforded by a small number of diagnostic finds. Layers forming the revetted trackway surface contained clay pipes dated 1660–1715 (Figs 118.20; 120.50, 52; 121.59). Within Tower 4 the stone floor, F81, sealed a pipe bowl dated 1640–90 (Fig 120.51). Late seventeenth-/early eighteenth-century pipes were found with earlier examples in the later dumps overlying the entrance (Figs 118.21 and 22; 120.49; 121.53–5). In Tower 5 a spur of *c* 1700 (Fig 115.36) was found in layer 891 beneath floor F890. Although the pottery associated with Period 8 layers was predominantly Civil War in date, diagnostic late seventeenth-century vessels and fabrics could be distinguished (p 209). Sherds of Mottled ware vessels, not dated earlier than 1690, occurred in Tower 4, in the entranceway layers, and in the overlying dumps (Fig 144.233–42). Amongst the other finds a later seventeenth-century date can be assigned to a group of copper alloy pins (Fig 101.44–7), three from Tower 5, and one from Tower 4; some of the window leads with glass (Fig 104.85); and eight hinges from the same con-

Fig 91 Outer Gateway: Period 8 floor F81 in Tower 4, vertical view (Photo P Hough)

text in Tower 4 (Fig 94.24–31) (p 138). The condition of coins of Charles II and William III (p 133, nos 27 and 29) found in later layers suggests deposition not at this period but in the later eighteenth century.

Analysis of the clay pipe evidence (M2:G3) suggested that the gatehouse was left by its inhabitants some time before the new access route was cut, if the latter event can be linked with the deposition of layer 6. The evidence suggested a date around 1700. Clay pipes in layer 6 (Fig 118.21, 22) differed from those associated with the gatehouse reoccupation, and may indicate that the road was cut c 1720.

Period 9: Eighteenth to twentieth centuries

Inner Ward

Within the towers there was no evidence of use later than the Civil War until repointing work in this century, evidence of which was apparent in the West Gatehouse Tower. A few postholes on the north side were recorded, perhaps associated with a rebuilding of the north curtain wall noted in the east part of the north wall. Here, in area W, the wall was seen to rest on a crumbled mortar and stone foundation, and the evidence suggested a modern rebuild on the remains of the medieval wall.

At the east end of the Inner Ward were deep deposits deriving from the clearances of the well in 1842 and 1935 (p 104). The earlier work was clearly more extensive, judging by the quantity of spoil. These layers were noted in area A as layers 1, 2, 3, 4, and 5 (Figs 77, Sections 2 and 4, and 78, Section 3), of which layer 2 represented a turf line formed following the nineteenth-century work. During the second of these clearance processes the well housing was reconstructed sealing the fill of the Period 7 cut F57.

The finds made in these layers overwhelmingly reflect the Civil War occupation, although some, most obviously the coin of Henry III found in A 5, must indicate medieval use. None amongst them could be clearly attributed to Periods 8 and 9 with the exception of the telescope eyepiece and the fob (Fig 103.80 and 81), attesting the presence of day visitors. A coin of George II is thought to be a late eighteenth-century loss (p 133, no 30). A few eighteenth-century clay pipes were found in Period 9 layers, but the majority of the pipes were nineteenth or early twentieth century in date (Fig 119.26, 28–30). The sherds of Victorian pottery found here may be attributed to the nineteenth-century fairs.

Outer Gateway (Fig 89)

The burying of the Period 8 entrance beneath layer 6, and the provision of a new entranceway involving the

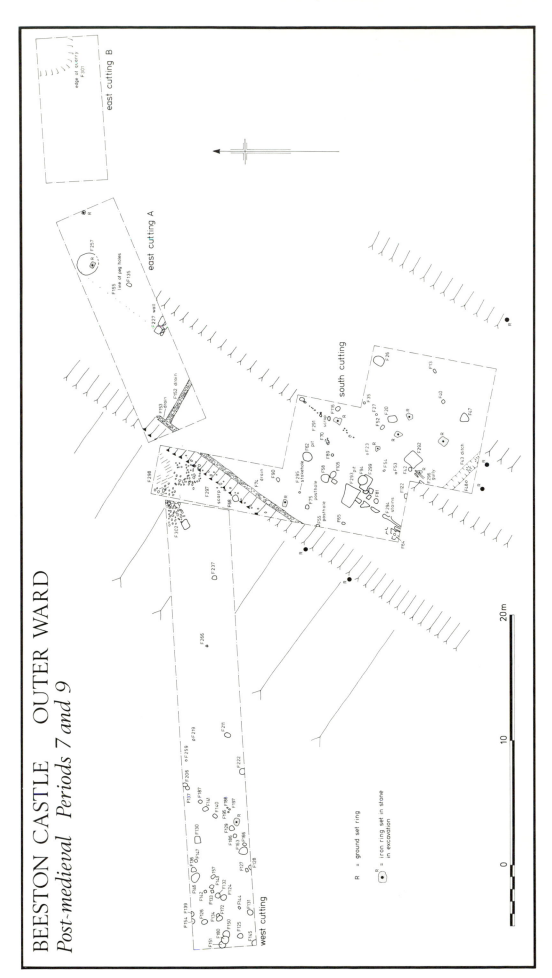

Fig 92 Outer Ward: Periods 7 and 9; scale 1:300

partial demolition of Tower 3, may be associated. As noted above (Period 8), clay pipes in layer 6 may indicate a date of *c* 1720 for the new route (M2:G3). The construction of the new track is likely to have caused the revetting of the standing part of Tower 3, while to the rear of the gateway the new hollow-way cut through to a level below the medieval ground surface.

A possible structure to the rear of Tower 4 can be attributed to the recent period. Above the Period 7 levels represented by layer 34, a succession of dumps brought the ground level up by 0.5m (Fig 19, Section 7). On this surface the remains of a stone wall, F27, running west from the medieval tower were recorded. Too little survived to suggest its function, although the presence of a layer of coal, 11, may indicate that it formed a containing wall for a coal dump, the coal perhaps being used as fuel by coal-burning traction or crane engines involved in the quarrying.

The curtain wall 6m north of Tower 3 appears to be a recent rebuilding. A straight joint was recorded here, with a different mortar used to bond coursed walling little different to that to the south. The joint coincides with foundation trenches, F819 and F688, on both sides of the wall (Fig 18, Section 1) at a change in alignment. On the east side of the wall the medieval offset continues in a straight line north beneath the rebuilding. The extent of the additional walling northward is not clear. It may have stopped at the sharp change of direction just south of Tower 2. The rebuilding may be attributed to nineteenth-century consolidation of the castle fabric, as with the work in the Inner Ward.

Amongst other evidence of recent activity was a group of pits, F412, F416, F422, and F549, filled with modern rubbish, and a pit, F78, located in Tower 4, possibly representing part of a robbing trench for stone from the tower (Fig 19, Section 7). West of Tower 4, a large pit, F23, was recorded filled with layers of sand and rubble (Fig 19, Section 7).

At Tower 7 the upper layers contained modern material, and formed a surface over the Period 7 level.

Period 9 layers and features at the Outer Gateway again produced a large assemblage of pottery, clay pipes, and other finds of Civil War date. Coins of George III and Victoria were found, as well as modern whiteware pottery, a handful of nineteenth-century clay pipes, and a spoon stamped Beeston Castle (Fig 105.98). A walking stick ferrule (Fig 103.82) was found in Tower 7.

Outer Ward (Fig 92)

In West Cutting a group of postholes and possible pits were recorded cut into the subsoils underlying the topsoil (Table M35, M2:E10–11). Of these a line of eight postholes was recorded running parallel to the terracing to the east, and separated from a second group of post and stakeholes by a 4m gap to the west. A tent placement may be located here. Stone spreads, F302, at the east end of the West Cutting, and F297, in the north part of South Cutting, indicated recent hardcore on the pathway.

Period 9 features in South Cutting comprised groups of linear marks of red sand, F294; a stone spread, F291, along the foot of the upper terrace; postholes; stakeholes; and pits (Table M36, M2:E12–13). East Cutting A features included a line of probable tent-peg holes, F155, and a large pit, F257, while in East Cutting B the south-west corner of a large quarry, F301, was excavated (Table M37, M2:E13).

In all the excavated zones iron rings set in large stones were recorded, and others were located in the ground beyond the excavation limits. The rings were aligned with the terraces and a number were placed on the terrace edges.

The various stake and postholes and the iron rings are likely to indicate the position of temporary tent structures, all associated with the nineteenth-century fairs held annually on Beeston crag. The rectilinear stains may indicate the position of stalls, while the pits were presumably dug to dispose of rubbish collected from the fair.

Finds of nineteenth-century pottery and clay pipes were made in all the Outer Ward excavation areas. These were vertically distributed throughout the sandy layers overlying bedrock. Analysis of the soil layers (p 83) suggested that this material was carried down through the loose soils by natural processes, and not as a result of wholesale levelling.

The finds included a number of coins comprising one of George III, three of Victoria, and one each of George V and VI; a large group of nineteenth and twentieth-century clay pipes (Figs 118.24–5; 121.62–6); and modern pottery including a cup and saucer printed with the words 'Beeston Castle Festival' (Fig 145.251).

Table 38 Deposit periods of the pre-Hanoverian coins

Coins	Deposited	No of coins and list no
Short Cross coinage	before c 1247	2 (1–2)
Long Cross coinage	before c 1279	1 (3)
Edward I	before c 1300	1 (4)
Edward I and II (inc. jetton)	c 1325–50	5 (5–8 and 44)
Elizabeth I	seventeenth century/Civil War	2 (9–10)
Jettons	seventeenth century/Civil War	7 (11–16 and 45)
James I	seventeenth century/Civil War	5 (17–21)
Charles I	seventeenth century/Civil War	5 (22–6)
Charles II	later eighteenth century	2 (27–8)
William III	later eighteenth century	1 (29)

7 The finds

The coins
by Marion Archibald

Catalogue

1 John, cut halfpenny, class Vbii, Winchester or Lincoln mint, moneyer Andreu; ref: North (1980, 970); wt 0.68g; c 1205–10. Some wear, could have been deposited at any time until the end of the coinage, 1247, but possibly earlier rather than later within the possible bracket. OG 304, Period 8.

2 Henry III, Short Cross issue, class 7b, London mint, moneyer Giffrei; ref: North (1980, 979); wt 0.30g; c 1217–42. Deposited before 1247. IW, B3, Period 9.

3 Henry III, Long Cross penny, class 5g, London, moneyer Renaud; ref: North (1980, 997); wt 1.36g. This coin was struck in the late 1260s and was certainly lost before 1279. IW N9, Period 5.

4 Edward I, halfpenny, class IIIc, 1280; ref: North (1960, 1045); wt 0.70g. Unworn, probably deposited shortly after issue, say c 1280–1300, but condition of halfpennies can be deceptive so a later deposit cannot be ruled out. IW F3, Period 5.

5 Tiny fragment of edge of Edward I, penny, Class II, 1280, mint name illegible; wt 0.24g. OG 84, Period 7.

6 Edward I, penny, class IVc(?), Canterbury mint, c 1282–3; ref: North (1960, 1025); wt 0.74g. Corroded but apparently not much worn and unclipped, probably deposited c 1300–25 but certainly before c 1350. OG 893, Period 7.

7 Edward I, penny, class IXb (no star), London mint, c 1300; ref: North (1960, 1037); wt 1.30g. Little wear, was probably deposited c 1325–50. OG 84, Period 7.

8 English sterling jetton, official type as coins of class XI, c 1310; ref: Berry type 1 (1974, pl 2 and 4); wt 3.33g. Sterling type with pellets in place of legend both sides. OG 51, Period 7.

9 Elizabeth I, penny, initial mark illegible; wt 0.28g. Worn, could have circulated into the Civil War period. OG 46, Period 8.

10 Elizabeth I, groat, initial mark illegible; wt 1.14g. Very worn, could have circulated into Civil War period. OG 57, Period 9.

11 Nuremberg jetton, poor style; wt 1.45g; diam 24mm; 16th century. Blundered legends, Reichsapfel/three crowns and three lis type. OG 55, Period 7.

12 Nuremberg jetton, Wolfgang Laufer, fl 1612–32; ref: Barnard (1916, 88); wt 1.47g; diam 22mm. Obv: rosette GOTTES SEGEN MACHT REICH, as no 13. Rev: rosette WOLF LAVFER IN NVRNBERG RECH, as no 13. OG 22, Period 8.

13 Nuremberg jetton, Hanns Krauwinckel, fl 1586–1635; ref: this common reverse is not in Barnard (1916); wt 1.45g; diam 22mm. Obv: rosette GOTT.ALLEIN.DIE EER.ESEI Reichsapfel. Rev: rosette HANNS.KRAVWINCKEL.IN.NVR (correct legend punched over erroneous spelling, KRAWINCKEL), three crowns and three lis around rosette. OG 1, Period 9.

14 Nuremberg jetton; wt 0.78g (corroded); diam 21mm. Details as no 13 above except ends at IN (without NVR) on reverse. IW area A, F1, period 7.

15 Nuremberg jetton; wt 1.04g. As no 13 except rev legend ends IN NV (NV over VN). Found on Beeston crag by a visitor.

16 Nuremberg jetton; wt 1.32g; diam 22m. Details as no 14 above. IW area A, F1, Period 7.

17 James I, half-groat, first issue, initial mark, lis 1604; ref: North (1960, 2076); wt 0.48g. Worn, could have circulated into the Civil War period. OG 54, Period 7.

18 James I, penny, second coinage, initial mark, escallop; ref: North (1960, 2106); wt 0.47g; 1606–7. Worn, could have circulated into the Civil War period. OG 353, Period 7.

19 James I, half-groat, second coinage, initial mark, co-ronet; ref: North (1960, 2106); wt 0.48g; 1607–9. Worn, could have circulated into the Civil War period. OG 353, Period 7.

20 James I, farthing, details uncertain; wt 0.26g. IW area A, F1, Period 7.

21 Contemporary forgery of a farthing of James I of rough, unofficial style; wt 0.43. IW EGT 3, Period 7.

22 Charles I, farthing, Richmond type 1624–34, type Ic, initial mark, fish hook; ref: Peck (1964, 163); wt 0.39g IW EGT 3, Period 7.

23 Charles I, farthing, Richmond type 1625–42, Ic initial mark, dagger; ref: Peck (1964, 158); wt 0.63g OG 1, Period 9.

24 Charles I, half-groat, initial mark, eye, 1645; ref: North (1960, 2258); wt 0.83. This coin is hardly worn and was probably deposited shortly after issue. OG Tower 5, GHT 5, Period 9.

25 Charles I, Scottish coinage, third coinage (lozenge above and below XX); ref: Stewart group 1 (1967); wt 0.19g. OW 543, Period 9.

26 Contemporary forgery of Charles I Scottish coinage 20 pence piece, second or third issue; wt 0.56g. The unofficial style of this piece identifies it as a contemporary imitation. It has been bent which may indicate that it was suspected of being a counterfeit. OG 51, Period 7.

27 Charles II, farthing; wt 4.85g. The volume of the left-facing head suggests Charles II, and this coin is typical of the condition of farthings of this reign which survived in circulation into the late eighteenth century. OG 1, Period 9.

28 Charles II, farthing; wt 4.93g. Found on Beeston crag by a visitor.

29 William III, halfpenny; wt 8.39g. Very worn, probably deposited in the later eighteenth century. OG 30, Period 9.

30 George II, halfpenny, 1746–9; wt 8.31g. Very worn, a late eighteenth century loss. IW Q +, Period 9.

31 Very corroded copper coin, almost certainly George III 'Cartwheel' penny, 1797; wt 20.40g. OG 30, Period 9.

32 George III, halfpenny, 1806; wt 8.31. IW Z +, Period 9.

33 George III, halfpenny, 1806; wt 8.62. IW surface find.

34 George III, shilling, 1816; wt 5.17g. Worn, probably a Victorian loss. OW 522, Period 9.

35 Victoria, penny, 1861; wt 8.34g. Found with no 36 and both very worn, probably twentieth-century losses. OW 557, Period 9.

36 Victoria, penny, 1861; wt 8.17g. See no 35. OW 557, Period 9.

37 Victoria, halfpenny, 1862; wt 5.18g. Very worn, a twentieth-century loss. IW W +, Period 9.

38 Victoria, halfpenny, 1862; wt 4.82g. OW 523, Period 9.

39 Victoria, halfpenny, 1875; wt 4.23g. OG 30, Period 9.

40 Victoria, penny. 1885; wt 9.22g. OG 30, Period 9.

41 George V, halfpenny, 1914; wt 4.80g. OW 500, Period 9.

42 George VI, threepence, nickel-brass type, 1941; wt 6.50g. OW 521, Period 9.

43 Elizabeth II, florin, 1955; wt 11.25g. Intrusive in OG 231, Period 7.

Coins from Beeston village

44 Edward I, penny, class IXb, Hull mint, c 1300; ref North (1960, 1037; wt 1.32g. Some wear, unclipped, probably deposited c 1325–50. Find from Beeston village.

45 Nuremberg jetton, very corroded; wt 0.55g; diam 20mm (edges corroded, originally 22mm?). Uncertain legends Reichsapfel ?crowns and lis type. Find from Beeston village.

46 George III, Irish farthing, 1806; wt 4.03g. Find from Beeston village.

Discussion

The earliest coin from the site is a cut-halfpenny of Short Cross type, class Vb, struck c 1205–10 (no 1). This coin is relatively unworn, and although a deposit date at any time before c 1247 must be allowed, it is more likely to have been deposited relatively early within the possible bracket, and could therefore have been lost during the earliest building phase in the 1220s. The other Short Cross coin (no 2) is a later type but again certainly deposited before c 1247 (Table 38).

Only one coin of the Long Cross type was found (no 3) but this need not signify any decline in activity or prosperity on the site as this coinage was of much shorter duration than its predecessor. It is a late coin of the type giving a very narrow deposition bracket of c 1269–79.

There is just one coin (no 4), apparently deposited in the period c 1280–1300, but it is possible that this coin, being a halfpenny, whose currency pattern is less reliable, may be a survivor in unusually good condition and may in reality belong in the same deposit period as the following group. The absence otherwise of coins apparently deposited in the period 1280–1325 is likely to indicate some change in the nature of the activity on the site.

Four coins (nos 5–8) appear to have been deposited between c 1325 and c 1350. These coins are all unclipped and unlikely to have survived in this condition after the reduction on the standard weight of the penny in 1351. The contrast with the previous period seems to indicate renewed coin-using activity on the site at this period.

The complete absence of any later medieval coins either struck or deposited after 1325–50 certainly points to a change in the nature of the occupation of the site.

The numismatic evidence suggests a revival in activities requiring coin in the Stuart period. The Krauwinckel jettons (nos 11–16) have not been narrowly dated and all the jettons could have been around in the Stuart period. The Elizabethan coins (nos 9–10) are all well worn and are likely to have been deposited well into the seventeenth century, probably into the Civil War period. To this same general period belong the common copper farthings of James I and Charles I (nos 17–26). It is not possible to assess the likely duration in circulation of these coins as their corroded condition precludes any estimate of the wear. The James I farthings were demonetised by the Charles issue and so theoretically might have suggested an earlier seventeenth-century period of activity.

There is then another coinless period between c 1650 and the later eighteenth century in which the very worn coppers of the end of the previous century were deposited (nos 27–30). There is thereafter a continuous trickle of coin losses down to the present day (nos 31–43).

The coin list therefore seems to fit the known history of the site – the earliest coinciding with the foundation in the 1220s, lively occupation in the earlier fourteenth century, followed by a long period of apparent lack of activity from the mid-fourteenth century to the Civil War. The context of the sixteenth- and early seventeenth-century coins is in most cases Civil War layers, and the recognition of this group of coins as having been in use in the Civil War is of considerable numismatic interest. The late seventeenth-/early eighteenth-century occupation does not seem to be reflected in the coin evidence, unless the later seventeenth-century coins are regarded as early eighteenth-century losses, a circumstance rendered unlikely by the degree of wear on the coins.

The medieval and post-medieval objects
by Paul Courtney

Introduction

The medieval and post-medieval objects are presented by material and type rather than by stratigraphic group since many of the finds are in residual contexts. Iron objects are catalogued in one section, copper alloy, silver, lead, and lead alloy objects in a second, and bone and ceramic objects in a third. Weaponry, regardless of material, is discussed in a fourth section, and spurs and fragments of armour are the subjects of separate reports (pages 161 and 165 respectively). Catalogue entries are followed by the context number preceded by the excavation location (IW Inner Ward, OW Outer Ward, OG Outer Gateway, ID Inner Ditch). The contexts for the

Inner Ward and the excavations by Laurence Keen at Towers 5 and 7 on the outer curtain are preceded by the area letter. These finds letters have not been altered in the catalogue but the simplifications used in the report text should be noted (p 13). Thus area A amalgamates excavated areas A, B, D, E, L, and R; area H, areas H, G, and Z; area X, areas X and Y; area K, areas M and K; and finally area W, areas F, J, Q, and W. Area N remains unaltered. The few objects deriving from medieval contexts comprised iron objects (Figs 93.1; 97.95; 98.123; 108.16–18), a silver tag-end (Fig 103.84), a lead disc (Fig 104.94), bone objects (Fig 106.1 and 19), and a ceramic marble and counter (Fig 107.25 and 28). There were equally few objects in later layers which were recognisably of medieval date. These included iron (Figs 93.3; 98.123) and copper alloy objects (Figs 100.2, 3, 15, 17–27; 101.38 and 49). The fact that the will of 1627–8 refers to 'two poore kinsmen' living in the castle suggests that some seventeenth-century finds could be earlier than the Civil War, although it is uncertain which part of the castle was occupied (p 98). Some items from later post-medieval contexts may be related to the reoccupation of the Outer Gateway after the Civil War, among them the pins (Fig 101.44–7) and the window leads with glass (Fig 104.85), or to nineteenth-century activity on the hill (Figs 95.51; 103.80–2; 105.98). However, the overall impression is that the Civil War period, 1643–5, accounts not only for the large number of finds found in Period 7 contexts but also for a large proportion of the small finds found in later layers. It is significant that those items which can be dated, for example the spurs, are overwhelmingly of Civil War date, as too are the weapons (p 156), which are perhaps the easiest category of artefact to assign to the Civil War occupation, even when they derive from residual contexts.

Of the other categories of finds, five buckles can certainly be ascribed to the Civil War period (Figs 97.76–9; 100.1). The latter is gilt and possibly from the dress of an officer. However, many of the buckles in later contexts in the Outer Gateway could be residual, and most of the Inner Ward collection probably also dates to the Civil War. It is extremely difficult to distinguish clothing and harness buckles. As noted above, the spurs are a definite Civil War group and the many stirrups found could also be of Civil War date.

Outer Gateway contexts of Civil War date produced six knives with bolsters (Fig 93.2, 4–7, 9), which were probably the main eating implements of both the ordinary soldiers and the officers. A razor or penknife was also recovered from the Inner Ditch Civil War horizon (Hough 1978, 21, fig 1.5) as well as two knives with bolsters, one with silver inlay (ibid, fig 1.6–7). The Inner Ditch produced a crude lead spoon, cut from sheet, in a Civil War context (ibid, no 1). The pewter porringer (Fig 105.99) from the Inner Ward probably dates to the Civil War period on typological grounds. As the name suggests it was probably used for eating porridge rather than as a bleeding bowl, as is sometimes suggested. The hooks and eye (Fig 97.97 and 98) are possibly associated with the seventeenth-century clothing. Finally the spatula (Fig 95.43) is likely to represent an object in use in the Civil War.

Numbers of eighteenth- and nineteenth-century artefacts were also recovered from the excavations,

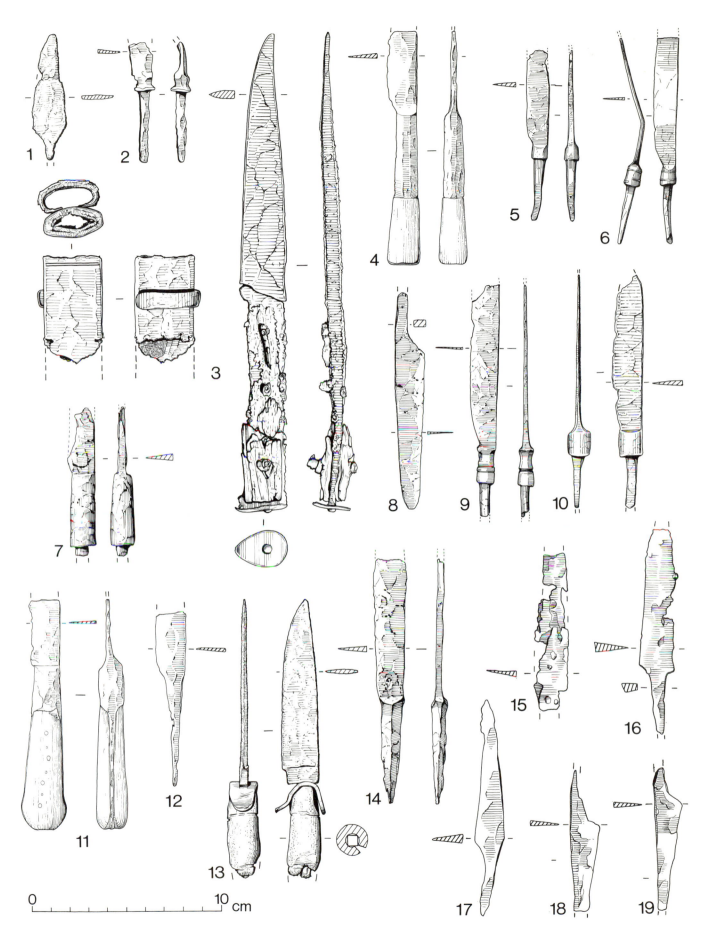

Fig 93 Medieval and post-medieval iron objects: knives and shears; scale 1:2

perhaps losses during the stone quarrying which occurred on the hill in the eighteenth and nineteenth centuries. However, the rise of the Romantic Movement in the late eighteenth century, and the consequent arrival of middle-class visitors in search of the picturesque, are a more likely explanation for many of the lost objects. In the nineteenth century visitors were also attracted by the annual fair.

Catalogue

Iron objects

Knives and shears (Fig 93)

The knives and shears come mainly from contexts associated with the Civil War occupation, or appear to derive from them. One knife (Fig 93.1) came from a medieval context, although both no 3 and probably no 15 are likely to be medieval and therefore residual. The knives have either whittle or scale tangs, most of them with a bolster between blade and tang. The bolster was an innovation in hafting which was introduced into knife manufacture during the sixteenth century (Hayward 1957, 4), and different forms, varying in length and shape, became fashionable. The range of bolster shapes among the Beeston Castle knives (Fig 93.2, 4–7, 9–11) is broad and is similar to that on knives from Civil War deposits at sites such as Basing House, Hants (Moorhouse and Goodall 1971, 36–8, fig 17.1–5, 8–11), and Sandal Castle, W Yorks (I Goodall 1983, 242, fig 6.73–84). The moulded form of the bolster on no 9 is unusual for its date: such shaping was more common in the late seventeenth and early eighteenth centuries (Hayward 1957, 15–16, pl IX–XII, XVI, XVII). The decorative copper alloy bands on the bolster of no 6 are unusual: silver encrustation, as on a knife from the Inner Ditch Civil War horizon (Hough 1978, 21, fig 1.6), was more usual though never common. The bolster sometimes developed into a solid iron handle (Moorhouse and Goodall 1971, 36, fig 17.6, 7) and no 14 may be of this type. Knives 1, 3, 12, and 15–17 lack bolsters and have either whittle or scale tangs; of these no 1 is medieval and nos 3 and 15 might be. Nos 18 and 19, and perhaps 8, are shears blades. See also the bone handles (Fig 106.2–10).

1   Whittle-tang knife. OG 617, Period 4.

2   Whittle-tang knife with bolster. OG 54, Period 7.

3   Knife with copper alloy end cap on scale tang which retains remains of wooden scales attached by four iron rivets. A scabbard mount was found with the knife. It has an attachment loop welded to the back and a mineralised textile lining. This knife and scabbard mount are probably residual finds of fourteenth- or fifteenth-century date (Cowgill *et al* 1987, 26–32). OG 891, Period 7.

4   Broken knife with long bolster of hexagonal section and short bone handle mounted on a whittle tang. Early to mid-seventeenth-century type (Moorhouse

and Goodall 1971, 36–8, fig 17.4). OG 51, Period 7.

5   Broken knife with whittle tang and bolster of circular cross-section. OG 51, Period 7.

6   Broken knife with whittle tang. Bolster of circular cross-section inlaid with two decorative copper alloy bands. OG 51, Period 7.

7   Broken knife with oval-sectioned bolster and broken whittle tang. OG 51, Period 7.

8   ?Shears blade. OG 51, Period 7.

9   Knife with bolster and broken whittle tang. OG 51, Period 7.

10 Whittle-tang knife with bolster. OG 6, Period 8.

11 Broken knife with scale tang and bone handle held by iron rivets. The bolster, of oval cross-section, showed traces of silvering or tinning on the X-ray. OG 22, Period 8.

12 Broken knife with whittle tang. OG 74, Period 8.

13 Whittle-tang knife with broken bone handle and copper alloy hilt guard. The bone handle has two crudely cut lines around its circumference. OG 801, Period 9.

14 Knife, perhaps with incomplete solid iron handle. OG 1, Period 9.

15 Knife blade with broken scale tang and one iron rivet. IW N +, Period 9.

16 and 17   Whittle-tang knives. IW H 4, Period 7.

18 and 19   Shears blades, broken. IW E 6, Period 7.

Chains (Fig 94)

20 Two S-shaped links with central collars. OG 51, Period 7.

21 Hook, S-shaped link, and circular link. OG 74, Period 8.

22 Elongated figure eight-shaped link. OG 6, Period 8.

Hinges and straps (Fig 94)

The hinge and strap fragments, although almost without exception from Periods 8 and 9, include many which must come from the decay or demolition of earlier features. The hinges which retain their means of support include no 28 which has a looped hanging eye which fitted over a hinge pivot; and nos 23, 31, 33–4, and 37–40, which are pinned hinges with integral pins which are self-supporting. The shape of the hinges and strap fragments varies. The long straps of nos 23, 28, and 31–6 could be either medieval or post-medieval (Holden 1963, 169, fig 36.9; Moorhouse and Goodall

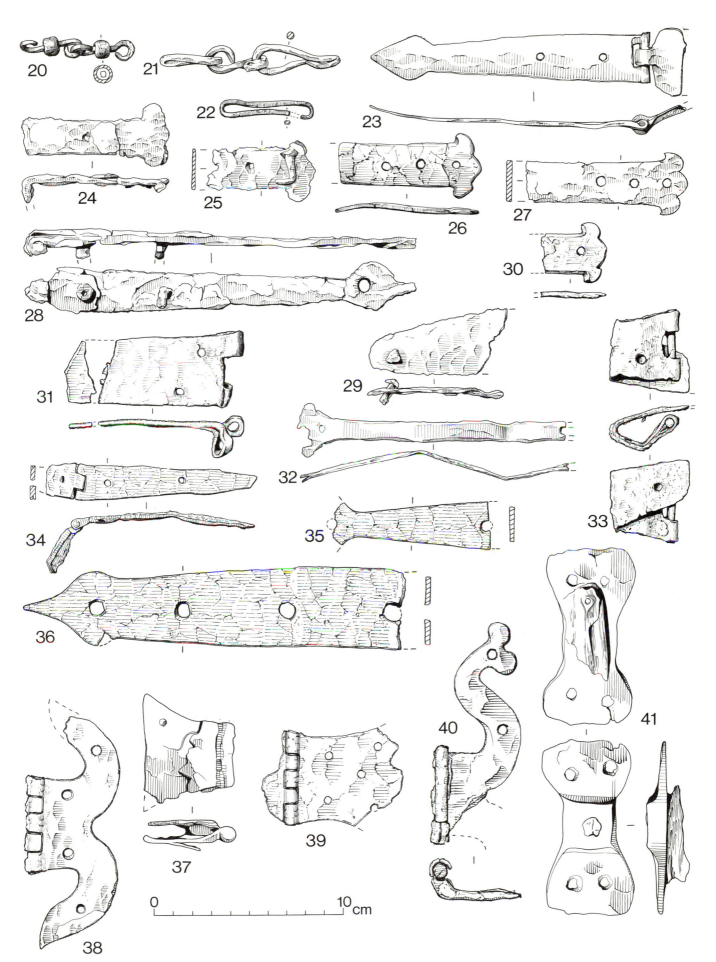

Fig 94 Post-medieval iron objects: chains and hinges; scale 1:2

1971, 41, fig 19.43, 44; Goodall 1976a, 26, fig 13.24; Goodall 1983, 246, fig 7.112, 113) but the trifid form of nos 24–7 and 30, the butterfly shape of nos 37 and 39, and the cockshead shape of nos 38 and 40 are all post-medieval. The trifid shape recalls the shape of some late seventeenth- and eighteenth-century spoon handles (Snodin 1974, 29–31), suggesting that the straps may be contemporary with their contexts, but the butterfly and cockshead forms could be of Civil War or later date (Moorhouse and Goodall 1971, 41, 43, figs 18.40, 41; 19.48; Goodall 1978, 143, fig 30.5; Goodall 1976a, 26, fig 14.28, 29).

23 Pinned hinge with one complete and one broken strap. OG 304, Period 8.

24–27 Strap fragments with trifid terminals. OG 22, Period 8.

The above four hinges are virtually identical except that no 24 is slightly smaller. All four come from the same layer as do the four following.

28 Strap hinge with shaped terminal and looped eye. OG 22, Period 8.

29 Fragment of tapering strap hinge. OG 22, Period 8.

30 Strap fragment with trifid terminal. OG 22, Period 8.

31 Broken strap from pinned hinge. OG 22, Period 8.

32 Hinge strap with shaped terminal. OG 46, Period 8.

33 Distorted single leaf from pinned hinge. OG 40, Period 9.

34 Pinned hinge, both straps broken. OW 543, Period 9.

35 Strap fragment with broken terminal. OW 543, Period 9.

36 Strap fragment with shaped terminal. OW 523, Period 9.

37 Pinned butterfly hinge. IW E 6, Period 7.

38 Single leaf from pinned cockshead hinge. Non-ferrous coating visible. IW W +, Period 9.

39 Single leaf from pinned hinge, probably of butterfly form. Non-ferrous coating visible. IW W +, Period 9.

40 Single leaf from pinned cockshead hinge. IW G/E 4, Period 9.

41 Plate with mineralised wood surviving on back. IW SET 4, Period 7.

Tools and domestic items (Fig 95)

42 Broken looped handle from scissors. OG 353, Period 7.

43 Double-bladed spatula. OG 51, Period 7.

44 Spud with broken tang. OG 51, Period 7.

45 Sickle blade. Tower 5, OG SGT 7, Period 8.

46 Socketed hoe. OG 60, Period 7.

47 Claw hammerhead with side straps and fragment of wooden handle in eye. OG 30, Period 9.

48 Awl. OG 5, Period 9.

49 Incomplete object. OG 1, Period 9.

50 Curved, double-bladed spatula. OG 67, Period 9.

51 Iron tip with two rivets for attachment to tip of a wooden post. It may be associated with the nineteenth-century fair in the Outer Ward. OW 521, Period 9.

52 Awl. OW 445, Period 9.

53 Object of square cross-section developing from a socket. OW 524, Period 9.

54 Tool with whittle tang, perhaps a file with all trace of its teeth lost, or an incompletely forged knife. IW W +, Period 9.

55 Reamer or pick. IW H 4, Period 7.

56 Axe. IW N 2, Period 9.

Building fittings (Fig 96)

57 Broken piece of hinged candlestick stem. Compare with no 61. OG 60, Period 7.

58 Wall anchor with perforated head. OG 30, Period 9.

59 Wall anchor with perforated head set at an angle to the tang. OG unstratified.

60 Window bar fragment. OG 41, Period 9.

61 U-shaped, twisted arm from a combined rush and candle holder. The socket held a candle, whereas the clip above the hinge originally formed a pair with a second clip and held the rushlight. Seventeenth- and eighteenth-century examples took a variety of shapes (Lindsay 1964, 44–5, figs 229, 234, 238–42). OG 31, Period 9.

62 Door bolt with holes for handle and for pivot. IW EGT 3, Period 7.

Locks and keys (Fig 96)

63 U-shaped padlock bolt, leaf springs lost. OG 51, Period 7.

64 Lock with decorative lock plate with keyhole and hole for staple of hasp; cased mechanism attached to rear. The toothed bolt of the mechanism passes

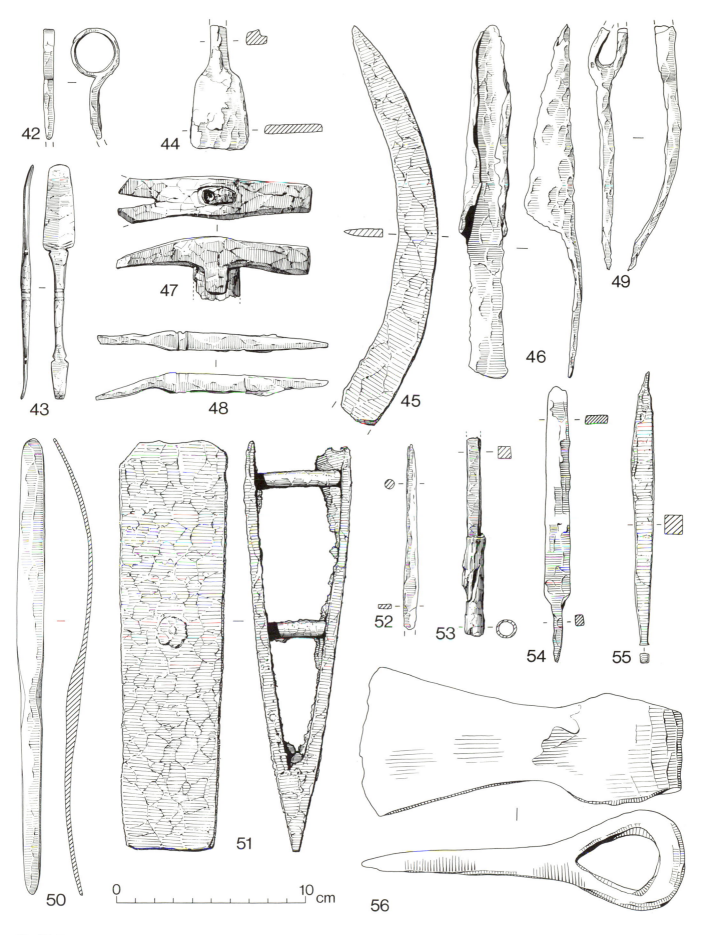

Fig 95 Post-medieval iron objects: tools; scale 1:2

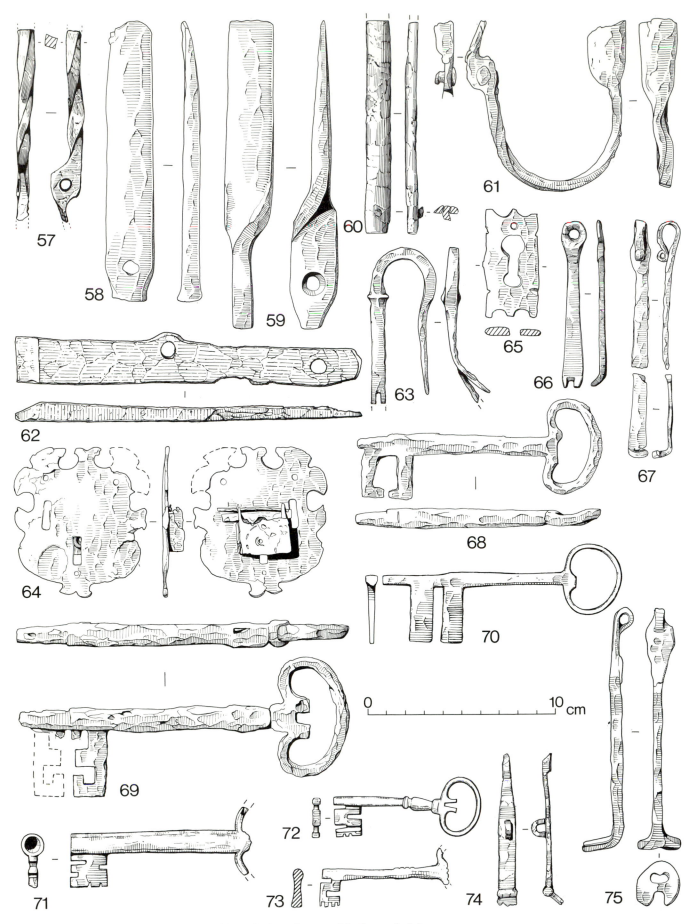

Fig 96 Post-medieval iron objects: building fittings, keys and locks; scale 1:2

through the case and is held by a back spring, carried on its top edge, to hold it securely in both the locked and unlocked positions. The lock mechanism has a pair of collars surrounding the keyhole. Non-ferrous coating. OG 353, Period 7.

65 Keyhole plate. OG 353, Period 7.

66 Barrel padlock key with looped terminal. OG 166, Period 7.

67 Barrel padlock key with hooked terminal. OG 103, Period 7.

68 Key with solid stem and symmetrical bit capable of opening a lock from both sides. OG 22, Period 8.

69 Key with solid stem and broken symmetrical bit. Non-ferrous coating. OW 10, Period 9.

70 Key with solid stem and symmetrical bit. Tower 1, unstratified.

71 Key with broken bow, hollow stem and asymmetrical bit. OG, Tower 5, GHT 5, Period 9.

72 Key with solid, moulded stem and asymmetrical bit. IW G/E 4, Period 9.

73 Key with broken bow, solid stem, and asymmetrical bit. IW EGT 2, Period 9.

74 Stapled hasp from lock, the broken strap attached by a pinned hinge. The hasp has a moulded tip which acted as a fingerhold. Non-ferrous coating. IW D 5, Period 7.

75 Barrel padlock key with hooked terminal. IW D 5, Period 7.

Buckles and furniture fittings (Fig 97)

The buckles, which may be either personal or from harness, are similar in their range of shapes to those from Sandal Castle, W Yorks (I Goodall 1983, 248, fig 9.178–99). The commonest shape is rectangular (nos 76, 77, 93, and 94), but others are variously double-looped (nos 85, 86, and 92), trapezoidal (no 88), and D-shaped (nos 91 and 95). Most are plain but the decoration on no 94 is exceptional for an iron buckle. No 87 is a buckle plate, similar to those still attached to nos 86 and 95.

Nos 78–84 and 89 are variously complete and incomplete fittings similar in overall form and detail and probably from small chests. The bent round sheet-iron plates generally have a single rivet through each side, and they wrap round rectangular frames. The plates retain mineralised wood on their inner faces, and mineralised textiles on one external surface. The rectangular frames are not buckles since none has a pin, but they may have served to guide and hold leather straps around chests. No 90 is a handle, most probably from a door or drawer, as are a pair from Ardingly, Sussex (Goodall 1976b, 60–1, fig 9a.30, 31). Similar handles, but usually of copper alloy, such as one from

Southampton (Harvey 1975, 265, fig 245.1864), also formed part of chafing dishes (Lewis 1973).

76 Rectangular buckle with pin and revolving sheet-iron cylinder. OG 103, Period 7.

77 Square buckle frame with revolving sheet-iron cylinder, pin lost. OG 54, Period 7.

78 Plate with rectangular frame. OG 54, Period 7.

79 Pair of plates, each with rectangular frames. Fortuitously corroded together. OG 54, Period 7.

80 Plate with two nail holes and rectangular frame. OG 22, Period 8.

81 Plate with rectangular frame out of place within it. OG 66, Period 8.

82 and 83 Plates with rectangular frames, one broken. Mineralised wooden cores and mineralised textile on one exterior surface of each plate. OG 22, Period 8.

84 Plate, rectangular frame lost. Mineralised wood core; mineralised textile on one exterior face. OG 3, Period 9.

Also (not illustrated) two plates identical to nos 82–4. OG 22, Period 8. All have mineralised wood remains on the inside and mineralised textile on the upper surface of their exteriors. Elisabeth Crowfoot reports on the textile remains (Crowfoot 1983):
82 Area 50 × 44mm, Z/Z, tabby weave, thread count 13/12–13 on 10mm; 83 Area 41 × 32mm, Z/Z, fine tabby, even weave, count 16/16; 84 Z/Z, tabby, count 15–16/14–15. In all these the spin is very loose. Of the unillustrated fragments: 1 Area 47 × 32mm, Z/?, open tabby weave, count *c* 14–15/14 per 10mm, corroded; 2 Area 55 × 28mm, Z/Z, appearance suggests wool, tabby, close, even, count 10–12/10 per 10mm. The latter is a good garment weight woollen.

85 Irregularly-shaped double-looped buckle with broken pin and rotating sheet-iron cylinder. OG 6, Period 8.

86 Double-looped buckle with buckle plate and incomplete distorted pin. OG 6, Period 8.

87 Buckle plate. OG 74, Period 8.

88 Trapezoid buckle frame with fragment of pin loop. OG 245, Period 8.

89 Broken plate with mineralised wood on both sides. Elisabeth Crowfoot reports on mineralised textile on the plate (Crowfoot 1983): lying in two folds, only 6 × 5mm clear, Z/Z, fine tabby, estimated count *c* 22/18 on 5mm. OG 806, Period 9.

90 Door or drawer handle with looped staple for attachment (cf Harvey 1975, fig 245.1864). OG 57, Period 9.

91 D-shaped buckle frame. OG 41, Period 9.

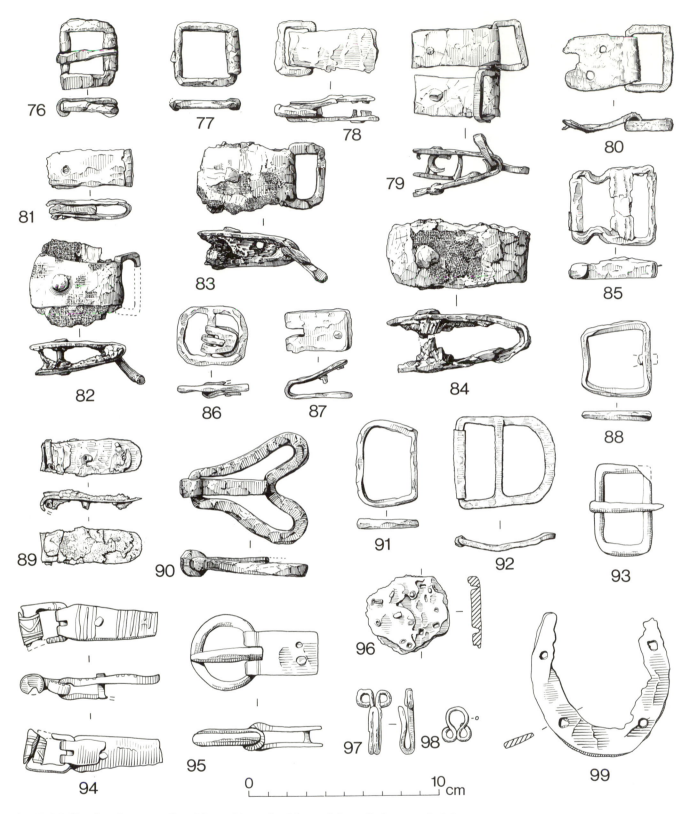

Fig 97 Medieval and post-medieval iron objects: buckles and dress fittings; scale 1:2

92 Double-looped buckle with revolving sheet-iron cylinder, pin lost. OG 806, Period 9.

93 Rectangular buckle with pin. IW SWT 3, Period 7.

94 Buckle with broken frame with sheet-iron cylinder
   and long, incomplete buckle plate. The plate and
   cylinder are inlaid with silver wire. IW D 3, Period 9.

95 Buckle with pin and attachment plate. IW SWT 8,
   Period 5.

Dress fittings (Fig 97)

Hooks and eyes similar to nos 96–8 are still used today
for fastening clothing. In the early post-medieval period
they were used for fastening bodices and doublets as

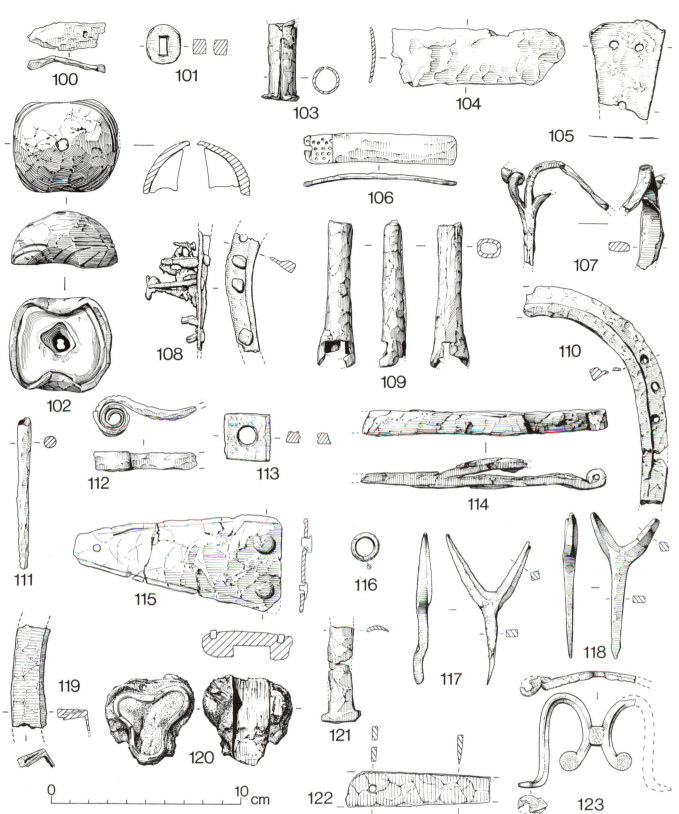

Fig 98 Medieval and post-medieval iron objects: miscellaneous; scale 1:2

well as holding up breeches (Cunnington and Cunnington 1973, 51–2 and 152: Bradfield 1968, 15). The large size of the Beeston examples suggests that they were used for hanging breeches, a fashion of the sixteenth and seventeenth centuries. From around the beginning of the eighteenth century breeches merely hung from the waist (Cunnington and Cunnington 1964, 66–9). Smaller-sized hooks were used for fastening a possible

Civil War oxhide 'buffcoat', as worn by musketeers, which is preserved in Worcestershire County Museum (Bullard 1967).

96 Fragment of mineralised shoe leather set with studs. OG 304, Period 8.

97 Fastening hook. OW 153, Period 9.

Also four other examples, not illustrated, of similar size: OG 46 (two), OG 66 (with non-ferrous plating), and OG 22, all Period 8.

98 Eye, used with fastening hook similar to no 97. OG Tower 5, GHT 5, Period 9.

99 Boot heel. IW SET 4, Period 7.

Miscellaneous (Fig 98)

100 Piece of plate iron. OG 89, Period 7.

101 Hilt plate from a whittle-tang knife. OG 803, Period 7.

102 Hemispherical weight comprising a lead core and an iron shell with decorative grooves. Traces of brazing occur on the exterior surface but large amounts around the underside edge suggests that it was brazed to its opposite side. Two indentations indicate it had been compressed with a pair of pincers. It has a central perforation which widens out towards the centre. The object weighs 298g, too heavy for a sword pommel or pistol butt. Its function remains uncertain. OG 51, Period 7.

103 Tubular sheet-iron spout. OG 51, Period 7.

104 Slightly curved iron plate. OG 51, Period 7.

105 Iron plate with three holes. OG 51, Period 7.

106 Strip with indented decoration at one end. OG 54, Period 7.

107 ?Distorted pricket candlestick. OG 311, Period 7.

108 Curved binding strap fragment with thickened inner edge, the flange pierced by three nails; other nail fragments are attached by corrosion. Similar to no 110. OG 803, Period 7.

109 Rolled sheet-iron spout, brazed along the join. OG 92, Period 7.

110 Curved binding strap fragment with thickened inner edge, the flange perforated. Similar binding straps are common on Civil War sites (see Goodall 1983, 248, fig 8.165–70 and references). OG 60, Period 7.

111 Iron rod. OG 49, Period 7.

112 Rolled strip. OG 46, Period 8.

113 Square washer with screw through to central hole. OG 25, Period 8.

114 Candlestick, pricket and stem broken. OG 22, Period 8.

115 Triangular riveted iron plate with decorative groove on outer face. OG 12, Period 8.

116 Buckle frame. OG 66, Period 8.

117 and 118 Tanged objects with V-shaped heads, seemingly too small to be pitchforks, but perhaps musket rests. OG 304 and 4, Period 8.

119 Vessel rim. OG 806, Period 9.

120 Trefoil-shaped iron band, perhaps plated, attached to block of mineralised ?oak. OG 7, Period 9.

121 Iron strip with terminal. OG 24, Period 9.

122 Scale-tang knife, blade and tang broken. OW 543, Period 9.

123 Handle, possibly from a box or chest. Similar objects from Eynsford Castle, Kent and Writtle, Essex are medieval in date; one from Sandal Castle, W Yorks, is from a context of 1485–*c*1600 (Rigold 1971, 147, fig 9.20; Rahtz 1969, 85, fig 47.57; I Goodall 1983, fig 8.161). IW H 3, Period 5.

Horse furniture (Fig 99)

Stirrups are the most numerous items of horse furniture apart from the spurs (p 165), and nos 124–8 are all of the same type with rectangular loops for the stirrup leather, curved sides, and, but for no 124, flattened and expanded treads. No 129 is the mouthpiece of a bridle bit. Nos 130 and 131 are horseshoes with an inner keyhole shape which was introduced in the seventeenth century and remained popular in the eighteenth century. They may be compared with contemporary examples from Sandal Castle, Yorks (I Goodall 1983, 251, figs 9.220, 10.221–5) and with a wider range from Williamsburg, Virginia (Chappell 1973, 102–4, figs 1, 2, 4).

124 Incomplete stirrup with rectangular loop for stirrup leather. OW 199, Period 9.

125 Part of stirrup with expanded tread. OW 10, Period 9.

126 Complete iron stirrup with expanded tread and rectangular loop for stirrup leather. OG 304, Period 8.

127 Expanded, slightly arched tread from stirrup. OG 7, Period 9.

128 Stirrup with rectangular loop for stirrup-leather and flat tread. IW EGT 2, Period 9.

129 Mouthpiece from bridle bit. IW EGT 2, Period 9.

130 and 131 Horseshoes with rectangular nail holes and inner keyhole shape. IW SET 4, Period 7.

Copper alloy objects

Buckles (Fig 100; see also iron buckles Fig 97.76–7, 85–8, 91–5)

1 Alison Goodall writes: gilt buckle with ornate cast decoration on the loops consisting of rosettes and husks. An almost identical buckle was found at Humberstone, Leicester (Rahtz 1959, 19, fig 13.3); this

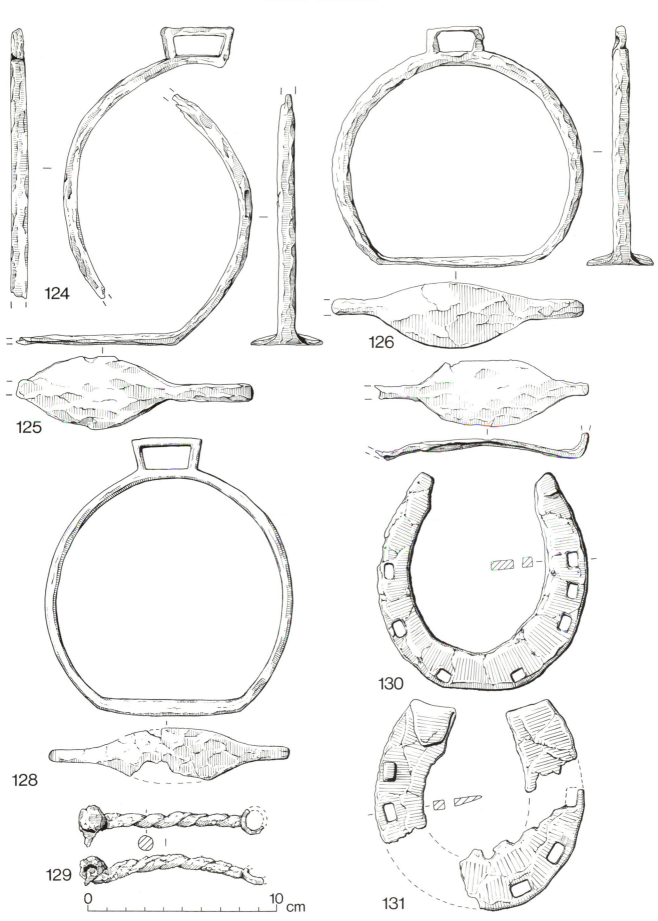

124

125

126

128

129

130

131

0   10 cm

Fig 99 Post-medieval iron objects: horse furniture; scale 1:2

is so similar as to suggest that both buckles came from the same manufacturer, if not the same mould, and dates from the sixteenth to seventeenth century. Another example, from Baconsthorpe, Norfolk, is similar but not identical, and a buckle from Exeter (Goodall 1984, 339, fig 190.M81) of late sixteenth- to seventeenth-century date, is also of similar type. OG 51, Period 7.

2 Buckle and pin, minus plate. The front of the buckle frame is heavily moulded and of thirteenth-century type (Fingerlin 1971, 218, and kat nos 211, 231, 535, and 553). OG 166, Period 7.

3 Buckle plate with traced decoration of correct size and type to have been attached to no 2 above. OG 103, Period 7.

4 Blanche Ellis writes: spur buckle. This is a common type with the sides of its frame extended into decorative curls. Similar buckles can be seen on seventeenth-century spurs in many museums in England and western Europe, including an example in the Royal Armouries (VI-427). OG 101, Period 7.

5 Part of tinned double-looped buckle (broken). Central bar (lost) was made separately. Sixteenth- or seventeenth-century. OG 66, Period 8.

6 Lightweight double-looped buckle with separately made central bar (lost). OG 169, Period 9.

7 Double-looped buckle. A find from Beeston village.

8 Single-looped buckle. IW E –, Period 9.

9 Buckle plate or strap end with two copper alloy rivets and three other rivet-holes. Decorated with rows of punched triangles. Used with a buckle which did not have a pin, or with a ring or strap distributor, since there is no slot or hole in the folded end of the plate. IW D 3, Period 9.

10 Buckle plate with two copper alloy rivets and incised zig-zag decoration. IW E 7, Period 7.

11 Broken buckle loop. IW D 3, Period 9.

12 Buckle, incomplete. Compare with two buckles from Basing House, Hants, destroyed in 1645 (Moorhouse 1971, fig 25.169–70). A closer parallel came from Sandal Castle, W Yorks, in a medieval context but almost certainly of post-medieval date (A Goodall 1983, fig 1.11-14). IW N 1, Period 9.

13 Gilded buckle with pin missing. Integral plate with two rivet-holes and a third hole for the pin. The buckle is of medieval type. IW D 5, Period 7.

14 Strap end. IW D +, Period 9.

Bindings (Fig 100)

The small strap or belt ornaments are common medie-val finds and all the Beeston forms are widely paralleled (Goodall 1981, 67–8; Fingerlin 1971, 375, 377–8; Ward Perkins 1940, 195–8). However, the rosette type, at least, continued into the sixteenth century as the finds at Whitefriars in Coventry show (Woodfield 1981, nos 73–83). Similar fittings are also common on sixteenth-century armour in use as strap studs, and rosettes have been recovered from the Armada wreck *Trinidad Valençera* (Flanagan 1988, fig 10.6–9).

15 Fleur-de-lis strap or belt ornament (cf no 27 which may be from same mould). OG 54, Period 7.

16 Fitting of curved cross-section with large rivet or nail hole. OG 166, Period 7.

17 Rosette-shaped strap or belt ornament. OG 51, Period 7.

18 Rosette-shaped strap or belt ornament. OG 92, Period 7.

19 Fragment of rosette-shaped strap or belt ornament. OG 89, Period 7.

20 Strap or belt ornament with remains of two rivets. OG 54, Period 7.

21–26 Five embossed belt or strap ornaments with a rivet *in situ*, plus a further loose rivet. These fittings probably come from the same belt. OG 803, Period 7.

27 Fleur-de-lis strap or belt ornament (cf no 15). OG 28, Period 8.

28–30 Embossed circular fittings or flattened rosettes. OG 801 (two) and 806, Period 9.

31 Decorative fitting with two attachment spikes, one broken and the other bent, cast as part of the object. The size of the spikes suggests it was attached to a wooden, rather than leather, object. A similar fitting was found at Nonsuch Palace (Goodall forthcoming) in a garderobe deposit dated *c* 1665–82/3. OG 238, Period 9.

Rings (Fig 101)

32–36 Rings. All are from the Outer Gateway: no 32 from OG 51, Period 7; nos 33 and 34 from OG 22, Period 8; nos 35 and 36 from OG 5 and OG 1, Period 9.

37 Gilt ring, cast with evidence of filing. IW SWT 4, Period 7.

Book fittings (Fig 101)

38 Book-clasp decorated with concentric lines, traced zig-zag lines, and what appear to be punched roses, acorns, and tiny bosses. It is paralleled in form and style of decoration by a find from Exeter in an undated context (Goodall 1984, fig 191.M143). Less exact parallels are probably of late medieval or early

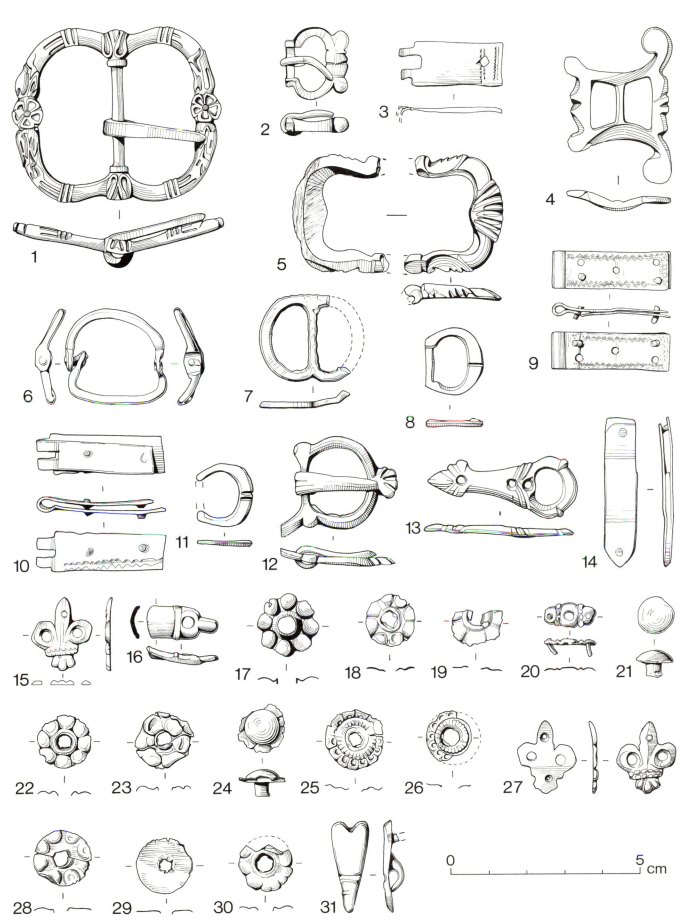

Fig 100 Medieval and post-medieval copper alloy objects: buckles and bindings; scale 1:1

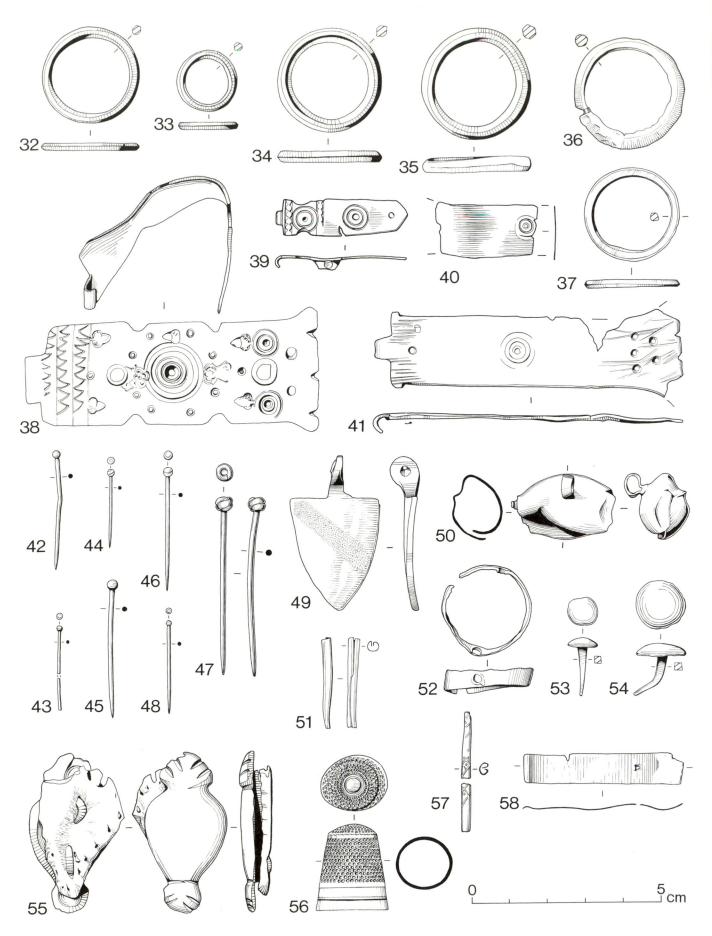

Fig 101 Medieval and post-medieval copper alloy objects: rings, book fittings, pins and miscellaneous; scale 1:1

modern date (see Moorhouse 1971, no 162 and Harvey 1975, fig 245.188). OG 32, Period 9.

39 Book-clasp. IW EGT 2, Period 9.

40 Fragment of book-clasp. IW D 3, Period 9.

41 Book-clasp. IW EGT 3, Period 7.

Pins (Fig 101)

42 Complete pin with partially worked wound wire head (Caple and Warren 1982, type C). OG 54, Period 7.

43 Fragments of pin (ibid, type B). OG SGT 7, Period 8.

44 Complete pin with partially-reworked wound wire head (ibid, type B). OG Tower 5 SGT 9, Period 8.

45 Complete pin with wound wire head completely reworked to hide coils (ibid, type C). A seam exists down the pin shaft resulting from the drawing of the wire. OG Tower 5 SGT 6, Period 8.

46 Complete pin with partially wound wire head (ibid, type C). OG Tower 5 SGT 9, Period 8.

47 Large pin with a head of spiral-coiled wire and partially worked wire (ibid, type B). Both the shaft and head show evidence of continuous lateral seam indicating the wire was made from a ribbon drawn into a circular form. OG 22, Period 8.

Nos 44–7 are probably associated with the late seventeenth-early eighteenth-century occupation at the gatehouse.

48 Pin with partially reworked wound wire head (ibid, type C). IW N 3, Period 9.

Miscellaneous (Figs 101–3)

49 Heraldic pendant from horse harness of common medieval type. A dark blue (heraldic azure) enamel setting forms a bend sinister. It is uncertain if the two fields were painted (see Ward Perkins 1940, 118–22 for a range of parallels) or gilded. OG 273, Period 9.

50 Bell of sheet metal made in two halves brazed together, with separately made suspension loop. OG 89, Period 7.

51 Lace tag-end. OG 54, Period 7.

52 Binding from circular shaft with two rivet-holes. OG 54, Period 7.

53 Stud with slightly domed head. OG 92, Period 7.

54 Stud with turned down domed head. OG 110, Period 8.

55 Harness mount attached by two bent tangs to fragment of leather with stitch holes (see Noel Hume 1970, fig 76.4, for an eighteenth-century example; see also no 67 in this section). OG Tower 5 SGT 9, Period 8.

56 Thimble, cast in one piece. Post-medieval. OG 22, Period 8.

57 Two tag-ends of folded sheet, one with stamped decoration of cross-hatching with central bosses. OG 23, Period 9.

58 Length of copper alloy strip with a single hole cut with a square sectioned punch. OW 501, Period 9.

59 Button with soldered loop. The upper surface is silver-plated and the stamped underside reads AT?D. The piece is nineteenth-century in date. Elisabeth Crowfoot reports on the attached textile: threads broken off, area 10 × 8mm, longest thread 10mm, coarse wool, Z-spun, mid-brown, no weave remaining, but scrap of ?hide attached. Fibre (identification by H M Appleyard FTI): wool, fine to medium, with medullation in some of the coarsest fibres; no dye detected (examination by Penelope Walton). Perhaps torn from a hide garment or glove with wool lining (Crowfoot 1983). OW 522, Period 9.

60 Decorated button cast with shank in one piece, and the hole drilled. Because of corrosion, it is difficult to tell how the decoration was applied. The button has an attached wire link and is probably part of a cufflink. Compare hexagonal-shaped cufflinks from an eighteenth-century context in Portsmouth (Fox and Barton 1986, fig 150.12). The decoration suggests an eighteenth or early nineteenth-century date. OW 161, Period 9.

61–64 Four bindings from wooden shaft with copper alloy rivets. Mineralised wood remains on interior. IW area A, F 1, Period 7.

65 Personal seal with broken attachment loop. The emblem is in the form of a rampant lion. This form of seal had a long period of currency. It is possible that the device was not specific to a particular person or family. IW WGT 3, Period 9.

66 Hollow button made of two cast pieces brazed together, with a loop soldered on. The two holes in the back are to allow gases to escape during bronzing. Seventeenth- or early eighteenth-century (Noel Hume 1970, 90). IW area H, Period 9.

67 Part of cast bridle boss, one attachment hole surviving (cf Goodall 1984, fig 192.M148 and Noel Hume 1970, fig 76.1–2, both in seventeenth-century contexts). IW Q 1, Period 9.

68 Mount for a harness pendant. The pendant would have hung from a pin, possibly of iron, passing through the hinge. IW G/E 4, Period 9.

69 Hook for attachment to a belt. IW area A, F 1, Period 7.

70 Gilded hook, with swivel. IW E 1, Period 9.

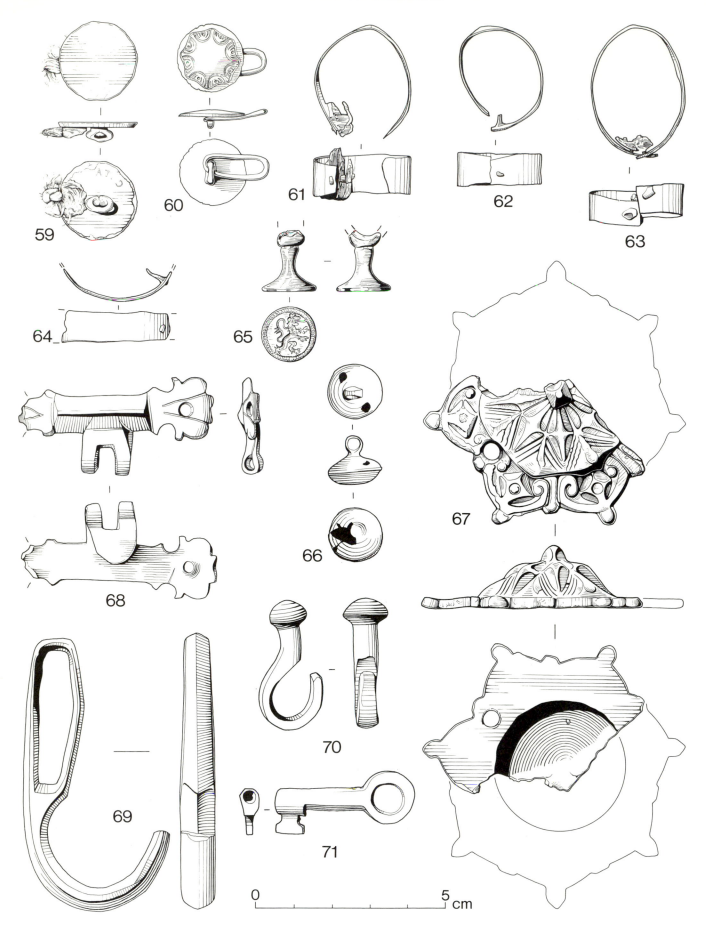

Fig 102 Post-medieval copper alloy objects: miscellaneous; scale 1:1

71 Key with ?drilled stem, possibly for use with chest. IW A 6, Period 7.

72 Gilt curved strip or plate rim with five rivet-holes. IW, layer EGT 2, Period 9.

73 Patch with two sheet copper alloy rivets and three other rivet-slots. IW N 5, Period 9.

74 Stud (see also nos 53 and 54). IW N 3, Period 9.

75 Needle. IW area A, F 1, Period 7.

76 Decorative disc with perforations for attachment rivets. IW B 1, Period 9.

77 and 78   Two pierced fragments. IW W +, Period 9.

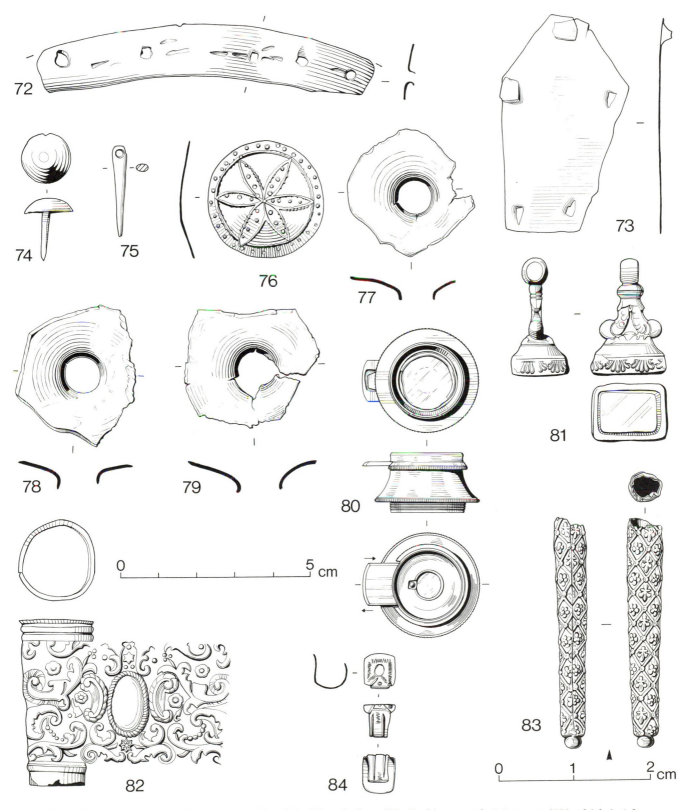

Fig 103 Medieval and post-medieval copper alloy (72–82) and silver (83–4) objects; scale 1:1 except (83) which is 1:2

79 Pierced fragment. IW B 3, Period 9.

80 Telescope eyepiece in brass with a single glass lens. It has a screw fitting for attachment to the telescope tube and a sliding lens protector; nineteenth-century. IW K 2, Period 9.

81 Fob with topaz, nineteenth-century. Fobs were worn on the end of watch chains often, unlike this example, with the owners initial engraved on the gem. Nos 80 and 81 were presumably lost by visitors to the castle. IW N +, Period 9.

82 Walking stick ferrule of impressed sheet copper alloy, silvered or more likely silver-plated on both sides. It has a perforation for a pin or nail to attach it to the stick. The decoration is in the Mannerist style of the late sixteenth/early seventeenth centuries (Jones 1856, 130–4), but the piece is probably late nineteenth-century in date. OW Tower 7, layer 1, Period 9.

Nos 80–2 are illustrated by colour photographs in the Beeston Castle guide book (Weaver 1987, 22).

Note: see also post-medieval domed weight (Fig 34.6).

Silver objects (Fig 103)

83 Object of rolled and embossed silver. Possibly a case for a valued steel needle (see Groves 1966, 18–23), or an aiglet – an ornamental tag (usually of gold or silver) used to ornament clothing (Cunnington and Cunnington 1973, 22 and 194). OG 311, Period 7.

84 Tag-end with perforation for attachment, presumably to leather or textile, and engraved decoration. IW H 3, Period 5.

Lead objects (Fig 104)

All the window leads are of post-medieval, milled type with H-shaped profiles, and straight mill marks occurring at 20 per 20mm (Knight 1984). The bulk of the window lead finds were from Civil War contexts. They appear to represent scavenging of windows as a source of lead for shot, and may have been brought in from elsewhere. However, the three sets of leads with panels of glass are all from Period 8 layers and may come from windows in use during the late seventeenth-/early eighteenth-century occupation. The lead discs (88–94) could all have been used as weights.

85 Window lead with triangular green glass pane. OG 6, Period 8.

86 Window lead with triangular green glass pane. OG 24, Period 9.

Not illustrated: fragment of green glass pane with attached lead. OG 12, Period 8.

At the Outer Gateway other pieces were found in Period 7 layers 92 (1 piece), 34 (2 pieces), 51 (1 piece), 54 (3 pieces), and in Tower 5 (8 pieces) and layer 4 (15 pieces). In the Inner Ward window leads were found in trenches E (15 pieces – 23g) and N (7 pieces – 33g).

87 Bar of square cross-section, decorated on two sides. Incised zig-zags on one face and crosses on the reverse. OG 54, Period 7.

88 Lead disc with cut/scratch marks on both surfaces. OG 61, Period 8.

89 Button-like lead disc, probably sewn into the hem of a long dress to weight it down (Peacock 1978, 16). OG 888, Period 9.

90 Perforated disc. OG Tower 5, SGT 5, Period 9.

91 Disc with cross formed by punched pits (V-shaped in horizontal plane). IW N 5/2, Period 9.

92 Disc with cross-like decoration. IW N 2, Period 9.

93 Disc with inscribed decoration on one face. IW R –, Period 9.

94 Disc with central perforation. IW N 6, Period 5.

95 Triangular lead sheet pierced by several holes. IW Q +, Period 9.

96 Plumb-bob. IW Q 1, Period 9.

Objects of lead alloy (Fig 105)

97 Top of lead alloy bottle cap. Early parallels include finds from the wreck of the Dutch ship *Jacht Vergulde Draecht*, which was sunk off western Australia in 1656 (Green 1977, 215), although this find could be nineteenth-century. OG 9, Period 9.

98 Spoon with BEESTON C[ASTLE] stamped on handle. It is made of an unidentified lead alloy and is probably a memento of the nineteenth-century Beeston fair. OG 13, Period 9.

99 Pewter porringer with a maker's mark on the upper side of the handle, in the form of a hammer. The form, with its straight sides and flat base, suggests a date in the first half of the seventeenth century (Michaelis 1971, 61–2). IW SWT 2, Period 9.

Bone objects (Figs 106–7)

1 Die, made from cutting a cube from a long bone and blocking the medullary cavity with a bone-plug (MacGregor 1985, 131). OG SGT 15, Period 6.

2 Handle from whittle-tang knife. OG 60, Period 7.

3 Fragment of ivory handle from scale-tang knife with iron pin and partial remains of two further holes. OG 65, Period 8.

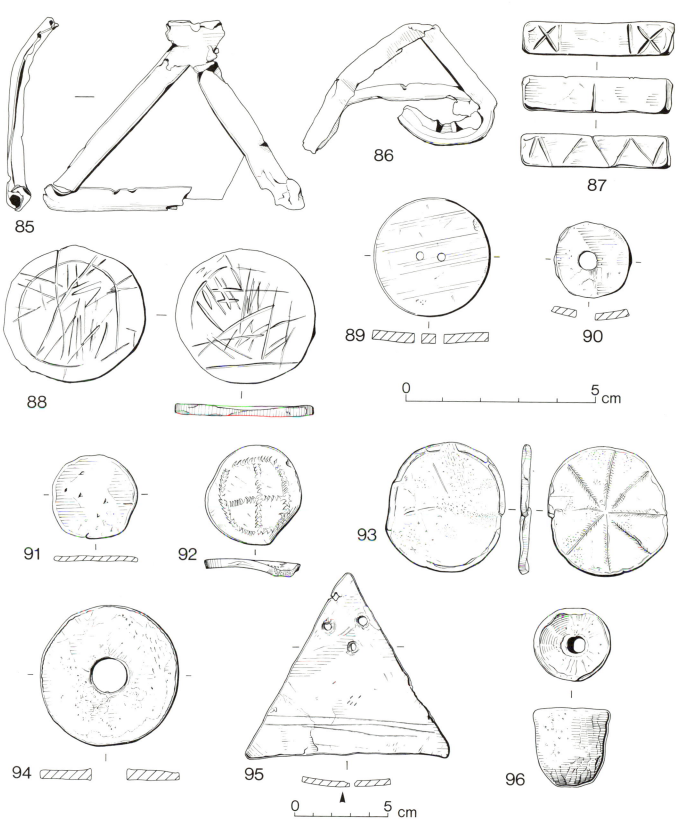

Fig 104 *Medieval and post-medieval lead objects; scale 1:1 except (95) which is 1:2*

4 Fragment of bone handle from whittle-tang knife. OG 54, Period 7.

5 Fragment of turned bone handle. OG 22, Period 8.

6 Fragment of turned handle from whittle-tang knife. OG 6, Period 8.

7 Handle from whittle-tang knife, probably with bolster. OG 25, Period 8.

8 Decorated handle of rectangular cross-section with whittle tang still inside. OG 46, Period 8.

9 Part of handle from scale-tang knife. It has four iron rivets and a hole for a fifth as well as light, small

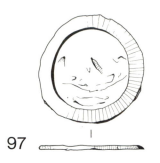

97

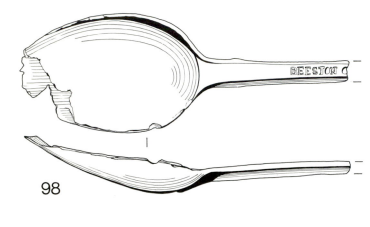

98

99

Fig 105 Post-medieval lead alloy objects; scale 1:1 except (99) which is 1:2

copper alloy studs (one lost) of a purely decorative nature. OG 24, Period 9.

10 Piece of crudely decorated bone, possibly from handle of scale-tang knife. OG 13, Period 9.

11 Fragment of double-sided comb with remains of eight coarse teeth along one side and 32 fine teeth on the other. OG 9, Period 9.

12 Fragment of bone object decorated with cut cross-hatching, possibly a handle, of uncertain age. OW 587, Period 9.

13 Broken bone handle from whittle-tang knife. IW SET 4, Period 7.

14 Broken bone pin or parchment pricker. The object closely resembles a group of iron-tipped objects used to prick parchment by scribes laying out their lines (MacGregor 1985, 124–5). IW EGT 3, Period 7.

15 Ivory peg, probably from a stringed musical instrument. IW EGT 3, Period 7.

16 Broken bone peg with incised ring decoration. The broad head has the remains of a central notch. IW G 1, Period 9.

17 Fragment of two-sided comb. IW EGT 2, Period 9.

18 Ear scoop. MacGregor (1985, 99) suggests that these became popular from the sixteenth century onwards. IW B 3, Period 9.

19 Ivory die. IW N 6, Period 5.

20 Ivory die, probably one of a pair of dice with no 19, both from the same trench. IW N 5, Period 9.

21 Bone washer showing wear from a nut. IW D 3, Period 9.

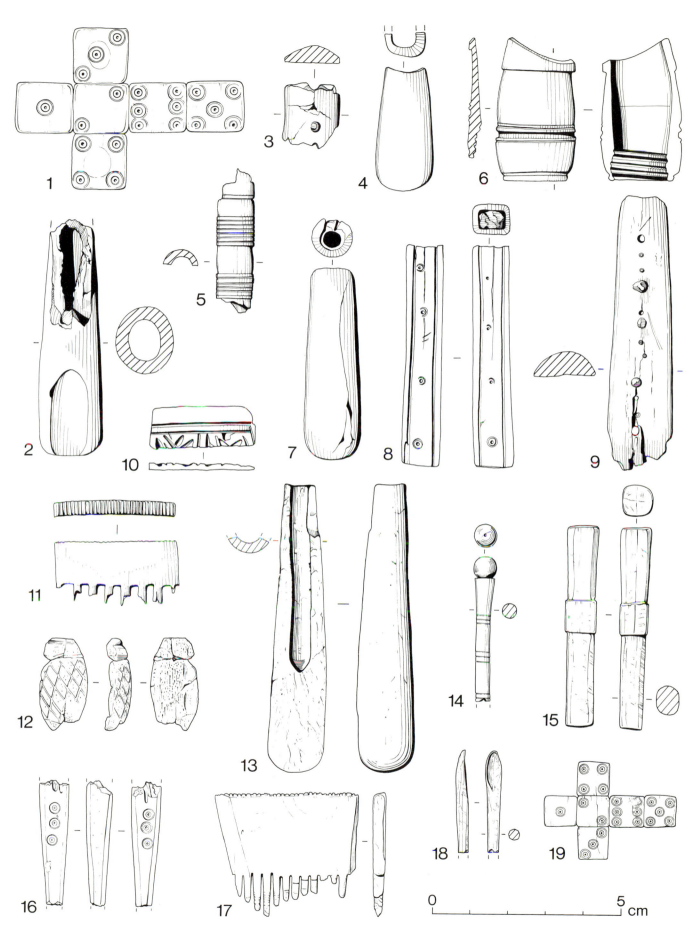

Fig 106 *Medieval and post-medieval bone objects; scale 1:1*

22 Waste offcut from the production of bone discs, for buttons or counters (c 19mm diam). The profile of the cutaway shows that the discs were drilled from both sides, leaving the flange in the middle, presumably using a centre bit. IW H 4, Period 7.

23 U-shaped bone object with one broken tang. OG Tower 5 SGT 5, Period 9.

Mother-of-pearl objects (Fig 107)

24 Buckle, probably of a purely decorative character, with no provision for a cross-bar. It may have come from a shoe, or a hat-band, and was presumably attached by stitching. OG 32, Period 9.

Ceramic objects (Fig 107)

25 Marble in red fabric with white slip blob and transparent lead glaze. Possibly post-medieval and intrusive in this context. IW M 3, Period 5.

26 Marble in white fabric, unglazed. IW SWT 4, Period 7.

27 Marble in white fabric with red streaks, unglazed. IW M +, Period 9.

28 Ceramic disc or counter, cut from glazed medieval jug (fabric C). OG Tower 5 SGT 15, Period 6.

Weapons and weapon accessories (Figs 108–9)

The excavations at Beeston Castle have produced a major assemblage of Civil War artefacts, both from mid-seventeenth-century and residual contexts. Excavated military artefacts of this period are particularly important in offering a contrast to the high-quality equipment preserved in collections such as the Royal Armouries, London. Iron artefacts are particularly prone to decay, and small fragments of armour, for example, may be difficult to identify. Particular care has therefore been taken to illustrate iron fragments from seventeenth-century contexts. Other objects of military function such as brushes for cleaning powder pans and vent-cleaning pricks (possibly domestic pins) would also be extremely difficult to identify conclusively.

The Outer Gateway produced four powder pan parts from matchlock muskets (nos 21–4), a breach plug from a musket (no 25), an exploded pistol barrel (no 27), a snaphance or flintlock jaw screw (no 26), a scourer (no 29), and a worm (no 31), for cleaning gun barrels, and three powder flask nozzles (nos 39–41). The Outer Gateway also produced two sword chapes (nos 44 and 45), probably of Civil War date, a buckle from a pikeman's armour (no 47), and the remains of a jack of plate armour (p 161). Gun accessories from the Outer Ward comprised a powder flask nozzle (no 38) and four powder holder caps, including nos 42 and 43, probably from the same bandolier. A further barrel scourer was found in the Inner Ditch (no 30), while the Inner Ward produced a powder pan cover (no 28), and part of a sword hilt (no 46).

Both the gun parts and flattened shot were concentrated in the Outer Gateway area. Their distribution (Table 39) suggests that the Inner Ward was occupied by troops, but confirms the documentary evidence that the bulk of the fighting took place at the Outer Gateway (p 98). Waste from lead shot production (nos 32 and 33), and lead rods (nos 36 and 37), point to the production of shot in the Inner Ward, while finds of window leads, scrap lead, and lead rods (nos 34 and 35) from Civil War contexts at the Outer Gateway suggest production there as well (p 124).

Many of the finds of gun parts may have been accidentally mislaid or lost in the heat of battle. The preponderance of priming pan parts may be the result

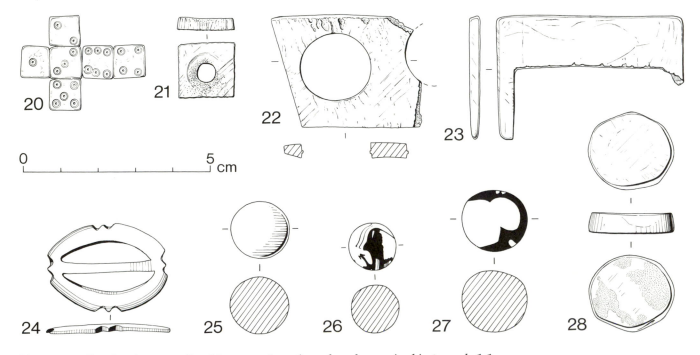

Fig 107 Medieval and post-medieval bone, mother-of-pearl, and ceramic objects; scale 1:1

of muskets exploding, or they may have been deliberately knocked off to render the weapons inoperable on surrender.

Catalogue

Arrowheads and crossbow bolts (Fig 108)

1–20 Arrowheads 1 and 5 have copper alloy pins in their sockets for attachment to wooden shafts. X-rays of nos 3 and 6 show faint traces of brazing on their sockets. The range of forms includes barbed and socketed heads (nos 1, 16–20); short pointed (nos 3 and 9); long bodkin (nos 2, 4, 5, and 10–15); and blunted practice heads (nos 6 and 7). No 9 has a slight flange, and no 8 is notable for its width but the broken cross-section suggests a bodkin arrowhead or possibly a crossbow bolt rather than a spearhead.

The low weight and narrow diameter of the Beeston projectile points, with the possible exception of no 8, would theoretically be more suitable for arrowheads than crossbow bolts. However, bolt and arrowhead forms overlapped, and barbed heads could be used for both weapons (Blackmore 1971, 193–7). There are few medieval projectiles with original shafts and thus the separation of crossbow bolts from arrowheads is often difficult.

The pointed and long bodkin forms of projectile were designed for their armour-piercing qualities, while the barbed examples were used for both military and hunting purposes (Ward Perkins 1940, 65–73; Hardy 1976, 201). Nos 6 and 7 with their blunt ends may have been practice heads as at Sandal Castle, W Yorks (Credland 1983, 265, fig 12.32–3). While nos 16–18 are from medieval contexts, the remainder are from residual contexts and cannot be closely dated. Robert Ascham describes pointed, barbed, and blunted arrowheads as all being in use in 1545 (Arber 1868, 135–9).

Nos 16–18 came from a Period 5 layer IW N 4. From Period 7 contexts came nos 12 and 13 both from IW D 5, and no 7 from OG 51. The remaining objects came from Period 8 and 9 layers: nos 1–6 from the Outer Gateway, no 8 from the Outer Ward, and nos 9–11, 14, 15, 19, and 20 from the Inner Ward.

Gun parts – iron (Fig 108)

The remains of three or four matchlocks of seventeenth-century date were recovered and are almost certainly from the Civil War occupation. Comparable remains of matchlocks have been excavated at Basing House, Hants (Dufty and Reid 1971, 52, fig 23.127–8), and Sandal Castle, W Yorks (Credland 1983, 264, fig 12.15–17). The snaphance or flintlock may be of Civil War date, particularly if it is from a pistol or carbine rather than a musket, although it could be an eighteenth-century piece. In the earlier snaphance the steel and pan were made separately, while in the flintlock they were combined in a single piece.

21 Powder pan cover from a matchlock musket. OG 92, Period 7.

22 Powder pan and rotating baffle or flashguard (broken) from a matchlock musket. OG 24, Period 9.

23 Powder pan with pan cover and broken baffle from a matchlock musket. OG 57, Period 9.

24 Pin from rotating baffle on a matchlock musket. OG 49, Period 7.

25 Breach plug from a musket. The diameter of the screw-thread is about 20mm suggesting that it belonged to a 12-bore musket. Mr R Ellis (pers comm) suggests that the thread shows signs of stretching, possibly as a result of an explosion in the barrel. OG 41, Period 9.

26 Jaw screw from cock of a snaphance or flintlock weapon with broken screw-thread. The jaw held the flint in position. Its small size suggests a light lock mechanism suitable for a pistol, carbine, or fowling piece. For the use of snaphance weapons in the Civil War see Blackmore 1961, 24–5. OG 45, Period 7.

27 Burst pistol barrel. Gauge of 0.5 in. OG 806, Period 9.

28 Powder pan cover. IW EGT 2, Period 9.

Gun accessories – iron (Fig 108)

The scourer and worm formed part of a standard musketman's kit but do not normally survive even in armouries. An archaeological parallel comes from Wolstenholme site H (Martin's Hundred) in Virginia and is believed to have been discarded c 1620–2 (Noel Hume 1982, 270–2). Noel Hume also points to many surviving examples in the Landeszeughaus arsenal at Graz in Austria (ibid, 305). Scourers and worms are illustrated in many seventeenth-century military manuals, notably *Kriegskunst zu Fusz* (von Wallhausen 1971), and many similar works derived from it. One of these manuals appears to have been the source for a group of weapons, including a scourer and worm, in a Restoration stained glass window in Farndon church, Cheshire. The weapons form part of a scene depicting Royalist troops and heraldic shields associated with the siege of Chester (illustrated in Weaver 1987, 20).

29 Barrel scourer. This object was screwed into the end of a ramrod and then used to clean scale from gun barrels. The remains of a screw-thread are visible on the X-ray. OG 51, Period 7.

Table 39 Distribution of gun parts, gun accessories, and flattened shot

	No of gun parts	No of gun accessories	No of flattened shots
Outer Gateway	7	5	8
Inner Ward	1	—	1
Inner Ditch	—	1	1
Outer Ward	—	5	1
Total	8	11	11

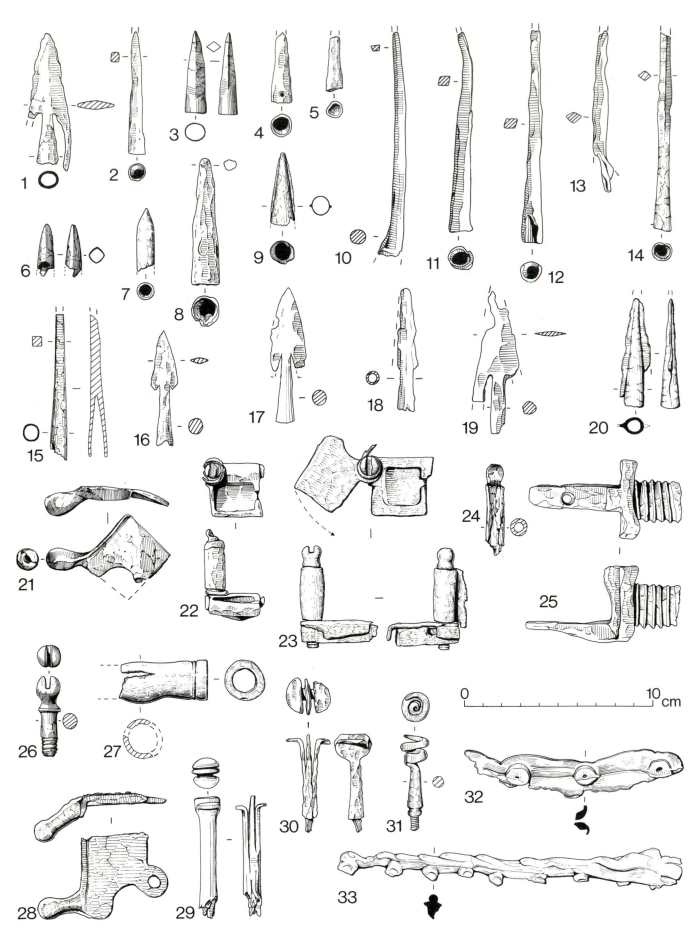

Fig 108 Medieval and post-medieval weapons: projectiles, guns, gun accessories, and gun shot; scale 1:2

30 Barrel scourer from an Inner Ditch Civil War context. This object was published in Hough 1978, fig 1.8, but not then identified.

31 Worm. This tool also screwed into the end of a ramrod and was used for cleaning out the used wadding from the gun barrel. OG 24, Period 9.

Gun shot (Fig 108)

A total of 70 lead gun shot were recovered from the excavations. These included 11 impacted shot (Table 39). A single, failed casting was found in layer 3 of the East Gatehouse Tower of the Inner Ward. This was a split and hollow ball of about 16mm diameter. The non-impacted shot were distributed as follows: Outer Gateway (23), Outer Ward (6), Inner Ditch (11), and Inner Ward (8). There was no observable pattern in the distribution of different shot sizes.

The calibre of seventeenth-century guns was far from standardised despite repeated attempts to impose uniform standards, eg the 1630 Council of War 'Orders for the general uniformatie of all sortes of armes both for horse and foote', summarised in Blackmore (1971, 24). Ideally each musketeer had his own bullet mould although it is uncertain whether this was achieved in practice, especially with local militias.

The most reliable way of assessing shot is by diameter as the weights for shot of the same size vary owing to distortions in shape, air bubbles, and possibly the purity of the lead used. The Beeston shot dimensions are summarised in Table 40. The shot falls into three main size ranges: 11–13mm, 15–16mm, and 18–19mm. The larger size (approximately 12-bore) was suitable for muskets, and the 11–13mm shot (around 48-bore) for pistols. A problem is posed, however, by the middle-sized shot (around 20-bore). At Sandal Castle and Marston Moor, 20-to-the-pound shot predominates. Credland (1983, 261–3) suggests that it was manufactured for use in muskets to save lead or to overcome the problem of the unstandardised weapons used by local militias. The problem may have been aggravated by the central supply of shot by the barrel to regional garrisons (cf *Calender of State Papers Domestic 1644–5*, 535).

At Beeston 12-to-the-pound shot predominates but at least some appears to have been manufactured on the site. The smaller 20-to-the-pound shot may represent centrally supplied 'general purpose' shot or may have been used in antique arquebuses. Another possibility is that it was fired from fowling pieces, long-barrelled guns known to have been used for sniping in the Civil War (George 1947, 28, 34, and 46; Blair 1983, 85).

The balls were cast in two-piece moulds (probably hinged and made of iron) and frequently have traces of a casting seam where the metal penetrated into the mould seam, as well as showing traces of the casting runner which was cut off with pincers on cooling. In addition several pieces of casting waste, comprising the header with multiple runners, nos 32–3, were found, showing that the balls were cast in multiple moulds although none of these sets of runners was definitely complete. Three sizes of shot are represented and at least four or five moulds. The distribution of the waste may indicate casting sites in the East Gate Tower and the South-West Tower, and in area N (Fig 71).

32 Header with three runners spaced at 180mm intervals. Also two other headers (not illustrated) one with four runners at 180mm, and one with three runners at 200mm. IW N 3, Period 9.

Not illustrated: header with two runners spaced at 180mm intervals. IW and presumably intrusive in N 4, Period 5.

These were used to produce shot of c 180mm diam (12-to-the pound).

33 Header with nine runners spaced at 100mm intervals. Also three others with 5, 8, and 10 runners all at 100mm. IW EGT 2, Period 9. These would have produced shot of under 100mm diam, probably for use in a cannon.

Not illustrated: header with two runners spaced at 195mm to produce 12-to-the-pound shot though from a different mould to no 32; and header with single runner, probably a different mould to those above. IW SWT 4, Period 7.

Lead rods (Fig 109) are known from Civil War contexts at Montgomery Castle (J Knight, pers comm). It seems likely that they represent material intended for manufacture as shot.

34–37 Rods of circular cross-section, weighing respectively 40.5g, 21.5g, 54g, and 24g. Nos 34 and 35 from OG 152 and 51, Period 7; nos 36 and 37 from IW EGT 2, Period 9.

Bandolier accessories – lead (Fig 109)

The lead nozzle finds at Beeston and Sandal Castles suggest that lead was adopted in preference to iron for the cheap mass production of nozzles in the Civil War. The flask body would have been likewise cheaply constructed with little elaboration as shown by the remains of a Civil War flask body from Ewenny, Mid Glamorgan (Sell 1983).

One of the Beeston powder holder covers, no 43, and one of the powder flask nozzles, no 38, show traces of a casting seam and runner. Two powder holder covers,

Table 40 Weight and dimensions of the lead shot

Size		Weight		Nos
mm	*in*	*g*	*oz*	
11	0.43	8.50	3.3	1
12	0.47	8–10	3.2–3.9	2
13	0.51	13	5.1	2
14	0.56	—	—	—
15	0.60	18–22	7.1–8.7	8
16	0.63	21.5–26	8.5–10.2	11
17	0.67	26.5	10.4	1
18	0.71	33–36.5	13–14.4	17
19	0.75	34–40	13.4–15.8	16
20	0.79	40	15.8	1
			Total	59

from Laugharne Castle in Dyfed, were also cast, in contrast to the use of sheet lead at Sandal Castle (Credland 1983, fig 12.1–5).

38 and 39   Nozzles from powder flasks of leather or wood, with two loops for attachment to bandolier (only one loop on no 39 surviving). No 38 from OW 7, Period 9; no 39 from OG 92, Period 7.

40–43   Powder holder covers with two attachment loops (one on no 41 damaged, only one on no 43 surviving). No 40 from OG SGT 5, Period 9 and no 41 from OG SGT 9, Period 8 (both Tower 5); no 42 from OW 523, Period 9; and no 43 from OW 543, Period 9.

Not illustrated: two flattened powder holder caps both OW 543, Period 9.

Swords (Fig 109)

The two chapes are of a common early post-medieval form but are not closely datable on typological grounds. They may be compared with similar post-medieval

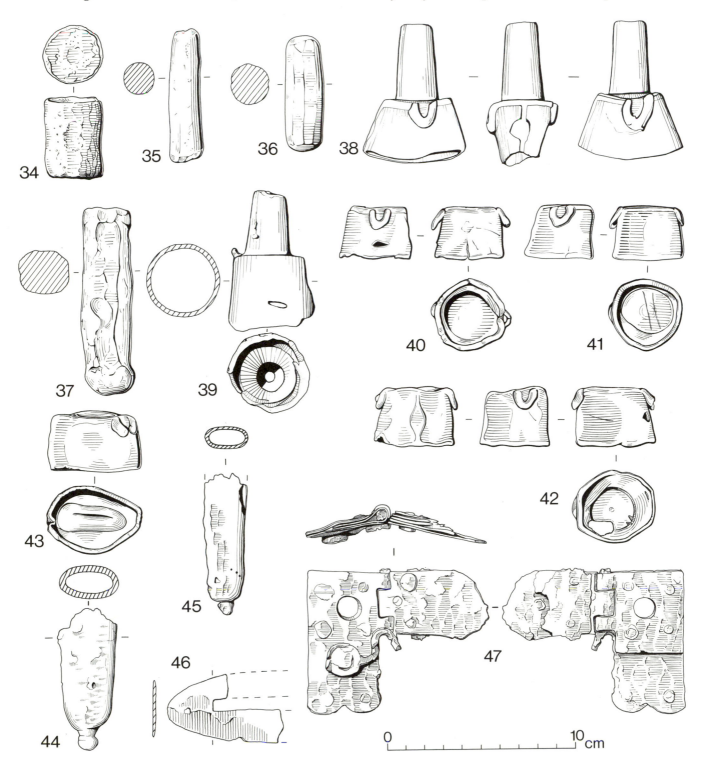

Fig 109   Post-medieval weapons: lead rods, bandolier accessories and swords; scale 1:2

chapes from Chelmsford, Essex (Goodall 1985, 57, fig 34.84) and Basing House, Hants (Moorhouse and Goodall 1971, 54, fig 24.141). Chapes without the knobbed terminal come from Sandal Castle, W Yorks (Goodall 1983, 248, fig 9.201–4).

44 and 45   Iron sword chapes with knobbed terminals. Both OG Tower 5, SGT 5, Period 9.

46   Iron hilt guard plate (broken), from a sword, dagger, or heavy knife. Of uncertain type or date though probably post-medieval. IW N +/1, Period 9.

Armour (Fig 109)

47   Iron buckle from pikeman's armour. This buckle was riveted to the top of the tasset or skirt and was used to fasten it to the cuirass or bodypiece. Loops on the cuirass slipped through the holes on the buckle and were fastened by the rotating catch (Norman and Wilson 1982, 39; Dufty and Reid 1968, pls LX1V–LXV; and Noel Hume 1982, pl 13.2). OG 46, Period 8.

The jack of plate
by Ian Eaves

Among the many pieces of iron excavated from the approaches to the Outer Gateway of Beeston Castle were large numbers of small plates, or fragments of them, which could be identified, either firmly or tentatively, as deriving from armour. Recognition of the type of armour involved has led to a reconsideration of late medieval armour, focusing particularly on the jack of plate and the brigandine, which it would be inappropriate to present here. A shortened version of the original report is presented here, while the reconsideration, together with further details of the material, described below, and full references to support the theories outlined, is presented elsewhere (Eaves 1989).

The majority of the finds were recovered from layers 51 and 54, located immediately to the east of the gateway. These layers contained demolition rubble and dated to the middle of the seventeenth century, immediately after the Civil War. A single piece was found in layer 89, predating layers 51 and 54 although still a seventeenth-century context, while further pieces were found in the same area in eighteenth-century and topsoil contexts. A topsoil layer within Tower 4 produced a further fragment. South of the main group three further pieces were found in ditch F198, which was filled in soon after the Civil War. The homogeneity of the pieces suggests that the great majority were deposited together, with subsequent disturbance redistributing some of the pieces.

All the plates are now extensively or entirely oxidised. Although corrosion products and encrustations obscure much of their detail, X-ray photographs provided excellent evidence of their outline and principal features. With certain important exceptions, discussed below, the majority of the plates are more or less square in shape (Fig 110.2–8). Their sides are typically 35mm long but vary from 25mm to 40mm. Each is pierced through its centre with a hole approximately 4.5mm ± 1mm in diameter. Many of the plates are pierced with further, smaller holes having a diameter of about 2mm ± 0.5mm. Although these smaller holes sometimes form a regular pattern within a given plate, their occurrence from one plate to the next is entirely arbitrary. In a few instances, where the plates retain something of their original form and remain relatively free of encrustations, their thickness may be tentatively estimated at about 1.5mm. This dimension is likely to have been the subject of some variation, however.

Traces of fabric are in evidence on both sides of the plates. Textile remains on 21 plates were examined by Elisabeth Crowfoot at the Ancient Monuments Laboratory (Crowfoot 1985). She reports that although all the fibres were replaced by metal oxides and in some cases the impressions were negative only, it was possible to distinguish two different tabby weaves. These were both Z-spun in warp and weft but with thread counts of c 20/16–18 per 10mm and 12/10–12 per 10 mm, the first noticeably finer than the second. The counts and, as far as could be seen, the style of the yarns, were consistent with vegetable fibre, the finer fabric probably flax, and the coarser either a rough-quality flax or possibly hemp. The presence and position of the two weaves suggested that one weave, perhaps the finer, could have been the lining and covering, between which the plates were fastened by sewing, in slightly overlapping rows, while the other might represent a loose wrapping, perhaps a sack.

The plates described above are readily identifiable from their characteristics as those of a jack of plate, although most if not all of them have been cut from earlier forms of armour, including the brigandine. The jack of plate, like the brigandine, was a canvas doublet reinforced with small, overlapping iron plates (Fig 111.20). Instead of being riveted to the doublet however, the plates were sewn between two layers of its fabric (Fig 111.21). They were typically square in shape, with roughly cropped corners, and each was pierced through its centre with a hole to receive the stitches.

References to jacks occur as early as the third quarter of the fourteenth century but these relate to quilted jacks. The jack of plate seems not to be recorded before the first quarter of the sixteenth century, and not with frequency until the mid-sixteenth century. Its use remained widespread among the lower classes of English and Scottish soldiery until the end of the century, when its manufacture was evidently discontinued. Although its use persisted until the first quarter of the following century, it became increasingly rare thereafter, and was to all intents and purposes obsolete by the time of the Civil War. The precise dating within this timespan of anything other than complete specimens is impossible.

The majority of the plates found at Beeston conform to the typical pattern of a jack of plate described above, although the absence of cropping of the corners indicates a cruder construction. Sharp corners would have been more likely to wear and tear through the enclosing fabric. Some of the Beeston plates are oblong rather than square, and are pierced with two holes instead of one (Fig 110.1, 9–13). These may have formed part of a pair of arm defences worn with the jack, although the Beeston examples are generally twice as wide as other

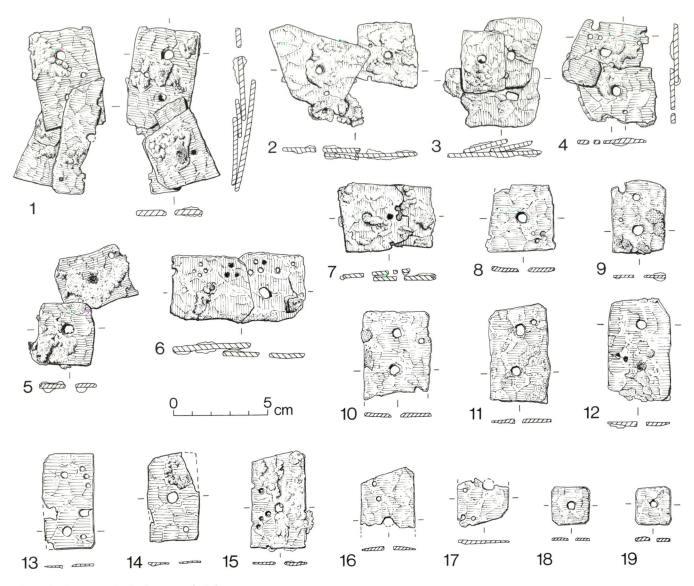

Fig 110 Armour: jack plates; scale 1:2

known examples. The illustrated arrangement of plates in the sleeve (Fig 111.22) is based on that used in a Royal Armouries example (No III–1885 A and B), although in that case the plates have only one hole.

Two plates having the same square, centrally pierced form as a normal jack plate are unusually small, measuring 20mm square (Fig 110.18 and 19). These plates, unlike the others, have cropped corners, and one was found in an earlier context than the others, suggesting that they may have no connection with the jack.

It remains to be determined, however, whether the plates found at Beeston Castle represent parts of a single garment, or were merely fragments of a series of decayed or decaying garments of the same general type that had been cast out together. The latter situation is only likely to have occurred in a well-established armoury where a number of jacks had been kept together for several years. Since Beeston Castle had evidently remained unused by the military for over 100 years before its reoccupation during the Civil War, when the plates were most probably deposited, the requisite conditions seem not to have prevailed, and there is consequently some reason to suppose that the plates in

question could have derived from a single defence, despite some significant differences in their individual form.

The number of plates required to make a complete jack would normally have been over 1000, whereas the Beeston fragments number no more than 160 pieces. The difference between the number of plates actually recovered from the site and the number of plates which might theoretically have occurred there may be greater than can be explained by destruction in the soil or subsequent disturbance. It is possible that the Beeston jack was incomplete when deposited and thus cast aside as unwanted rubbish rather than accidentally lost.

By that time it must have been of considerable age. As previously mentioned, no evidence exists for the manufacture of the jack of plate beyond the sixteenth century. Although it continued to be worn into the early years of the following century, any examples still in use at the time of the Civil War must have been 50 or more years old, and of exceptional rarity. They would have been old-fashioned to the point of inviting ridicule, and probably in a parlous condition. Nevertheless, so great was the shortage of armour during the Civil War years that even those who had the means and inclination to purchase their equipment anew were not always able to do so readily, and were sometimes compelled by circumstances to resort to reusing, and if necessary amending, old pieces of armour of the sixteenth and even earlier centuries. Thus if a jack of plate in anything remotely suggesting usable condition had still existed at that period, it is not improbable that it would eventually have been brought into service, even if, because of its age, it soon disintegrated beyond repair so that its fragments were cast aside. It is conceivable that the fragments of the jack found at Beeston Castle came to be deposited there through such circumstances.

When complete the jack would have resembled a contemporary civilian doublet. It would have possessed a short skirt, divided at either the sides, the rear, or both; an upstanding collar, probably divided at either the sides or the rear; and short extensions around the tops of the armholes, probably divided at their apexes (Fig 111.20). Although the skirts and collars of some jacks of plate were stuffed with mail rather than with plates, no mail was found in association with the pieces under discussion, and it may reasonably be concluded that they derive from a jack armoured with plates throughout. Although five wire hooks were found in the same general area as the jack plates, they occurred in later contexts, were on average twice the size of known hooks from such defences, and are therefore unlikely to be associated with the jack. It is probable that the Beeston jack was fastened down the centre of the chest, or a little to one side of it, by means of laces.

As noted above, such indications as have been preserved suggest that the canvas which formerly enclosed the plates was covered by a coarser fabric, perhaps sacking, and was not covered over with any finer material. The rough character of the plates themselves would lend support to the view that the Beeston Castle jack was a particularly humble specimen of its kind.

As has already been mentioned, jack plates were often made by cutting up old armour, and this is certainly true of most, if not all of the plates recovered from Beeston Castle. The small holes which occur arbitrarily in so many of them served no purpose in the jack, but originally held rivets when these plates formed parts of other kinds of armour. In the case of the finds from Beeston it is clear that the majority of the pieces were cut from brigandine plates. The characteristic profile of the brigandine has been preserved in several instances where the jack plate has been cut from the end of a brigandine plate. The size of the brigandine plates recovered suggests that they belong to armour produced in the fifteenth century.

Some support for this dating is provided by the pattern of rivet-holes discernible in the X-ray photographs of the plates. A triangular rivet configuration, widely used from the second to the last quarter of the fifteenth century, can be readily recognised on some of the reused plates.

At what date these brigandines and other pieces of armour were cut up to make the Beeston Castle jack is not easily determined, in so far as the plates themselves provide no evidence of the overall form, and therefore the fashion, of the latter. The jack of plate, as previously stated, may already have been in use as early as the first quarter of the sixteenth century, and was certainly being made by the second quarter of the century. It enjoyed its greatest popularity from the middle to the late sixteenth century, and it is perhaps from this period that the Beeston Castle jack is most likely to date.

Considering the tens of thousands of jacks of plate that must have been in use in England and Scotland at that period, and the millions of plates that would have been required to make them, it is a little surprising that no plates of this kind seem hitherto to have been reported from British archaeological excavations, although a small number have been recovered from a colonial site in Virginia (Noel Hume, 1982, fig 13.5). It is therefore to be hoped that the publication of this major group from Beeston Castle will prompt the recognition of further jack plates from sixteenth- and seventeenth-century sites in this country.

The illustrated fragments (Figs 110 and 111)

1–7 Connecting plates, nos 1 and 3 oblong, the remainder square; two holes apparent on oblong plate of no 1, remainder with single central hole. Note additional smaller rivet-holes from earlier use. AM Lab nos 803211, 803229, 803231, 803233, 803239, 803240, 803242, OG 54, Period 7.

8 Square plate, single central hole; also shows triangular group of rivet-holes. AM Lab no 803189, OG 54, Period 7.

9–13 Oblong plates pierced with two holes; also shows smaller rivet-holes in every case. AM Lab nos 803219, 803183, 803188, 803288, 811800, OG 54, Period 7, except no 13, OG 103, Period 7.

14 and 15 Oblong plates pierced with single hole; also shows smaller rivet-holes in both cases. AM Lab nos 803154, 803227, OG 54, Period 7.

16 and 17 Plate fragments, broken through central hole; also show smaller rivet-holes. AM Lab nos 803150, 803184, OG 54, Period 7.

18 and 19 Two smaller plates, central hole and cropped edges. Possibly not connected with jack and representing fragments of a separate defence. AM Lab nos 811734 and 812004, no 18, OG 89 Period 7, no 19 OG 41, Period 9.

20 Jack of plate: front view of armour based on a jack of plate in the Royal Armouries (No III–1884).

21 Arrangement of stitches and plates for jack body; based on Royal Armouries example noted above.

22 Arrangement of stitches and plates for jack sleeve; based on an example in the Royal Armouries (No III–1885 A and B).

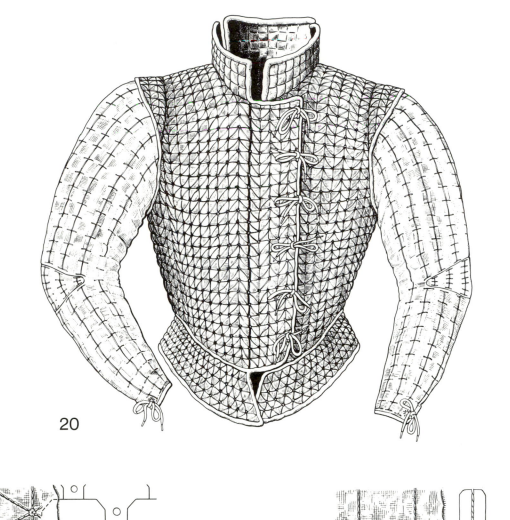

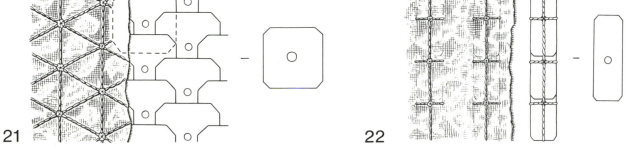

Fig 111 *Jack of plate reconstructions based on extant examples: front view of armour (20) , arrangement of stitches and plates for body (21), arrangement of stitches and plate for the sleeve (22)*

The spurs
by Blanche Ellis

(For details of the spurs and their measurements see M2:E14–F9)

Introduction

With the exception of nos 1, 18, and 36, all the Beeston Castle spurs are likely to have been worn during the Civil War. In addition to their importance as aids for riding horses, spurs were also accessories for fashionable men who wore them with boots even when not riding during the first three-quarters of the seventeenth century. Figs 112.2–4 and 114.23–4, are clearly decorative as well as functional, and the remaining undecorated spurs were all originally elegantly formed, many bearing traces of tin plating used both to protect the spur and enhance its appearance (Jope 1956, 35–42).

Twenty of the spurs were found at the Outer Gateway, fourteen came from the Inner Ward and one from the Inner Ditch. The eight examples found in the lower room of the South-East Tower of the Inner Ward may indicate an equipment store.

The spur sides curved around the heel, with their terminals, to which leathers were attached, at the front, and the necks supporting the rowels at the back. Usually a plain strap was worn under the sole of the boot attached to the lower rings of the spur terminals. The rowel box contained the rowel held by its pin. The upper leather was attached to the top ring of the terminal on the inner side of the wearer's foot, and passed over the instep to the buckle fitted on to the top ring of the outer terminal. During the seventeenth century the upper leathers were extended into broad flaps which covered the top of the foot and front of the ankle. Buckles were worn on the outside of the foot. Only occasional traces of the spur leathers have survived, and only two buckles associated with these spurs, although a further spur buckle is separately described (Fig 100.4, p 146).

Catalogue (Figs 112–15)

Medieval

1 Rowel-spur fragments; iron. This is the earliest type of rowel-spur, of thirteenth- or early fourteenth-century date, since rivet attachments were discontinued fairly soon after the introduction of the rowel in the thirteenth century. Similar to an example in the Museum of London (Ward Perkins 1940, 100, fig 30.6). IW area A, unstratified.

Post-medieval

2 Rowel-spur decorated with fluting; iron. OG 51, Period 7.

3 Rowel-spur with elaborate terminals; copper alloy. IW SET 4, Period 7.

Nos 2 and 3 share a number of similarities and may be compared with copper alloy spurs found at Canterbury (Marlowe site, SF 268) and North Elmham Park, Norfolk (Wade-Martins 1980, 505, fig 264.60); with an unprovenanced copper alloy spur in the Royal Armouries in the Tower of London (No VI–298); and with a fluted gilt copper alloy spur in the Museum of London from the site of the Rose Theatre, built in 1587 in Southwark. The unusual terminals and other similarities in detail suggest a common place of manufacture for all six. The latter example has the central curve of each elongated terminal closed to form a third ring. Its buckle, two attachments, and part of its leather survive, but its neck is broken. Medieval and post-medieval spurs with fluted or roped surfaces, although uncommon, are known. Those described here are likely to be dated c 1620–46. Spurs with fluted decoration comparable to No 2 can be seen on contemporary portraits of Sir Richard Graham (collection of Sir Fergus Graham) and George Gordon (collection of Duke of Buccleuch), both painted by D Mytens.

4 Silver-encrusted rowel-spur; iron. A damaged silver-encrusted spur of this type has been found at Hull (Armstrong 1977, fig 28.95). Encrusting with silver was a common way of decorating spurs in the late sixteenth and seventeenth centuries (Norman 1980, 360). This example dates to the first half of the seventeenth century. IW SET 4, Period 7.

The following small iron spurs, (5–22), each have horizontally straight sides of flattened D-section, deepest at their junction behind the wearer's heel and tapering towards their terminals. Where the terminals survive each is formed as two rings set like a figure eight projecting equally above and below the front of the spur side. The necks are slender and rounded, starting horizontally straight and tapering towards their downward bent rowel boxes. The few surviving rowels are small.

Although an iron spur of similar form to nos 5–22 came from what is probably a mid-sixteenth-century context at Somerby, Lincolnshire (Mynard 1969, fig 11.IW 23), this type was not common until the period 1620–60. Similar spurs have often been found in the same contexts as definite seventeenth-century spurs, for example at Kettleby Thorpe, Lincolnshire (Russell 1974, fig 41), Basing House, Hampshire (Moorhouse 1971, fig 21), and Sandal Castle, Yorkshire (Mayes and Butler 1983, 253–8, fig 11). Typologically no 12 probably dates from the first half of the seventeenth century. A spur very similar to no 20 was found in a Civil War context at Sandal Castle, Yorkshire (Mayes and Butler 1983, 256 and fig 11.10). The shallow sides and overall proportions of no 18 suggest manufacture in the late seventeenth or early eighteenth century.

5–8 are from IW SET 4, Period 7; 9 and 10 from IW EGT 2, Period 9; 11–13 from IW A 4, Period 9; 14 from OG 54, Period 7; 15 from OG 80, Period 7; 16 from OG 353, Period 7; 17 from OG 54, Period 7; 18 from OG 6, Period 8; 19 from OG 22, Period 8; 20 from OG 66, Period 8; 21 from OG 5, Period 9; and 22 from OG 385, Period 9.

23 Spur fragment; copper alloy. IW A 4, Period 9.

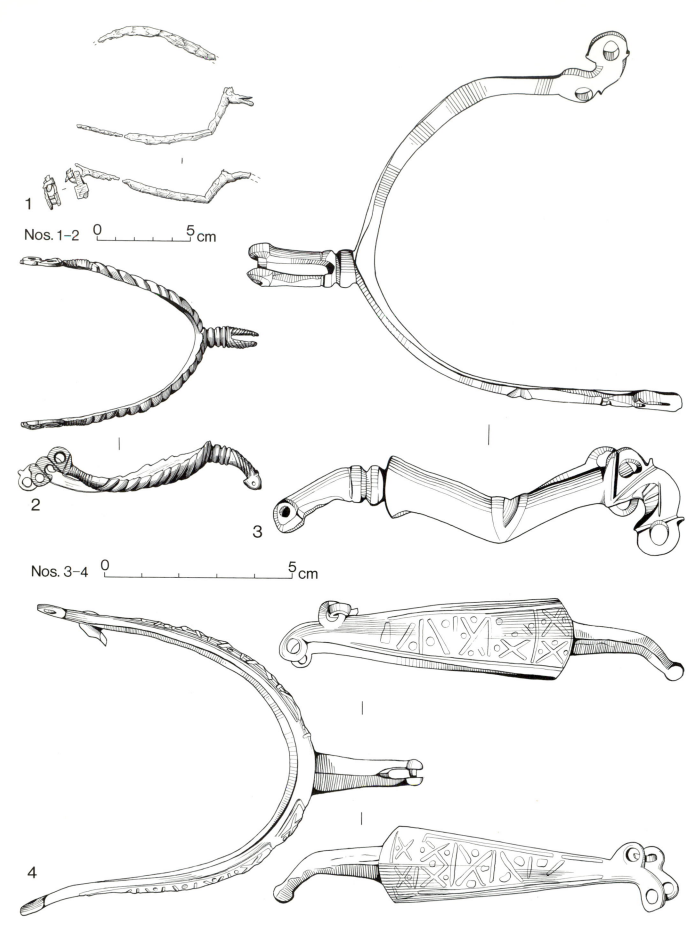

Nos. 1–2

Nos. 3–4

Fig 112 Medieval (1) and post-medieval (2–4) spurs; scale 1:2 (1–2) and 1:1 (3–4)

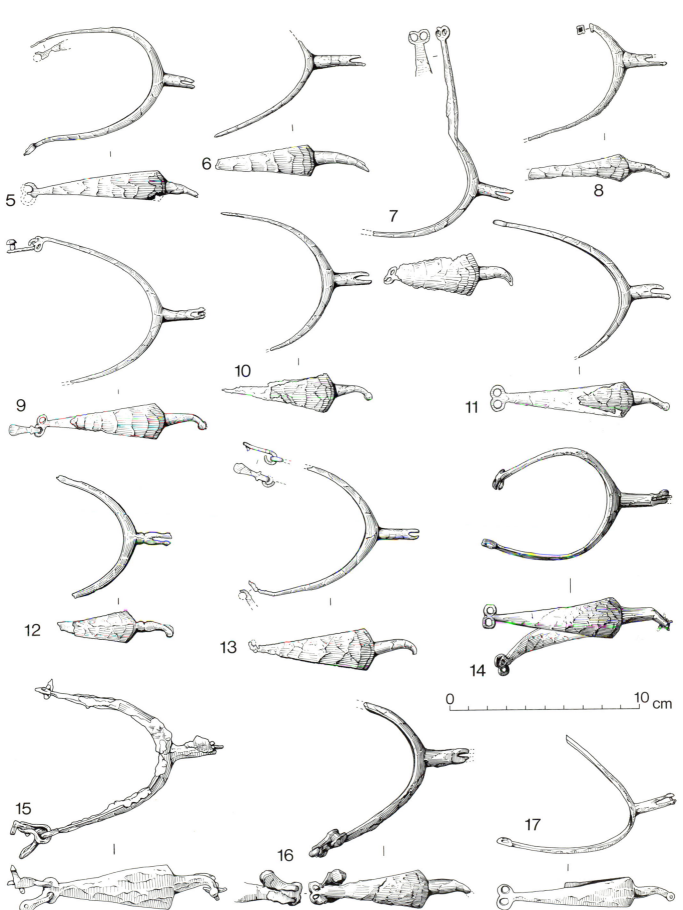

Fig 113 Post-medieval spurs; scale 1:2

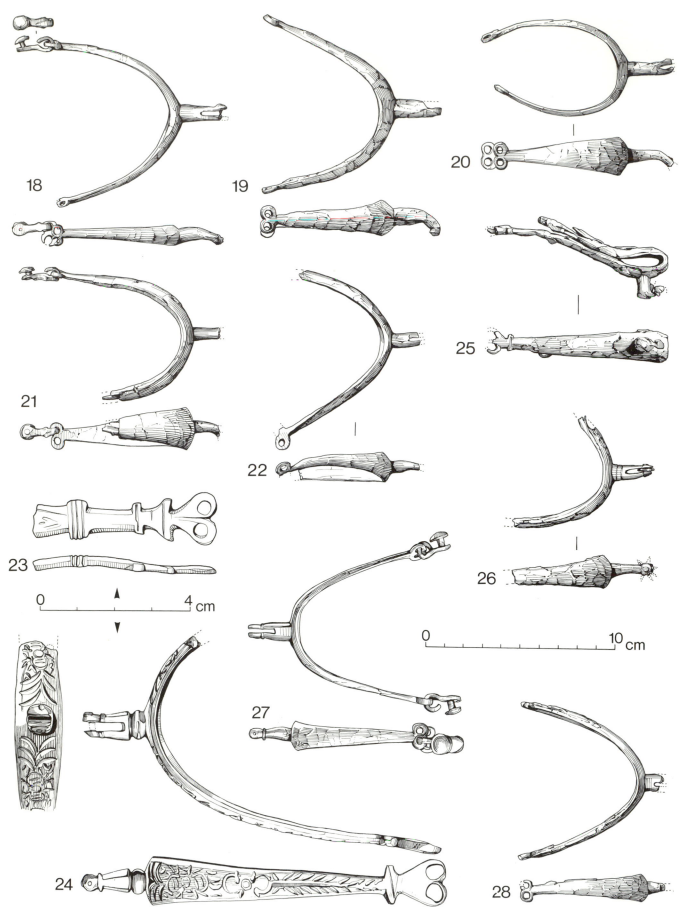

Fig 114   *Post-medieval spurs; scale 1:2 except (23–4) which are 1:1*

24 Rowel-spur; copper alloy. OG 74, Period 8.

25 Rowel-spur; iron with traces of lead and tin plating. OG 32, Period 9.

Nos 23–5 are likely to date from the Civil War. Straight-sided spurs were used increasingly throughout the seventeenth century. The unusual terminal of no 24 is paralleled by a copper alloy spur from London (Roach Smith collection, British Museum No 56.71.2546).

26–29   Rowel-spurs; iron. Surface traces of lead and tin on nos 26–8. 26 is from OG 353, Period 7; 27 from OG 60, Period 7; 28 from OG 11, Period 9; and 29 from the Inner Ditch, unstratified.

Nos 26–9 have straight sides of flattened D-section tapering from junction to terminal. They differ from nos 5–22 in that their round necks are horizontally straight. They are also mid-seventeenth-century types.

30 Spur side; iron. IW SET 4, Period 7. Mid-seventeenth century.

31 Spur fragment; iron. IW SET 4, Period 7. The evenly set terminal suggests a mid- to late seventeenth-century date.

32 Spur fragment; iron. OG 353, Period 7. Probably mid-seventeenth-century.

33 Spur fragment; iron with widespread surface traces of lead and tin plating. OG 54, Period 7, Probably mid-seventeenth-century.

34 Spur fragment; iron with surface traces of lead and tin plating. OG 51, Period 7. Mid-seventeenth-century.

35 Spur fragment; iron with slight traces of lead and tin plating. OG 304, Period 8. Probably seventeenth-century.

36 Rowel-spur; iron. OG Tower 5 GHT 9, Period 8. C1700.

37 Stud attachment for a spur leather; iron, tinned with traces of lead. OG 76, Period 7. Stud attachments were used from the late sixteenth century and were common during the seventeenth and eighteenth centuries. This attachment is similar to the one on no 21.

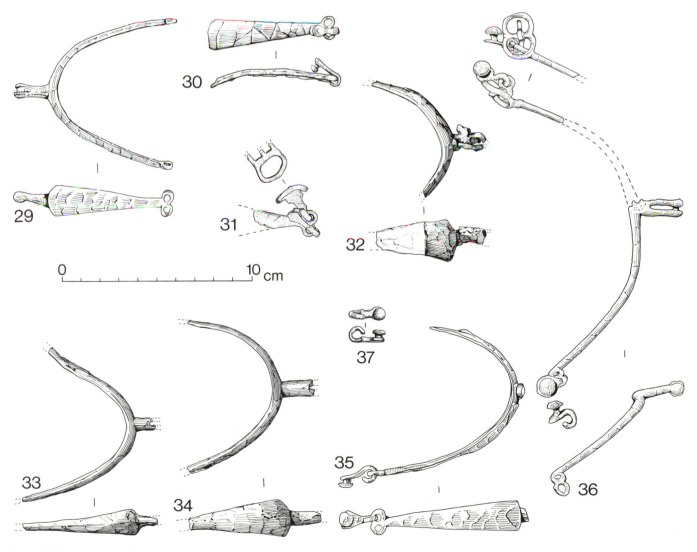

Fig 115 Post-medieval spurs; scale 1:2

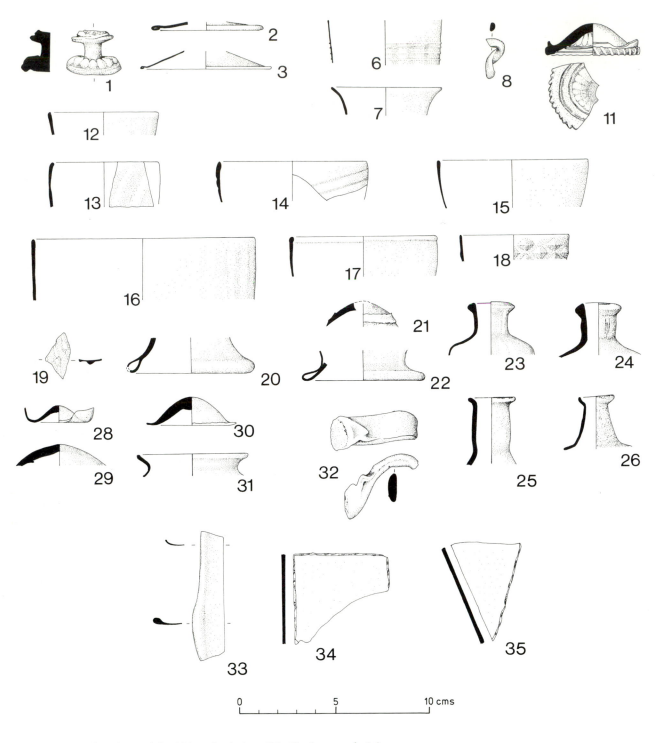

Fig 116　Post-medieval vessel (1–32) and window (33–5) glass; scale 1:2

The seventeenth-century glass
by Robert Charleston

Venetian and *façon de Venise* glass (Fig 116)

A few of the Beeston Castle glass fragments represent the colourless soda-lime glass (in reality usually tinged with brown or grey) called by the Venetian glass-makers *cristallo*, and exported by them to most of Europe and parts of Asia from the fifteenth century until their industry declined towards 1700 (Charleston 1984, 52-71). The three-piece wine glass composed of bowl, stem, and foot was the dominant form created by the Venetians in the course of the sixteenth century and maintained through most of the seventeenth century. Among the Beeston fragments is the top portion of a 'lion mask' stem (Fig 116.1), a hollow-blown baluster-shaped stem representing on two faces lions' masks with festoons between: here only the upper border of gadrooning survives. These finds probably mark the *terminus post quem non* for these stems (Charleston 1984, 57; Moorhouse 1971, fig 27.1–3). The type is common throughout the second half of the sixteenth and the first half of the seventeenth centuries. In addition three foot fragments (Fig 116.2 and 3 and no 4, not illustrated) with narrow edge folds represent three glasses, one of them probably associated with the lion mask stem. A mould-blown fragment with a vertical rim (no 5, not illustrated) perhaps came from the bowl of a goblet, but is too small to permit a reconstruction. A further fragment (Fig 116.6), from a glass of fine quality, is decorated with four turns of self-coloured applied thread. Whereas the diameter of the fragment (c 65mm) suggests the bowl of a wine glass, it is not impossible that it came from a beaker with flaring lip of a type found in the Gracechurch St hoard (Oswald and Phillips 1949, 35), dating mainly from the first half of the seventeenth century. These beakers, however, are usually of less fine *cristallo*, characterised as beige-white in colour and probably of English manufacture. The fragment (Fig 116.8), formed part of an elaborate stem, made by coiling a long ribbed tube into a complicated composition of superimposed loops, in the style which fell within the category called at the time 'of extraordinary fashion'; such glasses seem to fall within the first half of the seventeenth century.

A single foot fragment of a beaker glass (Fig 116.11) in *cristallo* belongs to a well-known group of 'chequered spiral trail' glasses, in which a thread is applied in a spiral to the outside of the vessel, which is then forced into a ribbed mould which indents the trail to give a modified chequered appearance. The Beeston Castle fragment shows the end of the trail, and the impressions of the vertically ribbed mould underneath the foot, the edge of which is finished with a thicker applied overlapping thread ornamented with a notched pattern produced by a 'rigaree' (a metal milled wheel resembling a pastry cook's wooden wheel). These glasses are usually in the form of small cylinders with a slightly domed 'kick' under the foot, and were probably referred to as 'mortar glasses'. This is a shape proper to northern Europe, and was not part of the Venetian repertoire, although it should be borne in mind that the Venetians were adept at making glass to suit their northern customers. From 1608 Edward Salter worked a glasshouse in London which specialised in beakers and cylindrical beer glasses in crystal; these were specifically mentioned as being not in the Venetian style (Charleston 1984, 61–2). On the other hand, the English site most prolific in producing such glasses is Plymouth (Charleston 1986, figs 9.16–31, and 15.4), a location which suggests the possibility of trade. It should also be borne in mind that glasses of this type are not infrequently represented in Netherlands paintings. On balance, these glasses seem most likely to have been English-made. As this suggests, the Venetian style of glass-making was copied in many countries in northern Europe, including England, and it is often impossible to be certain whether a fragment is part of an imported Venetian glass or of a homemade product; however, those of the finest quality, of thin and colourless metal (Fig 116.7), are likely to be imports.

A fine manganese purple fragment (Fig 116.12), part of the rim of a cylindrical vessel, may be of either Venetian or English origin. The possibility of its being English is supported by the existence of another purple glass, presumed to be of sixteenth-century date and known to have had a continuous history in England; glass coloured by manganese was certainly being made in England towards the end of the seventeenth century (Charleston 1984, 59–60, 132). There seems therefore no intrinsic reason why a fragment of such glass found in a mid-seventeenth-century context should not be English-made.

Green glass (Fig 116)

Of quite a different nature is the usually green glass made in the English country glasshouses, originally scattered in the woodlands of the Weald and a number of Midland and northern counties, including Cheshire. This naturally coloured, potash-lime glass was used throughout the Middle Ages for windows, and for utilitarian vessels such as lamps, bottles, and urinals (Charleston 1983, 112–4). In the second half of the sixteenth century, however, it was also used for drinking vessels, the most common type being a tall, roughly cylindrical beaker with slightly inward-slanting rim (Fig 116.13–15, 17), the base formed from the same bubble of glass as the body of the beaker, by pushing the base inwards and upwards to form a pedestal foot of double thickness (Fig 116.20, 21). Although most specimens are hopelessly fragmented, one or two survive in sufficiently complete state to indicate the general order of shape (Noel Hume 1962, 269–70). A less common second type has a shorter, more flaring, funnel-shaped body and the same foot formation. A more or less complete glass of this type was found at Nonsuch Palace. The finding of a foot fragment without sufficient wall fragments to indicate the bowl profile makes positive identification uncertain, although the tall beaker with inward-sloping rim seems much the commoner. The tall beaker may be plain or decorated with mould-blown ribbing, either vertical or 'wrythen' spirally (Fig 116.13); or may be decorated with various types of mould-blown diaper (Noel Hume 1962, figs 1 and 2). Two Beeston Castle fragments display a sharply defined relief lozenge diaper on a good-quality green metal (Fig 116.18, 19). These glasses probably date from the first half of the seventeenth century (Crossley and Aberg 1972, figs 64 and 65). An exceptionally fine-quality, glossy green pushed-in foot (Fig 116.22) may come from the base of a flask rather than a beaker, and is possibly an import, perhaps from Germany.

In the second half of the sixteenth century cylindrical beakers were joined by a different type of container, the tallish, vertical-sided body mould-blown in a square or hexagonal mould, with the short neck everted and roughly cut off. These square 'case bottles' were intended for grouping in pairs or fours in canteens or 'cases' for protection (Charleston 1984, 91–2). Flasks of similar capacity, however, could also be made with cylindrical body. In the absence of any clear indication of their appearance in cross-section, it is impossible to say to which type the neck or base fragments of such flasks belong (Fig 116.23–6, 28–30). The Beeston Castle examples are probably all of seventeenth-century date. Of the same green glass, wide-mouthed jars of *albarello* type were also made for apothecaries' use (Fig 116.31, of seventeenth-century date). Also in green glass is a fragmentary handle, perhaps of a jug (Fig 116.32).

A curiously amorphous oblong fragment of pale green glass (Fig 116.33) is probably to be interpreted as the edge of a window pane produced by the 'muff' technique, in which a long cylinder of glass is split longitudinally while hot and then opened out into a rectangular panel (Charleston 1984, 13–14, 38–9). The two vertical edges produced by this technique are frequently considerably thickened, and are liable to distortion during the flattening process. A number of fragmentary, lozenge-shaped 'quarries' are also included among the finds (Figs 116.34 and 35). All probably date from the first half of the seventeenth century.

The principal pieces are listed in the catalogue (M2:F10–13). Other non-diagnostic but probably seventeenth-century pieces, and the later glass, were briefly examined and are listed in the archive. Window glass fragments other than those described here are also separately listed in the microfiche (M2:G1–2).

The clay pipes
by Peter Davey

Introduction

The text is divided into two main sections. The first deals with the evidence the pipes provide towards the interpretation of the archaeological contexts in which they occur, including a detailed analysis of the stem-bore results (Fig M122, M3:A3; Tables M41 and M42, M3:A4–6). This section is available in full in the microfiche (M2:G3–M3:A7), and the information from the pipe analysis has been integrated in the stratigraphic text. The second section offers an assessment of the local and regional significance of the pipes themselves, and is presented here.

Although two previous reports, one (unpublished) on the 1968–73 excavations (Arnold 1975) and the other on the 1975/6 seasons in the Inner Ditch (Davey 1977b), have formed starting points for this report, all the material has been studied afresh.

Summary

The Beeston clay pipes provide the largest and most significant dated groups from the North West, outside Chester. They suggest that whilst the supplies, if not the occupants, of the castle during the Civil War came from the south east, probably Nantwich, those for its demolition gangs came from the Rainford area to the north. Only a handful of seventeenth-century pipes were made in Chester. The reoccupation of the Outer Gateway was also supplied from the Nantwich area and beyond. Although some Chester material is included amongst the sporadic finds of the eighteenth and nineteenth centuries, this is overshadowed by the volume of Broseley products which succeeded in reaching the site.

The pipes in their regional context

The clay pipes from Beeston Castle are important in providing a large collection of closely dated and well stratified groups from an area of Cheshire at some distance from the well-studied production centres at Chester (18km), Rainford (35km), Newcastle-under-Lyme (34km), and Broseley (55km – all as the crow flies). They provide both an opportunity to test existing dating assumptions, particularly for the mid-seventeenth century, and the chance to assess the strength of the competing local industries over time.

The Civil War groups

At least 166 definable pipes of this period were recovered, 73 of which were from closed Civil War deposits (Table 43). They consist of a variety of simple, undecorated, heeled and spurred pipes as described in the microfiche (M2:G3). In general terms they are equivalent to Forms 15–20 in the Chester type series (Rutter and Davey 1980, 216, fig 76), which are dated, on Chester evidence, to 1630–50. The Beeston evidence, which proves that the use of these pipes predates 1646, confirms the Chester dating. In a number of respects, however, the pipes are unlike those published from Chester. The rather sharp tapering of the bowl towards the mouth from a midway position on some examples (Fig 117.3–5), reminiscent of the Dutch 'biconical' forms, is not met with in Chester. Although some of the Beeston shapes are similar to those from Chester – in particular Fig 117.12 is very close to Chester Form 9 (ibid) – most cannot be closely paralleled. In addition, Chester groups of this period normally include a reasonable number of well-finished and milled examples. The Lower Bridge Street pit group, for example, has 9 out of 25 pipes with milling (36%), while the probable kiln group from Princess Street, which may be slightly later in date, has 42 out of 107 milled examples (39% – ibid, 57–70). Only one of the Beeston Civil War finds is milled (<1%) and this example (Fig 119.33) is certainly not a Chester product. There is a single example of a Chester-type NE stamp (Fig 119.39). Other common early Chester stamps, such as OP, SE, and AL are completely lacking. The AL stamp was the one most commonly produced in Chester from around 1630–64 when its maker, Alexander Lanckton, left the city. Only one of these was found at Beeston, from a Period 9 context (Fig 120.41). Thus it seems likely that, with a few exceptions, most of the pipes from the Civil War deposits were not made at Chester.

Only five marked pipes are from Period 7 contexts. One is a nine-spoked wheel mark of a type common throughout England during the first half of the seventeenth century (Fig 119.31). Another is a heel stamped DB on a non-local form. Another example of this pipe and mark was recovered from Civil War deposits at Dudley Castle (Higgins 1987, 596, fig 82.2) which suggests that it is a West Midlands import. The third marked pipe came from entranceway layers at the Outer Gateway (OG 89). It is fragmentary and carried the letters HH in relief on the heel (Fig 119.38). It is similar to another fragmentary HH-marked pipe from the post-Civil War accumulations in the Inner Ditch (Fig 119.37). The other two marked pipes from this period were both recovered from the upper Civil War layers of the South-East Tower (SET 4). One has a Rainford type GL mark (Fig 120.43) and is probably the

Table 43 Clay pipes: the main datable types of pipe and stamp by area and period

	Bowl date range	Period 7	8	9	Total
Inner Ward					
Small plain heeled	1630–50	13	—	17	30
Small spurred	1630–50	2	—	4	6
Rainford-type (plus stamps)	1650–70	—	—	7	7
Later seventeenth-century	1660–90	—	—	—	—
Seventeenth to eighteenth-century	1690–1720	—	—	—	—
Nineteenth-century types	1800–1900 plus	—	—	16	16
Total		15		44	59
(milled pipes)		(—)		(8)	(8)
Outer Ward					
Small plain heeled	1630–50	—		10	10
Small spurred	1630–50	—		—	—
Rainford-type (plus stamps)	1650–70	—		8	8
Later seventeenth-century	1660–90	—		—	—
Seventeenth to eighteenth-century	1690–1720	—		—	—
Nineteenth-century types	1800–1900 plus	—		74	74
Total		—		92	92
(milled pipes)		(—)		(6)	(6)
Inner Ditch					
Small plain heeled	1630–50	6	—	—	6
Small spurred	1630–50	—	—	—	—
Rainford-type (plus stamps)	1650–70	—	4	1	5
Later seventeenth-century	1660–90	—	2	—	2
Seventeenth to eighteenth-century	1690–1720	—	—	—	—
Nineteenth-century types	1800–1900 plus	—	—	9	9
Total		6	6	10	22
(milled pipes)		(—)	(3)	(1)	(4)
Outer Gateway					
Small plain heeled	1630–50	42	29	25	96
Small spurred	1630–50	8	7	2	17
Rainford-type (plus stamps)	1650–70	?2	5	13	20
Later seventeenth-century	1660–90	—	14	3	17
Seventeenth to eighteenth-century	1690–1720	—	12	4	16
Nineteenth-century types	1800–1900 plus	—	—	2	2
Total		52	67	49	168
(milled pipes)		(2)	(11)	(8)	(21)
All areas					
Small plain heeled	1630–50	62	29	52	143
Small spurred	1630–50	10	7	6	23
Rainford-type (plus stamps)	1650–70	1	9	29	39
Later seventeenth-century	1660–90	—	16	3	19
Seventeenth to eighteenth-century	1690–1720	—	12	4	16
Nineteenth-century types	1800–1900 plus	—	—	101	101
Total		73	73	195	341
(milled pipes)		(2)	(14)	(23)	(39)

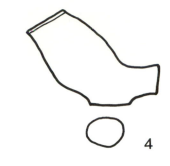

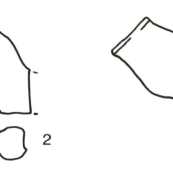

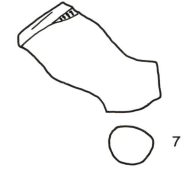

1

2

3

4

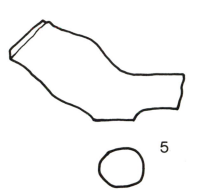

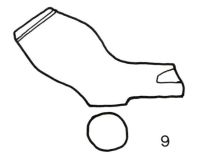

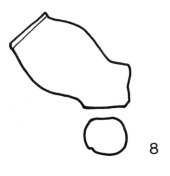

5

6

7

8

9

10

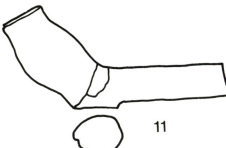

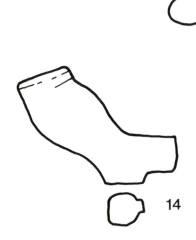

11

12

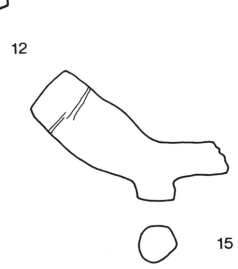

13

14

15

Fig 117 Clay tobacco pipes; scale 1:1

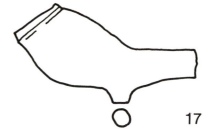
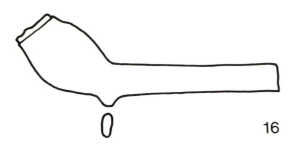
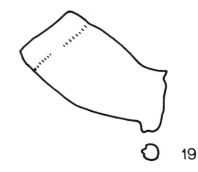
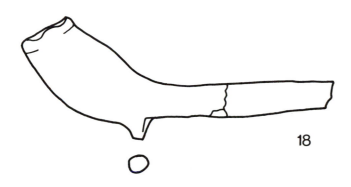
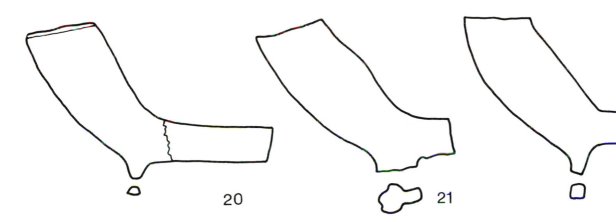
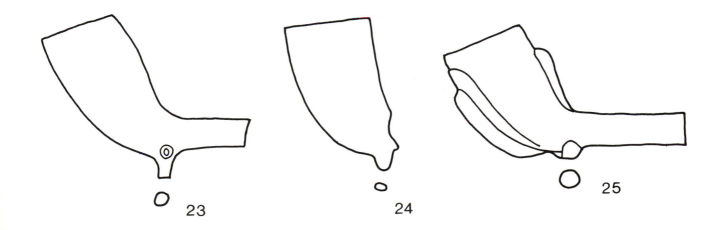

Fig 118 Clay tobacco pipes; scale 1:1

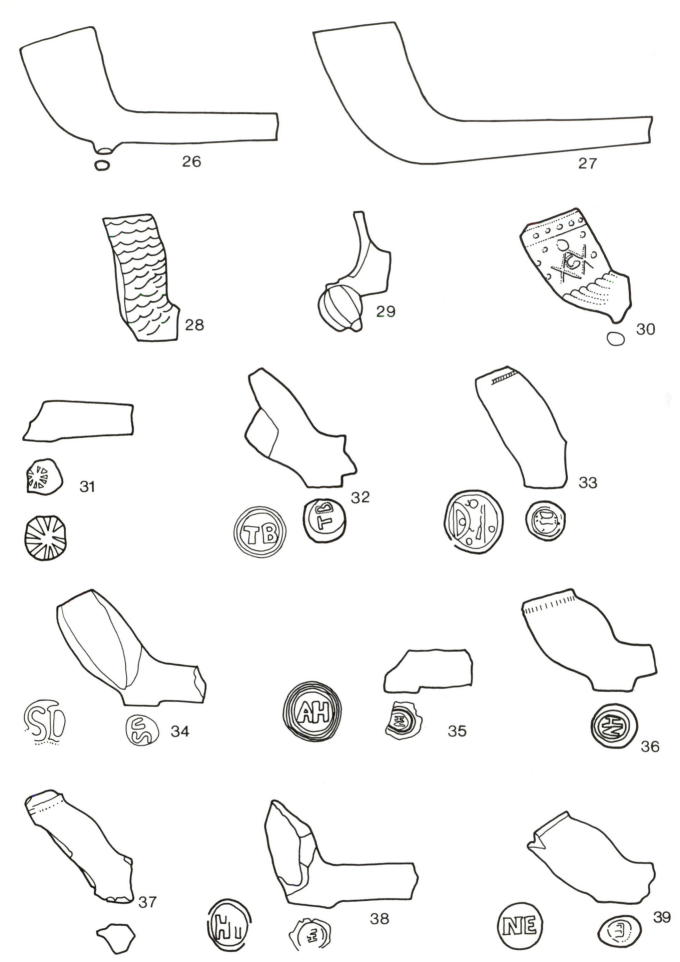

Fig 119 Clay tobacco pipes; scale 1:1 except stamps which are 2:1

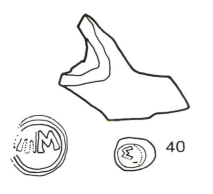

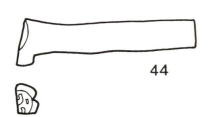
40

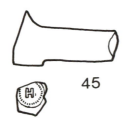
41

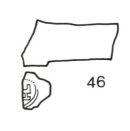
42

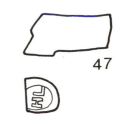
43

44

45

46

47

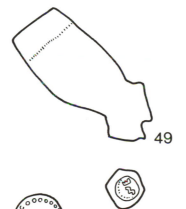

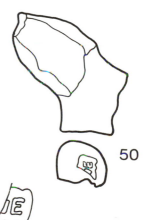

48

49

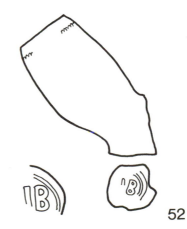
50

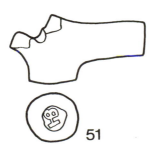
51

52

Fig 120 Clay tobacco pipes; scale 1:1 except stamps which are 2:1

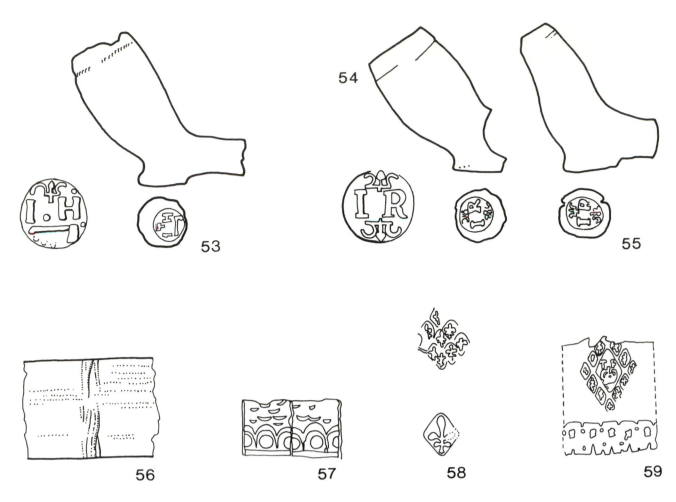

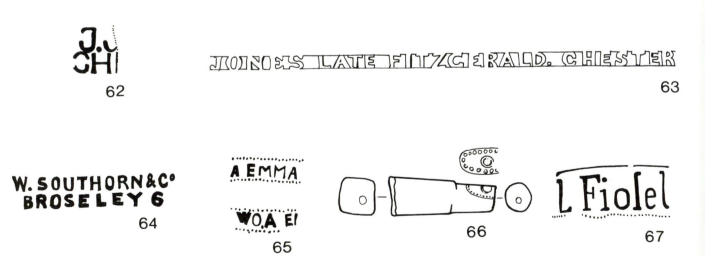

Fig 121 Clay tobacco pipes; scale 1:1 except stamps which are 2:1

product of one of the Lyon family who were working in south Lancashire by the 1640s. The other, marked NE, is the only Chester-marked pipe from this period (Fig 119.39). The contexts of these latter three marked pipes suggest that they may well be associated with the destruction of the castle in 1646 and after, rather than with its occupation during the various sieges. None of these marks gives any indication as to the source of the bulk of the pipes smoked by the defenders of the site during the Civil War.

A comparison of the Beeston finds with early material from other neighbouring centres is also unrewarding. The mid-seventeenth-century Rainford kiln group has distinctive stamps, forms, and fabrics, none of which can be observed in the Beeston finds (Higgins 1982). Although exhaustive study of the pipe-makers of Newcastle-under-Lyme (Barker 1985) showed that pipe-making had begun there by 1637, no marked pipes dating to earlier than 1650 have been recovered. The earliest forms of pipe associated with the Charles Riggs stamps are as different from the Beeston finds as are the Chester examples (ibid, 264–7). Similarly, the early heeled forms from Broseley do not compare at all closely with those from Beeston (Atkinson 1975, 24). Further afield, the Beeston forms are distinct from those of London (cf Atkinson and Oswald 1969, 8–9, figs 1 and 2) and Bristol (cf Jackson and Price 1974, 88–109). This leads inevitably to the conclusion that the Beeston pipes mostly derive from a maker or makers unknown, and from a centre or centres unknown. Perhaps the most likely contender is the town of Nantwich, 13km to the south-east of the castle. Although no attempt has been made to locate a possible industry there at this period, it is known that at least one pipe-maker was working in the town by the early eighteenth century (McNeil-Sale et al 1980, 29). Small groups of distinctive pipes have been recovered from excavations in the town centre (McNeil-Sale et al 1979, 190).

The Rainford type pipes

A minimum of 39 examples of this group of forms and stamps was found. A number (9) were directly associated with the final Civil War occupation and demolition; most (29) came from Period 9 contexts (Table 43). A wide range of makers seems to be represented, including TB, SD, AH (2), HM, GL (3), and HL (3) (Figs 119.32, 34–6; 120.40, 42–7 respectively). This confirms the impression from other excavated groups, such as those from the Isle of Man (Davey 1989) and Drogheda, north of Dublin (Norton 1984), that the south Lancashire makers probably employed middlemen to market all their products and did not trade independently at a distance. The Beeston finds are useful in confirming the documentary evidence that some of these makers were in production by the middle of the seventeenth century. It also establishes that their trading area extended well south of the Mersey and beyond sites such as Norton Priory and village, where they have already been noted in some numbers (Davey 1985).

The late seventeenth-century pipes

The 19 examples that can be dated to the period 1660–90

are more amorphous than the Rainford types. Apart from a single late Rainford form (Fig 120.52), most exhibit southern influences, particularly Broseley. There is an unstamped example of a Broseley Type 2B (Fig 117.15; Atkinson 1975, 25) and one certain Broseley product (Fig 120.51) made by Henry Bradley (Higgins 1987, 190–248). The remaining six stamp types have strong Broseley affinities but do not appear to be Broseley products (Higgins 1987, 329). They have already been recorded in either Chester or south Cheshire and include three WE dies (Fig 120.48–50), two pipes stamped IR in well-executed lettering divided by a tripartite floral symbol above and below (Fig 121.54 and 55), and a single pipe stamped IH with a hatchet or pipe beneath the initials (Fig 121.53). There is a single, unprovenanced example of this stamp on a similar bowl in the Grosvenor Museum, Chester (Rutter and Davey 1980, 113, fig 38.57), and the recovery of a full name stamp marked IERE HATCHETT at Buckley (Clwyd) (Bentley et al 1980, 276, fig 3.20) on a Broseley Type 5 bowl led to the supposition that this IH mark represented the same maker and that the symbol beneath the initials was a hatchet. Excavations in Nantwich (McNeil-Sale et al 1979; 1980), however, rather tend to question this argument. The Wood Street excavations produced 18 examples of this mark from at least five different dies, and three examples of a GH mark with similar symbolism (McNeil-Sale et al 1980, 29). This makes it more likely that the symbol beneath the letters is actually a pipe. Recent examination of a large collection from two fields in Willaston, 4km north of Nantwich, provided a further 103 examples of the IH mark, one pipe with the IR mark, and a number of other initials with the same dividing symbols as nos 54 and 55. This suggests very strongly that the Beeston pipes were produced in a south Cheshire centre, probably Nantwich, by an industry strongly influenced by Broseley forms and mark types. This possibility reinforces the idea that the Civil War period pipes from Beeston may have come from the same source.

Three Dutch pipe fragments (Fig 121.57 and 58 – two examples) also probably belong to this period and again emphasise the very slight Dutch penetration into the north-west of England, compared, say, with the south-west peninsular or north-east Scotland (cf Norton Priory, Cheshire, Davey 1985; Plymouth, Oswald 1979; and Aberdeen, Davey 1982b).

Eighteenth-century types

Sixteen early eighteenth-century pipes were recovered from the site (Table 43), almost all of which appear to derive from Chester. These start with the Chester lozenge stamp and early border (Fig 121.59), and include a number of very elegant, thin-walled bowls (Fig 118.21 and 22). Later eighteenth-century activity is suggested by the presence of a single bowl from the Outer Ward (Fig 118.23) and three Chester roller-stamped stems which probably date from the middle of the century (Fig 121.60–61).

The nineteenth-century and later pipes

Altogether fragments of at least 101 nineteenth-century

or later pipes were recovered, the majority from the Outer Ward, probably associated with the Bunbury Fair which was established after 1851. Most are plain types. Of the 11 maker-marked stems, two are Chester products both apparently made by John Jones II who was working at the Newgate from 1840–69 (Fig 121.62 and 63). The latter stem can be dated fairly precisely to 1840 when the maker took over the factory from Joseph Fitzgerald II (1792–1840). Two of the marked stems are imports from Fiolet of St Omer in the Pas de Calais (Fig 121.67). The remaining seven were made by W Southorn and Co of Broseley, a company which was marking pipes in this manner, with its name and a code number, from around 1850–1960. The example illustrated here (Fig 121.64) bears the number 6; others in the collection are marked 4 and 18. The precise meaning of these numbers is not known.

In addition there are a few mould-decorated nineteenth-century pipes and stems. One bowl has an all-over fish-scale surface (Fig 119.28), another has a football at the end of the heel (Fig 119.29), and another appears to bear Masonic symbols (Fig 119.30). A stem carrying part of the chorus of a popular music hall song of the 1850s – 'Oh! Emma! Whoa! Emma!' – (Fig 121.65; cf Higgins 1988, 8–9), and a curious, partially square-sectioned, black stem with a moulded legend, or possible maker's name, beginning with 'O', complete the collection (Fig 121.66).

The medieval pottery
by Paul Courtney

A discussion of the residuality of the pottery, the detailed fabric descriptions, and the catalogue of illustrated vessels are in the microfiche (M3:A8–C3).

Introduction

The medieval pottery examined in this report came from all the Beeston Castle excavations of recent years. Material is reported on here from the Inner Ditch excavations (Hough 1978), as well as from the Inner and Outer Ward and Outer Gateway excavations. The overall size of the assemblages is tabulated (Table 44). Considerable post-depositional movement and marked residuality in most contexts was a feature of all the excavated areas. The only fairly reliable ceramic groups came from the construction trenches and even this material is small in volume, fragmented, and difficult to date closely. Of the reconstructed vessels only five were estimated to comprise over 20% and, not surprisingly, all came from the Inner Ward, three primarily from deposits in the South-West Tower (Figs 123.10; 124.24 and 26; 127.93 and 97; Table M45, M3:A9).

Methods

The Inner Ward pottery was only made available for study after the other pottery had been analysed and catalogued, and had therefore to be sorted into vessels independently of the Inner Ditch material. Exhaustive attempts, however, were then made to cross-reference

Table 44 Medieval pottery: quantity and minimum vessel counts by area

	Sherds	Minimum vessels
Inner Ward	4516	240
Inner Ditch	504	208
Outer Gateway	1168	275
Outer Ward	109	13
Total	6297	711

any vessel linkage between the two sites. The Inner Ditch pottery came from sections through the ditch deposits on either side of the causeway, the bridge pit, and a small amount from the Outer Ward north-west cutting at the approach way. In addition considerable amounts of unstratified material were subsequently recovered from clearance of the Inner Ditch to the west of the causeway by machine or labourers. Some of the spoil from these clearances, and from non-archaeological work in the Inner Ward, was dumped downhill at the Outer Gateway, and it is possible that unstratified finds from the Outer Gateway include material from the Inner Ward and Ditch.

The pottery was quantified by sherd count and by sorting into minimum vessels, necessitating the laying out of all sherds from the site and cross-referencing between layers. Each vessel was given a unique number and its fabric, form, decoration, and context details were entered on a *pro forma*.

Regional background

Beeston Castle commands the main Chester-to-Nantwich road artery (Fig 1) as it passes through a gap in the Peckforton hills (Hindle 1982, 211–13). Tarporley (4km) and Nantwich (13km) are the nearest boroughs (Beresford and Finberg 1973, 75–6). Medieval kiln sites are known at Ashton (Rutter 1977b), Arrowcroft, Chester (J Rutter, pers comm), Audlem (Webster and Dunning 1960), and Brereton Park (McCarthy and

Table 46 Medieval pottery: numbers of sherds and minimum vessels in each fabric

Fabric	Sherds (%)		Minimum vessels (%)	
A	531	(8)	64	(9)
B	3490	(55)	433	(61)
C	396	(6)	37	(5)
D	940	(15)	34	(5)
E	15	(<1)	5	(<1)
F	351	(6)	62	(9)
G	6	(<1)	4	(<1)
H	535	(8)	65	(9)
I	29	(<1)	4	(<1)
J	1		1	
K	1		1	
L	1		1	
Total	6296	(100)	711	(100)

Brooks 1988, 360–1; J Rutter, pers comm), all in Cheshire, as well as at Rhuddlan in Clwyd (Miles 1977). The date of kiln material from Sneyd Green, Stoke-on-Trent remains uncertain (Middleton 1984), although some of the Sneyd forms suggest a fourteenth- or fifteenth-century date, especially the conical jugs, a bottle, and a handled storage vessel (Middleton 1984, figs 2.1 and 2, 3.6, 4.13). Late medieval kilns are known at Ewloe, Clwyd (Harrison and Davey 1977; Davey and Morgan 1977), and at Eaton, 5km from Beeston (McCarthy and Brooks 1988, 360–1; J Rutter, pers comm). Ewloe forms include storage vessels, with applied thumb-impressed strips around the rim, and jugs, including narrow baluster or bottle forms. Eaton produced cisterns and storage vessels in a thick gritty fabric with glossy green glazes. Important comparative groups of excavated material come from Nantwich (Nailor 1983), Chester, Norton Priory near Runcorn, and a number of castle and monastic sites in north Wales (Davey 1977a).

Both Sneyd Green and Ewloe wares derive from relatively iron-free Coal Measure clays. Most pottery from the Cheshire Plain tends to be in relatively iron-rich fabrics derived from petrologically undistinctive clays of Pleistocene or recent origin (Earp and Taylor 1986; Poole and Whiteman 1966). Inclusions in all fabrics are usually restricted to rounded quartz sand, with some mica, felspar, and iron minerals (McCarthy and Brooks 1988, 359–61).

Assemblage details by fabric (Table 46)

Fabrics A (Figs 123.1, 11, 13–20; 124.21), B (Figs 123.2–7 and 12; 124.22–34; 125.35–52; 126.53–81; 127.82–92), and C (Figs 123.8; 127.93–6)

Fabrics A, B, and C are variants of the same sandy fabric and only differ in the degree of oxidisation or reduction: Fabric A is oxidised, Fabric B has reduced cores, and Fabric C is reduced. It is uncertain whether these variations resulted from accidents or from deliberate control of the firing. It is not possible to see any clear correlation of fabric colour with form or decorative style. These fabrics account for 75% of the minimum vessels at Beeston Castle. The distribution of the fabrics by site is shown in Table M47 (M3:A11).

The form analysis (Table 48) shows that jugs comprise almost 90% of the vessels in these fabric types. Twelve cooking pots were identified, of which nine had interior glazes and two were definitely unglazed. Two cooking pots showed evidence of having been wheel-thrown (Figs 126.54; 127.92). One internally glazed cooking pot had been burnished on the exterior (not illustrated). However, a further 28 unglazed vessels of uncertain form may have been cooking pots and one pipkin handle was found but could not be ascribed to a minimum vessel (Fig 127.91). Pipkins from the site have been included under cooking pots because of the difficulty of distinguishing them apart (see discussion of Fabric H, p 190). Other forms include drip pans (Figs 128.131 and 135; 129.141 and 144) and small glazed jars (Fig 126.55–7).

Most of the jugs are very fragmentary and it is difficult to reconstruct their forms. The majority appear to be coil-made, and a few vessels show evidence of the actual coils, owing to poor finishing on the interior (Fig 125.46). A few coil-made vessels appear to have had their rims finished on a wheel; this is particularly noticeable on one vessel (Fig 126.76). Wheel finishing of hand-made jugs in the early thirteenth century is also reported from Stafford (McCarthy and Brooks 1988, 359). It is impossible to calculate with any accuracy the proportion of wheel-made to coil-built vessels owing to the fragmentary nature of many pots and the occasional use of wheel finishing. However, under 20% of the jugs in these fabrics showed any positive sign of having been wheel-thrown in whole or part.

The change from coil-made to wheel-thrown jugs in the West Midlands seems to have occurred in the thirteenth century. Wheel-thrown jugs made at Worcester and in the Montgomery area can be dated to the second quarter of the thirteenth century (Vince 1984, 673–8; Knight 1982, 7). The Beeston Castle construction groups contain 15 jugs in Fabrics A, B, and C, none of which shows evidence of having been made on a wheel although two Fabric F whiteware jugs (Fig 123.9 and V2485, not illustrated) appear to be wheel-thrown. However, the Beeston Castle construction deposits, as discussed below, cannot be closely dated within the thirteenth century.

The jugs, whether coil-made or wheel-thrown, tend to have patchy splashed glazes with much pitting of the ceramic surface. On one jug (not illustrated) granules of lead up to 1.5mm in size were left on the surface owing to imperfect formation of the glaze, as was the case with two vessels in Fabric H. Similar splashed glazes are a common feature of twelfth- and early thirteenth-century jugs in northern England, for instance in the Nottingham, Derby, Lincoln, and York areas (Coppack 1980). Splashed glazes, with pitting and lead globules, are also a feature of London ware jugs of the thirteenth and fourteenth centuries (Pearce *et al* 1985).

Experimental work by Anne Woods (pers comm) of Leicester University has produced all these features (splashing, pitting, and lead globules) using powdered galena applied in a flour and water mixture to provide adhesion. This seems more practical than the direct application of dry powdered galena to the pot, which is often speculated to have been the method used. The galena (PbS) is oxidised to PbO during an initial stage of firing, then reduced to the metallic lead which jumps

Table 48 Medieval pottery: forms represented in Fabrics A, B and C (by minimum vessels)

Jugs	470
Cooking pots	13
?Cooking pots	30
Drip pan	7
Small glazed jars	6
Uncertain	8
Total	534

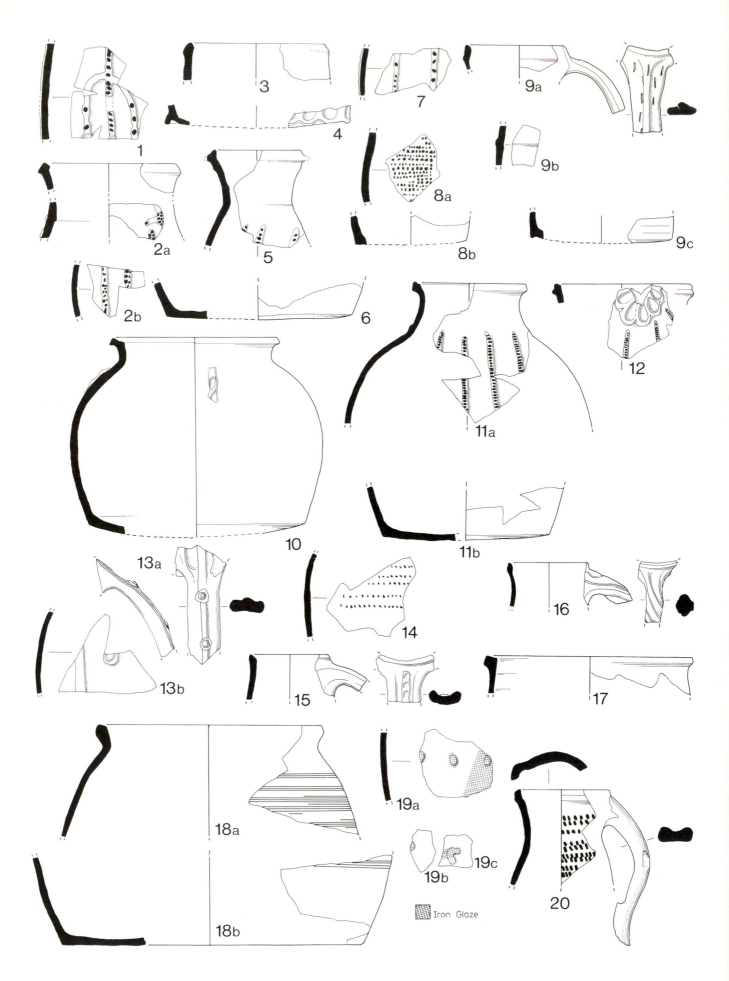

Fig 123 Medieval pottery: Fabric A (1, 11, 13–20), Fabric B (2–7, 12), Fabric C (8), Fabric F (9) Fabric H (10); scale 1:4

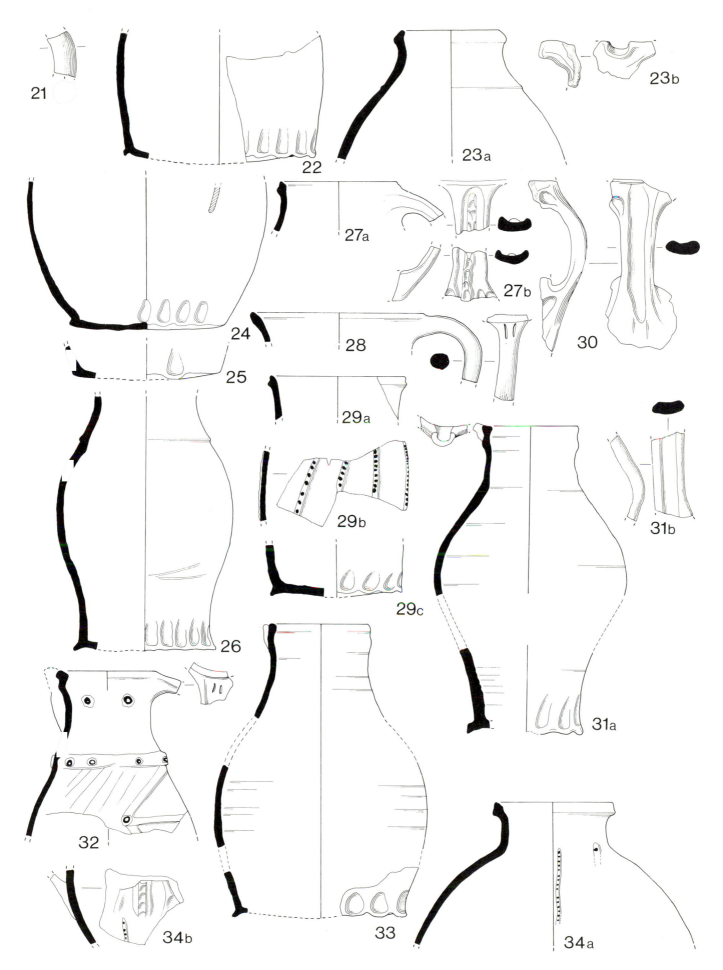

Fig 124 Medieval pottery: Fabric A (21) , Fabric B (22–34); scale 1:4

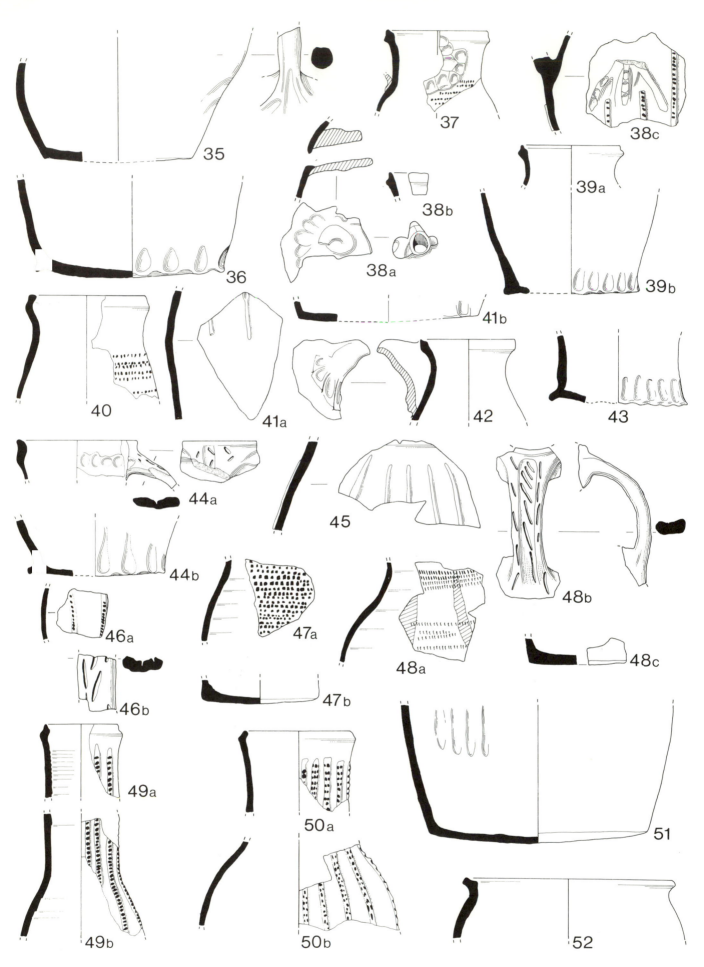

Fig 125 Medieval pottery: Fabric B; scale 1:4

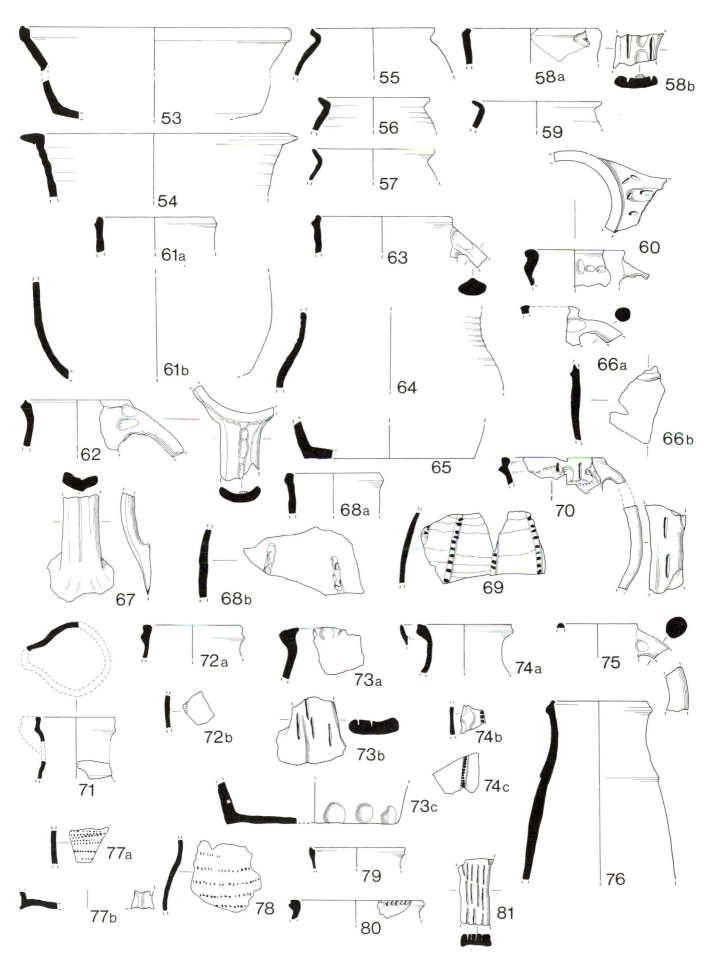

Fig 126 *Medieval pottery: Fabric B; scale 1:4*

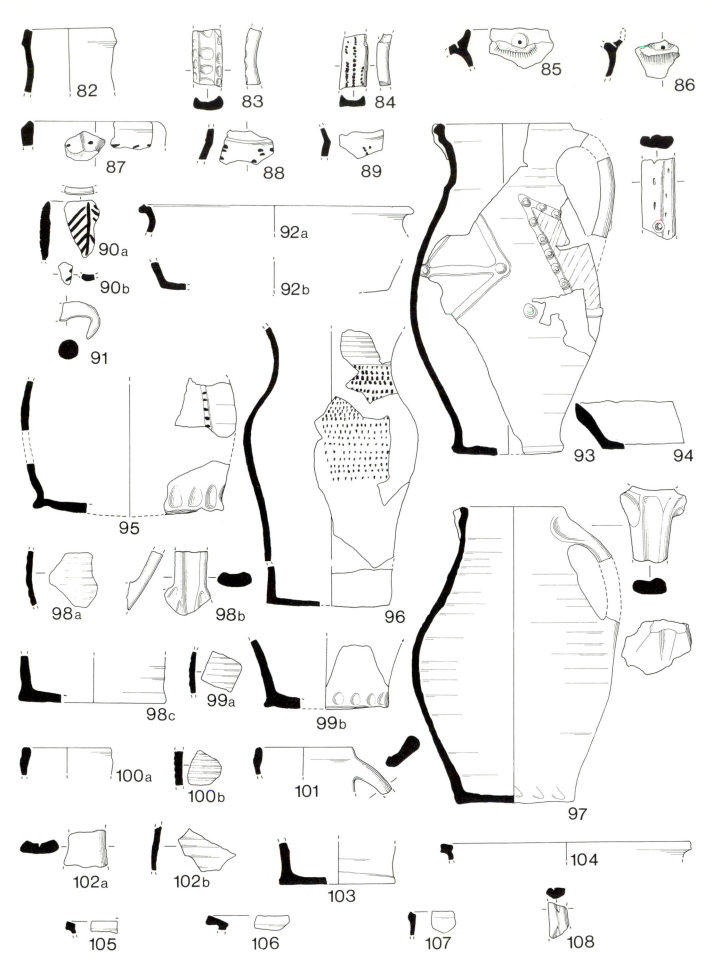

Fig 127 Medieval pottery: Fabric B (82–92), Fabric C (93–6), Fabric D (97–103), Fabric E (104–8); scale 1:4

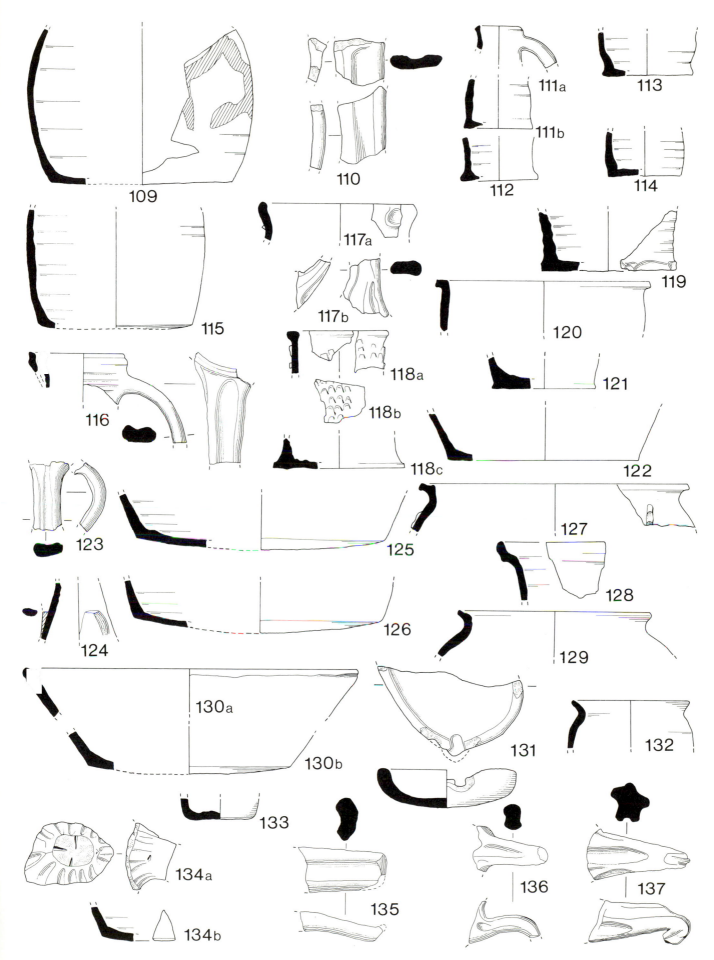

Fig 128 Medieval pottery: Fabric F (109–20), Fabric G (121–4), Fabric H (125–37); scale 1:4

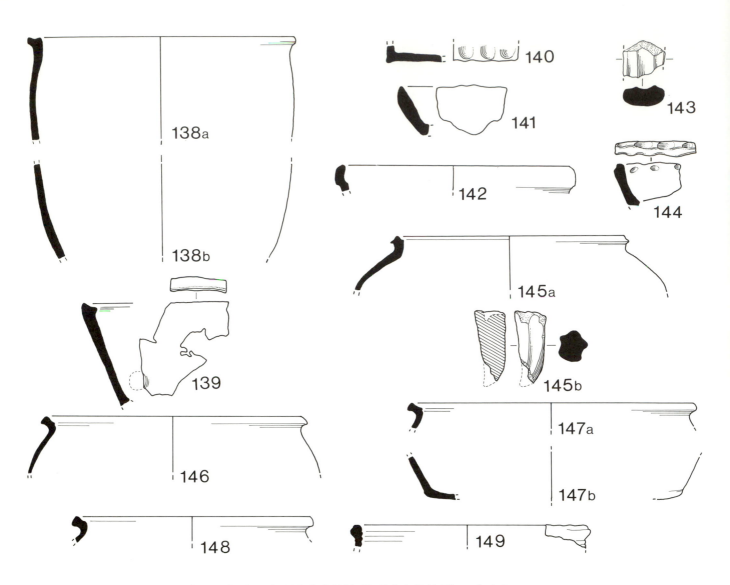

Fig 129 Medieval pottery: Fabric H (138–45), Fabric I (146–8), Fabric L (149); scale 1:4

around the kiln producing pitting. Improved glazes were probably the result of better preparation of glazing materials although the control of firing conditions may also have played a part. The more evenly glazed successors of splashed ware may have been produced by using finely powdered galena suspended in a slip (Hayfield 1985, 106–9), although other glazing compounds such as lead oxides and carbonate may also have been used (McCarthy and Brooks 1988, 35–9).

Eleven vessels, comprising nine jugs (Fig 123.19 and 20) and two drip pans (Fig 129.141), had yellow speckled glazes apparently caused by fissuring in the glaze. One jug handle had hard, angular, calcareous white fragments up to 3mm in size within the glaze (Fig 126.67). An internally glazed cooking pot (not illustrated) had angular quartz grits up to 2mm in size set in its glaze presumably for grinding food. Seventeen jugs had vertical applied strips. These were normally pinched, in some cases by rotating a tool around the pot leaving horizontal grooves in the body (Fig 126.69). In only 25 cases were the applied strips coloured with an iron compound. One vessel had a thumbed horizontal strip below its rim (V2210, not illustrated).

Rouletting occurred on 19 jugs. On one vessel it can be seen that the handle was added after the rouletting (Fig 123.20). Other forms of jug decoration included stabbed crescents (Fig 127.88), stabbing below the rim (Fig 127.87), applied pellets on the body (Fig 127.89), and thumbing below the rim (Fig 126.60). One vessel had painted iron-brown stripes in addition to rouletting (Fig 125.48). Of note is a group of highly decorated jugs with applied strips, stamps, and incised lines (Figs 123.13; 124.32; 127.93).

Most jugs had simple pinched spouts but four had applied frills (Figs 123.12; 125.37 and 42). This feature has wide regional parallels including the Audlem and Rhuddlan kiln material (Webster and Dunning 1960, fig 40.7; Miles 1977, no 5; Rutter 1977a, no 15; and Talbot 1977, nos 11–14). Two jugs had tubular spouts formed out of folding a clay slab with applied ear-like decoration (Fig 125.38).

Six jugs had rod handles including one with a twisted handle (Fig 123.16). Seventy had strap handles, often stabbed. Eight strap handles had applied central thumbed strips (Fig 123.15; 124.27; 126.62), and four had thumbing (Fig 127.83). One had multiple pinched applied strips (Fig 125.38). Two jugs, probably by the same potter, had punched holes near the top of their handles (Fig 127.85 and 86). The jug bases were flat or slightly convex. Fifty-seven were thumbed and 19 were plain. One jug had weaving impressions on its base, probably from a grass mat (V2393, not illustrated).

Fabric D (Fig 127.97–103)

The 34 vessels in this fabric are all similar jugs with little stylistic variation and may be the work of a single potter or family. The fabric is sandy, generally oxidised, and crumbly, and is represented by tiny sherds. The vessels all have strap handles, and bases may be plain or thumbed. They are all wheel-thrown and have thick, pitted, glossy glazes varying from pale green to orange in colour on oxidised bodies. Some splashing occurs at glaze margins and under handles although the pits are smaller and more closely spaced than on Fabrics A, B, and C.

Some vessels had dark green streaks in their glazes. These may be owing to the addition of copper filings or perhaps result from the reduction of iron minerals in the clay body (Dawson and Kent 1986, 34), but the cause is difficult to assess without chemical analysis. The fact that these vessels are wheel-thrown suggests that they are unlikely to have been made before the end of the thirteenth century, but their precise chronology remains unclear.

Fabric E (Fig 127.104–8)

This fabric group comprises only five vessels, four from the Inner Ditch (Fig 127.105–8) and a fifth from the Inner Ward (Fig 127.104). It is a poor-quality fabric (soft, reduced, and sandy) and the vessels could be a poorly fired Fabric H group. However, the distinctive form of two of the vessels (nos 105 and 107) suggests a different fabric. The vessels comprise three jugs and two cooking pots. One of the jugs has traces of a degraded lead glaze (Fig 127.107). At least some of the vessels are handmade (Fig 127.105). All the sherds in this fabric clearly come from residual contexts. It is not clear how significant the localised distribution of the ware is in terms of use or chronology.

Fabric F (Figs 123.9; 128.109–20)

This group is composed of wheel-thrown pots made in relatively iron-free Coal Measure-derived clays with sand inclusions. Beeston lies between two possible sources, the Flintshire and West Midlands coalfields, and it is not possible to distinguish between them on petrological grounds. Although future research may alter the picture, the Beeston Castle narrow vessel forms

Table 49 Medieval pottery: forms represented in Fabric H (by minimum vessels)

Cooking pots	26
?Cooking pots	28
Drip pans	7
Bowl	1
Jugs	3

Table 50 Medieval pottery: forms represented in the assemblage (by minimum vessels and %)

Jugs	573	(80)
Cooking pots	50	(7)
?Cooking pots	58	(8)
Drip pans	14	(2)
Small jars	6	(<1)
Bowl	1	
Uncertain	11	(1)
Total	713	

seem closest to Flintshire examples. The Ewloe kiln products may be taken as typical of north-east Wales, with narrow bottle jugs and storage vessels predominating. Glazes are patchy and splashed although pitting is rare. The Ewloe products are closely paralleled at Beeston Castle. Bottle and baluster jugs appear to be relatively uncommon West Midlands whiteware forms, although two narrow jugs from Montgomery are likely to be Shropshire products (Courtney and Jones, forthcoming), and there is a single example in the Sneyd Green kiln group (Middleton 1984, fig 3.6). At Beeston Castle there were at least 15 bottle jugs and a further six probably indicated by rod handles. One cooking pot (Fig 128.120), a handled, glazed 'storage vessel' with external sooting (Fig 128.117), and two internally glazed vessels of uncertain form were also found. Ewloe-type wares are in evidence at Chester by the mid-fourteenth century (Rutter 1977a; 1977c), and may have continued as late as the sixteenth century.

The high-quality jugs from Beeston, however, have broader forms and may come from the West Midlands, eg the group of six wheel-thrown vessels with dark streaked green glazes (possibly owing to the addition of copper). Two of these vessels came from construction contexts (Fig 123.9 and V2485, not illustrated). They are closely paralleled by two vessels recovered in recent excavations by J Manley at Caergwrle Castle (Clwyd), 22km to the west. This castle was built c 1278 and its small ceramic assemblage is dominated by local handmade pots, comparable to Fabrics A, B, and C apart from the two wheel-thrown, streaky glazed, whiteware jugs. Three jugs from Beeston have painted iron-stained stripes (Fig 128.109). Two jugs (Fig 128.118 and 119), the former with applied fish-scale decoration, are similar to vessels from Montgomery Castle (Knight 1982, 48).

Fabric G (Fig 128.121–4)

This group consists of four highly-fired vessels. These include a strap handle (Fig 128.123), a jug base (Fig 128.121), a jug or storage vessel base (Fig 128.122), and a bottle jug, possibly an overfired 'Ewloe' type in Fabric F (Fig 128.124). None of these wheel-thrown pots was glazed, and a late medieval or transitional medieval/post-medieval date is likely.

Fabric H (Figs 123.10; 128.125–37; 129.138–45)

This coarse-sandy fabric can be regarded as a coarser variant of Fabrics A, B, and C. The fabric appears to have been used for kitchen-related forms such as cooking pots and drip pans (Table 49). At least 16 of the cooking pots (eg Fig 123.10) had internally glazed bases and two were definitely unglazed. Three cooking pots were wheel-thrown (Figs 128.128; 129.142 and 145). The drip pans also had internal glazes and in two examples lead pellets were left on the surface (Fig 129.140). Two bowls (Fig 128.130; 129.139) and three jugs (Figs 128.133; 129.140), the former a bottle form, were recognised. In only two cases could pipkin-like handles be definitely associated with body sherds (Figs 128.134; 129.145). This leaves a further six handles (Fig 128.135–37) although the flatter ones are probably from drip pans.

Fabric I (Fig 129.146–8)

This group comprises wheel-thrown cooking pots in a distinctive reduced sandy fabric which appears to be paralleled (on the published description only) by some of the Nantwich Wich House pots (Nailor 1983, fig 14.44, 45, and 47). Sherds of one of the Beeston vessels found before excavation began have been suggested as Low Countries Greyware (Davey 1980, 211, table 12.1), but close examination of the fabric and the finding of further examples suggests a local origin. The same may be true for another suggested Low Countries Greyware sherd from Nantwich (ibid).

Fabric J

This group comprises an unidentified single sherd in a fine-sandy orange fabric with fine throwing lines on the interior surface suggesting wheel-thrown manufacture (not illustrated).

Fabric K

A single small sherd of Oxford AM ware in a pink, sandy fabric (not illustrated) comes from a highly decorated jug (Hinton 1973, pl 13). The wheel-thrown sherd has a green glaze and an iron-coloured vertical rouletted strip. It dates to the mid- to late thirteenth century and is a product of the Brill and Boarstall area (Mellor 1980; identification confirmed by M Mellor). The original vessel was possibly brought to the castle in the personal luggage train of a visitor from the Oxford region.

Fabric L (Fig 129.149)

A single sherd in a soft, reduced, coarse-sandy fabric was found, probably from a cooking pot. It is a hand-made rim with horizontal nail marks on the rim interior. The fabric and form would suggest a Saxo-Norman date in many parts of the country, but it is best regarded as of uncertain date, since there are no local parallels, and it was found in a residual context. Even if this is indeed from a pre-thirteenth-century vessel, its presence on Beeston crag need imply no more than a casual visit to the hill.

Discussion

Forms

The Beeston assemblage is clearly dominated by jugs (Table 50), a feature shared by other sites in the Cheshire Plain. Cooking pots form between 6% and 15% of the assemblage, depending on how fragmentary unglazed body and base sherds are assigned. The probable pipkins and late medieval 'storage vessel' forms have not been divided up separately and are included under the cooking pots.

Many of the pipkins/cooking pots had interior glazed bases, and the presence of sooting on the outside of some shows that they may have been deliberately intended to provide non-stick cooking surface. Other forms include a bowl, drip pans, and small glazed jars. No appreciable difference could be observed between the Inner Ward and Inner Ditch area, and the Outer Gateway area. The presence of cooking pots and drip pans in Outer Gateway deposits indicates that cooking was carried out here as well as in the Inner Ward.

Sooting and scaling

Traces of sooting or carbon-like deposits in the assemblage were difficult to interpret due to the fragmentary state of much of the pottery. Sooting occurred on only 26 vessels; certain or possible cooking pots, but also on six jugs, a jar, and a drip pan.

Some of the sooting especially on the jugs may have occurred after breakage but this could not be proven. On many of the cooking pots definite indications of their use in a fire could be seen, with sooting being confined to the base and lower half of the body. Sooting on one drip pan (V 191) was on its side only, suggesting that it had stood under a spit next to a fire (Moorhouse 1986, 110). Two vessels, both in Fabric H, showed water-scale deposits from the boiling of water.

Provenance

The bulk of the pottery from Beeston Castle, although petrologically undistinctive, almost certainly derived from clays of the Cheshire Plain, and could have been made in the immediate locality of the castle. It is notable that no pottery from the castle can be assigned to any of the known Cheshire kilns, despite stylistic similarities, and this may reflect the highly localised nature of potting at least until the fourteenth century. The known kiln sites, however, are probably only a small proportion of those which existed. Apart from the Oxfordshire jug (Fabric K), the most distinctive non-local pottery is the Coal Measure ware (Fabric F) from north-east Wales and/or the West Midlands. There is a notable lack of imports on the site despite their importance at Chester. The same absence is noted at the nearby town of Nantwich (Nailor 1983; Davey 1983). This must presumably be because imports were unloaded for sale in Chester with no effort to market them inland, a common feature of medieval ceramic trading patterns. It is also possible that their total absence reflects few visits by the castle's feudal overlords who might have been expected to bring more exotic pots in their baggage trains.

Dating

A small group of pottery comes from deposits associated with the construction of the castle, which began in the 1220s but which the evidence suggests may have continued throughout the century. Certainly the two wheel-thrown Fabric F (whiteware) vessels from a definite Outer Gateway construction deposit and a possible Inner Ward construction layer would seem more likely to belong to the second half of the thirteenth century on current evidence. They are closely paralleled, alongside local coil-made products, at nearby Caergwrle Castle, built c 1278. The absence of later stratified levels makes the establishment of a chronological sequence for the pottery difficult. On external evidence it may be suggested that Fabric G is late medieval and that the narrow Ewloe-type jugs of Fabric F are from the fourteenth century or later. Although stylistic change may have been slow, the similarity of much of the pottery, notably the jugs in Fabrics A, B, and C, to that in the construction deposits, and its stylistic similarity to wasters from the Rhuddlan kiln of mid-thirteenth-century date (Miles 1977), as well as the high proportion of coil-made vessels, suggest that much of the pottery assemblage dates to the thirteenth century.

The post-medieval pottery
by Penny Noake

Introduction

This report describes all the post-medieval pottery from the excavations with the exception of the published Inner Ditch material (Hough 1978). The excavations produced in excess of 10,000 sherds from which a minimum number of 1052 vessels could be established, representing activity at the castle from the seventeenth to the late nineteenth century (Table M51, M3:C8–9).

A Civil War date for the Period 7 assemblage is attested by its association both with specifically military material amongst the small finds (p 134), and with datable clay pipes (p 173). Although much of the pottery from later horizons is clearly residual from the Civil War, it was possible to identify distinctively new pottery in Period 8 layers at the Outer Gateway, most obviously the Mottled ware vessels. Period 9 was marked by the presence of modern industrial wares. While the Outer Gateway pottery was found to be widely dispersed through a number of layers (one vessel, Fig 134.76, was reconstructed from 122 sherds deriving from 19 different contexts), at the Inner Ward less post-depositional movement seemed to have taken place.

Details of the ware and fabric groups, by the author and Jane Edwards, many of the statistical tables (Tables M51, M52, M56, and M57), the catalogue of the illustrated vessels, and a discussion of the Beeston Castle evidence, are available in the microfiche (M3:C4–F8).

Methods

The pottery was divided into 13 basic wares representing well-established post-medieval pottery types: Blackware, Midland Purple ware, Tinglaze ware, Slipware, Midland Yellow ware, Martincamp Flasks, Early Stoneware, Mottled ware, Coarseware, Porcelain, Whiteware, Earthenware, and Late Stoneware. Each was separated into broad fabric divisions, and matching sherds from individual vessels grouped together. A large number of vessels could be distinguished, although none could be completely reconstructed, and only in a few cases could as much as 50% of the vessel be recovered. However, it was possible in almost all cases to establish the vessel form which was catalogued according to a simple form series. Of the 1052 vessels, the form and function of 943 could be recognised.

Pottery use at Beeston Castle

Period 7 (Table 53)

All the pottery thought to have been in use in the Civil War is discussed here. The vessels found in Period 8 and 9 layers are distinguished from the stratified material.

Table 53   Post-medieval pottery: the Civil War assemblage (Periods 7–9), forms and wares

	Blackware	Midland Purple	Tinglaze Ware	Slipware	Midland Yellow	Martincamp Flask	Early Stoneware	Total	(% of identified vessels)
Storage jar	136	124	—	10	13	—	—	283	(43)
Ointment pot	—	—	—	—	23	—	—	23	(3)
Jug	32	2	1	3	1	—	3	42	(6)
Pancheon	8	—	—	—	—	—	—	8	(1)
Dish/bowl	13	—	5	99	19	—	—	136	(21)
Drinking vessel	128	—	2	7	—	—	—	137	(21)
Bottle/flask	—	—	—	—	—	4	20	24	(3)
Costrel	1	—	—	—	—	—	—	1	(<1)
Candlestick	—	—	—	1	1	—	—	2	(<1)
Lid	—	—	—	1	—	—	—	1	(<1)
Cooking vessel	—	—	—	—	1	—	—	1	(<1)
Chafing dish	—	—	—	—	2	—	—	2	(<1)
Unidentified	45	—	—	15	9	—	—	69	—
Total	363	126	8	136	69	4	23	729	

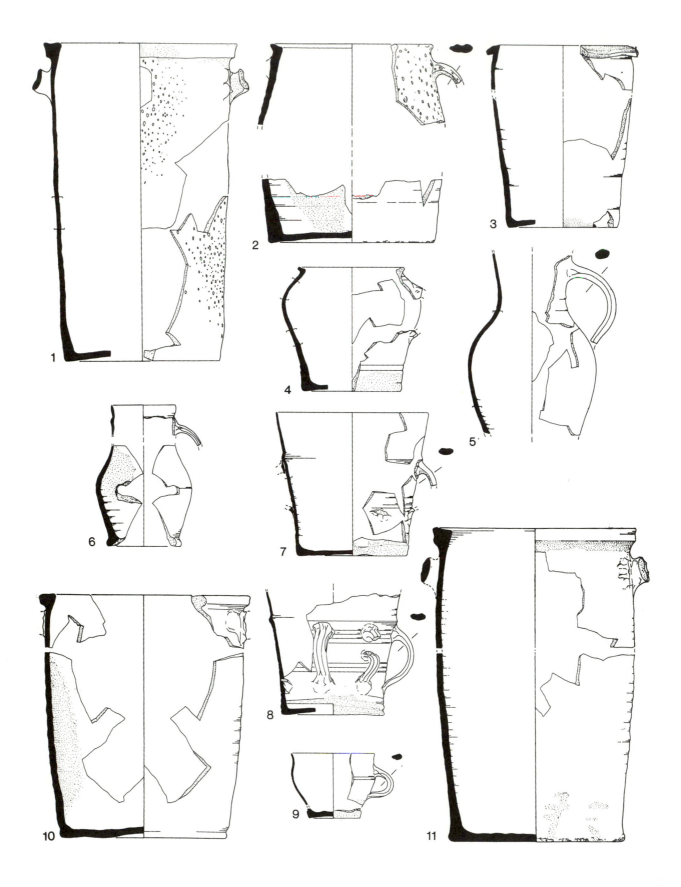

Fig 130 Post-medieval pottery: Period 7, Blackware; scale 1:4

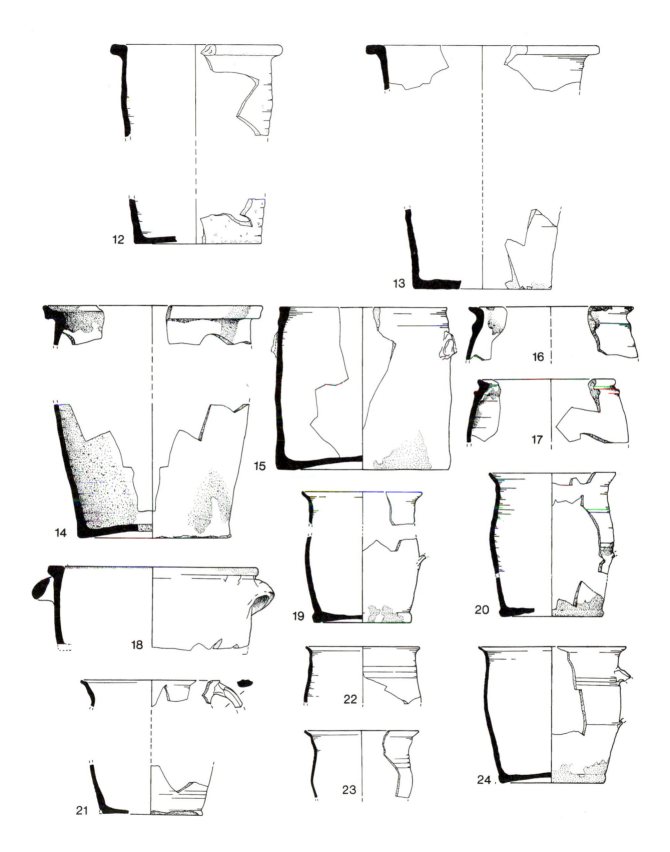

Fig 131 Post-medieval pottery: Period 7, Blackware; scale 1:4

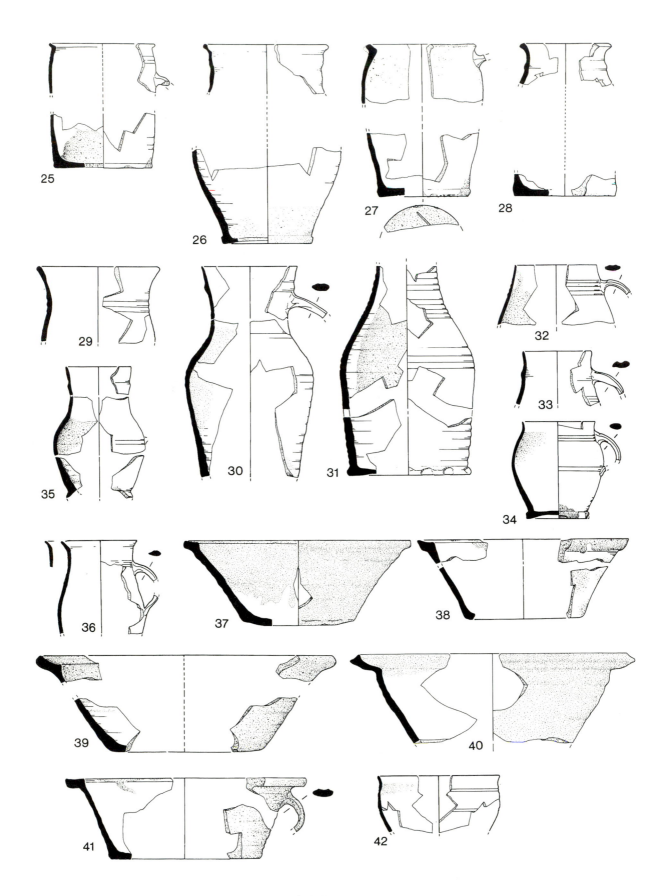

Fig 132 *Post-medieval pottery: Period 7, Blackware; scale 1:4*

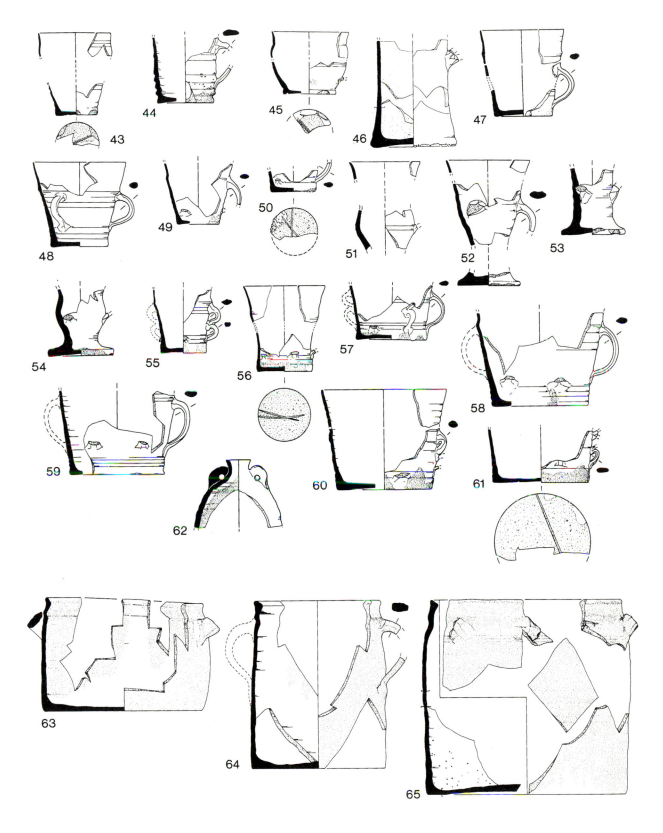

Fig 133 Post-medieval pottery: Period 7, Blackware (43–62), Midland Purple (63–5); scale 1:4

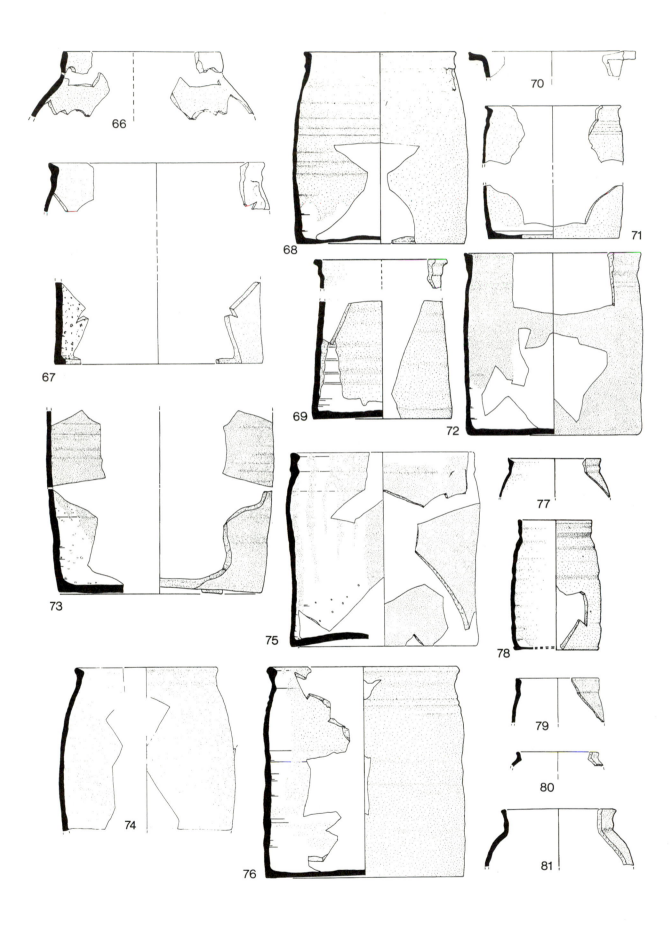

Fig 134 Post-medieval pottery: Period 7, Midland Purple; scale 1:4

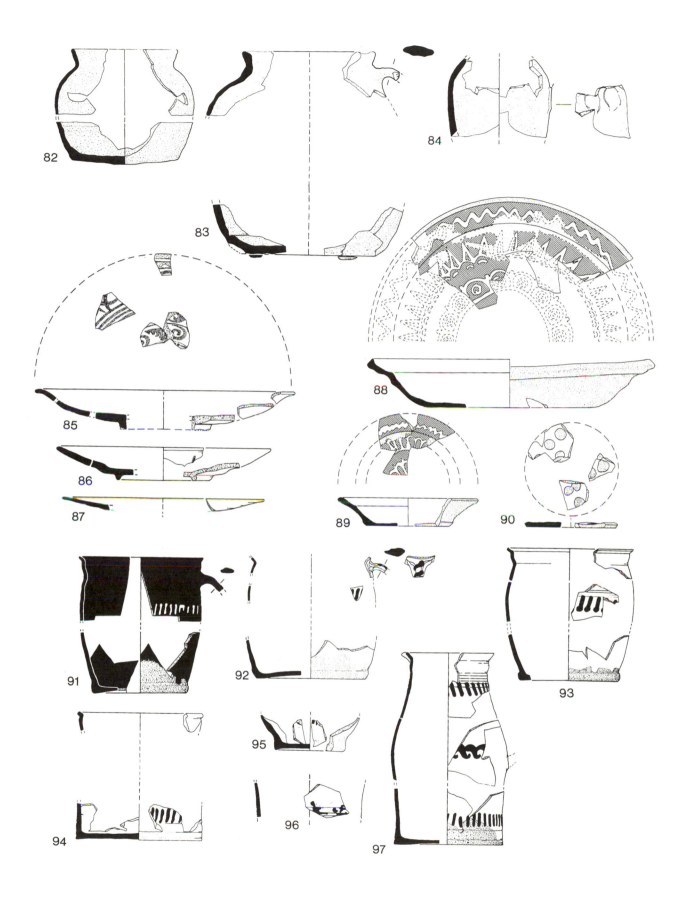

Fig 135 Post-medieval pottery: Period 7, Midland Purple (82–4), Tinglaze (85–7) , Slipware (88–97); scale 1:4

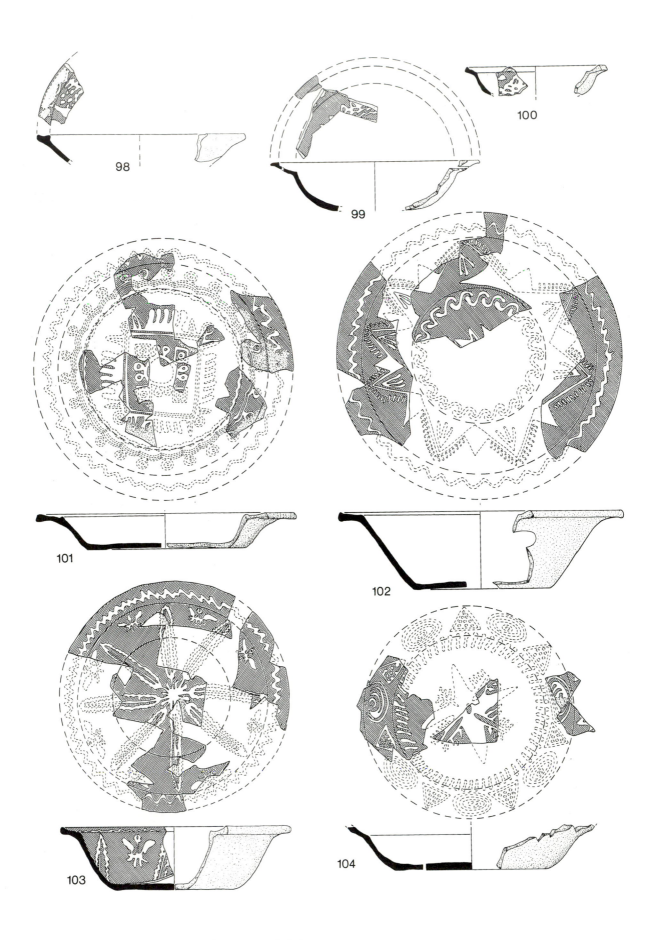

Fig 136 Post-medieval pottery: Period 7, Slipware; scale 1:4

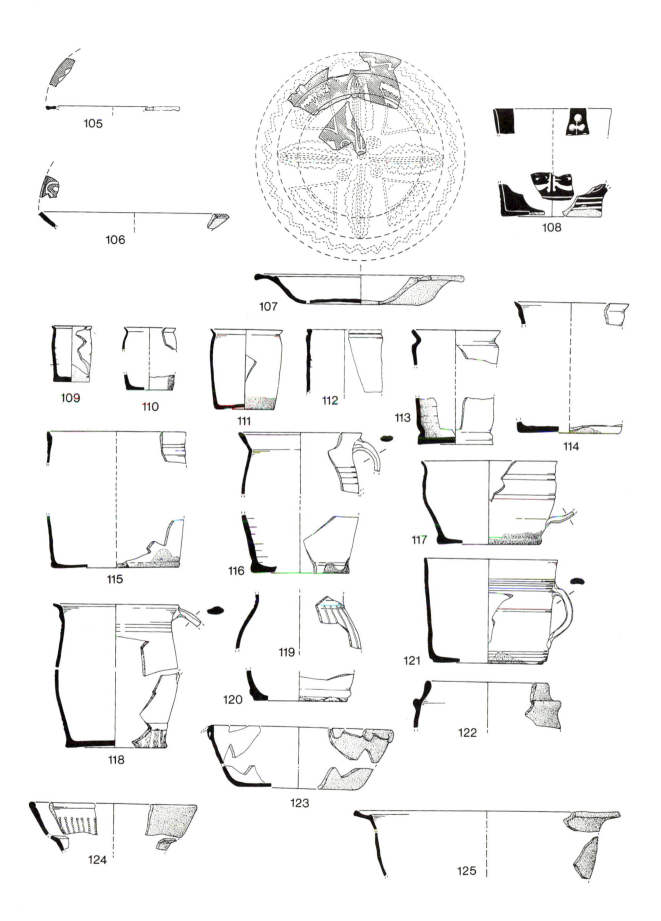

Fig 137 Post-medieval pottery: Period 7, Slipware (105–8), Midland Yellow (109–25); scale 1:4

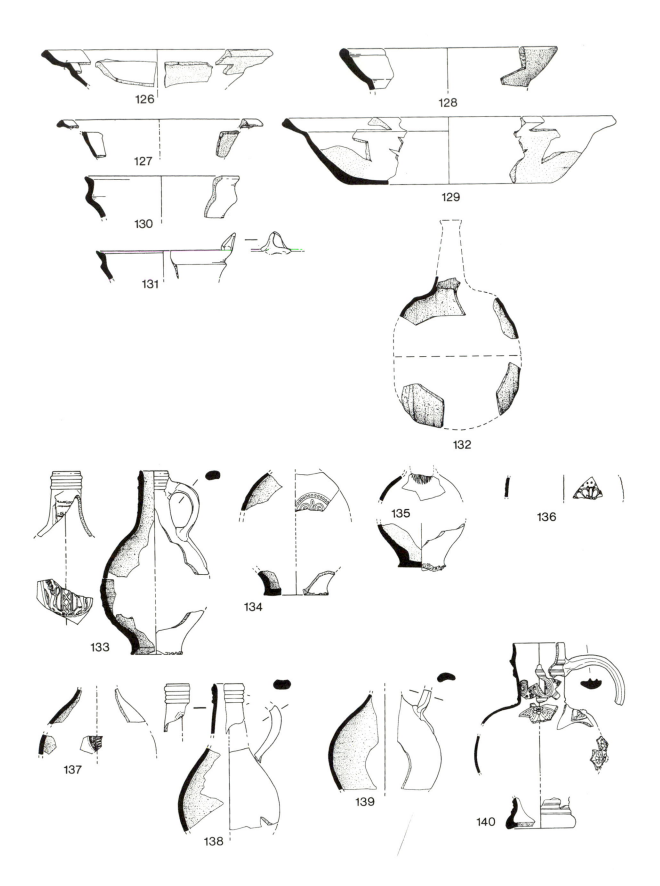

Fig 138 Post-medieval pottery: Period 7, Midland Yellow (126–31), Martincamp Flask (132), Stoneware; (133–40); scale 1:4

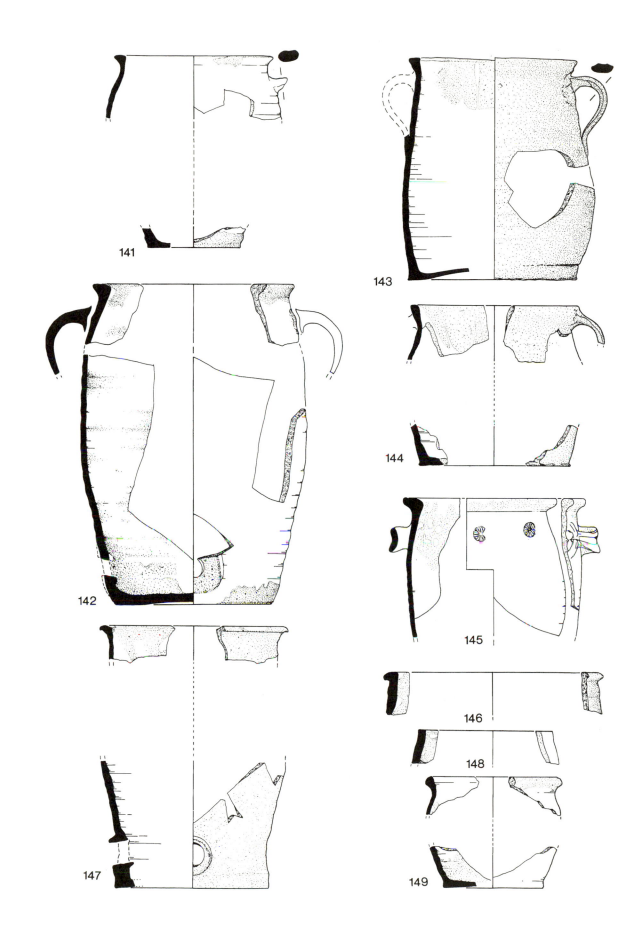

Fig 139 Post-medieval pottery: Period 8, Blackware; scale 1:4

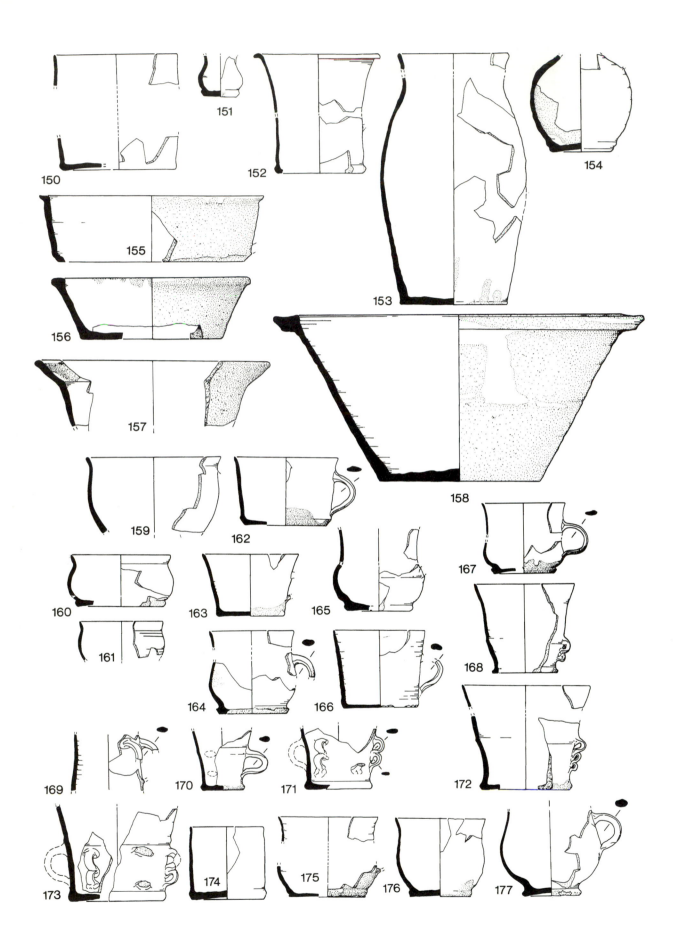

Fig 140 Post-medieval pottery: Period 8, Blackware; scale 1:4

Blackwares (Figs 130, 131, 132, 133.43–62)

The predominant forms represented were large storage vessels, straight-sided drinking vessels, and smaller jugs and jars. The large storage jars were tall and slightly rounded, with club rims and opposed horizontal handles (eg Fig 130.11). Glaze flows and unreduced circles on the bases indicate that some of the vessels were inverted in the kiln and some would have acted as saggars. Only two decorated examples were found, one with wheel-like impressions near the rim, in a Period 8 context (Fig 139.145), and the other with an incised wavy band produced by a comb-like tool (V1009). Blackware jars have a long manufacturing tradition continuing into this century (the Buckley pan-mug, for instance). The Beeston examples are closely paralleled by those found at Rainford (Liverpool Museum). Two vessels with interesting forms are Figures 131.15 and 18, the former paralleled by a vessel found at Hanley (Kelly and Greaves 1974, fig 20.180) and imitating the cylindrical Midland Purple form with thumbed horizontal strap handles, although coated in a thick black glaze. These vessels are sometimes referred to as butter pots.

The smaller storage vessels include a group of single-handled everted-rim jars of good quality (Fig 131.19–24), the form also occurring in Slipware and Midland Yellow. Parallels are known at Eccleshall Castle (Stoke-on-Trent City Museum and Art Gallery), but the function of these vessels is not clear. Calcium carbonate deposits were found in two examples (Fig 131.20 and 24) suggesting their possible use as lime-wash containers. Ten globular jugs with small pedestal bases were found in fabrics similar to the single-handled jars. Two different neck forms (Fig 132.34 and 35) were noted. The form of these jugs may imitate pewter vessels. A similar storage jar to Figure 131.17 was found in a pre-1600 context at Norton Priory (B Noake, pers comm).

The drinking vessels are either multi-handled and wide-rimmed (Fig 130.7) or single-handled straight-sided tankards (Fig 133.44). The base diameter of the multi-handled vessels ranges from 50–130mm. The larger vessels have six alternating single- and double-looped handles (Fig 130.8), or, less often, single-looped handles only (Fig 133.58). The smaller vessels normally have three single-looped handles (Fig 133.48). One exception (Fig 133.55) has four alternating single- and double-looped handles, while another vessel was noted with five single-looped handles (Fig 133.56). Four pedestal-base drinking vessels (Fig 133.51–4) are closer to the original tyg tradition. Three have rounded bodies while the fourth is more trumpet-shaped, and all probably had flaring rims. These and the larger multi-handled vessels occur in Staffordshire and may originate from there, although a north-western origin for the vessels is as likely.

The upper part of a pierced lug-handled costrel (Fig 133.62), with fabric and brown glaze reminiscent of Cistercian Ware pottery, was in a form comparable to Brears type 8 (1971, 37).

Seventeen of the vessels, principally the drinking vessels but also some jars, showed evidence of a linear scoring under the base, most in the form of a long shallow cross (Figs 132.27; 133.45, 50, 56). Many of the handled vessels have a band of grooves at the handle terminals perhaps to indicate the attachment position.

Midland Purple (Figs 133.63–5; 134; 135.82–4)

Large cylindrical jars were predominant (Fig 134.66, 67, 69, 71–3, 75), the bases typically c 200mm in diameter reducing to as narrow as 100mm for the smaller examples (Fig 134.78). The larger vessels often have two applied strap handles attached just below the rim, although one from the Inner Ward, most unusually, has possibly five strap handles (Fig 133.65). Three other Inner Ward vessels have untypically distorted forms, including Figure 133.63. A number of the jars are narrow-necked and resemble medieval cooking pot forms (Fig 135.82 and 83), and some do in fact have sooting, indicating that they were used for cooking.

None of the vessels were decorated. Some may be Midlands products (eg Fig 134.76) but the more rounded, coarser vessels are more likely to have been locally produced. One jug of medieval character (Fig 135.84) has a highly fired fabric similar to Midland Purple vessels although the form is not typical of the ware. Similarly a vessel in a Period 8 context (Fig

Table 54 Post-medieval pottery: the Period 8 assemblage (Civil War pottery excluded)

	Blackware	Midland Purple	Slipware	Late Stoneware	Mottled Ware	Coarseware	Total	(% of identified vessels)
Jar	11	1	5	1	1	—	19	(13)
Jug	2	—	3	—	1	—	6	(4)
Pancheon	4	—	—	—	—	—	4	(3)
Dish/bowl	3	—	6	—	—	—	9	(6)
Drinking vessel	29	—	30	—	10	—	69	(48)
Chamber pot	9	—	1	—	—	—	10	(7)
Plate	—	—	12	—	—	—	12	(8)
'Owl mug'	—	—	1	—	—	—	1	(<1)
Lid	—	—	—	—	1	—	1	(<1)
Cooking vessel	1	—	—	—	—	10	11	(8)
Unidentified	—	—	1	—	5	—	6	—
Total	59	1	59	1	18	10	148	

141.184), in an atypical Midland Purple form, has similarities to medieval vessels, suggesting that it is early post-medieval rather than late seventeenth/early eighteenth-century.

Tinglaze (Fig 135.85–7)

Three plates (Fig 135.85–7) are probably of London or Dutch origin (L Burman, pers comm). A malling jug (V1204), coloured blue, is likely to be a Netherlands import (J Hurst, pers comm). Similar examples are dated by hallmarked silver mounts to the late sixteenth century (Garner and Archer 1972, 4). A blue decorated rim sherd (V1676) may represent a blue dash charger, while fragments of a cup in a Carrickfergus fabric (V1679) were also noted.

Slipware (Figs 135.88–97; 136; 137.105–8)

Flange-rim dishes are predominant in the Period 7 assemblage. They are glazed on the interior, the glaze sealing geometrical designs of yellow trailed slip. None of the designs are wholly similar although there are recurring elements. Almost all have a continuous wavy line round the rim. Sooting is apparent on the outside of nine vessels, usually beneath the flange and on the side, presumably resulting from being placed beside a fire or on a chafing dish. The slipware dishes are comparable to those found at Norton Priory (B Noake, pers comm); to vessels found at Montgomery Castle in layers dated to the 1640s (Knight 1982, fig 4.42); and to pottery found at the Hill Top kiln site, Burslem (Kelly 1969).

Some slipware forms and fabrics have their counterparts in Blackware vessels. Single-handled jars comparable to the Blackware jar Figure 131.24 are either black with yellow dashes (Fig 135.91), or yellow with brown dashes (Fig 135.93), only the former sharing fabrics with the Blackware vessels. A tall jug with handle and pulled spout (Fig 135.97) is similar in character and decoration to the single-handled jars, and another jug with similar simple decoration but of coarser appearance is most probably residual in its Period 8 context (Fig 141.188).

Only one drinking vessel was found (Fig 137.108), sharing both form and fabric with Blackware examples, although, by contrast, single-handled. A vessel with a rudimentary star design of brown slip (Fig 135.97) is similar to those noted at Woodbank St, Burslem (Greaves 1976, fig 10.80).

A fragment of a lid or candlestick base (Fig 135.90) was found in the Inner Ward.

Midland Yellow (Figs 137.109–25; 138.126–31)

Thirteen flange-rim dishes were found as well as a number of jars. Of the former the great depth of one example (Fig 137.125) and the thickness of two of the rims are unusual (Figs 137.124; 138.128). In common with the slipware dishes, many of the rims show sooting beneath the rim. A parallel to Figure 137.123 was found at Woodbank St, Burslem (Greaves 1976, fig 7.47), and was comparable to a similar dish found at Eccleshall Castle in a probably pre-1643 context. The larger jars are single-handled and are either squat (Fig 137.117 and 121), or taller and slightly rounded (Fig 137.116 and 118), and the smaller jars are straight-sided or slightly rounded drug or ointment jars (Fig 137.110, 111, 113). Amongst the taller vessels, Figure 137.116 and 118 have parallels in the Blackware and Slipware vessels. Figure 137.121 is paralleled by an example found at Nottingham. Most of the seven small pots are of common form (Fig 137.110 and 111), and all have a groove at the rim to secure a fabric lid.

There were two chafing dish fragments (Fig 138.130 and 131). The latter has a plain support attached to the rim, and was fired under reduced conditions causing the green coloured glaze. The shoulder of a possible jug with incised line decoration (Fig 137.119), and a possible pipkin (Fig 137.122) were also found. A similar form was found in a pre-1649 context at Montgomery Castle (Knight 1982, fig 4.34). A small, shallow, wavy-walled pot was found in Period 9 layers in the Inner Ward (Fig 145.247), while a candlestick base was found in Period 8 layers (V 1191).

Martincamp Flask (Fig 138.132)

Sherds from two flasks were found (Fig 138.132 and V1529), both Hurst Class II (Hurst 1966, 54–9). A further Class II flask (V1518) together with a Class III flask (V1789) were recovered from Outer Gateway Period 9 layers.

Table 55   Post-medieval pottery: the Period 9 assemblage (Outer Ward vessels in brackets)

	Late Stoneware	Whiteware	Porcelain	Mottled Ware	Blackware	Total (%)	
Storage jar	5	2 (2)	—	—	—	7	(5)
Drinking vessel	—	44 (21)	1	2	—	47	(33)
Plate	1	25 (4)	—	—	—	26	(18)
Saucer	—	13	—	—	—	13	(9)
Bottle	46 (29)	—	—	—	—	46	(33)
Tea/coffee pot	—	1 (1)	—	—	—	1	(<1)
Candlestick	—	—	—	1	—	1	(<1)
Unidentified	5	26	—	2	1	34	
Total	57	111	1	5	1	175	

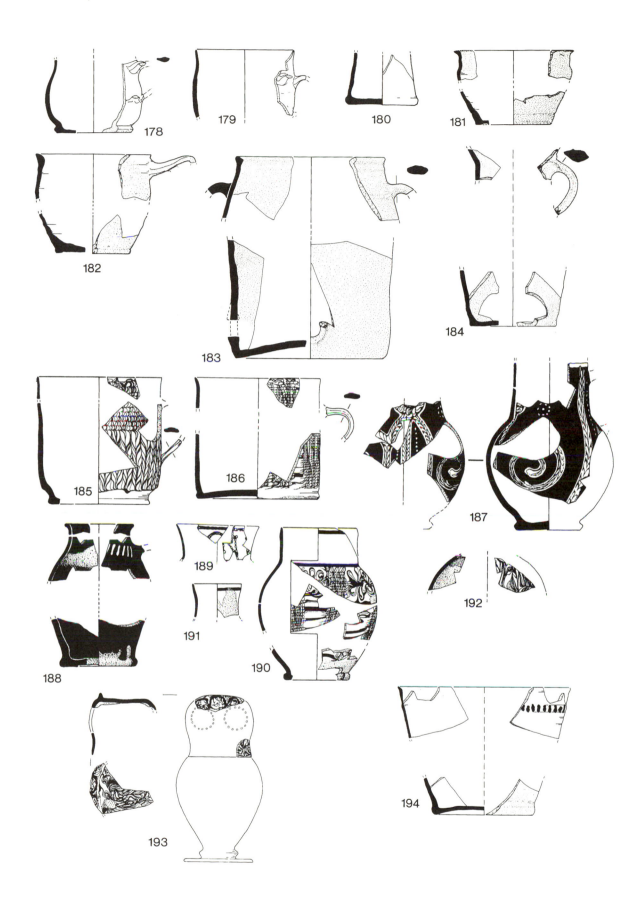

Fig 141 Post-medieval pottery: Period 8, Blackware (178–82), Midland Purple (183–4), Slipware (185–94); scale 1:4

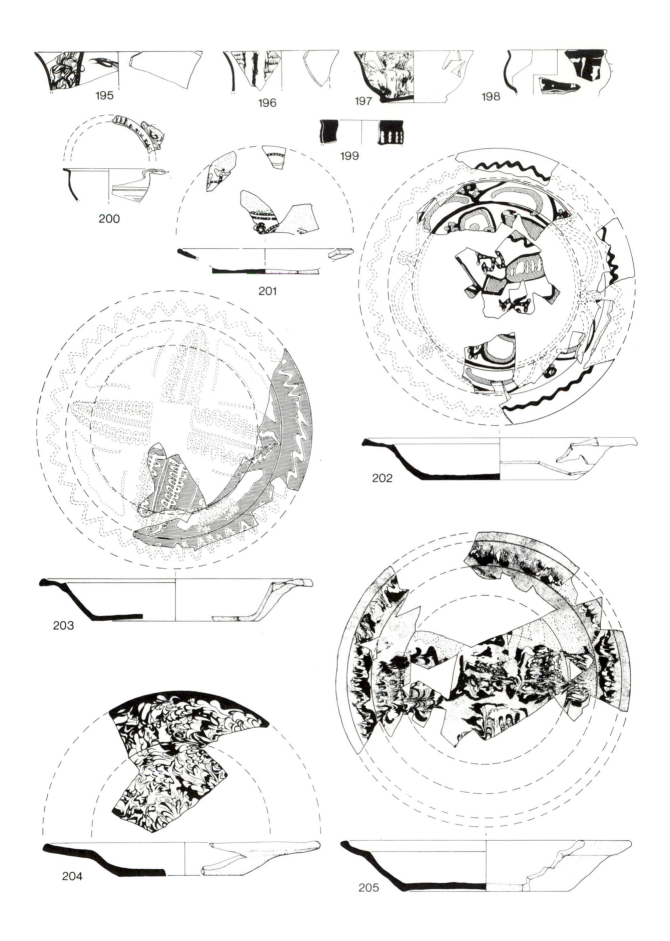

Fig 142 Post-medieval pottery: Period 8, Slipware; scale 1:4

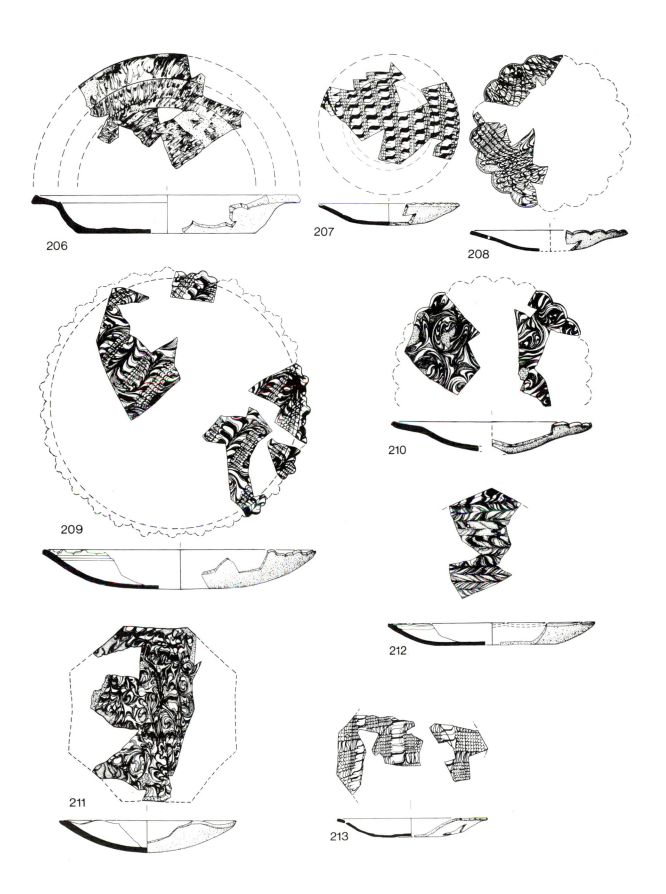

Fig 143 Post-medieval pottery: Period 8, Slipware; scale 1:4

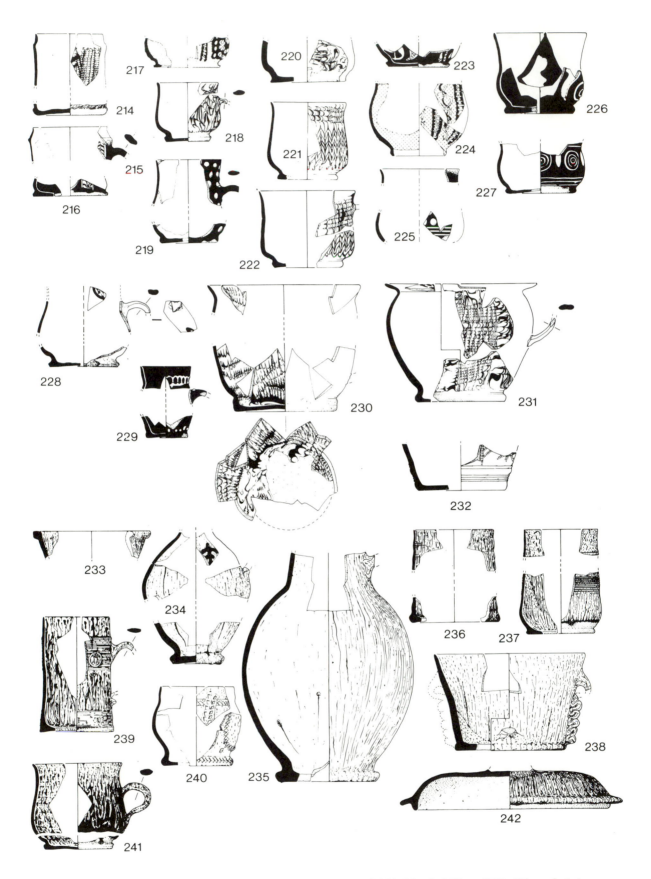

Fig 144 Post-medieval pottery: Period 8, Slipware (214–31), Stoneware (232), Mottled Ware (232–42); scale 1:4

Early Stonewares (Fig 138.133–40)

Fifteen vessels were found in Period 7 contexts. The majority were Frechen Bellarmine types with applied masks and medallions, one (Fig 138.133) bearing the arms of Amsterdam and dating from the first half of the seventeenth century. A possible Siegburg product with an applied blue wafer was found (Fig 138.137). A Westerwald vessel (Fig 138.140) showed an unusual combination of applied press-moulded decoration (usually seventeenth-century) and stamped decoration (usually early eighteenth-century). Another example

was found in Period 7, and a similar though wider necked vessel, with applied decoration only, was found in Period 9 layers at the Outer Gateway.

Period 8 (Table 54)

The identifiable late seventeenth-/early eighteenth-century pottery, all from the Outer Gateway, is described here. The large assemblage of residual Civil War pottery found in Period 8 layers has been discussed above.

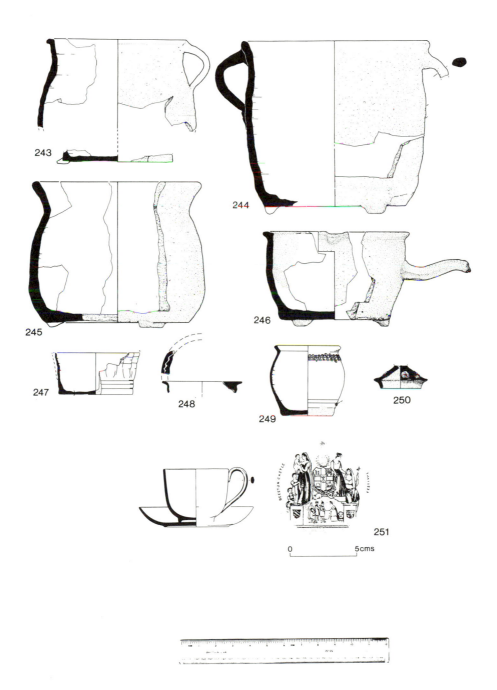

Fig 145 *Post-medieval pottery: Period 8, Coarseware (243–6), Period 9 Whiteware (247–51); scale 1:4 except (251) which is 1:2*

Blackware (Figs 139, 140, 141.178–82)

In general glazes on the later Blackware vessels were denser in colour than the Civil War vessels. Amongst the drinking vessels a small pronounced foot appears on thin-walled waisted cups and on the multi-handled vessels, and the handles are more decorative (eg Fig 140.172). The single-loop handles are less elongated (eg Fig 140.170). Parallels for the Period 8 drinking vessels are provided by those found at the Marquis of Granby hotel site, Burslem (Mountford 1975, figs 2 and 4). Other new forms include a small rounded bowl (Fig 140.160), an everted rim-handled jar (Fig 140.152), and chamber pots. Figure 141.181 and 182 may be of Buckley origin (P Davey, pers comm) in which case other vessels in these fabrics (A3 and A7) may also be from Buckley.

Midland Purple (Fig 141.183–4)

Manufacture of cylindrical jars continued into the eighteenth century with few alterations. Figure 141.183 has vertical handles and a spigot-hole near the base.

Slipware (Figs 141.185–94; 142; 143; 144.214–31)

A wider range of forms and more elaborate decoration distinguishes the Period 8 slipwares. White clays appear to have been more widely used. Flange-rim dishes with light and dark brown slips trailed on a yellow background may be distinctively Period 8 vessels especially in conjunction with jewelling (Fig 142.201 and 202), and when different coloured slips are combed together (Figs 142.204; 143.206). Similar decoration is found on a number of waisted and straight-sided cups (Fig 144.227 and 228), large single-handled jars (Fig 141.185 and 186), chamber pots (Fig 144.230 and 231), a jug (Fig 141.190), and on an owl jug and cup (Fig 141.193; Parkinson 1969). The press-moulded plates (Fig 143.207–13) are distinctively late seventeenth-/early eighteenth-century, and have a thick glossy glaze and methodically executed decoration. Some of these plates (Fig 143.213) have pierced rims, presumably to facilitate hanging on a wall. Other drinking vessels and a large jug (Fig 141.188) are decorated with yellow slips on a black background.

Figure 144.229 is closely paralleled by a pot from Woodbank St, Burslem (Greaves 1976, fig 9.72); Figure 142.198 by a pot from Albion Square, Hanley (Celoria and Kelly 1973, fig 72.165); and Figure 141.190 by a pot from the Sadler teapot manufactory site, Burslem (Mountford 1975, fig 8.45).

Mottled Ware (Fig 144.233–42)

The Beeston vessels are all likely to belong to the earlier part of the date range of Mottled Ware (c 1690–1780). Many of the 23 vessels found are fine drinking vessels, eg the rounded, waisted cup (Fig 144.241) and the straight-sided tankard (Fig 144.239). The latter has an applied press-moulded wafer excise mark, AR, surmounted by a crown (Bimson 1967, 165), and similar tankard forms were found at Swan Bank (Kelly 1973, fig 25.108). Less typical are a vessel with four alternating single- and multi-loop handles (Fig 144.238) and a vessel decorated with a diamond-shaped stamp on applied wafers (Fig 144.240). Neither is paralleled by Staffordshire products, unlike the lid (Fig 144.242), a bottle (V1026), the very large jug (Fig 144.235), and the smaller, brown slip decorated jug (Fig 144.234). All of these have Staffordshire counterparts (S Greaves, pers comm). A similar jug to the last of these was found at excavations at Chester Castle in 1984.

Coarseware (Fig 145.243–6)

Of the nine large rounded vessels found, two had tripod feet and opposed vertical handles (Fig 145.243 and 244), a further two had tripod feet only (Fig 145.245), while two others had opposed vertical handles. A smaller squat pot with tripod feet, a pouring lip, and a horizontal rod handle was also found (Fig 145.246).

These vessels are almost certainly from the Buckley kilns where the type was manufactured possibly from as early as 1640 (Amery and Davey 1979, 80), although not used at Beeston till the late seventeenth century.

Other wares (Fig 144.232)

The base of an English Stoneware vessel was found (Fig 144.232). A single sherd (not tabulated) of Japanese peasant ware porcelain was found showing the outline of a clenched hand (V1712).

Period 9 (Table 55)

Blackware

No Blackware products of the nineteenth century could be distinguished, with the exception of a lug handle from an unidentified vessel (V4673).

Whiteware (Fig 145.251)

The predominant Period 9 material was the transfer-printed whiteware from the Staffordshire potteries. This group comprised drinking vessels, jars, plates, saucers, and a tea or coffee pot. Of particular interest was a cup and saucer over-glaze printed 'Beeston Castle Festival' (Fig 145.251).

Later Stoneware

A number of Stoneware bottles were found, as well as storage jars and a plate.

Other wares

A further fragment of porcelain was found, as well as five mottled ware vessels. Sherds representing over 80 earthenware vessels were also found, principally at the Outer Gateway and the Outer Ward. These have not been included in the overall quantification.

8 Discussion of the medieval and post-medieval evidence

Construction and medieval use of the castle

by Laurence Keen

When building started in the 1220s, Beeston crag appears to have been covered with more trees than it now is (p 85). Although the tumbled boulders and hillwash layers at the Outer Gateway suggest that the prehistoric defences were very much eroded, they were still sufficiently prominent to dictate the position of the medieval outer curtain wall. The Outer Gateway excavations showed that the prehistoric entranceway continued in use. With the exception of sherds from a single vessel there was no medieval pottery from the excavations that need be earlier than the thirteenth century and, as has been noted in Part I, it would seem unlikely that the hilltop had been used since the Iron Age for anything more than pasture, and possibly cultivation in the Roman period.

The documentary, structural, and archaeological evidence all suggest that the construction of the castle did not take place in one building operation, and that the castle was never completed to its original design. The change in ownership from the earls of Chester to the Crown, and with it the alteration of the castle's role and function, undoubtedly changed the original concept. The evidence makes it difficult to discuss the castle as a structure of the 1220s alone, but, unfortunately, there are few archaeological, structural, and historical details on which to construct a complete picture of the castle's development.

The context of the construction of Beeston Castle in the 1220s by Earl Ranulf was his systematic reorganisation of the earldom on returning from the crusades. The castle site was not chosen to protect the earldom from Llywelyn: Ranulf had already initiated the process of association with Llywelyn by his treaty of 1218. The choice of site reflects the need to control one of the main medieval routes linking Chester with the Midlands and the South of England.

Having chosen the site for his new castle, the plan Earl Ranulf devised was undoubtedly influenced by the line of the surviving prehistoric earthworks. These dictated the position of the curtain wall of the Outer Ward which, although not completed until later, determined where the Outer Gate was to be built. The location of the Inner Ward was dictated by the commanding position and defensive capabilities of the summit of the hill.

Ranulf's plan in the 1220s had no provision for a larger tower or 'keep': the major and strongest element in the castle's defences was the series of formidable gatehouses of the Inner and Outer Wards. The gatehouses were to be connected to the curtain walls, with sturdy round-fronted towers projecting from them. These two elements anticipated the designs of the castles built by Edward I in the last quarter of the thirteenth century, in which gatehouses of enormous strength and complexity were an essential part of a castle's plan.

A similarly innovative plan was devised by Earl Ranulf for his castle at Bolingbroke, Lincolnshire, where an unencumbered site allowed him a free hand. Here a large gatehouse and five stone-backed mural towers enclose a polygonal courtyard (Thompson 1966, fig 62; Drewitt 1976, fig 1). The plans of Beeston and Bolingbroke Castles are in marked contrast to that of the castle at Chartley, Staffordshire, where the existing earthworks dictated its form.

At Beeston the gatehouses to the Inner and Outer Wards clearly belong to Earl Ranulf's first building operations. As a major element in the castle's defences the Inner Ward gatehouse was no doubt the first to be constructed. This is confirmed by the excavation of a curbed entrance track which ran beneath the Outer Gatehouse, suggesting that the defences of the Outer Ward were not started until those of the Inner Ward had been completed.

The gatehouses, with rounded towers and solid rear walls on either side of the entrance passage, are similar in plan to those at Bolingbroke and Chartley. The defensive arrangements are simple and those of the Inner Ward gatehouse suggest the details missing from the Outer Gateway, where less survives: a pair of gates opening outwards with a drawbar, followed by a portcullis, and finally another pair of gates. These arrangements are among the earliest in the development of gatehouses, which was to reach a peak with the gatehouses of Edward I, in which elaborate drawbridges, several portcullises, gates, and machicolations were to increase defensive capabilities (Mesqui 1981). That Earl Ranulf's gatehouses were built to an 'up-to-date' plan may be seen by comparing them with, for instance, the Inner gatehouse at Henry III's new castle at Montgomery, built in the later 1220s (Colvin 1963, ii, 739–42). Here, flanked by solid three-quarter round towers, the narrow entrance passage has a portcullis, a pair of gates with a drawbar, and then another pair of gates.

Earl Ranulf's gatehouse design provided the inspiration for Llywelyn ab Iowerth's castle at Criccieth, built about 1230. The plan is similar to that at Beeston – two round-fronted towers with an entrance passage between, defended by a portcullis and a pair of gates. At Criccieth, as at Beeston, the entrance passage had a wooden ceiling: there are three arrow-loops in each tower, in contrast to the two in each of the Beeston towers (Avent 1983, 17).

As at Montgomery and Criccieth, the gatehouses at Beeston provided some of the principal accommodation. The chamber in the Inner Ward gatehouse was connected by the parapet walk to a chamber with a garderobe on the first floor of the South-East Tower, and to a chamber with a fireplace on the first floor of the South-West Tower. All three curtain wall towers in the Inner Ward at Beeston are similar in plan, with solid rear walls and two arrow-loops in the rounded front walls. Only the East Tower is different internally, with three straight front walls instead of the rounded surfaces of the other towers. This need not suggest that the tower is of a different date: the gatehouse at Criccieth has exactly the same plan.

From the overall plan it appears that the Inner Ward gatehouse and the three towers are all of the same date. Such a view, however, would not explain the presence, in the foundation trench of the west wall of the South-West Tower, of a Henry III Long Cross penny, struck in the late 1260s and lost before 1279 (p 132, coin no 3); nor would pottery of Fabric F, dating to the second half of the thirteenth century (p 190), from construction levels beneath the mortar floor of the same tower, help this interpretation. There remains the possibility that the coin and pottery may have been deposited during later repair work and modifications to the tower. Although the mortar and sandstone floor of the tower looks primary, it need not be so.

Tower 2 of the Outer Ward, with a solid rear wall, is similar in scale to the towers in the Inner Ward and may be assigned with some confidence to Earl Ranulf. Like the Outer Gatehouse, it would have been constructed after the Inner Ward.

In 1237, when Earl John died, the castle passed to the Crown. The extent to which Earl Ranulf's original plan had been completed is largely a matter for speculation, but clearly considerable sums of money were spent on Beeston Castle by Henry III. The fact that the expenditure is included, more often than not, with that spent on other royal castles, and that the details are imprecise, does not help the identification of those parts of the castle which were built during Henry III's reign. Nor is the unravelling of the building sequence any easier, since over half of the curtain wall of the Outer Ward no longer survives.

The architectural details which remain demonstrate that buildings had been planned in the Inner Ward but were never built. Coin evidence suggests that the north curtain wall of the Inner Ward was constructed after 1280 (p 132, coin no 4). This may indicate that, even at this time, buildings were still envisaged: the north curtain wall has tusks for a building in the north-west corner of the Inner Ward, and there are two windows in the north-east corner. No buildings were found in these areas during the excavations.

Along the curtain wall of the Outer Ward, Towers 1 and 6–10 are all very similar in plan, particularly in the fact that they have no back walls. In this and in scale, the towers are unlike the towers which, with some confidence, may be assigned to Earl Ranulf. To what period do they belong?

In November 1241 the justiciar of Chester and *custos* of Beeston Castle received 250 marks (£166 13s 4d) towards the fortification of Beeston and Rhuddlan Castles. Between Christmas 1241 and Christmas 1242, £410 12d was spent on strengthening the two castles, and in 1242 two turrets at Beeston were finished. The defences of Rhuddlan Castle, at least in part, were of wood as late as 1241–2 (Taylor 1987, 5), so one may propose that the greater part of this expenditure was for Beeston Castle. Furthermore, the reference to finishing two turrets at Beeston in 1241 may possibly suggest that the expenditure was on the curtain wall towers of the Outer Ward. If this is correct the six surviving towers (1 and 6–10) may be assigned to 1241–2.

Of interest are references to a prison in 1246/7 and 1249, and to a chapel in the accounts for 1245–6, 1246–7, and 1247–50. The location of the prison is now difficult to establish. No building in the Inner Ward is an obvious candidate: the inward-facing doors with internal drawbars in all the ground floor chambers of the towers and gatehouse disqualify these as possible candidates. Similarly the ground floors of the towers and gatehouse of the Outer Ward could never have been used for prisoners. The only possible candidate is Tower 5, an addition to the Outer Gatehouse. Here the basement chamber, originally unlit, would have served well as a prison. The archaeological evidence for the dating of the tower is inconclusive: it has been assigned to Period 6 (later medieval) but may well belong to Period 5. There is no reason to consider the tower as post-medieval, as Ridgway and Cathcart King suggested before archaeological investigations began (1959, 19: Tower 4a).

The payments to chaplains serving the chapel at Beeston raise the question of where the chapel was. The lack of halls, service blocks, and kitchens implies that the chapel is unlikely to have been a free-standing structure since it would presumably not have been built before other free-standing structures such as these. More likely, the chapel may have been in one of the curtain towers or gatehouses. It would have followed the usual liturgical arrangement with an altar to the east. The East Tower in the Inner Ward could have provided such an arrangement, but access to a chapel in an upper chamber would not have been convenient. The most likely location is in one of the upper chambers of the Outer Gatehouse, which could most easily have accommodated the required orientation and to which access would have been easy.

After Edward I created his son Prince of Wales and Earl of Chester in 1300/1, major alterations were carried out to the buildings of the Inner Ward. But no new buildings were constructed there: the areas clearly intended for buildings were left empty and the Ward still contained only its gatehouse and three towers.

The three towers were heightened and then crenellated to give them flat roofs, since they had 'high wooden surfaces' before (p 96). As the upper parts of the towers no longer survive it is difficult to establish of what these alterations consisted. 'High wooden surfaces' implies some kind of pitched roof, which would have given very little usable space below; the heightening and provision of flat roofs was clearly intended to provide extra accommodation in the highest parts of the towers. The towers would undoubtedly have been crenellated from the start. It would appear, therefore, that the crenellations were filled in, the towers heightened overall, and then flat or very low-pitched roofs constructed.

Repairs carried out to the Outer Gate in 1304–5, expenditure in 1324–5, the 'covering' of towers in 1326, works to the 'houses, chambers, turrets and other buildings' in 1328, and expenditure in 1359–60 cannot be related to any of the surviving fabric. What seems clear is that although parts of the castle were repaired, or even slightly altered, no major building was carried out after 1303–4. Even then Beeston Castle still lacked the halls, kitchens, and service blocks which would have been necessary for use on the scale originally intended by Earl Ranulf in the 1220s. When the Earl of Chester's castle passed to the Crown in 1237 it was necessary only to complete the basic fortifications. Greater resources were expended on the castle at Chester, conveniently situated as a base for Henry III's wars against the Welsh. As the supply base for Edward I's conquest of Wales, Chester Castle was where royal accommodation was needed. This was why Beeston Castle was largely superfluous to royal requirements, why it was never provided with the full complement of buildings expected in a royal castle, and why it was neglected during the later medieval period. Beeston Castle's strategic location, however, was to be of great importance in the Civil War, seeing far greater use and military activity than it ever had done in the Middle Ages.

Civil War and later
by Peter Ellis

The historical role of the castle in the Civil War is well documented. The location of a ditch on the east side, intended to act as a major protection for the walls, demonstrates the scale of the work carried out. The slight works around the entrance may be unfinished defensive works. The suggested gateposts perhaps indicate a hurried defence erected at the entrance. The scale of the postpits, contrasted with the *ad hoc* impression given by the work, gives some indication of the difficulties faced in bringing the castle into service again. Arrow-loops were enlarged, presumably for muskets, and some appear to have been blocked. The provision of gunports is suggested at the Inner Ward.

It is not clear whether the refortification elements can be assigned to the initial Parliamentarian occupation. There is documentary evidence that the walls and defences were refurbished, but there are also references suggesting that the castle was not ready to withstand a Royalist attack. It is possible that the gateway and the slight trenches either side, together with some blocking of the curtain, was all that was carried out initially. The ditch and outer bank and the Inner Ward gunports may represent the later Royalist work.

The distribution of the finds has been examined to see if any particular use areas can be recognised or if certain areas were allocated to certain ranks. The findspots of military gear might imply that the officers were stationed in the Inner Ward. Here the spurs found in the South-East Tower contrast with the equipment, particularly the outmoded armour, found at the Outer Gateway. The suggestion is supported to some extent by the slight differences in the pottery assemblages for the Inner Ward and the Outer Gateway (Table M56, M3:D2). However, any such difference in allotted quarters may only have been for the period of the Royalist occupation, since the Parliamentarian governor was lodged in the Outer Gateway when the castle was seized by the Royalists.

Occupation in the Outer Ward, on the terracing, is suggested by the excavations. The scale of the terracing not only indicates the numbers of troops involved, but suggests that there were no pre-existing prepared occupation zones for troops, whether in a ruinous condition or not. The lowering of the floor of the Outer Gateway gatehouse rooms is not easily explicable, and it is possible that, as at the Inner Ward South-East Tower, this was an original medieval feature. The south room

appears to have been used for storage and not for defence. Preparation of musket shot and other activities appear to have taken place in a second phase. The burials in the Inner Ward must represent casualties of the Civil War.

The pottery and clay pipe evidence suggests that their supply to the castle was maintained from the same source (for the pottery see M3:C12; for the pipes see p 173). Neither assemblage shows any signs of being divisible into Parliamentarian and Royalist groups, nor are there indications of a change in the source of materials. Although it is possible that an initial supply of clay tobacco pipes and pottery vessels was sufficient for the whole occupation period by both sides, it would seem more likely that an initial provision was followed by further supplies from the same source. This must suggest that the economic network survived the military and political changes of the period, indeed may have been largely unaffected by them. Some supplies, however, were provided by force, for there is evidence, in the form of petitions heard at the Quarter sessions, of enforced work and service during the Royalist occupation. The reuse of window leads for shot may suggest that the locality was scoured for suitable material. However, it seems possible that larger-scale economic supply was maintained throughout the conflict.

An occupation in the period following the capitulation of the Royalists is evidenced solely by a group of clay pipes (p 179). These Rainford style pipes are spread throughout the sites and may have been brought in the baggage of a team employed to demolish the castle. It is possible to speculate further on the basis of these finds. At the end of the siege, the abandonment of armour, spurs, and other equipment indicates that the material was of little or no commercial interest in the post-war period; or that there was a strong prescription against entrance to the castle for a period; or, alternatively, that all the material was deliberately broken (as indicated by the number of matchlock priming pan parts). The castle may have been kept closed until the arrival of a group employed for the purpose of clearing the material left from the occupation, and ensuring that no further occupation could take place. The clay pipes used by the demolition gang show that they came from some distance. It is possible that demolition was deliberately contracted out to teams from outside the area who would be unlikely and unable to use the opportunity to advance any local interests. The presence of Rainford style pipes at the Outer Ward terraces may indicate where the workers were stationed, while the governor maintained the Outer Gateway as his residence for a time.

The new layout of entrance steps, the provision of stone floors in ground floor rooms, and the suggested landscaping below the Outer Gateway, all indicate that the reoccupation following the Civil War was to a wealthy standard within what must have been a comfortably refurbished building. It would appear that the gate towers were not extensively damaged following the Civil War since there were no demolition layers between Civil War and Period 8 levels. Those finds that can be demonstrated to be later than the Civil War seem to indicate an establishment of some quality (eg hinges, Fig 94.24–31, pins, Fig 101.44–7, and pottery, p 209).

In contrast, the Civil War levels in the Inner Ward lay directly beneath demolition layers, and there were no finds of distinctive Period 8 pottery. The slight evidence of Period 8 activity outside the towers clearly suggests temporary work on a different scale to that at the Outer Gateway. Clay pipes suggesting the presence of the demolition gangs were found here.

The dating evidence from beneath the new stone floor in Tower 4 suggests that it was not laid until after 1680. In Tower 5, spur 36, predating the floor, provides a *terminus post quem* of *c* 1700, while the clay pipe finds associated with the entrance track are similarly confined to the last decades of the seventeenth century (M2:G12). It is not possible to provide a definite date for the abandonment of the gatehouse but it seems to have taken place early in the eighteenth century, judging from the date of finds associated with the layers sealing the steps.

An association between the refurbishment of the Gateway and the documented references to a residence 'by the castle gate' by George Walley (p 98) makes an attractive hypothesis. There is, too, an interesting link with the Thomas Walley who took over the Castle following the departure of the Royalists, although there is clearly a hiatus between the two occupancies. This association, however, may be mistaken. Despite the difficulties with the dating of the relevant documents (and one may be as late as 1759) it would certainly seem indisputable that they refer to some structure at the Outer Gateway, but the described rented house and the 'tenement called Walleys' are hard to reconcile with the scale of occupation revealed by excavation. The evidence suggests a reoccupation of the gatehouse around 1680 by someone who owned the building, and occupa-

tion for perhaps two or three decades thereafter. It is possible that the occupants of the gatehouse were members of the Beeston family. Disuse of the entrance steps seems to be associated with the provision of a new entrance track, and that provision clearly involved the demolition of the gatehouse. It is possible that the documentary accounts of George Walley's residency refer to subsequent rented occupation of a cottage formerly associated with the then partially demolished gatehouse; indeed, the Walleys may have lived at some site on the lower slopes below the castle from the end of the Civil War.

Later use of the hilltop is represented by the quarries, by the features at the Outer Ward, and by the finds. Survey work by Peter Hough in the Outer Ward suggested the position of some structures (Fig 63), and others are represented in part on Ordnance Survey maps. Examination of the quarry faces demonstrated the use of gunpowder charges: the evidence for this was quite different to the medieval stoneworking marks visible in the Inner Ditch (M2:E5). Contemporary engravings and visitors' items found witness the beginnings of antiquarian and Romantic interest, and there are two examples of rebuilding of the curtain wall which must date from this period. The exploration of the well in 1842 marks the first attempt to understand the structural remains, even if motivated by the search for treasure. A different use of the hilltop was for the Bunbury Temperance fairs, and for major local celebrations of national events. On these occasions, for a day or so each year, Beeston crag saw a gathering of the local population, an echo of the more permanent settlement there in prehistory.

Summary

The ruins of the medieval fortress of Beeston Castle are situated on a rocky outcrop overlooking the Cheshire plain 16km south-east of Chester. The site was purchased by the state in the 1950s, and, following the provision of new access routes and consolidation of the fabric, was opened to the public in the 1980s. Archaeological excavations were carried out in advance of clearance work in two campaigns, between 1968 and 1973, and from 1975–85. No previous archaeological work had been undertaken, although the structural remains have been discussed by a number of authorities.

The earliest excavated features, a levelled area and a handful of postholes and pits, were Neolithic, dated by pottery and a radiocarbon date. Flint microliths suggested some Mesolithic activity, and flint tools and pottery indicated Early and Middle Bronze Age occupation, but these finds were found out of context in later features or in the subsoil.

The medieval castle's outer defences were found to overlie a sequence of prehistoric defences. An undated palisade trench with associated postholes was overlain by a slight bank with timber strapping, dated to the Late Bronze Age by a radiocarbon date and two Ewart Park axes. Within the defences, a spread of refractory debris and copper alloy objects intended for remelting indicated a metalworking area; another was suggested just to the rear of the bank.

The bank was buried beneath two phases of the defences of an Iron Age hillfort. An initial bank and ditch with a defended inturned entrance was later reconstructed with a rubble bank built in boxed sections and revetted by two lines of large boulders. It was surmounted by large posts with some evidence of an additional timber structure at the entranceway. A group of radiocarbon dates from the second phase centred around 400 BC.

In the interior, where there was no intact stratigraphy, nine round houses are hypothesised from amongst almost 150 postholes, many stone-packed. Two differing radiocarbon dates suggested that these structures dated from the Late Bronze Age to the later Iron Age. The report on finds of charred plant remains concludes that corn was processed and stored at a large storage centre at the hillfort, and that the charring may have resulted from an accidental fire. The date of this centre remains unknown within the Late Bronze Age and Iron Age. A major pottery assemblage included salt container 'VCP' fabrics found throughout the Iron Age sequence. From a late Iron Age context behind the rampart came fragments of a drinking vessel. The hillfort was abandoned by the Roman period, when there was some evidence for a settlement with Iron Age antecedents at the foot of the crag. Iron, shale, stone, and clay objects of Bronze Age and Iron Age date are reported on, and the evidence from analysis of the soils is presented.

The medieval castle was built by Ranulf de Blundeville, the sixth Earl of Chester, in the 1220s, and is comparable with other newly built castles within his Earldom at Chartley, Staffordshire and Bolingbroke, Lincolnshire. At his death, his lands were taken over by the Crown. There are documentary references to further building works in the thirteenth and early fourteenth centuries but no evidence of a hall or kitchen were found and the castle was never completed.

The surviving remains comprise an Inner Ward defended by a wall with half round towers and dominated by a gatehouse with two projecting round towers. A large rock-cut ditch divides the Inner Ward from an Outer Ward enclosed by a curtain wall, part of which survives, including the remains of an Outer Gateway similar in character to the Inner. A later attached tower is interpreted as a prison. Projecting half round towers along the outer curtain wall are open-backed. The excavations produced medieval pottery, metal finds, and coins, most in residual contexts.

Documentary evidence shows that the castle site was bought from the Crown by the Beeston family in the sixteenth century. There was no indication of occupation until the Civil War, when the castle was commandeered by the Parliamentarians in 1643, taken by the Royalists in 1644, and finally won back in 1645 after a long siege. After the Civil War an order was given for the castle to be slighted. Excavation showed, however, that the Outer Gateway was reoccupied from the end of the seventeenth century into the early years of the eighteenth.

Archaeological evidence of the Civil War was seen in structural alterations, three graves, and large numbers of finds, most attributable to the Civil War with some from the later reoccupation. These comprised weapon parts, fragments of a jack of plate armour, spurs, other metal objects, coins, pottery, vessel glass, and a major group of clay pipes amongst which those used in the Civil War could be distinguished from demolition and reoccupation groups.

The site of the Bunbury Fair, an annual Temperance Festival held in the later nineteenth century, yielded finds of pottery, clay pipes, and metal objects.

The industrial residues and the human and animal bones from the medieval and post-medieval periods are reported on; some of the finds reports and the detailed stratigraphic data are presented in microfiches.

The significance of the excavations lies firstly in the recognition of the Late Bronze Age origins of a major hillfort, with evidence for metalworking and crop processing, the data supported by a number of radiocarbon dates; secondly in the detailed analysis of the castle structure and the medieval documentary evidence; and thirdly in the important group of finds closely datable to the Civil War period of 1643–45.

Résumé

Les ruines de la forteresse médiévale de Beeston Castle se trouvent sur un affleurement rocheux qui domine la plaine du Cheshire à 16km au sud-est de Chester. L'état a acquis ce site dans les années 50, et, après avoir aménagé de nouvelles voies d'accès et consolidé l'édifice, il en a autorisé l'accès au public dans les années 80. Des excavations archéologiques avaient été effectuées, avant les travaux de dégagement, au cours de deux campagnes de fouilles, entre 1968 et 1973, et à partir de 1975 jusqu'en 1985. On n'avait tenté aucune exploration archéologique auparavant bien qu'un certain nombre d'experts aient débattu des vestiges d'édifices.

Les plus anciens éléments mis à jour consistent en une aire aplanie et une poignée de trous de poteaux et de fossés, grâce à la poterie et à une datation au radiocarbone, on a pu établir qu'ils dataient du néolithique. Des microlithes de silex témoignent d'une activité au mésolithique, de plus, des outils en silex et de la poterie révèlent que le site était occupé au début et au milieu de l'âge du bronze, mais ces trouvailles ont été découvertes hors contexte, au milieu de structures plus récentes ou dans le sous-sol.

On a découvert que les ouvrages de défense extérieurs du château médiéval recouvraient une série de fortifications préhistoriques. Une tranchée avec palissade non datée et les trous de poteaux correspondants avaient été recouverts par un léger talus renforcé avec du bois que l'on a pu dater de la fin de l'âge du bronze grâce è une datation au radiocarbone et à deux haches de type 'Ewart Park'. On a trouvé, éparpillés à l'intérieur des ouvrages de défense, des débris réfractaires et des objets en alliage de cuivre destinés à être refondus; ce qui indique la présence d'un atelier où on travaillait le métal; on a suggéré l'existence d'un autre juste derrière le talus.

Le talus était enseveli sous deux phases de la fortification d'une forteresse de l'âge du fer. Le talus et le fossé d'origine avaient une entrée fortifiée rentrante, cet ouvrage fut reconstruit plus tard avec un talus de remblais bâti en sections emboîtées et garni de deux rangées de grosses pierres. Il était surmonté de gros poteaux et on a trouvé quelques vestiges d'un édifice supplémentaire, en bois, à l'entrée. Une série de dates au radiocarbone concernant la seconde phase se concentrent autour des années 400 av.J–C.

A l'intérieur, là où la stratigraphie avait été perturbée, on a émis l'hypothèse de l'existence de neuf maisons rondes à partir de presque 150 trous de poteaux, dont beaucoup avaient été remblayés avec des pierres. Deux datations au radiocarbone divergentes laissent supposer que la date de ces structures se situerait entre la fin de l'âge du bronze et la fin de l'âge du fer. Le compte-rendu portant sur les restes de plantes carbonisées qui ont été trouvés conclut que le blé était transformé et conservé dans un grand centre de stockage à l'intérieur du fort, et que la carbonisation pouvait être le résultat d'un incendie accidentel. La date de ce centre reste indéterminée entre la fin de l'âge de bronze et l'âge du fer. Une importante collection de poteries comprenant des récipients destinés à contenir du sel en poterie très grossière était présente partout dans la sé-quence de l'âge du fer. Des fragments d'un gobelet proviennent d'un contexte de la fin de l'âge du fer situé derrière le rempart. L'abandon de la forteresse précède l'époque romaine, mais on a recueilli des témoignages d'une occupation au pied du rocher à cette date avec antécédents remontant jusqu'à l'âge du fer. Le compe-rendu comprend des rapports sur des objets en fer, schiste, pierre et argile de l'âge du bronze et de l'âge du fer, et on présente les résultats de l'analyse des sols.

Le château médiéval a été construit par Ranulf de Blundeville, sixième comte de Chester, dans les années 1220, et il ressemble à d'autres châteaux de construction récente de son comté, Chartley dans le Staffordshire et Bolingbroke dans le Lincolnshire. A sa mort, ses terres échurent à la couronne. Des documents font référence à des travaux de construction supplémentaires au treizième et au début du quatorzième siècle, mais on n'a pas trouvé de traces de l'existence d'une grande salle ou d'une cuisine et le château n'a jamais été terminé.

Les vestiges qui ont survécu comprennent une cour intérieure protégée par un rempart jalonné de tours semi-rondes et dominé par un poste de garde flanqué de deux tours rondes saillantes. Un grand fossé taillé dans le roc sépare la cour intérieure d'une cour extérieure limitée par un mur d'enceinte dont une partie a survécu, cela comprend les vestiges d'une porte extérieure d'un style semblable à celle de l'intérieur. Une tour, qui a été ajoutée plus tard, semble avoir servi de prison. Les tours semi-rondes saillantes qui flanquent le mur d'enceinte extérieur sont ouvertes à l'arrière. Les fouilles ont révélé de la poterie médiévale, des objets en métal et des monnaies, la plupart des trouvailles se trouvaient dans des contextes résiduels.

Des documents prouvent que le site du château a été acheté à la couronne par la famille Beeston au seizième siècle. Il n'existe pas de preuve d'occupation jusqu'à la guerre civile, durant celle-ci le château fut réquisitionné par les Parlementaires en 1643, repris par les Royalistes en 1644, et finalement reconquis en 1645 après un long siège. Après la guerre civile on a donné l'ordre de raser le château. Les fouilles ont toutefois montré que la porte extérieure avait été réoccupée à partir de la fin du dix-septième jusqu'au début du dix-huitième siècle.

Voici les preuves archéologiques que la guerre a laissées: des modifications des structures, trois tombes et un grand nombre de trouvailles dont la plupart peuvent être attribuées à la guerre civile bien que quelques unes datent d'une réoccupation ultérieure. Celles-ci comprennent des éléments d'armes, des fragments d'un jaque d'armure à plaques, des éperons, d'autres objets en métal, des monnaies, de la poterie, du verre à gobelets, et un important assortiment de pipes en terre parmi lesquelles il fut possible de différencier celles utilisées pendant la guerre civile de celles associées aux périodes de démolition et de réoccupation.

Le site de la foire de Bunbury, un festival annuel de la tempérance qui avait lieu à la fin du dix-neuvième siècle, a fourni des trouvailles en poterie, des pipes en terre, et des objets en métal.

On commente les résidus industriels et les os humains et animaux des époques médiévale et post-médiévale; certains des rapports concernant les découvertes et les renseignements détaillés sur la stratigraphie sont présentés sous forme de microfiches.

L'importance de ces fouilles tient, premièrement, dans la reconnaissance du fait que l'origine d'une importante forteresse se situait à la fin de l'âge du bronze, avec des témoignages de travail du métal et de transformation des récoltes, ces données s'appuient sur un nombre de dates au radiocarbone; deuxièmement, dans l'analyse détaillée de la structure du château et des preuves documentaires médiévales, et troisièmement dans l'important assortiment de trouvailles qu'on peut dater très précisément de l'époque de la guerre civile, entre 1643 et 1645.

Zusammenfassung

Die Ruinen der mittelalterlichen Befestigung Beeston Castle liegen auf einem Felsenvorsprung, der 16 Km südöstlich von Chester die Cheshire Ebene überragt. Das Denkmal wurde in den fünfziger Jahren durch den Staat erworben, und dann, nachdem neue Zugangswege hergestellt und die Ruinen saniert worden waren, in den achtziger Jahren der Öffentlichkeit zugänglich gemacht. Archäologische Ausgrabungen wurden in zwei Phasen zwischen 1968 und 1973 und von 1975 bis 1985 in Vorbereitung für die Sanierungsarbeiten durchgeführt.

Archäologische Untersuchungen hatten bis dahin nicht stattgefunden, obwohl die aufstehenden Überreste mehrfach von Sachkundigen diskutiert worden waren.

Die ältesten ergrabenen Reste, ein geebnetes Areal mit Pfosten-löchern und Gruben, gehörten ins Neolithikum. Diese Datierung wurde durch Keramik und ein Radiokarbondatum gesichert. Mikrolithische Feuersteinartifakte lassen auf Aktivität während des Mesolithikums schließen, während Feuersteinwerkzeuge und Keramik auf Besiedlung in der frühen und mittleren Bronzezeit deuten. Diese Fund wurden jedoch ohne Zusammenhang jüngeren Horizonten oder aber dem Unterboden entnommen.

Es zeigte sich, daß die Führung der äußeren Befestigungsanlagen der mittelalterlichen Burg über einer Reihenfolge von vorgeschichtlichen Verteidigungsanlagen verlief. Ein nicht datierter Palisadengraben mit dazugehörigen Pfostenlöchern lag unter einem niedrigen Erdwall mit Holzverankerung, der durch ein Radiokarbondatum und zwei "Ewart Park" Äxte in das späte Bronzezeitalter datiert wird. Innerhalb dieser Verteidigungsanlagen deutete eine Streuung von Schamottbrocken und Gegenständen aus Kupferligierung, die wohl zum Einschmelzen vorgesehen waren, auf eine Metallverarbeitungsstätte hin. Ein zweite Arbeitsstätte scheint nicht weit von der Rückseite des Walles gelegen zu haben.

Der Erdwall lag unter zwei Befestigungsphasen des eisenzeitlichen Rigwalles begraben. Eine anfängliche Wall-und Grabenanlage mit eingezogener Toranlage wurde später durch einen Geröllwall in Holzrahmenkonstruktion ersetzt, der durch zwei Reihen von Felsblöcken abgestützt war. Er wurde von großen Pfosten und Anzeichen für einen zusätzlichen Holzbau an der Toranlage überragt. Eine Gruppe von Radiokarbondaten der zweiten Konstruktionsphase konzentrieren sich in den Zeitraum um 400 n.Chr.

Im Innern konnte keine ungestörte Stratigraphie festgestellt werden. Aus den 150 Pfostenlöchern, viele mit Packsteinen, mutmaßt man neun Rundhäuser.

Zwei unterschiedliche Radiokarbondaten deuten darauf hin, daß die Nutzung dieser Häuser in den Zeitraum zwischen der späten Bronzezeit und der späten Eisenzeit fällt. In dem Bericht, der sich mit den Funden verkohlter pflanzlicher Reste befaßt, wird gefolgert, daß Getreide auf einem großen Vorratsplatz innerhalb des Ringwalles umgeschlagen und aufbewahrt wurde, und daß die Verkohlung durch ein Brandunglück entstanden sein kann. Das Datum für diesen Vorratsplatz kann in dem gegebenen Zeitraum zwischen der späten Bronzezeit und der Eisenzeit nicht festgelegt werden. Eine größere Ansammlung von Keramik enthielt "VCP" Scherben von Salzbehältern, wie sie durch die gesamten Serien der Eisenzeit auftreten. Aus einem späteisenzeitlichen Kontext hinter dem Verteidigungswall stammen Scherben eines Trinkgefäßes. Der Ringwall wurde während der Römerzeit aufgegeben. Für diesen Zeitraum gibt es jedoch Anhaltspunkte für eine Ansiedlung mit eisenzeitlichen Vorläufern am Fuß des Felsvorsprunges. Gegenstände aus Eisen, Tonschiefer, Stein und Ton mit Datierungen in die Bronze-und Eisenzeit werden beschrieben, und der Befund aus den Bodenanalysen wird vorgelegt.

Die mittelalterliche Burgenlage wurde von Ranulf de Blundeville, dem sechsten Earl von Chester um 1200 erbaut. Sie kann mit anderen neuangelegten Burgen in seiner Grafschaft - Chartley in Staffordshire und Bolingbroke in Lincolnshire - verglichen werden. Nach seinem Tode fielen seine Besitzungen an die Krone. Weitere Bautätigkeit im 13. und frühen 14. Jahrhundert ist dokumentarische belegt, doch wurden keine Spuren für einen Palastbau oder eine Küche gefunden und die Burg ist nie fertiggestellt worden.

Die überkommenen Reste bestehen aus einer Hauptburg, die durch eine Mauer mit halbrunden Türmen und einem beherrschenden Torbau mit zwei vorspringenden, runden Türmen geschützt wird. Ein tiefer, in den Fels eingeschnittener Graben scheidet die Hauptburg von der Vorburg. Diese wird von einer Ringmauer, die zum Teil noch aufsteht, umgeben und besitzt einen Torbau, der dem der Hauptburg ähnelt.

Ein später eingefügter Turm wird als Kerker angesehen. Die vorspringenden, halbrunden Türme entlang der Ringmauer sind auf ihrer Rückseite offen. Die Ausgrabungen erbrachten Keramik, Metallfunde und Münzen, der größte Teil davon in residualen Ablagerungen.

Die dokumentarischen Quellen belegen, daß das Burggelände im 16. Jahrhundert durch die Familie Beeston von der Krone erworben wurde. Die Burg scheint bis zu Beginn des Bürgerkrieges, wenn sie 1643 durch die Parlamentarier beschlagnahmt wird, unbewohnt gewesen zu sein. 1644 wird sie dann von den Royalisten eingenommen und 1645 nach langer Belagerung wiederzurückerobert. Nach Ende des Bürger-krieges wurde die Burg auf Befehl hin geschliffen. Die Ausgrabungen zeigen jedoch, daß das äußere Torhaus von Ende des 17. Jahrunderts bis in das frühe 18. Jahrhundert neu bewohnt worden war.

Archäologische Zeugnisse für den Bürgerkrieg wurden deutlich in den struktuellen Änderungen, drei Grablegungen und einer großen Anzahl von Funden, die hauptsächlich in die Zeit des Bürgerkrieges zu datieren sind, mit einigen zusätzlichen Gegenständen aus der späteren Nutzung. Zu diesen Funden gehören Waffenteile, Teile einer Brigantine (jack of plate armour), Sporen, andere Metallgegenstände, Münzen, Keramik, Glasgefäße und eine umfangreiche Sammlung von Tonpfeifen, in der sich die Pfeifengruppe aus dem Bürgerkrieg deutlich von den Gruppen der Abbruchs- und Neunutzungsphasen abzeichnet.

Der Standort des "Bunbury Fair", einer jährlichen Versammlung der Abstinenzbewegung im ausgehenden 19. Jahrhundert, erbrachte Keramik, Tonpfeifen und Metallgegenstände.

Der Gewerbeabfall, sowie die menschlichen und tierischen Skelett reste aus den mittelalterlichen und nachmittelalterlichen Phasen werden beschrieben; einige der Funde in diesen Beschreibungen und die eingehenden stratigraphischen Daten werden auf Mikrafischen beigefügt.

Die Bedeutung dieser Ausgrabungen liegt in erster Linie in der Festlegung der spätbronzezeitlichen Anfänge eines bedeutenden Ringwalles, den Hinweisen auf Metallverarbeitung und Getreideumschlag, sowie den Befunden, die durch eine Anzahl von Radiokarbondaten untermauert sind. Von gleicher Bedeutung sind die eingehenden Analysen der Bausubstanz der Burg und der schriftlichen mittelalterlichen Quellen und die wichtigen Fundgruppierungen, die direkt in die Zeit des Bürgerkrieges 1643-1645 datiert werden können.

Bibliography

Primary sources

Beeston Field Centre: manuscript account of well investigations
Cheshire Record Office: DTW Acc 2477
Mostyn estate records: nos 4270, 5385, 6085, 6089, 8847
British Library, Harley 2111

Printed sources

Alcock, L, 1967 Excavations at Degannwy Castle, Caenarvonshire, 1961–6, *Archaeol J*, **124**, 190–201

—, 1971 Excavations at South Cadbury Castle 1970: summary report, *Antiq J*, **51**, 1–7

Amery, A, and Davey, P J, 1979 Post-medieval pottery from Brook-hill, Buckley, Clwyd, *Medieval and later pottery in Wales*, **2**, 49–85

ApSimon, A M, and Greenfield, E, 1972 The excavation of the Bronze Age and Iron Age settlement at Trevisker Round, St Eval, Cornwall, *Proc Prehist Soc*, **38**, 302–81

Armstrong, P, 1977 Excavations in Sewer Lane, Hull, 1974, *East Riding Archaeol*, **3**

Arber, E (ed), 1868 Robert Ascham, *Toxophilus*, London

Arnold, C J, 1975 Beeston Castle, Cheshire: report on the clay tobacco pipes, unpubl

Arnold, D E, 1981 A model for the identification of non-local ceramic distribution: a view from the present, in *Production and distribution: a ceramic viewpoint* (eds H Howard and E L Morris), BAR, Int Ser, **120**, 31–44, Oxford

Ashbee, P, and ApSimon, A M, 1958 Barnby Howes, Barnby, East Yorkshire, *Yorkshire Archaeol J*, **39**, 9–31

Askey, D, 1981 *Stoneware bottles 1850–1949*, Brighton

Atkin, S, and Davey, P J, 1985 Clay tobacco pipes from a 17th-century well/cesspit on St Stephen's Street, Norwich, in *More pipes from the Midlands and southern England: the archaeology of the clay tobacco pipe, 9* (ed P J Davey), BAR Brit Ser, **146(ii)**, 309–24

Atkinson, D R, 1975 *Tobacco pipes of Broseley, Shropshire*, Saffron Walden

Atkinson, D R, and Oswald, A, 1969 London clay tobacco pipes, *Brit Archaeol Assoc J*, third ser, **32**, 1–67

Avent, R, 1983 *Castles of the princes of Gwynedd*, Cardiff

Avery, B W, 1980 *Soil classification for England and Wales*, Soil Surv Tech Monogr, **14**, Harpendon

Avery, B W, and Bascomb, C L (eds), 1974 *Soil survey laboratory methods*, Soil Surv Tech Monogr, **6**, Harpendon

Avery, M, 1976 Hillforts of the British Isles: a student's introduction, in *Hillforts: later prehistoric earthworks in Britain and Ireland* (ed D W Harding), 1–58, New York

Badham, K, and Jones, G, 1983 An experiment in manual processing of soil samples for plant remains, *Circaea*, **3(1)**, 15–26

Banks, P J, and Morris, E L, 1979 Iron Age pottery and briquetage, in *Fisherwick* (ed C Smith), BAR, Brit Ser, **61**, 45–57, Oxford

Barker, D, 1985 The Newcastle-under-Lyme clay tobacco pipe industry, in *More pipes from the Midlands and southern England; the archaeology of the clay tobacco pipe, 9* (ed P J Davey), BAR, Brit Ser, **146(i)**, 237–89, Oxford

—, 1986 *North Staffordshire post-medieval ceramics: a type series*, Stoke-on-Trent City Mus and Art Gallery New Series Rep, **3**

Barnard, F P, 1916 *The casting counter and the counting board*, Oxford

Barraclough, G, 1951 The earldom and County Palatine of Chester, *Trans Hist Soc Lancs and Chesh*, **103**, 23–57

Barrett, J, 1979 The pottery – discussion, in Coombs and Thompson 1979, 44–9

Bartlett, A, 1981 *Beeston Castle, Cheshire: geophysical survey*, Ancient Monuments Lab Rep 3369

Bayley, J, 1985 *Analysis of a glass bead from Beeston Castle, Cheshire*, Ancient Monuments Lab Rep 4575

—, J, 1987 *Glass beads and miscellaneous finds from Beeston Castle, Cheshire*, Ancient Monuments Lab Rep 9/87

Belcher, J, and Jarrett, M C, 1971 Stem-bore diameters of English clay pipes: some northern evidence, *Post-Medieval Archaeol*, **5**, 191–3

Bentley, J, Davey, P J, and Harrison, H M, 1980 An early clay pipe industry in North Wales, in Davey 1980, 273–82

Beresford, M B, and Finberg, H P R, 1973 *English medieval boroughs: a handlist*, Newton Abbot

Berry, G, 1974 *Medieval English jettons*, London

Beswick, P, 1975 Report on the shale industry at Swine Sty, in Machin 1975, 207–11

Bimson, M, 1967 The significance of ale measure marks, *Post-Medieval Archaeol*, **4**, 165

Blackmore, H L, 1961 *British military firearms 1650–1850*, London

—, 1971 *Hunting weapons*, London

Blair, C (ed), 1983 *Pollard's history of firearms*, Feltham, Middlesex

Boardman, S, and Jones, G, 1990 Experiments on the effects of charring on cereal plant components, *J Archaeol Sci*, **17**, 1–11

Boon, G C, and Savory, H N, 1975 A silver trumpet brooch from Carmarthen, and a note on the type, *Antiq J*, **55**, 41–61

Booth, P H W, 1981 *The financial administration of the lordship and county of Chester 1272–1377*, Chetham Soc, third ser, **28**, Manchester

Booth, P H W, and Carr, A D, 1991 *Account of Master John de Burham the younger, Chamberlain of Chester, of the revenues of the counties of Chester and Flint, Michaelmas 1361 to Michaelmas 1362*, Lancashire Cheshire Rec Soc, **125**

Bradfield, N, 1968 *Costume in detail: women's dress 1730—1930*, London

Bradley, R, 1975 Maumbury Rings, Dorset: the excavations of 1908–-13, *Archaeologia*, **105**, 1–98

Bradley, R, Lobb, S, Richards, J, and Robinson, M, 1980 Two Late Bronze Age settlements on the Kennet gravels: excavations at Aldermaston Wharf and Knight's Farm, Burghfield, Berkshire, *Proc Prehist Soc*, **46**, 217–96

Branigan, K, and Bayley, J, 1989 The Romano-British metalwork from Poole's Cavern, Buxton, *Derbyshire Archaeol J*, **109**, 34–50

Brears, P C D, 1971 *The English country pottery: its history and techniques*, Newton Abbot

Brewster, T C M, 1963 *The excavation of Staple Howe*, Scarborough

Briggs, C S, Leahy, K, and Needham, S P, 1987 The Late Bronze Age hoard from Brough-on-Humber: a reassessment, *Antiq J*, **67**, 11–28

Britton, D (ed), 1968 *Late Bronze Age finds in the Heathery Burn cave, Co Durham*, Inventaria Archaeologica GB55, British Museum

Brunaux, J L, and Rapin, A, 1988 *Gournay II; boucliers et lances, dépôts et trophées*, Paris

Bullard, D, 1967 Notes on a buff coat *c* 1645 in the Worcestershire County Museum, *Post-Medieval Archaeol*, **1**, 103–4

Bullock, P, Fedoroff, N, Jongerius, A, Stoops, G, and Tursina, T, 1985 *Handbook for soil thin section description*, Wolverhampton

Burgess, C B, 1982 The Cartington knife and the double-edged knives of the Late Bronze Age, *Northern Archaeol*, **3**, 32–45

Burgess, C B, and Miket, R, 1976 Three socketed axes from north-east England with notes on faceted and ribbed socketed axes, *Archaeol Aeliana*, **4**, fifth ser, 1–10

Burley, E, 1958 A catalogue and survey of the metalwork from Traprain Law, *Proc Soc Antiq Scot*, **89**, 118–226

Burne, R V H, 1962 The monks of Chester, in *The history of St Werburgh's Abbey*, London

Burstow, G P, and Hollyman, G A, 1957 Late Bronze Age settlement on Itford Hill, Sussex, *Proc Prehist Soc*, **23**, 167–212

Caple, C, and Warren, S E, 1982 Technical observations on the method of production and the alloy composition of later and post-medieval wound wire headed pins, *Proc twenty-second symp archaeom*, 273–83, University of Bradford

Carver, M O H, 1991a Prehistory in lowland Shropshire, *Shropshire Archaeol Nat Hist Soc Trans*, **67**

—, 1991b A strategy for lowland Shropshire, in Carver 1991a, 1–8

Celoria, F S C, and Kelly, J H, 1973 *A post-medieval pottery site with a kiln base found off Albion Square, Hanley*, City of Stoke-on-Trent Mus Archaeol Soc Rep, **4**

Chappell, E, 1973 A study of horseshoes in the Department of Archaeology, Colonial Williamsburg, in *Five artifactual studies* (ed I Noel Hume), 100–16, Charlottesville, Virginia

Charleston, R J, 1983 Vessel glass, in *Bayham Abbey* (A Stretton), Sussex Archaeol Monogr, **2**, 112-4

—, 1984 *English glass*, London

—, 1985 Vessel glass, in *Battle Abbey* (J N Hare), HBMC Archaeol Rep, **2**, 139-44

—, 1986 Glass from Plymouth, in *The medieval waterfront* (C Gaskell Brown), Plymouth Archaeol Ser, **3**

Christie, R C (ed), 1886 *Annales Cestrienses: or chronicle of the Abbey of S Werburg, at Chester*, Lancashire Cheshire Rec Soc, **14**

Clark, A J, Tarling, D H, and Noel, M, 1988 Developments in archaeomagnetic dating in Britain, *J Archaeol Sci*, **15**, 645–67

Clarke, M V, 1931 The Kirkstall Chronicle, 1355–1400, *Bull John Rylands Lib Univ Manchester*, **15**, 100–37

Clarke, M V, and Galbraith, V H, 1930 The deposition of Richard II, *Bull John Rylands Lib Univ Manchester*, **14**, 125–81

CLibR *Calendar of Liberate Rolls 1226–1240*, Hen III, **1**, 1916; 1240–1245, Hen III, **2**, 1930; 1245–1251, Hen III, **3**, 1937

Coles, J M, 1978 *Somerset Levels papers*, **4**, Hertford

Colquhoun, I, 1979 The Late Bronze Age hoard from Blackmoor, Hants, in *Bronze Age hoards: some finds old and new* (eds C B Burgess and D Coombs), BAR, Brit Ser, **67**, 197–220, Oxford

Colvin, H M (ed), 1963 *The history of the king's works*, London

Coombs, D G, and Thompson, F H, 1979 Excavation of the hillfort of Mam Tor, Derbyshire, *Derbyshire Archaeol J*, **99**, 7–51

—, 1991 Bronze objects, in *The Breiddin hillfort: a later prehistoric settlement in the Welsh Marches* (C R Musson), CBA Research Rep **9**, 132-9

Coppack, G, 1980 The medieval pottery of Lincoln, Nottingham and Derby, unpubl PhD thesis, Univ Nottingham

Corcoran, J X W P, 1952 Tankards and tankard handles of the British Iron Age, *Proc Prehist Soc*, **18**, 85–102

Cornwall, I W, 1958 *Soils for the archaeologist*, London

Cotton, M A, 1947 Excavations at Silchester 1938–39, *Archaeologia*, **92**, 121–67

—, 1954 British camps with timber-laced ramparts, *Archaeol J*, **111**, 26–105

Courtney, P, and Jones, N, forthcoming The Clwyd-Powys medieval fabric series, in *Medieval and later pottery in Wales*

Courty, M A, Goldberg, P, and Macphail, R, 1989 *Soils and micromorphology in archaeology*, Manuals in archaeol ser, Cambridge

Cowell, M R, 1977 Energy dispersive X-ray fluorescence analysis of ancient gold alloys, in *X-ray microfluorescence applied to archaeology* (eds T Hackens and H McKerrell), 76–85, Strasbourg

Cowgill, J, de Neergaard, M, and Griffiths, N, 1987 *Knives and scabbards: medieval finds from excavations in London*, **1**, London

CPR *Calendar of Patent Rolls 1232–1247*, Hen III, **3**, 1906; *1247–1258*, Hen III, **4**, 1908; *1258–1266*, Hen III, **5**, 1910

CR *Calendar of Close Rolls 1231–1234*, Hen III, **2**, 1905; *1234–1237*, Hen III, **3**, 1909; *1237–1242*, Hen III, **4**, 1911; *1242–1247*, Hen III, **5**, 1919; *1254–1256*, Hen III, **9**, 1931; *1272–1279*, Edw I, **1**, 1900; *1279–1288*, Edw I, **2**, 1902; *1318–1323*, Edw II, **3**, 1895; *1323-1327*, Edw II, **4**, 1898; *1327–1330*, Edw III, **1**, 1896; *1330–1333*, Edw III, **2**, 1898

Credland, A G, 1983 Military finds, in Mayes and Butler 1983, 259–66

Crossley, D W, and Aberg, F A, 1972 Sixteenth-century glass-making in Yorkshire: Hutton and Rosedale, North Riding, 1968–71, *Post-Medieval Archaeol*, **6**, 107–59

Crowfoot, E, 1983 *Textile remains on metal, Beeston Castle*, Ancient Monuments Lab Rep 4118

—, 1985 *Textile remains on jack-plates, Beeston Castle*, Ancient Monuments Lab Rep 4651

Cunliffe, B W, 1974 *Iron Age Communities in Britain*, London

—, 1984a Iron Age Wessex: continuity and change, in *Aspects of the Iron Age in central and southern Britain* (eds B W Cunliffe and D Miles), OUCA Monogr, **2**, 12–45, Oxford

— (ed), 1984b *Danebury: an Iron Age hillfort in Hampshire, vol 2: The finds*, CBA Res Rep, **52**, London

Cunliffe, B W, and Phillipson, D W, 1968 Excavations at Eldon's Seat, Encombe, Dorset, *Proc Prehist Soc*, **34**, 191–235

Cunnington, C W, and Cunnington, P, 1964 *Handbook of English costume in the eighteenth century*, London

—, 1972 *Handbook of English costume in the seventeenth century*, third edn, London

Cunnington, M E, 1923 *The Early Iron Age inhabited site at All Cannings Cross Farm, Wiltshire*, Devizes

Curle, J, 1911 *A Roman frontier post and its people. The fort of Newstead in the parish of Melrose*, Glasgow

Dalton, H, 1794 *The new and complete English traveller*

Davey, P J, 1973 Bronze Age metalwork from Lincolnshire, *Archaeologia*, **104**, 51–127

—, 1975 Stem-bore analysis of Chester clay tobacco pipes, *Cheshire Archaeol Bull*, **3**, 29–34

— (ed), 1977a *Medieval pottery from excavations in the North West*, Liverpool

—, 1977b Clay tobacco pipes from Beeston Castle, *Cheshire Archaeol Bull*, **5**, 14–18

—, 1981 Guidelines for the processing and publishing of clay pipes from excavations, *Medieval and later pottery in Wales*, **4**, 65–88

—, 1982 The clay pipes, in *Excavations in the medieval burgh of Aberdeen 1973–1981* (J C Murray), Soc Antiq Scot Monogr Ser, **2**, 216–23

—, 1983 Later medieval imported pottery in the Irish Sea province, in *Ceramics and trade. The production and distribution of later medieval pottery in North-West Europe* (eds P J Davey and R Hodges), 209–18, Sheffield

—, 1985 Clay pipes from Norton Priory, Cheshire, in *More pipes from the Midlands and southern England: the archaeology of the clay tobacco pipe, 9* (ed P J Davey), BAR, Brit Ser, **146(ii)**, 157–236, Oxford

—, 1989 The ceramic evidence from Peel Castle, Isle of Man, in Freke forthcoming

Davey, P J, and Forster, E, 1975 *Bronze Age metalwork from Lancashire and Cheshire*, University of Liverpool, Department of Archaeology worknotes, **1**

Davey, P J, and Morgan, D E M, 1977 Hen Blas, in Davey 1977a, 42—7

Davies, R I, 1970 The podzol process, *Welsh Soils Discuss Group*, **11**, 133–42

Davies, R R, 1987 *Conquest, coexistence and change in Wales 1063—1415*, History of Wales, **2**

Dawson, D, and Kent, O, 1986 Experiments in reduction firing: the Bickley Project, *Bull Exp Firing Group*, **5**, 34–41

Dimbleby, G W, 1962 *The development of British heathlands and their soils*, Oxford

Dixon, P, forthcoming *Crickley Hill, vol 1: the hillfort defences*

Dore, R N, 1965-6 Beeston Castle in the great Civil War, 1643—46, *Trans Lancashire Cheshire Antiq Soc*, **75–6**, 103–22

—, 1984 *The letter books of Sir William Brereton, I*, Lancashire Cheshire Rec Soc, **123**

—, 1990 *The letter books of Sir William Brereton, II*, Lancashire Cheshire Rec Soc, **128**

Drewitt, P, 1976 The excavation of the Great Hall at Bolingbroke Castle, Lincolshire, 1973, *Post-Medieval Archaeol*, **10**, 1–33

Driver, J T, 1971 Cheshire in the late Middle Ages, 1399—1540, in *A History of Cheshire*, **6**, Chester

Dufty, A R, and Reid, W, 1968 *European armour in the Tower of London*, London

—, 1971 Military equipment, in Moorhouse 1971, 52–4

Dugdale, W, 1817–30 *Monasticon Anglicanum*, ed J Caley, H Ellis, and B Bandinel

Dunning, G C, 1934 The swan's-neck and ring-headed pins of the Early Iron Age in Britain, *Archaeol J*, **91**, 269–95

Eales, R, 1986 Henry III and the end of the Norman earldom of Chester, in *Thirteenth-century England, I* (P R Coss and S D Lloyd), 1, 100–12

Earp, J R, and Hains, B A, 1971 *The Welsh borderland*, British Regional Geology, third edn, London

Earp, J R, and Taylor, B J, 1986 *Geology of the area around Chester and Wimsford*, Brit Geol Surv Sheet Mem, **109**

Eaves, I, 1989 On the remains of a Jack of Plate excavated from Beeston Castle in Cheshire, *J Arms Armour Soc*, **13**, no 2, 81—154

Ehrenberg, M R, 1977 *Bronze Age spearheads from Berks, Bucks and Oxon*, BAR, Brit Ser, **34**, Oxford

Ellis, P, Evans, J, Hannaford, H R, Hughes, E G, Jones, A E, forthcoming Excavations in the Wroxeter hinterland 1988–1990: the archaeology of the A5, *Shropshire Archaeol Nat Hist Trans*

Elsdon, S M, 1979 Iron Age pottery, in Excavation at Willington, Derbyshire 1970–1972 (H Wheeler), *Derbyshire Archaeol J*, **99**, 162–78

Erdeswicke, S, 1717 *A survey of Staffordshire ... with a description of Beeston Castle in Cheshire*, London

Evans, J, 1975 *Beeston Castle, Cheshire: mollusca*, Ancient Monuments Lab Rep 1776

Fasham, P J, and Ross, J M, 1978 A Bronze Age flint industry from a barrow site in Micheldever Wood, Hampshire, *Proc Prehist Soc*, **44**, 47–67

Fingerlin, I, 1971 *Gürtel des Hohen und späten mittelalters*, Berlin

Flanagan, L, 1988 *Ireland's Armada legacy*, Gloucester

Foedera Foedera, Conventiones, Litterae ... (ed A Clarke and F Holbrooke), **I**, 1816

Forde-Johnston, J, 1962 The Iron Age hillforts of Lancashire and Cheshire, *Trans Lancashire Cheshire Antiq Soc*, **72**, 9–46

Fox, R, and Barton, K J, 1986 Excavations at Oystermouth St, Portsmouth, Hampshire, 1968–71, *Post-Medieval Archaeol*, **20**, 31—256

Freke, D, forthcoming *Excavations at Peel Castle 1981—86*, Liverpool

—, and Holgate R, 1991 The excavation of two second millennium BC mounds at Winwick, Cheshire, *J Cheshire Archaeol Soc*, **70**, 9–30

French, D H, 1971 An experiment in water sieving, *Anatolian Studies*, **21**, 59–64

Furness, R R, 1978 *Soils of Cheshire*, Soil Surv Bull, **6** Harpendon

Garner, F H, and Archer, M, 1972 *English Delftware*, London

George, J N, 1947 *English guns and rifles*, London

Gillam, J P, 1976 Coarse fumed ware in north Britain and beyond, *Glasgow Archaeol J*, **4**, 57–80

Girling, M A, 1985 *Investigation of insect attack on charcoal from Beeston Castle, Cheshire*, Ancient Monuments Lab Rep 4585

Goodall, A R, 1981 The medieval bronzesmith and his products, in *Medieval industry* (ed D W Crossley), CBA Res Rep, **40**, 63–71, London

—, 1983 Non-ferrous metal objects, in Mayes and Butler 1983, 231–8

—, 1984 Objects of non-ferrous metal, in *Medieval and post-medieval finds from Exeter 1971–1980* (J P Allan), Exeter Archaeol Rep, **3**, 337–48, Exeter

—, forthcoming Objects of copper alloy, in *The palace of Nonsuch, ii: The domestic occupation* (M Biddle), London

Goodall, I H, 1976a Metalwork, in Drewitt 1976, 26–9

—, 1976b The metalwork, in The excavation of Ardingly Fulling mill and forge: 1975–6 (O Bedwin), *Post-Medieval Archaeol*, **10**, 60–4

—, 1978 Iron objects, in An excavation at Chapel Garth, Bolton, Fangfoss, Humberside (G Coppack), *Yorkshire Archaeol J*, **56**, 140–5

—, 1983 Iron objects, in Mayes and Butler 1983, 240–52

—, 1985 Ironwork, in *Post-medieval sites and their pottery: Moulsham Street, Chelmsford* (C M Cunningham and P J Drury), CBA Res Rep, **54**, 51–7

Greaves, S J, 1976 *A post-medieval excavation in Woodbank St, Burslem*, City of Stoke-on-Trent Mus Archaeol Soc Rep, **10**

Green, J N, 1977 *The* Jacht Vergulde Draecht *wrecked off western Australia 1656*, BAR, Supp Ser, **36**, Oxford

Greig, J R A, 1991 The British Isles, in *Progress in Old World palaeoethnobotany: a retrospective view on the occasion of 20 years of the International Work Group for Palaeoethnobotany* (eds W van Zeist, K Wasylikowa, and K-E Behre), Rotterdam, 299–334

Griffith, N G L, Halstead, P L J, MacLean, A C, and Rowley-Conwy, P, 1983 Faunal remains and economy, in Mayes and Butler 1983, 341—8

Grimes, W F, 1930 Holt, Denbighshire: the works depot of the twentieth legion at Castle Lyons, *Y Cymmrodor*, **41**

Grinsell, L V, 1985 Carrying flint cores to Mendip, *Lithics*, **6**, 15–17

Groves, S, 1966 *The history of needlework tools and accessories*, London

Guido, M, 1978 *The glass beads of the prehistoric and Roman periods in Britain and Ireland*, Rep Res Comm Soc Antiq, **35**

Guilbert, G, 1976 Moel y Gaer (Rhosesmor) 1972–1973: an area excavation in the interior, in *Hillforts: later prehistoric earthworks in Britain and Ireland* (ed D W Harding), 303–17, New York

—, 1981 Double ring roundhouses, probable and possible, in prehistoric Britain, *Proc Prehist Soc*, **47**, 299–317

—, 1982 Post ring symmetry in roundhouses at Moel y Gaer and some other sites in prehistoric Britain, in *Structural reconstruction: approaches to the interpretation of the excavated remains of buildings* (ed P J Drury), BAR, Brit Ser, **110**, 67–86, Oxford

Hall, J (ed), 1889 *Memorials of the Civil War in Cheshire*, Lancashire Cheshire Rec Soc, **19**

Harding, J M, 1964 Interim report on the excavation of a Late Bronze Age homestead in Weston Wood, Albury, Surrey, *Surrey Archaeol Collect*, **61**, 10–17

Hardy, R, 1976 *Longbow: a social and military history*, Cambridge

Harrington, J C, 1954 Dating stem fragments of the 17th–18th-century clay tobacco pipes, *Q Bull Archaeol Soc Virginia*, **9**, 1

Harrison, H M, and Davey, P, 1977 Ewloe Kiln, in Davey 1977a, 92—9

Harvey, Y, 1975 The small finds catalogue, in *Excavations in medieval Southampton 1953–1969, vol 2: The finds* (C Platt and R Coleman-Smith), 254–95, Leicester

Hayfield, C, 1985 *Humberside medieval pottery*, BAR, Brit Ser, **140**, Oxford

Hayward, J F, 1957 *English cutlery: sixteenth to eighteenth century*, London

Henderson, J D, 1988 *Beeston Castle, Cheshire – the human bone*, Ancient Monuments Lab Rep 62/88

Hewitt, H J, 1929 *Medieval Cheshire: an economic and social history of Cheshire in the reigns of the three Edwards*, Chetham Soc, New Ser, **88**

Higgins, D A, 1982 Reconstruction and interpretation of the pipes, in *More pipes and kilns from England, the archaeology of the clay tobacco pipe, 7* (ed P J Davey), BAR, Brit Ser, **100**, Oxford, 197–209

—, 1987 The interpretation and regional study of clay tobacco pipes: a case study of the Broseley district, unpubl PhD thesis, Liverpool University

—, 1988 Song pipes, *Society for clay pipe research newsletter*, **19** (July 1988), 6–10

Higgins, D A, and Davey, P J, 1988 A new recording system for excavated clay tobacco pipes, unpubl, Univ of Liverpool

Hildyard, E J W, 1956 An enamelled fibula from Brough-under-Stainmore, *Trans Cumberland Westmorland Archaeol Soc*, New Ser, **55**, 54–8

Hillman, G C, 1981 Reconstructing crop husbandry practices from the charred remains of crops, in *Farming practice in British prehistory* (ed R J Mercer), 123–62, Edinburgh

—, 1991 Crop husbandry in the Late Iron Age at Breiddin hillfort, in Musson 1991

Hindle, B P, 1982 Roads and tracks, in *The English medieval landscape* (ed L M Cantor), 193–217, London

Hinton, D, 1973 *Medieval pottery in the Oxford region*, Oxford

Hodges, H, 1956 Studies in the Late Bronze Age in Ireland, part 2, *Ulster J Archaeol*, **19**, 29–56

Hodgson, J M, 1974 *Soil Survey field handbook*, Soil Surv Tech Monogr, **5**, Harpendon

Holden, E W, 1963 Excavations at the deserted medieval village of Hongleton, part I, *Sussex Archaeol Collect*, **101**, 54–181

Holleyman, and Curwen, E C, 1935 Late Bronze Age lynchet-settlements on Plumpton Plain, Sussex, *Proc Prehist Soc*, **1**, 16–38

Hough, P R, 1978 Excavations at Beeston Castle 1975–77, *J Cheshire Archaeol Soc*, **61**, 1–22

—, 1982 Beeston Castle, *Current Archaeol*, **91**, 245–9

Howard, H, 1983 The bronze casting industry in later prehistoric southern Britain: a study based on refractory debris, unpubl PhD thesis, Univ Southampton

Hughes, M J, Cowell, M R, and Craddock, P T, 1976 Atomic absorption techniques in archaeology, *Archaeometry*, **18**, 19–36

Hurst, J G, 1966 Imported flasks, in Kirkstall Abbey excavations, 1960–64 (C V Bellamy), *Publ Thoresby Soc*, **51**, 54–9

Hutchinson, M E, 1989 *The identification of 43 pieces of colourless material from Beeston Castle, Cheshire*, Ancient Monuments Lab Rep 73/89

Jackson, R G, and Price, R H, 1974 *Bristol clay pipes, a study of their makers and their marks*, Bristol City Mus Res Monogr, **1**

Jones, G D B, 1975 The north-western interface, in *Recent work in rural archaeology* (ed P J Fowler), 93–106, Bradford-on-Avon

Jones, G, and Milles, A, 1989 Iron Age, Romano-British and medieval plant remains, in The Collfryn hillslope enclosure, Llansantffraid Deuddwr, Powys: excavations 1980–82 (W Britnell), *Proc Prehist Soc*, **55**, microfiche 3.5

Jones, M K, 1981 The development of crop husbandry, in *The environment of man: the Iron Age to the Anglo-Saxon period* (eds M Jones and G Dimbleby), BAR, Brit Ser, **87**, 95–127, Oxford

—, 1984 The plant remains, in Cunliffe 1984b, 483–95

—, 1985 Archaeobotany beyond subsistence reconstruction, in *Beyond domestication in prehistoric Europe* (eds G Barker and C Gamble), 107–28, London

Jones, O, 1856 *The grammar of ornament*, London

Jones, P, 1897 *Incidents and accidents round about Beeston Castle*

Jones, R T, Wall, S M, Locker, A M, Coy, J, and Maltby, M, 1976 *Ancient Monuments Laboratory computer-based osteometry, data capture user manual*, Ancient Monuments Lab Rep 3342

Jope, E M, 1956 The tinning of iron spurs: a continuous practice from the 10th to the 17th century, *Oxoniensa*, **21**, 35–42

—, 1961 Daggers of the Early Iron Age in Britain, *Proc Prehist Soc*, **27**, 307–43

Keepax, C, 1978 *Beeston Castle, Cheshire: examination of biological remains*, Ancient Monuments Lab Rep 2449

Kelly, J H, 1969 *The hill top site, Burslem*, City of Stoke-on-Trent Mus and Archaeol Soc Rep, **3**

—, 1973 *A rescue excavation on the site of Swan Bank Methodist Church, Burslem*, City of Stoke-on-Trent Mus and Archaeol Soc Rep, **5**

—, 1975 *Post-medieval pottery from Newcastle St, Burslem*, City of Stoke-on-Trent Mus and Archaeol Soc Rep, **8**

Kelly, J H, and Greaves S J, 1974 *The excavation of a kiln base in Old Hall St, Hanley*, City of Stoke-on-Trent Mus and Archaeol Soc Rep, **6**

Kenward, H K, Hall, A R, and Jones, A K G, 1980 A tested set of techniques for the extraction of plant and animal macrofossils from waterlogged archaeological deposits, *Science and Archaeology*, **22**, 3–15

Knight, B, 1984 Researches on medieval window lead, *J Brit Soc Master Glass Paint*, **18**, 49–51

Knight, J K, 1982 Montgomery Castle: a provisional checklist of fabrics, *Medieval and later pottery in Wales*, **2**, 44–62

Leland, J, 1548 *Genethliacon Eaduerdi Principis*

le Saxon, J, 1895 *Cheshire, historical and picturesque*

Lewis, J M, 1968 The excavation of the new building at Montgomery Castle, *Archaeol Cambrensis*, **117**, 127–56

—, 1973 Some types of metal chafing-dish, *Antiq J*, **53**, 59–70

Lindsay, J S, 1964 *Iron and brass implements of the English home*, London

Liversage, D, 1980 *The archaeology of Sjaelland in the Early Roman Iron Age*, Nat Mus Denmark, Copenhagen

Longley, D, 1987 Prehistory, in *A history of the county of Cheshire, vol I* (ed B E Harris), 36–114, Oxford

Longworth, I, 1984 *Collared urns of the Bronze Age in Great Britain and Ireland*, Cambridge

Lumby, J R (ed), 1882 *Polychronicon Ranulphi Higden monachi Cestrensis ...*, 8, 1882, Chronicles and Memorials, **41**

McCarthy, M R, and Brooks, C M, 1988 *Medieval pottery in Britain AD 900–1600*, Leicester

McDonnell, J G, nd *Report on the slags and residues recovered during excavations at Beeston Castle, Cheshire*, Ancient Monuments typescript report

MacGregor, A, 1985 *Bone, antler and ivory: the technology of skeletal materials since the Roman period*, London

Machin, M L, 1971 Further excavations of the enclosure at Swine Sty, Big Moor, Baslow, *Trans Hunter Archaeol Soc*, **10** (1), 5–13

—, 1975 Further excavations of the enclosure at Swine Sty, Big Moor, Baslow, *Trans Hunter Archaeol Soc*, **10** (3), 205–11

Mackreth, D F, 1983 The Roman brooches, in Excavations at Poole's Cavern, Buxton: an interim report (D Bramwell, K Dalton, J F Drinkwater, M Hassall, K L Lorimer, and D F Mackreth), *Derbyshire Archaeol J*, **103**, 52–61

McNeil-Sale, R, Colledge, S, Coldwell, D, Gleave, M, Hutchins, P, Nailor, V, Pheasey, K, Streeter, A, and Wood, C, 1979 *Archaeology in Nantwich: Crown car park excavations interim report*, Liverpool

McNeil-Sale, R, Gleave, M, Hargrave, S, Hughes, C, Hutchins, P, Nailor, V, and Noake, P, 1980 *Wood Street salt works, Nantwich*, Cheshire County Council and Liverpool University

Macphail, R I, 1980 *Soil report on Beeston Castle, Cheshire*, Ancient Monuments Lab Rep 3235

—, 1981a *Soil report on Beeston Castle, Cheshire*, Ancient Monuments Lab Rep 3235

—, 1981b *Soil report on Beeston Castle, Cheshire*, Ancient Monuments Lab Rep 3565

—, 1983 *Soil report on Beeston Castle, Cheshire*, Ancient Monuments Lab Rep 4101

—, 1984 *Soil report on Beeston Castle, Cheshire*, Ancient Monuments Lab Rep 4441

—, 1987a A review of soil science in archaeology in England, in *Environmental archaeology, a regional review, 2* (ed H Keeley), HBMC Occas Pap, **1**, 332–79, London

—, 1987b *Soil report on Beeston Castle, Cheshire*, Ancient Monuments Lab Rep 173/88

Maltby, M, 1979 *The animal bones from Exeter*, Exeter Archaeol Rep, **2**, Exeter

Manby, T G, 1979 Neolithic and Bronze Age pottery, in Excavation at Willington, Derbyshire 1970–1972 (H Wheeler), *Derbyshire Archaeol J*, **99**, 146–62

—, 1980 Bronze Age settlement in eastern Yorkshire, in *Settlement and society in the British later Bronze Age* (J Barrett and R Bradley), BAR, Brit Ser, **83(ii)**, 307–70, Oxford

Manley, J, 1984 A Romano-British brooch from Llysfaen, Clwyd, *Denbighshire Hist Soc Trans*, **33**, 105–6

Manning, W H, 1976 *Catalogue of Romano-British ironwork in the Museum of Antiquities, Newcastle upon Tyne*, Newcastle upon Tyne

—, 1985 *Catalogue of the Romano-British iron tools, fittings and weapons in the British Museum*, London

Mayes, P, and Butler, L A S, 1983 *Sandal Castle excavations 1964–73*, Wakefield

Mellor, M, 1980 The pottery, in A beaker burial and medieval tenements in the Hamel, Oxford (N Palmer), *Oxoniensa*, **45**, 160–82

Mesqui, J, 1981 La fortification des portes avant la Guerre de Cent Ans, *Archéologie Médiévale*, **11**, 203–29

Michaelis, R F, 1971 *Antique pewter of the British Isles*, London

Middleton, S, 1984 The Sneyd Green medieval kilns: a review, *Staffordshire Archaeol Stud*, **1**, 41–7

Miles, H, 1977 Rhuddlan kiln, in Davey 1977a, 100–1

Mokma, D L, and Buurman, P, 1982 *Podzols and podzolisation in temperate regions*, ISM Monogr, **1**, International Soil Museum, Wageningen

Moorhouse, S, 1971 Finds from Basing House, Hampshire, c 1540–1645: part 2, *Post-Medieval Archaeol*, **5**, 35–76

Moorhouse, S, and Goodall, I H, 1971 Iron, in Moorhouse 1971, 36–57

—, 1986 Non-dating uses of medieval pottery, *Medieval Ceram* **10**, 85–124

Morgan, P, 1987 *War and society in medieval Cheshire 1277–1403*, Chetham Soc, Third Ser, **34**

Morris, E L, 1984 Petrological report for the ceramic material from the Wrekin, in Stanford 1984, 76–80

—, 1985 Prehistoric salt distributions: two case studies from western Britain, *Bull Board Celtic Stud*, **32**, 336–79

Morris, R H, 1923 The siege of Chester 1633–1646, *J Chester N Wales Architect Archaeol and Hist Soc*, **25**

Mountford, A R, 1975 *The Sadler teapot manufactory site, and the Marquis of Granby hotel site, Burslem*, City of Stoke-on-Trent Mus and Archaeol Soc Rep, **7**

Musson, C R, 1976 Excavations at the Breiddin 1969–1973, in *Hillforts: later prehistoric earthworks in Britain and Ireland* (ed D W Harding), 293–302, New York

—, 1991 *The Breiddin hillfort: a later prehistoric settlement in the Welsh Marches*, CBA Research Rep **76**

Mynard, D C, 1969 Excavations at Somerby, Lincs, 1957, *Lincolnshire Hist Archaeol*, **1**, 4

Nailor, V, 1983 The medieval pottery, in Two 12th-century Wich houses at Nantwich (R McNeil), *Medieval Archaeol*, **27**, 70–5

Needham, S P, 1986 The metalwork, in O'Connell 1986, 22–60

—, 1990 *The Petters Late Bronze Age metalwork: an analytical study of Thames valley metalworking in a settlement context*, British Museum Occas Pap, **70**, London

Needham, S P, Lawson, A J, and Green, H S, 1985 *Early Bronze Age hoards*, British Bronze Age metalwork, Associated Finds Ser A1–6, British Museum, London

Noel Hume, A, 1979 Clay tobacco pipes excavated at Martin's Hundred, Virginia, 1976–1978, in *The United States of America, the archaeology of the clay tobacco pipe, 2* (ed P J Davey), BAR, Brit Ser, **78**, 3–36

Noel Hume, I, 1962 Tudor and early Stuart glasses found in London, *The Connoisseur* (August 1962), 269–70

—, 1970 *A guide to the artifacts of colonial America*, New York

—, 1982 *Martin's Hundred*, New York

Norman, A V B, 1980 *The rapier and small-sword, 1460–1820*, London

Norman, A V B, and Wilson, G M, 1982 *Treasures from the Tower of London: arms and armour*, Norwich

North, J J, 1960 *English hammered coinage, 2*, London

—, 1980 *English hammered coinage, 1*, second edn, London

Norton, J, 1984 Appendix 1: report on clay pipes, in Archaeological excavations at Shop Street, Drogheda, Co Louth (P D Sweetman), *Proc Royal Irish Academy*, **84** (C), 199–206

O'Connell, M, 1986 *Petters sports field, Egham: excavation of a Late Bronze Age/Early Iron Age site*, Surrey Archaeol Soc Res, **10**

O'Connor, B, 1980 *Cross-channel relations in the later Bronze Age*, BAR, Int Ser, **91**, Oxford

Oldfield, F, Kwawiecki, A, Maher, B, Taylor, J, and Twigger, S, 1985 The role of mineral magnetic measurements in archaeology, in *Palaeoenvironmental investigations* (N R J Fieller, D D Gilbertson, and N G A Ralph), BAR, Int Ser, **258** (5A), 29–44, Oxford

Orderic Vitalis The ecclesiastical history of Orderic Vitalis (ed M Chibnall): **ii** (1968) (Books III and IV); **iii** (1972) (Books V and VI), Oxford

Ormerod, G, 1882 *The history of the County Palatine and city of Chester*, second edn (ed T Helsby)

Oswald, A, 1979 The clay pipes, in *St Andrew's Street, Plymouth: excavations 1976* (G J Fairclough), 114–19, Plymouth

Oswald, A, and Phillips, H, 1949 A Restoration glass hoard from Gracechurch Street, London, *The Connoisseur* (September 1949), 30–6

Parkinson, M R, 1969 *The incomparable art: English pottery from the Thomas Gregg collection*, City Art Gallery, Manchester

Peacock, D P S, 1977 Ceramics in Roman and medieval archaeology, in *Pottery and early commerce: characterisation and trade in Roman and later ceramics* (ed D P S Peacock), 21–33, London

Peacock, P, 1978 *Discovering old buttons*, Aylesbury

Pearce, J, Vince, A G, and Jenner, A, 1985 *A dated typeseries of London medieval pottery, part 2: London type ware*, London Middlesex Archaeol Soc Spec Pap, **6**, London

Pearson, W G, and Stuiver, M, 1986 High precision calibration of the radiocarbon time scale, 500–2500 BC, *Radiocarbon*, **28** (2B), 839–62

Peck, C W, 1964 *English copper, tin, and bronze coins in the British Museum, 1558–1958*, second edn, London

Pollard, A M, Bussell, G D, and Baird, D C, 1981 The analytical investigation of Early Bronze Age jet and jet-like material from the Devizes Museum, *Archaeometry*, **23**, **2**, 139–67

Poole, E G, and Whiteman, A J, 1966 *Geology of the country around Nantwich and Whitchurch*, Brit Geol Surv Sheet Mem, **122**

Price, G, 1856 *On fire and theft proof depositories and locks and keys*, London

Pryor, F M M, 1980 *Excavations at Fengate, Peterborough, England: the third report*, Toronto and Northampton

Radley, Y, 1969 A shale bracelet industry from Totley Moor near Sheffield, *Trans Hunter Archaeol Soc*, **9** (4), 264–8

Raftery, B, 1983 *A catalogue of Irish Iron Age antiquities*, Veröffentlichung des Vorgeschichtlichen Seminars Marburg, Sonderband 1

Ragg, J M, Beard, G R, Hollis, J M, Jones, R J A, Palmer, R C, Reeve, M J, and Whitfield, W A D, 1983 *Soils of England and Wales: Midlands and western England*, Southampton

Rahtz, P A, 1959 Humberstone earthwork, Leicester, *Trans Leicestershire Archaeol Hist Soc*, **35**, 1–21

—, 1969 *Excavations at King John's Hunting Lodge, Writtle, Essex, 1955–7*, London

Rahtz, P A, and ApSimon, A M, 1962 Excavations at Shearplace Hill, Sydling St Nicholas, Dorset, England, *Proc Prehist Soc*, **28**, 289–328

Ridgway, M H, and Cathcart King, D J, 1959 Beeston Castle, Cheshire, *J Chester N Wales Architect Archaeol and Hist Soc*, **46**, 1–23

Rigold, S E, 1971 Eynsford Castle and its excavation, *Archaeol Cantiana*, **86**, 108–71

Russell, E, 1974 Excavations on the site of the deserted medieval village of Kettleby Thorpe, Lincolnshire, *J Scunthorpe Mus Soc*, Ser 3, **2**

Rutter, J A, 1977a Chester: Old Market Hall pit group, in Davey 1977a, 18–21

—, 1977b Ashton, in Davey 1977a, 70–85

—, 1977c Chester: Upper Northgate St hoard pot, in Davey 1977a, 22–3

Rutter, J A, and Davey, P J, 1980 Clay pipes from Chester, in *Britain: the North and West, the archaeology of the clay tobacco pipe, 3*, BAR Brit Ser, **78**, Oxford, 43–282

Salzman, L F, 1967 *Building in England down to 1540*, Oxford

Savory, H N, 1976 Welsh hillforts: a reappraisal of recent research, in *Hillforts: later prehistoric earthworks in Britain and Ireland* (ed D W Harding), 237–91, New York

Schmidt, P K, and Burgess, C B, 1981 *The axes of Scotland and northern England*, Prähistorische Bronzefunde, **9** (7), Munich

Scrivener, A, 1896 Chartley earthworks and castle, *J Brit Archaeol Ass*, NS, **ii**, 53–9

Sell, S, 1983 A cache of Civil War armour from Ewenny, *Glamorgan–Gwent Archaeol Trust Annu Rep 1982–3*, 66–9

Skeat, W W (ed), 1886 W Langland, *The vision of William concerning Piers the Plowman ...*, Oxford

Smith, I F, 1965 *Windmill Hill and Avebury: excavations by Alexander Keiller 1925–1939*, Oxford

Snodin, M, 1974 *English silver spoons*, London

Stanford, S C, 1984 The Wrekin hillfort excavations 1973, *Archaeol J*, **141**, 61–90

Stanley, J, 1954 An Iron Age fort at Ball Cross Farm, Bakewell, *Derbyshire Archaeol J*, **74**, 85–99

Stead, I M, 1968 An Iron Age hillfort at Grimthorpe, Yorkshire, England, *Proc Prehist Soc*, **34**, 148–90

—, 1979 *The Arras Culture*, Yorkshire Philos Soc, York

Stewart, I, 1967 *The Scottish coinage*, second edn, London

Stewart-Brown, R (ed), 1910 *Accounts of the chamberlains and other officers of the county of Cheshire, 1301–1360*, Lancashire Cheshire Rec Soc, **59**

—, 1938 *Cheshire in the Pipe Rolls*, Lancashire Cheshire Rec Soc, **92**

Stone, J F S, 1941 The Deverel-Rimbury settlement on Thorny Down, Winterbourne Gunner, S Wilts, *Proc Prehist Soc*, **7**, 114–33

Stow, J, 1631 *Annales, or a general chronicle of England* (ed E Howes), London

Stuiver, M, and Pearson, G W, 1986 High precision calibration of the radiocarbon timescale, AD 1950–500 BC, *Radiocarbon*, **28** (2B), 805–38

Switsur, V R, and West, R G, 1975a University of Cambridge national radiocarbon measurements, X111, *Radiocarbon*, **17** (1), 35––51

—, 1975b University of Cambridge national radiocarbon measurements, XIV, *Radiocarbon*, **17** (3), 301–12

Talbot, E, 1977 Degannwy, in Davey 1977a, 30–3

Taylor, A, 1987 *Rhuddlan Castle*, Cadw (Welsh Historic Monuments), Cardiff

Thompson, E M (ed), 1904 *Chronicon Adae de Usk, 1377–1421*, second edn

Thompson, F H, 1965 *Roman Cheshire*, Chester

Thompson, M W, 1965 An alert in 1318 to the Constable of Bolingbroke Castle, Lincolnshire, in *Medieval Archaeol*, **9**, 167–8

—, 1966 The origins of Bolingbroke Castle, Lincolnshire, *Medieval Archaeol*, **10**, 152–8

Tylecote, R F, 1962 *Metallurgy in Archaeology*, London

—, 1980 *Beeston Castle, Cheshire, SJ5459*, Ancient Monuments Lab Rep 3176

—, 1987 *The early history of metallurgy in Europe*, London

Varley, W J, 1935 Maiden Castle, Bickerton, preliminary excavations 1934, *Ann Archaeol Anthropol Univ Liverpool*, **22**, 97–110

—, 1936 Further excavations at Maiden Castle, Bickerton, 1935, *Ann Archaeol Anthropol Univ Liverpool*, **23**, 100–12

—, 1948 The hillforts of the Welsh Marches, *Archaeol J*, **105**, 41–66

—, 1952 Excavations at Castle Ditch, Eddisbury, 1935–1938 *Trans Hist Soc Lancashire Cheshire*, **102**, 1–68

—, 1976 A summary of the excavations at Castle Hill, Almondbury, 1939–1972, in *Hillforts: later prehistoric earthworks in Britain and Ireland* (ed D W Harding), 119–31, New York

van der Veen, M 1992 *Crop husbandry regimes: an archaeobotanical study of farming in northern England 1000 BC–AD 500*, Sheffield Archaeol Monogr, 3

Vince, A G, 1984 The medieval ceramic industry of the Severn valley, unpubl PhD thesis, Univ Southampton

Vine, P M, 1982 *The Neolithic and Bronze Age cultures of the middle and upper Trent basin*, BAR, Brit Ser, **105**, Oxford

Wade-Martins, P, 1980 *North Elmham Park*, Norfolk Archaeol Unit Rep, Norwich

Wainwright, G J, 1979 *Gussage All Saints, an Iron Age settlement in Dorset*, DoE Archaeol Rep, **10**, London

von Wallhausen, 1971 *Kriegskunst zu Fusz* (ed J B Kist), Netherlands

Ward Perkins, J B, 1940 *London Museum medieval catalogue*, London

Watson, J, 1983 *Identification of charcoal from a socketed axe from Beeston Castle, Cheshire*, Ancient Monuments Lab Rep 4113

Weaver, J, 1987 *Beeston Castle*, English Heritage guide, London

Webb, J, 1824 Translation of a French metrical history of the deposition of King Richard the Second ..., *Archaeologia*, **20**, 1–423

Webster, G, and Dunning, G C, 1960 A medieval pottery kiln at Audlem, Cheshire, *Medieval Archaeol*, **4**, 109–25

Whimster, R, 1989 *The emerging past: air photography and the buried landscape*, London

White, J, 1976 King Stephen, Duke Henry and Ranulf Gernons, earl of Chester, *English Hist Rev*, **91**, 555–65

Whittaker, K M, undated A preliminary report on the pollen diagram from Beeston Castle, Cheshire, HBMC Central Excavation Unit Rep, unpubl

Woodfield, C, 1981 Finds from the Free Grammar School at the Whitefriars, Coventry, c 1545–1557/8, *Post-Medieval Archaeol*, **15**, 81–160

Index

Compiled by Lesley and Roy Adkins